BEING AND BECOMING HUMAN

BEHAVIORAL SCIENCE SERIES

BEING AND BECOMING HUMAN:
Essays on the Biogram

Earl W. Count

BEHAVIORAL SCIENCE SERIES

VAN NOSTRAND REINHOLD COMPANY
New York Cincinnati Toronto London Melbourne

FOR MAUDE—GRATEFULLY

Van Nostrand Reinhold Company Regional Offices:
New York Cincinnati Chicago Millbrae Dallas

Van Nostrand Reinhold Company International Offices:
London Toronto Melbourne

Copyright © 1973 by Litton Educational Publishing, Inc.

Library of Congress Catalog Card Number: 73-162
ISBN: 0-442-21718-8

Manufactured in the United States of America

Published by Van Nostrand Reinhold Company
450 West 33rd Street, New York, N. Y. 10001

Published simultaneously in Canada by Van Nostrand Reinhold Ltd.

15 14 13 12 11 10 9 8 7 6 5 4 3 2 1

Library of Congress Cataloging in Publication Data
Count, Earl Wendel, 1899–
  The biogram.

  (Behavioral science series)
  Includes bibliographies.
  1. Psychology, Comparative. I. Title.
  [DNLM: 1. Behavior—Essays. BF 149 C855b 1973]
  BF671.C66   156   73-162
  ISBN 0-442-21718-8

BEHAVIORAL SCIENCE SERIES

The Van Nostrand Reinhold Behavioral Science Series will publish a broad range of books on animal and human behavior from an ethological perspective. Although presently observable behavior is the focus of this series, the development of behavior in individuals, as well as the evolutionary history in various species, will also be considered. It is felt that such an holistic approach is needed to come to a fuller understanding of behavior in general. This series is a contribution toward this goal.

Erich Klinghammer, Consulting Editor
Purdue University

Preface

An author, boxed in between covers, sometimes finds in the Preface his opportunity to apologize for the urge to write a book; it is much more comfortable to explain why he has not written one.

The six essays that follow simply do better than that book would have done. They dot ten years of a quest that was older by a number more, and that continues. So, together they work upon a theme, yet each may be read without its demanding that the reader first have trudged through its predecessors; it only suggests, mildly, that he might have found himself aided had he done so. Furthermore (*confessio auctoris*), an idea is more intelligible if its *ontogenesis* has been traced. And yet more—an earlier *Urdummheit* is then on record, to be repaired later, while the reader watches, by the author himself if he is fortunate, or by other students who can see better. There is seminal virtue in a "primal stupidity."

The quest shall be indicated in due course. When at last it was under way, it justified an occasional report. There follow six of them.

I am profoundly grateful to my friend, Professor Erich Klinghammer, psychologist, of Purdue University, consulting editor of the Van Nostrand Reinhold Behavioral Science Series, for his appreciation of these and others of my essays, and his urging that the six join the company of the publications; and to Mr. George Narita, editor of the Professional and Reference Book Division, who is guiding the series into print. Its various authors are a goodly fellowship in which to find oneself.

A publication note. This collection was initiated by Professor Ilse Schwidetzky, head of the Anthropological Institute of Mainz University and by the S. Fischer Verlag, Frankfurt a/M (Ilse Grubrich-Simitis, editor in chief). Essays 1, 2, and 6 appeared, translated into German, as *Das Biogramn: Anthropologische Studien,* in Fischer's CONDITIO HUMANA series; numbers 3, 4, and 5 are freshly added to the present volume. Number 1 has never before appeared in English.

Berkeley, California   Earl W. Count

Introduction

In Search of the Biogram

There seem to be three kinds of approaches taken in textbooks that introduce college students to "anthropology": the evolution of man, from primate ancestry to modern races; "culture," commencing either with archeology or with ethnology; and a tandem of both.

Any and all three are discomforting to an alert mind—be he student or lifelong professional. For, he finds two loaded boxcars, one full of biology, the other of sociality. A college curriculum may indeed couple them, for the time being; the professional is at liberty to uncouple them forever afterward.

There is man—but no coherent image of him. Coupled boxcars do not demonstrate that the shape of human culture for all time to come was given when a particular animal form changed and developed in a way that predetermined a life mode that could have arisen in no other wise. The student will follow his senior professional in the belief that, sometime during the latest stages of that bodily evolution, a "new kind of evolution" took over, which led men even farther away from the collateral descendants of their common ancestry. Thus culture is the product of a unique mind; it has its own laws. A culturologist, if he so chooses (and he often does), is free to assert that in human evolution intelligence and environmental conditioning have superseded, even "dissolved," "instincts." We are still waiting to discover the precise meanings of these notions, however they be expressed. Lore and science do not mix well.

If our strictures are Draconian, it is because nothing less than a crucial issue of civilization is at stake, to which we must finally return. That aside—the gaunt condition just delineated impelled us, more than two decades ago, to a naive question. Surely, all the while those pre- and proto-humans were becoming what they did, their communal life-patterns continued, brain and behavior evolved concordantly; surely there could have been no time when some *tertium quid* slipped in, when something strange happened within a nervous system so that "instincts" waned as intelligence grew; did life-mode develop *genuinely* new ways of evolving?

There is a primitive wisdom of science that urges to naive questions, when we face a blank wall. The rest of the canon prescribes that there shall be only sophisticated answers to such questions. Wherefore, we shall not start from the premise that man's life mode is unique among all animals—any fool can see that—and shall refrain from telling students so. We ask: Is man's (social) behavior that of a primate, a mammal, a vertebrate even, as completely and unexceptionally as his body is, and for exactly the same fundamental reasons? Of course we know, and we are not forgetting, that man has his superlatives and his "uniquenesses," within some frame of discourse; that he has a capacity for creating values and living by them, or for destroying himself when he destroys them; that he has powers for "agony and ectasy"; that he is impelled to convert the means of livelihood away from animal simplicity and toward hugely elaborate efforts, which in the end give him exactly the same amount of sustenance as that of his far less endowed fellow creatures; that apparently he alone has anxieties about what his fellow humans think. All this, and much more, tolerates no simplistic explanation; yet the stubborn truth remains: Either we shrug the problem by invoking a *tertium quid,* or, because our mentation is scientific, we renounce any *ex nihilo* hypothesis, and insist on natural laws.

When, in 1951, our question first arose, interest in primate behavior was far less than it is today. Anthropologists, at least, got along very well without paying it mind. Very fortunately this is no longer true; yet primate behavior in its turn has hardly been cast in the larger mold of mammalian behavior. As for a cast of vertebrate configuration, the widest circle of all, there is none such. A science of general, comparative psychology does indeed exist, though still in its infancy. It is possible to hold symposia where papers on bees, fishes, dolphins, monkeys may all be poured out together; and ethologists have indeed been doing yeoman service among invertebrates and vertebrates alike. Still, we do not yet have in the behavioral sciences the equivalent of an evolutionary comparative morphology such as exists in the sciences of body. The reasons therefor are, of course, historical; but the condition is there.

The concept of the "biogram" is introduced in the first essay. In its broadest application, the term denominates the life-mode of any animal kind, considered as the expressed aspect of its physical morphology. More particularly, however, it is the behavior produced by that morphology and is exactly as configurative; for structure and function cannot but be one entity. Hence, in all its considerations there runs an undertone from the biological mechanisms that produce it.

As things turned out, a biogram of the vertebrates proved that it could be systematized in parallel with the morphology that forms the basis of taxonomic ordering. It proved feasible to reconstruct, at any rate in general outlines, a phylogenesis. And thereupon, if one juxtaposes an evolutionary account of the central nervous system, speculations become highly suggestive. Speculations they remain notwithstanding, until and unless neurology and psychology *together* can flesh them out

Precisely because it was an anthropologist who first asked the question, he turned his back on man; then, breasting the evolutionary current, he followed the vertebrates backward, down to the cyclostomes. It seemed that, as one progressed, the behaviors became simplified, stripped of a certain *quality* of details, while the gross pattern held throughout. Then, on touching bottom, one could reascend; this time, the "embellishments" added on again. Only after all this had been tried were man and biogram set to test each other. For whatever it may be worth, it seemed that a vertebrate-tetrapod-mammalian-primate "biogram" furnished an adequate structure upon which to continue attaching the particularly human "embellishments." Quite as importantly, there were found no "residuals"—no anomalies, no humannesses that refused accommodations. And there seemed to be a reverse dividend: without any anthropomorphizing whatever, the behaviors of nonhumans yet seemed, occasionally, more understandable (sometimes, even predictable!) from a human condition. Lorenz' "King Solomon's Ring" appeared unexpectedly potent.

Naturally, the hypothesis of the biogram cannot be validated by one, or by even a score, of researchers. Still, the next four studies put it to some testing; and on these occasions, with the frank intent of seeing whether man is the more intelligible from them. To wit:

Suppose that a certain behavioral complex is identifiable in nonhumans, who, however, are assumed to reflect fairly some ancient stem-ancestral pattern: What has happened to it, in the making of man? The second essay extracts from the primate reproductive cycle a segment which we labeled the "lactation complex"—clearly, a configuration at once anatomical, physiological, biochemical, psychological. Some of its ingredients are traceable even to the reptilian level; it becomes a definitive complex with the organization of the mammals; it undergoes some interesting and peculiar modifications as the primate order itself evolves; it changes hardly at all, physically, from the ape level to man. But *psychologically*, this mother-offspring relationship becomes markedly richer as the brains of monkeys and apes build upon it further interpersonal relations; and it is enormously magnified as the brain of *Homo sapiens* takes over.

The third essay picks up some observations dropped in the first one, concerning the evolution of the human version of primate familialism. It seemed to us that the lactation complex together with the sexuality dealt with in this note on incest, pretty much outline the essentials that are the seedbed of this fundamental of human sociality.

The fourth and the fifth essays, unlike the second, consider something about man that finds in apes none of a complex already and long since formed, which can be taken over, so to say, by an evolving human mentality. In the origin and evolution of the speech function ("phasia"), we have our safest encounter with a "break" or a "discontinuity" between ape and man; we may investigate more precisely just what such a discontinuity consists of. Yet we are committed, by hypothesis, to the speculation that this capacity too must have expanded, from an antecedent of not-speech. And now we find ourselves closely committed to an evolution of neuropsychological mechanisms. For, while indeed we may await eagerly whatever the students of primate psychology discover, if and as they crack the codes of utterances by monkeys and apes, instinctively we feel that such evidence cannot but be slender when the magnitude of the problem is realized.

"Lactation complex" and "phasia" together converge upon the proposition that at the core of the process which has made man lies the evolution of his power for making symbols so thoroughly that he has shaped his life by them. Certainly this is no new realization. But it is one thing to discourse, as anthropologists have done, on the cultural consequences of this power; it is quite another to see the brain as the maker of symbols—which anthropologists seem not to do.

From this standpoint, the human relations exemplified in all the latter four essays (2, 3, 4, 5) represent different *ad hoc* exercises of symbolopoea, at the *human* level. (We insert the "small print," in recognition that symbol-making seems not to be quite a human "patent.") The sixth essay (it was written before all but the first) is an attempt, not to build a bridge from the symbol-making brain to the cultural world it effects, but to place a few stepping-stones across the current, that there may be some gingerly, connecting passage. It continues to elude us all—this *aditus* between the scientific world of phenomena and the humanistic world of experiences and values. It had seemed to us worth the effort to register that an *aditus* there must nevertheless be.

The search for the biogram has eyed the question that every cultural tradition, Hottentot, "European," Papuan, Aztec must ask itself, each in its own way: What is man?[1] The answer may be hardly more than pragmatic; only philosophers give it a system of thought; the devoted may ponder it; it engages the chisel and the brush of the Australian and the Eskimo, and those of the Florentines and Umbrians. But unless a culture finds a viable answer, eventually it perishes. Every culture produces a mythology; it is always vaster than any of the media that essay to catch it. It is a defensible thesis that any culture may be given some appraisal in terms of the stature of the mythology it produces. A mythology is the truth as a culture sees it.

For it constitutes the world of symbols that man builds for himself to live in. It is an ecology that can occupy, full-time, students of brain-mind, anthropologists whose specialty is myths and rituals, humanists sensitive to the "affecting presence."[2]

We would bring these observations down to the here-and-now and the once-but-gone of the human image in our Occidental culture-tradition. It has had no coherent human image since the waning of the Middle Ages. This is not uttered in reproach, it is a statement of human condition. For a millennium or so, an image of man had stood amid a value system and a "sacred" world view. It began to crumble, at the onset of the Renaissance; for in the long run it could not cope with the crowding newer knowledge. Pieces of a more

[1]There was a striking echo of this when, in 1946, the United Nations was organizing itself. The Security Council had met to decide what should be the scope and nature of its agenda. The Western and the Communist blocs had each its dossier of proposals; quite pragmatic ones. The Lebanese delegate suggested that the Council should commence with the question, What is man? This the western bloc seemed to consider rather idle; the communist said that they already had a sufficient answer. Mrs. Roosevelt once remarked, in the writer's hearing, that the most stubborn difficulty that was plaguing the groundwork of this international body was its inability to arrive at common conceptual definitions.

[2]With thanks to Robert Plant Armstrong.

informed world view and human image there indeed are; we all are much aware, nonetheless, that ours is a day of self-doubt.

Occidental culture today is schizoid. A relatively simple and no longer controversial illustration will hint: In 1860, Thomas Huxley found himself unexpectedly pitted in debate against the Anglican Bishop Samuel Wilberforce, over the issues of Darwin's "The Origin of Species." The bishop was very knowledgeable in the facts of current science, and of course well educated in the traditions of his civilization, especially the "sacred" ones. According to the folklore of scientific history, Huxley's broadsword smote the enemy hip and thigh, and the victory lay with a relentless enlightenment over an obstinate and pious obscurantism. But this is not a very enlightened judgment. For, each of the debaters was the protagonist of a body of achieved values that is the very life-stuff of our civilization. But things had come to such a pass that an obsolescent, "sacred" world view stood against a newer but callow "secular" one. The debate was a skirmish in the self-defeat that our tradition was engaged in. The older view was worried and mistrustful of the younger; conversely, the latter had been finding the former no longer interesting.

The same *schisis* has another and familiar guise: incommunication between "science" and the "humanities." For want of better terms, we shall characterize the "sciences" as phenomenological knowledge, while the "humanities" are experiential. Science avoids value judgments; values are what the humanities live by. And a cultural anthropology has tried to be scientifically objective by developing the attitude of "cultural relativism," when values are the question. This does not promote an *entente* with the humanities, of either "sacred" or "secular" stripe. To draw a cleavage plane between phenomenological and experiential knowledge has been a great achievement, unique to Occidental culture-tradition and civilization; but the purchase price has been very heavy. The weakness of this achievement's strength has brought to us our desperation.

So, two anthropologies confront the novice at the university. In our time, it is the best that we can offer. Perhaps, in his or her time, or in that of their children's children, some one will do better. We shall hope that a *man-science* and the humanities will have entered upon goodly and continuing dialogue.

Earl W. Count

Contents

1 The Biogenesis of Human Sociality

An Essay in Comparative Vertebrate Sociology*

INTRODUCTION

One hundred years ago, Charles Darwin brought out his "The Origin of Species"; seven years later, Thomas Huxley followed it with "Man's Place in Nature." If a century afterwards we would no longer consider their evidence adequate proof of their thesis, it is because "species," "man," "nature" have gained far richer factual and theoretical content.

In Darwin's day, although Cuvier's dictum *"Il n'y a pas d'hommes fossiles"* already held premonitory cracks, nonetheless both speciation and the phylogenesis of man rested almost solely on comparative anatomy (including embryology). Since that time, however, processual sciences either have been born or have matured; indeed, their theoretical validation now rests, in part, upon their even-handed applicability to both man and other animals, by virtue of an assumed common phylogenetic relationship.

—Except for ethnology, or culturology. *"Il n'y pas d'animaux culturisés."* It is quite superfluous to remark that the students of human culture have made successful discoveries and analyses within their

*Published hitherto only in German translation. See *Homo* **IX**:129–146, 1958; **X**:1–35, 65–92, 1959.

own field of operations without ever anchoring them in biological premises. Yet if they were to study, instead, the life modes of any other animal species, they would consider themselves ecologists, ethologists, or other specialists within the science of biology. To be sure, the biological side of human living enlists plenty of study, for instance, by the medical sciences; but these in their turn are quite able to function without invoking ethnology. When, however, only pragmatic reasons can be adduced for making the life mode of man the one exemption in all nature from a primal dependency upon or rooting in biological regularities, the scientist cannot rid himself of a certain unease.

Ethnology treats a culturized life mode as though it were a *nova* in evolution. We repeat—this is allowable and fruitful, up to a point. But this is far from permitting one to erect some kind of "psychozoic era" as a capstone to the succession of life ages that parallel the geological series of rock formations. Of course, this is not something which we can lay at the door of the ethnologists; but rather at that of certain evolutionists. It deserves mentioning nonetheless; for it illustrates a certain trait of our Occidental cultural tradition. Our tradition starts with the distinctiveness of man over and against all other creation; so that only with reluctance has it come to recognize the weight of the similarities. In this, it betrays us. The reordering which scientific philosophy has brought to our tradition has lain in the principle that particularity must be identified and measured in terms of departure from a more embracive regularity already established, or established in the same operation that identifies the particularity.

In the study of man, we have not yet filled the gap between the primates with *no-culture* and the primates with culture. Until we have plausible speculation as to how the latter life mode has evolved out of the former, we cannot have a holistic anthropology.[1] The prehominid and protohominid bodies lived the lives of prehominid and protohominid primates. A *Ganzheitsanthropologie* is necessary if we are to "place" "man" in "nature."

Unfortunately, plausible speculation is as far as we can ever get; for there is no prospect of our ever recovering the life modes of fossils. Our speculations must continue to rest upon no more than a comparative biosociology of extant vertebrate forms. This fact we never dare forget.

Such a biosociology, however, is feasible. It is a comparative study of how the individuals and the groups of individuals within a given

---

[1]Cf. v. Eickstedt 1936: "Ganzheitsanthropologie."

animal species-community interreact, and how those interreactions stem from their biological constitutions.

We have the right to assume, as a working hypothesis until and unless proven wrong, that the architecture of the central nervous system common to the vertebrates functions essentially in the same way in all of them; and thus far all experimental work indicates that this is so. The present study (it is an abstract of a much more extensive one) considers "behavior" as the symptomatics of neurophsysiological processes that are externally observable. "Behavior" is no more all that takes place than pains, cramps, nausea are all there is to appendicitis or cholera. Behavior is the externalized portion of a syndrome which includes visceral and other physiological tonicities; the syndrome may include alterations of bodily appearance not under control of the voluntary nervous system: blushing, paling, melanophore intensification, enlargement and engorgement of wattles—to say nothing of changes in blood pressure and biochemical states of the blood, etc. If we care to distinguish between physical and behavioral changes, that is our privilege; it is also our artifact. It is justifiable pragmatically, but it distorts the reality. A situational approach, on the other hand, looks for a syndrome possessing a configuration.

Just as we find that bees and termites possess life modes that are part of their total organismal configuration, we have a right to look for a life mode among vertebrates that is part of their phyletic configuration. We may expect the evolution of vertebrate form to include evolution of life mode. And we have justification in expecting that man's vertebrate constitution, from which he obviously has never been emancipated, will include a life mode which, no matter how culturized, remains indissolubly a part of that constitution. In the course of this exploration, we may hope to discover the route by which a life mode of no-culture has naturally become culturized, in pace with the emergence of those (anatomically and physiologically quite secondary) peculiar modifications of the brain which distinguish man from his Primate relatives. Indeed, there is no other imaginable way by which we might make the discovery.

A "culturized" life mode which nonetheless is primate and vertebrate inevitably raises the question of "instinct" and "intelligence." Certainly it should not need to be said that the question is far beyond the scope and the capacities of the present study. Fortunately, however, thanks to the students of the psyche, our conception of both instinct and intelligence has become scientifically sophisticated. Besides this, the students of neurology are beginning to place their fingers upon the brain mechanisms which operate in the production of complex psychological phenomena. We can utilize their findings; but over and beyond this we can watch the vertebrates as they evolve ever richer content within their basic behavioral configuration, and note certain cerebral elaborations which have accompanied this evolution. We shall not try to establish cause-and-effect; but the mere act of juxtaposing has value—if for no better reason than that it seems never to have been done before.

THEORETICAL CONSIDERATIONS

Some theoretical propositions will be advanced first, without proof, to offer a point of view.

1. Anything less than organism-in-environment is an abstraction. Furthermore, every organism deals with two environments; the world about it and its own internal organization. The nervous system itself, a part of the latter, is the device whereby the organism mediates between these two environments. The organism, however, has an "interest" vested only in its own internal environment, which constitutes its self; and not in the external environment.

2. This hypothesis restores to the organism the autogenous character that is denied it by an approach which would view behavior merely as an adjustive response or reaction to an initiative coming from the environment. The external environment—the physical world —does not present "stimuli" to any organism. The external world, as far as the organism is concerned, is composed of regularized energies; it is the organism that converts them into stimuli by means of its own neural mechanisms. The process of "digesting" an energy and converting it into a stimulus begins with the sensory receptors; the rest of the nervous system is both a further digestive and an assimilative mechanism.

3. This affords theoretical backing to v. Uexküll's *"Umwelt"* and *"Merkwelt"* concepts, which we adopt.

4. Psychologists reject today the notion of there existing a special "social instinct." Nevertheless, it is universally true that individual animals "react" to their own kind with patterns of special behavior. This makes of every member of such a group an item of environment for all the other members, so that there is no essential difference between an organism and this social environment of which it is a part. We shall call this the "self-environment" or "autocoenosis" of the species.

Although peculiar reaction to one's own kind is social behavior, it still does not constitute social organization. The latter comes into existence when the total behavioral repertoire of the species is split up and distributed differentially among the member individuals, so that part of this total is elicited as an initiating act in one individual toward another, and another part is the response of the other to that act. Initiating and responding acts are different; and a response cannot occur without an initiation. This builds up a system of complementations, in which one act has but incomplete "meaning" without its complementation. Clearly this is much more than mere gregariousness, where each individual exercises the entire behavioral repertoire in the company of his fellows. Among lower (invertebrate) species, one often encounters animal activity within an *aggregation*; when numbers have assembled because one common stimulus draws them, we have a *congregation*;[2] but this is not social behavior, and cannot itself initiate social organization.

Two individuals thus *socially* interdependent may be considered a "minimum society," if one so chooses. A heterosexual pair of dung-beetles engaged in stocking a nest for eggs are such a society, though a temporary one. But among both insects and vertebrates, there are genera in which the behavioral repertoire is exercised completely only if the group is much more numerous. In such cases, we do not find the randomness, so to speak, of the "Brownian movement" seen among physical particles; instead, it runs through a programmatic course of behavior. This makes the configurative approach to the study of societies indispensable.

5. More analytic studies than the present one should find it convenient to treat a social group as a closed system or field, in which every individual is a nucleus of social energies, and the psychological orientations are taken as vectors. Thus, whenever individuals mobilize their energies toward some goal ("interests"), the vectors become polarized to produce subfields. If this closed system be passed through the time dimension, it will be found that the polarities of subfields undergo transformation; yet the transformations themselves are dependent functions of some dynamic pattern, some configuration, which "controls" the changes.

The annual cycles of vertebrate societies offer plenty of material for such analyses. If, in the springtime, lengthening daylight "activates" the pituitary gland and sets in motion the reproductive syndrome, it is after all the inherent constitution of the animal itself

2Cf. Allee, 1938.

which determines the particular course of actions which the animal will enter upon.

In terms of a field composed of social energies and vectors, the distances between the individuals represent equilibria between attractions and repulsions. In a highly gregarious society, the attractions are such that the individuals exist in close propinquity, the areal population is high, and interindividual energy discharges are frequent, which tend toward varietal reduction, to closer approaches to some stereotypic mean, as it were. In so-called "solitary" species, centrifugal energies carry the individuals farther apart before an equilibrium is achieved between attractions and repulsions. But all these balances change cyclically. For instance, at the onset of the sex cycle the individuals' psyche changes tonus; the animals tend to congregate until a set of internal tensions have been grounded. It needs emphasizing that dispersal and keeping distance between individuals is a social phenomenon quite as genuinely as interindividual attraction is. A period of the one condition is usually followed by a change and trend toward the other. The changes may occur in rapid or slow cycles.

The psychological life space does not coincide with the areal life space. The former extends over the area occupied at any time by the social group. A gregarious group such as bison may possess an enormous life space yet occupy but a fraction of it areally at any time; the herd then moves about more or less compactly: its psychological life space travels with it. For a species of solitary livers, on the other hand, the psychological life space is diffuse, and may practically coincide with the areal life space. Here individual ranges subdivide the areal life space of the species.

6. We accept the psychologists' conclusion that "social" behavior is but general behavior of the animal adapted to particular conditions and organized toward its fellows. At the same time we shall treat all behavior as but the externally visible symptomatics of neurophysiological processes; and therefore, like all symptoms, only a fraction of what is really going on. Moreover, one and the same symptom is capable of being produced by more than one internal process or state. Psychic responses are versatile; they may enter into the composition of different syndromal patterns.

7. We shall be much concerned with syndromal behavior. The greater bulk of laboratory experiments in psychology are concerned with items of behavior, and therefore are not designed to operate on the level of syndromal configuration. (This in no wise disparages those experiments. Without their results, we could never pass to the study of syndromes.)

Some new terms will be necessary.

a. There are no "gregarious" and "solitary" species—only societies that alter their degrees of individual dispersal and congregation periodically, according to their peculiar internal constitutions and the situational circumstances. All the members of a species must at some time and in some way react with their own kind; therefore any group that is being viewed as a social system in any state whatever is termed a *coenonia*. The penguin coenonia is continuously gregarious, the red deer coenonia lives as sex-societies when not in rut, and in small subgroups at that; but the sexes mingle in a way characteristic of the coenonia when rutting season is on. During sex quiescence, the coenonia of the Anolis lizard disperses, the individuals become solitary; which means that, not only does each live by itself, it also pays little attention when one of its own kind approaches. The term may be used generically or specifically; as—the coenonia of the genus *Homo,* or a coenonia composed of a group of intercommunicating villages. The term is dynamic, and not static, in that it emphasizes the reactivities of a group and not the numerical and corporeal composition of the group.

b. The life cycle of the individual, the life mode of the coenonia or species or even phylum, taken as a cycle, is its *biogram.* Only by following individual or group through a whole period until all the processes commence to repeat (i.e., over an entire cycle) can we record its biogram.

c. Such terms as "appetitive behavior" and "consummatory act" are adopted from Craig (1918) and from the ethologists.[3]

d. Complex behavior patterns are marshaled about some general and prolonged "interest" ("interest polarities"); hence a *syndrome;* for instance, the "reproductive syndrome." Implicit are the neurological mechanisms involved, and the endocrinal tonicities; in other words, the syndrome is a total psychologic and physiologic condition-and-process. Within the syndrome there are *psychodromes,* compounded in varying degrees. Here we are thinking of behavioral segments; for instance, the nesting, courting, parental psychodromes.

e. We shall find that the biogram of vertebrates contains two phases. Vertebrates signalize the onset of their reproductive periodicity and its cessation by changing the territory of operations. This is a "phase migration."

g. Putatively, sometime during the Miocene and Pliocene, the Homindae emerged from an ancestral alloprimate stock. The incipient stage is that of the *pre-;* the earliest and most primitive yet unmis-

---

[3]See Tinbergen, 1951, p. 104 ff.

takably hominid stage is that of *protohominids*. For our purposes, the terms need not be defined any more closely. They cover the period when there evolved those cerebral mechanisms that have made symbolizations, technologies, and all cultural skills possible. It is assumable that "brain does as brain is."

h. For the evolutionary process whereby the hominid emerged from the alloprimate, we shall adopt the Spanish term *hominación*; hence, *homination (sive Menschwerdung)*.

PROCEDURE

We shall gain perspective if we attack the subject of the biogram among insects, particularly the colonial forms, before moving on to a survey of the vertebrates. The latter survey will be interrupted to introduce the subject of the vertebrate brain in its relation with the evolution of social behavior, before we pass from brains without a developed neopallium to the mammals. We shall narrow the survey of the mammals progressively down to the primates and finally to men.

THE BIOGRAM OF INSECTS

Umwelt and Constitution

A horse and a bee sharing a meadow are in the same environment, but not the same *Umwelt*. They possess different ecological dimension ratios—the relativities of their bodily dimensions to the dimensions of the environmental details are obviously different: each organism constructs a different world-as-problem. For each, that world was to a certain degree predetermined for it when its aquatic palae-ancestors developed, respectively, a chitinous exoskeleton and a cartilage-calciferous endoskeleton. When once terrestrialized, the chitinous exoskelton permitted Orthoptera with a wingspread of 70 cm; the bony endoskeleton, the dimensions of Brontosaurus and of Baluchitherium. Let the arthropod exoskelton be cited in a spirit of *pars pro toto*: in reality it is an integral part of a more embracive configurative economy that explains at once the *Umwelt* of insects, their psychoneurological construction, and the devices which express their sociality.[4]

[4]Cf. Kennedy, 1927.

The joined exoskeleton allows, over the range of the insect class, an astounding variety of relatively gross movements, but a limited repertoire of these per individual. The insect is a peripatetic tool kit. When it alights from flying, or falls to the ground, the shock is absorbed by a passive and solid framework—in contrast to the performance of the vertebrate, which relies upon the psychomotor pilotage of a cerebellum.

The insect exoskeleton permits instantaneous access of oxygen to the bodily tissues, yet prevents the desiccation of a body possessing a large surface relative to small volume. The insect can range from relative quiescence to a blazing activity instantaneously.

The brain is, of course, calibrated to the quality and variety of possible bodily movements; yet, limited though it is in this direction, it has developed an astounding capacity for harboring complex behavior chains that are transmissible only via the gene constitution.

This capacity is indeed so extreme—particularly among the colonialized genera—that they seem to have trapped students of behavior into overspecifying the differences between "instinctive," "learned," and "intelligent" behavior. Later, there will be occasions to bring up this subject again; at the moment, suffice it to remark that "instinctive" behavior is now seen to be not nearly so completely automatic and rigid as was once believed.

Insects as Terrestrial Evolutes

The Phylum Arthopoda, like every other animal phylum, had its origin in the sea. With negligible exceptions, it is one of the only two phyla that have succeeded in establishing terrestrialized forms, the other of the two being the Chordata.

Sociality is never more than rudimentary among the aquatic classes of the phylum. Aggregations and congregations occur, but no societies. Societies—"colonies"—exist only among the insects; and then, as compared with the many noncolonial forms, they are actually rare, even though these colonial forms have proven enormously successful.

Wheeler[5] declares that socialization has been attempted by insects at least 30 different times, in 8 of the orders; and 12 of these attempts have eventuated in full-dress socializations. In other words, the arthropodal pre- or proto-insects became terrestrial animals long before they evolved social configurations. These social schemes, therefore, have been founded upon an already terrestrialized body form.

[5]1928; p. 16.

This is a cardinal point. As we shall see, the vertebrates possess a rudimentary social configuration while still aquatic—and this scheme has evolved apace with terrestrialization; it therefore is a built-in ingredient of the vertebrate form itself. There has been no chance for it to arise repeatedly on separate and independent occasions.

Despite the fact that various insect lines have developed socialized biograms separately, they all naturally have exploited only the arthropod architecture which their palae-ancestry has bequeathed to them. A number of tangible life features have been utilized, variously, to this end; and no one of them, but only the way in which they have been combined, is accountable for the colonizations of termites, ants, wasps, bees. This deserves a treatment, since it illustrates in a classic way the configurative nature of social evolution.

1. The arthropod body is metameric and the metameres prove capable of particular specializations, yet each conforming to an over-all bodily configuration. This capacity is older than the insects, who have continued to exploit it.

Coupled with this is the ontogenetic phenomenon that growth requires a periodic shedding of the old chitinous envelope and a secretion of a larger one (molting).

The most primitive orders of insects have perpetuated this combination (they are ametabolous); among the more derived ones, the young are but imperfectly adultiform; and by successive moltings they acquire additional bodily structures (e.g. wings) and capabilities (they are hemimetabolous). The transitional instars are *nymphs* or *naiads*. The most evolved insect orders are completely metabolous: Each successive instar is morphologically and biogrammatcally unique. During the phylogeny of these insects, the processes of ontogenesis have, so to speak, been sorted over and spread out on the table of time, that new ingredients may be introduced into the pattern. Thus we find the stages of larva-pupa-adult; both the larva and the adult are hatchlings, each with a behavioral repertoire almost complete on emergence, with very little room and need for learning adaptations.

Another consequence of the capacity for regional specializations of metameres is the polymorphism of the completely socialized genera. The insect class as a whole comprises a most astonishing range of bodily shapes and proportions; and within the species of Isoptera and social Hymenoptera, there are special body shapes with specialized functions ("castes").

For a socialized biogram, there is yet one other indispensable ingredient: that transgenerational provision made by elders for the young, usually seen as parentalism; but furthermore the life span of the elder must overlap that of the young.

The several successive steps of preparing a nest or chamber for the eggs, tending them during incubation, and even guarding the hatchlings until they begin to fend for themselves, occur already in as lowly an order as the Dermaptera; they occur in any number of more evolved orders, notably the Coleoptera, where there are degrees of cooperation between both parents.

Now, we may consider these features to be the resources from which colonialism may be built; yet none of them has been a *primum mobile* toward colonialization of the genus. Thus:

The Isoptera (termites) are no more than hemimetabolous. They are nonetheless thoroughly colonialized; and their behavioral repertoire surpasses, perhaps, the most evolved of all other insects. The termites have built for themselves exceedingly elaborate environments —vast chambers and galleries, where they cultivate "vegetable gardens" and raise "cattle." Their polymorphism, with its attendant specialization of functions, exceeds that of any other order. The young are born as nymphs, into an environment already engineered by the older generations; which means that they are actually heirs to a technologically produced economy and environment, which will be theirs to carry on. The more primitive care of the young by their parent has evolved into the impersonal parentalism of the colony.

It is to be noted carefully that, but for the artifactual environment already in existence, the instinctive behavior patterns of the hatchlings would not unfold properly. (Evidence has been gathering in recent years which proves that an elicitation from the environment must occur at the calendrical moment when an innate psychoneural mechanism has reached an operative level of maturity; otherwise it remains permanently distorted.) The difference between an insect colony and a human society is not that of a complex social automatism as against a culturized society—as indeed has been asserted on many occasions—but between a culture with a high instinctive component and low learning component and a culture with high learning component. (We defer comment on the instinctive component in human society.)

A termite colony starts from a heterosexual pair, which first digs itself the incipient home of the future colony. Once the female starts to lay eggs, she ceases ever to do anything else, her abdomen swelling to the size of a small finger. (The eggs appear with clocklike precision, up to 30,000 a day, and 100 million in a lifetime.) The male remains with her to replenish her with spermatozoa. The castes are all bisexual, though in the soldiers and workers the sex organs remain infantile. Members of the fertile castes eventually fly off and start new colonies. A colony, therefore, is constituted of a pair of parents plus their countless offspring.

The resemblance of this biogram to those of colonial Hymenoptera is striking; all the more in that the latter have evolved their schemes quite independently. There exist many noncolonial genera (although all of the Formicidae are colonial); so that the stages by which the colonial Hymenoptera have achieved their biograms can be reconstructed.

In generalized terms, a Hymenoptera colony begins with a fertilized female, who starts a "nest," lays eggs, and tends them; these run through larval and pupal stages, finally emerging as adults, who turn out to be sterile females. Thenceforth, they enlarge the home, tend the young, forage for food, defend the colony, even raid the colonies of other genera. Fertile females and males are produced but periodically (the latter by parthenogenesis); they swarm on the "nuptial flight," and thus a new colony-family-generation is seeded.

The two schemes are contrastive as well as similar. In both, there is polymorphism; the labor is divided between an egg-laying specialist (erroneously called a "queen"; she may just as well be called the gonad of a social organism) and sterile attendants who do everything else; the environments are artificial constructs which are more than incubating environments, since they continue to be referent environments for the individuals throughout their lives. The members of both these orders, evolutionarily poles apart, are agriculturists, herdsmen, and engineers. Impersonal parentalism exists; from a vertebrate standpoint, it is not "parental" but "sororal" care. But this is merely a semantic trick; for such terms are misapplications of the terminology of human society, where pragmatically "mother" and "sister" have social much more than biological meaning. In insect colonies, "kinship" is an empty and irrelevant term. In an insect colony, where status is determined by the rigidity of polymorphism and appropriately circumscribed and predetermined behavior, the rearing of offspring is a great, impersonal enterprise. Among vertebrates, by contrast, status is determined via psychological channels; and this leaves open the possibility of developing the familialism of the birds and mammals. Sex behavior and germ cell production have been eliminated (at least under regular living conditions of the colony) from the workers; while paradoxically, the care for young has been increased to what to us vertebrates looks like an "obsession."

There are also contrasts between the two orders. The Isoptera have retained both sexes for the work of the colony, though sexual behavior is as irrelevant to that work as it is among Hymenoptera. And while it undoubtedly is true that to develop the bodily mechanisms—anatomical and psychological—necessary for the life of the wasp and ant the immature must pass through a complete metamorphosis (larva and pupa), the Isoptera achieve the equivalent result with no more than a semimetabolous arrangement.

If we turn to the Lepidoptera (moths, butterfiies) we encounter as highly evolved a metamorphism and body morphology as that of the Hymenoptera; yet these insects never develop colonialism: The adults —by contrast with the Hymenoptera—are short-lived; the generations do not overlap; provision for the yet unhatched young is comparatively rudimentary. Complete metabolism has not produced a complex behavioral repertoire, but only a highly specialized body; yet there is no more polymorphism than that of sex monoecism. We note the contrast with the Isoptera; incomplete metamorphism has not prevented the development of these specialties.

Several points should now be clear, that are important for our appraisal of the vertebrates:

1. Within the class Insecta itself, we find that to possess a resource which in one order or family is exploited in the construction of a scheme of colonialism does not mean that this will happen in all others which possess it. Furthermore—

2. There is no simple correlation between degree of morphological evolution and psychological evolution.

3. Even though colonial configurations have evolved independently and repeatedly in the class, and present differences that are integral parts of the taxonomic differences within the class, they all prove to be variations upon the central theme of "Insect-ness."

4. Though colonialism (socialized living) is present in both the insects and the vertebrates, and although in both the social schemes are constructed out of such things as division of labor, hierarchies of status, parentalism, identification with territory and home, on inspection these turn out to be logical rather than phenomenal terms; each form of colonialism represents separate and independent evolutionary processes. The insect social configurations, no matter what the differences *inter se*, stand together over against the vertebrate social configuration.

It has been asserted repeatedly that human socialization has originated in answer to the lengthening of the infancy and childhood period, which has gone along with the enlargement of the brain. An analogous point is sometimes put forward to account for socialization among insects; the analogy being that elaboration of parental care is cardinal in both lines. Wheeler,[6] however, has remarked that in the evolution of insect colonialism, it is the adult stage of life that lengthened first, making social life possible; and that consequently it is already there to span the period of retarded ontogenesis, when that retardation comes about. From what has just been reviewed, it is clear that retarded ontogenesis can occur with and without a lengthened adult life span (Lepidoptera and Hymenoptera); that colonialism can occur with and without retarded ontogenesis (Isoptera and colonial Hymenoptera); and that lengthened adult life span, even with retarded ontogenesis, does not inevitably lead to colonialism (Coleoptera—who deserve far more attention than the present account accords them; many solitary Hymenoptera; Diptera. Even if the adult life spans of the latter are brief, they are several times the length of the ontogenetic life spans). As for the case of humans, and other vertebrates, the original statement above is oversimplified to the point of being fallacious. For, as we shall see, socialization in the lowest vertebrates starts among the young whose parents forsook them as soon as the eggs were laid. Human lengthening of the ontogenetic life span took place in an already favorable socialized environment, one that permitted it to happen. But socially living avian and mammalian genera are almost innumerable. The point that we may salvage from the apparent or spurious inconsistencies of the original claim is nevertheless important: When a species evolves, it is the entire constitution which makes a shift; it alters its ontogenesis, it alters its adult life mode, its movements, its psyche. These represent adjustments within itself. But it does much more: as an adult it alters adaptively toward the offspring it will produce; and that goes hand-in-glove with the offspring's altering adaptively toward the elder who is in process of producing it.

The female *Sphex*, for instance, goes through an elaborate behavior in preparing the nest chamber for her eggs. The acts are *telic*—that is, they have no meaning except in terms of what they accomplish for the future offspring; and the offspring are preadapted to exploit their mother's preparations. No mystical or metaphysical doctrine has to be adopted before this simple fact can be admitted. In the self-environment of animals, adjustive mutalisms—physiological and psychological both—are intragenerational; but they are also transgenerational.

[6]1923, p. 10; 1928, p. 14.

There are several further points. Among colonial insects, where a colony equals a generation, it is obvious that the "queen" lives as long as the colony; but from the standpoint of the developing larvae, the important thing is not the life spans of its nurses: It is that there shall be an uninterrputed succession of nurses, even if these should die.

And it is obvious that the insect scheme allows but a minimum opportunity for anything but biological heritage. (Cultural transmission of a sort and of a certain quantity does take place.)

In a socialized species—one which exists as interreacting groups of individuals, whether these be in close and constant association or related more diffusely—the total behavioral repertoire of the species is never expressed by every individual. Instead, there appear subtypes or subgroups, whose expressed repertoire represents a restriction. This may—and perhaps always does—accompany an expansion of the total repertoire of the species. This is much more readily visualized among insects than among vertebrates; for the polymorphism of insects obviously limits individuals to movements specialized with their bodily specialties. This, however, in no wise implies that their nervous systems *lack* the behavioral mechanisms which remain unexpressed; for the entire psychoneural potentialities of the species may well be present, though in many ways permanently latent. The point is of theoretical interest only, as far as these insects are concerned. But the nonsocialized Hymenoptera, though inferior as specialists, appear to be more versatile than their socialized cousins: It is as though they simply lack the bodily straitjacket imposed upon the individuals of a polymorphic genus. Among vertebrates, however, the point has livelier connotation. For the only heteromorphism of the subphylum is that of sexual dimorphism; and there is good evidence that the entire behavioral repertoire of a species is carried by every individual, and that part of it remains latent by virtue of bodily dimorphism. And it seems plausible that this lack of morphological specialization is correlated with their superior capacity for modifying their behavior.

THE BIOGRAM OF THE VERTEBRATES

Introduction

Theoretical biology has found it convenient to distinguish between those life processes which are concerned with the well-being of the individual and those by which the individual transmits its kind. In many animals, the reproductive process is but a relatively brief phase in the life cycle; among the colonial insects, it is concurrent with the life of the colony and is a major focus of social interests. The biogram of the vertebrates is engineered on the basis of a two-phase cycle: a phase of reproductive quiescence and a phase of reproductive activity. Each phase transpires under a different endocrine presidency; each is marked by peculiar behavioral patterns. These phases persist, no matter how gregarious or how solitary the life habits of the individuals may be.

The reproductive phase has received far more study than the non-reproductive. The former is the more dramatic: The agonisms of the individuals are more varied, more intense, more completely organized and patterned. In addition, there have been economic reasons for this one-sided interest: The fishing industries are concerned about the breeding habits of herring, salmon, tuna, mackerel; seals and mink are valued for their fur; huntsmen prey upon ducks, geese, and deer.

As may be expected, among the lower vertebrates the chief occupation of the nonreproductive phase is feeding. To the student, this lends it a monotony; yet it is not without a social structuring. For, if the group be small, the individuals may develop status hierarchies and leadership-followership. The individuals manifest practically no awareness of sex differences; so that if, in a bisexual group the males tend to dominate, it is by virtue of a generally higher metabolic rate and aggressiveness. But the difference becomes a relative and not an absolute one. However, from cyclostomes to mammals, the brain increases enormously in its capacity for versatility of conduct; so that the nonreproductive phase fills up with ever richer patterns of psyche, until, at the human level, it is in the nonreproductive field that culture has had the bulk of its development.

The vertebrates contrast with the insects in the following biogrammatic features:

All the adults, being fertile, engage in the reproductive activities of the coenonia. This is what makes the diphasic biogram operative. Vertebrates are homoiomorphic, no matter how solitary or gregarious be the life habits of a species at any time; except for the dimorphism of sex. Since any degree of bodily hetermorphism confines the individual to expressing less than the entire behavioral repertoire of the species, by this much the vertebrate species are functionally specialized. Here, of course, is the biosocial anlage which eventuates at the human level in the sex division of status and occupation—which is the most elemental and the universal functional specialization in human cultures. But no vertebrate species constructs its sociogram on a basis of a polymorphism.

Vertebrate homoiomorphy is even more thoroughgoing than this lack of polymorphy would indicate; for even the sex dimorphism is but a relative matter. For every vertebrate individual, without any known exceptions, is ambisexual—from his/her anatomy to his/her endocrinology.[7] Each possesses, as far as evidence indicates, potentially the entire psychoneurological and behavioral repertoire of the species (of course, with certain bodily performances excepted, which are anatomically impossible—for instance, a male mammal cannot give birth—and largely under autonomic nervous control). If in any species the sexes behave differently, it is because of a hormonal balance that is acting selectively upon a common psychoneurological repertoire. Egg incubation is a male role in the ostrich but a female role in the turkey-hen, because in each species the sensitivity of a certain element of psychoneurological mechanism to the respective hormonal balances is different. Ambisexualism manifests itself in countless ways: in the reversals of parental roles as just illustrated; in homosexual behaviors that are occasional or persistent: "effeminate" males and virilism among females. It may be involved in cases of males with some forms of low dominance drive and of females with some forms of high dominance drive—although in this matter we cannot be too cautious in our appraisals. At the human level, various social groups treat some of the manifestations of ambisexualism as social problems; other groups exploit them as a cultural asset. And ambisexualism has entered into the creation of the sublimest art, as well as having generated fathomless personal problems.

The vertebrates thus are seen to lack the capacity to develop stereotypic differentia like those of insects; so that a vertebrate society is organized upon a very different principle: that of *status,* which is determined through contact experiences between individuals, and so is subject constantly to realignment. Vertebrates living as groups whose individuals make repeated contacts arrange these statuses into hierarchies. This obtains from fish to bird to mammal. A vertebrate society thus gives the picture of being at any moment in a state of dynamic equilibrium.

When two individuals do not simply ignore each other's presence, but begin to adjust a portion of their behavior to the movements of the other, we may describe it as "taking each other's rhythm." The

[7]Myxine—a cyclostome—is even normally a hermaphrodite. Hermaphroditic Anura are not uncommon.

courting rituals of many animals[8] are intense and appetitive; but they are only special and dramatic cases of the more general phenomenon of interindividual reactivity. Particularly, Lorenz[9] has studied with insight the *"Kumpan"* among pairs of birds. On the avian and the mammalian levels, if not among the lower vertebrates, heterosexual as well as isosexual pairs perform a variety of activities in each other's presence that are not sexually directed, and so stimulate each other. A hen who is not hungry is impelled to eat if her companions are doing so. In the nonreproductive phase, quite a variety of mammals travel about in isosexual pairs or groups. After the brood period is over, bird mates may continue indefinitely to live together: among geese, even lifetime monogamies are established. The phenomena of rhythm-taking extends to groups. Excitement, even to the point of becoming hysterias, can spread through a flock or herd (stampedes). After the reproductive phase is over, migratory birds congregate into flocks and spend much time synchronizing their rhythms.

Primitive human societies make much more of communal dancing then do sophisticated societies. Among men there are the preparatory war dances; the boatmen's chanties that synchronize their paddling; marching songs; to say nothing of the sophisticated symphonic orchestras of Bali and Vienna. Women grind their corn and hoe while they sing in unison or antiphonally. Very significant are the communal dances executed by sex moieties: Here the sexes as such "take each other's rhythm."[10] The phenomena are real enough; what we lack is their study by scientific methods.

Whether or not interindividual behavior alters among insects with population density and quantity, this holds true for many vertebrates; possibly for all. Among small groups, opportunity exists for repeated contacts with the same individual which does not occur where the society is very numerous. Therefore the behavior of the individuals of a species may differ markedly, depending upon whether they form a large or a small group. One other variable is involved: the psychic caliber of the individuals themselves. Psychic caliber is further analyzable: there is the degree of innate gregariousness of the individual—

[8]Rhythm-taking is an essential ingredient of the mating rituals of a number of arthropod species—most spectacularly, of scorpions. This is true also of vertebrates; but the very fact that among the latter it is such a conspicuous factor in other situations as well, serves to emphasize its importance in the sociality of vertebrate species.

[9]1935.

[10]The effects of rhythm-taking can be seen in any enterprise of sophisticated societies, where man and women are assigned to a common task. If given their freedom, they will gradually gravitate toward a sex division of portions of the task—and always expect the other moiety to keep up its portion.

which, in turn, belongs within the range of gregarious propensity of the species. Yet further—the gregarious propensity may intensify or diminish relative to such things as the phase in which the social biogram (the sociogram) finds itself at any given moment; that is, one and the same society varies its degree of gregariousness cyclically. What is most essential to see, in all this, is the fact that the situation we are trying to grasp and describe is a fluid one; and all generalizations, essential though they be, are limited and even fluctuating.

An illustration may help here. A penguin society numbers countless thousands. While we know nothing about their social relationships during their phase of sex quiescence, the behavior of some species during their breeding season is rather well documented. Probably under the same pituitary activation that operates also among other birds, individuals are impelled to depart from their fellows for the distant breeding ground. But this social centrifugality strikes many of them simultaneously, so that while some departures are individual, most are group-wise. Arrived at the nesting sites, members of both sexes identify with territory individually, and tolerate the presence only of members of the opposite sex. When at last pairing has occurred, and the next stages of the reproductive syndrome are under way, individuals react most frequently with those who are their more immediate neighbors. While this produces dominance-subordinance reactions among neighbors, subgroups do not seem to form, apparently because after all the population is a continuum. No "tribal government" is ever in evidence: The penguin mentality is too small to encompass such numbers. Nonetheless, molar suggestibility is very strong: Penguins collect in informal and temporary groups for excursions of fun, and prior to migrations back to the territory of their other phase, they perform most astounding mass maneuvers that resemble those on a military parade ground. (These have been interpreted as a psychic survival from palae-ancestors who flew when migrating.)

A further variable in vertebrate conduct is its context; that is, when two individuals direct stimuli at each other, the conduct of the respondent incorporates situational factors into his answer. Contextual behavior occurs to some degree among at least the higher invertebrate phyla, if not in the lowest; but it is well developed even among the lower vertebrates. Illustratively—a fish, lizard, bird, or dog defending its home territory against an intruder of its own kind can usually defeat him (even when the latter is the more powerful); then, if the relations be reversed, the former loser is likely to be the victor.

Finally, I would suggest that what the psychoanalysts term the "ego" (*das Ich*) has its phyletic anlage in the status mechanisms indicated in the foregoing; perhaps—dare we say it?—the "super-ego" also.

Territorialism

It is characteristic for vertebrates, when they enter the other phase of their biogram, to change territorial setting for it. From cyclostomes to birds and mammals, this commonly means an actual migration to another territory; so that the habitat range is bipolar. But even in those cases where the species remains in the same physical location, it changes attitude toward its territory; we may say, therefore, that whether there is actual physical migration or not, there occurs a "psychological phase migration." Whether or not there is a physical migration, the new behavior toward territory is the same. It consists of individuals, particularly the males, appropriating for private occupation some spot that hitherto was "open" country, and exploiting it in the reproductive syndrome. The observer's first impression of this behavior, which he encounters in all the vertebrate classes, is likely to be that the society has temporarily dissolved. On second sight, he finds the home spots not maximally but only optimally separated; the owners may even keep in touch with each other by advertising calls, although this is not universal; there remains some communal territory; and the homeowner who is threatened by an intrusive danger often can "summon" his follows with his cries. The latter phenomenon occurs, at any rate, among reptiles (Caimans) and certainly among birds and mammals. This behavioral pattern retires with the passing of the reproductive phase.

Social Behavior During the Reproductive Phase

For the lower vertebrates, the reproductive phase is much the shorter. Why this is so, and what is involved when, among the higher vertebrates, it gradually usurps a greater share of the total time span of the diphasic cycle of the biogram, will appear when we come to examine the vertebrate taxonomic divisions *separatim*. At present, it is important that we recognize: (1) that there are patterns of behavior which break to the surface only during this reproductive phase; (2) that they are under the presidency of a hormonal syndrome which is active only at this time, and which is responsible for the activation of the neuropsychic syndrome; (3) that the reproductive phase thus is manifestly a *mood which periodically engages the sociography of a coenonia.* The implications for the evolution of human society should be clear. Primate society is an evolute from palae-ancestral mammalian society; human society is an evolute from palae-ancestral primate society. Phylogeny does not support the notion that human society has sprung from an amalgamation of familial units; it does support the notion that the human familial unit, like that of man's relatives, represents a patterned segregation of certain activities and interests within a society. Like other points of this essay, this one will be brought out more fully later.

The reproductive phase sees the hitherto homoiomorphous society (in terms of its behavior) developing sex moieties; passing of the phase witnesses the recession of this social dimorphism. This is but one facet of the heightened individualism that appears—that of the males "staking out" home grounds, in which they will tolerate no other male; and both sexes developing an intolerance of their iso-sexuals and an interest in their antisexuals—an identification which previously had been nonexistent or, rather, nonmanifest. Yet paradoxically, these antagonisms do not disrupt the society. In other words, there is a realignment of social vectors and tensors, but not a cancellation.

The conduct of both male and female vertebrates often appears so strangely "human" that it is easy to commit the blunder of anthropomorphizing. On the other hand, there is nothing unscientific about the notion that the similarities are due to a common vertebrate *souche*; and such recognition is the reverse of anthropomorphizing. It does not end up by reading into lowlier animal forms the psychic complexities of the higher; it does read into the psyche of the higher animal anlagen that have been derived from its palae-ancestors.

The point demands factual implementation. From fish to man, the agonistic behavior of males starts with "warning" signals: threat-postures and threat-sounds; very frequently—probably more often than not—these rituals are effective in resolving the agonistic behavior, so that fighting does not necessarily ensue. This is but one illustration among many. The behavior of vertebrate males bears comparison, not only in the progression of their agonistic rituals, but in what kind of things they fight about.

During the phase of sex activities, males and females seem never to develop the same agonistic patterns. From fish to bird and mammal, we frequently see the males first "fighting it out," then establishing territorial stations under a sort of "armed truce"; while the females of the same species either identify themselves with a male of their choice, or remain grouped and establish "peck orders" between them. Or they do both. This phenomenon, to be sure, is most clear-cut among the birds and mammals; but it has adumbrations among at least the amphibia and the reptiles. The very modes of fighting often differ in the sexes. Male penguins, for instance, stand chest-to-chest and flail each other unmercifully with their flippers; female penguins may sit on neighboring nesting sites and peck at each other's eyes until their faces are bloody. (But both sexes also administer "drubbings" with their flippers, in certain situations.) Roosters and hens, as anyone knows, do not duplicate each other's fighting methods, even though they possess certain features in common. Male Anolis lizards fight when establishing territorial claims during the mating season, but otherwise tend to leave each other alone; females, on the other hand, tend to quarrel at any time.[11]

Endocrines and Behavioral Homologues

This raises appropriately the question of what is homologous behavior. It has already been indicated that when once we have gone beyond the single act as a behavioral isolate and have recognized the syndromal pattern into which it fits, we are in position to perceive "meaning." The syndrome whereby males migrate, select nesting sites, repel isosexual intruders, build nests, court the females, tend eggs and hatchlings, differs in its details between birds and fishes, and even between genera of fishes. Yet the inciting agent is pituitary hormone, which is present in all vertebrates.

If testosterone (propionate) be injected into amphibian, bird or animal, it will elicit characteristic yet equivalent ("homologous") "male" behavior in each. But testosterone is a natural secretion also of lower vertebrates which has persisted as the higher have evolved, and continues to preside over these "equivalents" of conduct. Lactogen secretion is what induces both male and female pigeons to secrete "pigeon's milk" during the syndrome of caring for the young; it induces the female mammal to secrete "true" milk—even though in a different body region. The bullfrog secretes a pituitary lactogenous hormone which, experimentally, induces the pigeon's crop gland to secrete its "milk"—although this frog never tends eggs or cares for young. Lactogen injected into both hens and roosters makes them broody;[12] likewise jewel-fish.[13] Mammalian lactogen administered to

[11]Greenberg and Noble, 1944.
[12]Nalbandov and Card, 1945; Riddle, 1941.
[13]Noble, Kumpf and Billings, 1938.

Triturus induces this salamander to return to water and eject sperm or lay eggs.[14] Behind these phenomena lies the fact that the brain from fish to man has an essentially common architecture; and that the same thing holds for the endocrine system. Referring again to the instances just cited—prolactin secretion is indicated as being far more ancient a vertebrate property than the lactation of mammals is; and evolution should be written not merely in terms of anatomical transformations but in terms of transformations within provinces of hormonal presidencies; and these presidencies cut across anatomical, physiological, biochemical, and psychological phenomena.

Is Vertebrate Mateship Socially Structured?

Primitive reproductive behavior, whether of animals in general or of the most unsophisticated human societies, has so often been labeled "promiscuous" that the term calls for an appraisal. Its validity at any time will depend upon how it is defined. Beginning with the cyclostomes, we already fail to find the mere extrusions of spermatozoa and ova which characterize many invertebrates; nor yet the apparent helter-skelter of the nuptial flight among bees, or the massed courting of termites.[15] When a male fish builds a nest, stays by it, invites any female who swims through his territory to deposit eggs, drives her out after she has done so, then repeats the performance with the next oncoming female; while each female repeats her share of the performance as another batch of eggs ripens within her, but now at another nest—the whole drama has an orderliness about it; it has not the randomness of chaos. These are serial reproductive matings. On the other hand, when the term "promiscuity" is applied to human situations, usually it connotes the disordered violation of a moral code which is held either by the culture in which it is occurring, or by the commentator; that is, it is judged to be chaotic. The term cannot therefore be used for both a culturized and also for a nonculturized situation without appropriate redefinition; but if this is done, what we have is no longer the same word: We have, so to speak, *two words that are homonyms.* In any event, there is no vertebrate class wherein sex activity is unassociated with other, adnex or associated activity so as to compose a regular behavioral syndrome.

[14]Chadwick, 1941.
[15]For that matter, these insect courtings are not exactly promiscuous either; actually, they are a case of "sorting" which starts as a random affair but winds up nevertheless with a monopolostic pairing of a male with a female.

Parentalism

a. Any provision made by an elder for its offspring is an act of parentalism.[16] At the cyclostome level, this consists of males selecting nesting sites, constructing a nest, inviting a female to lay eggs, and milting. The father may linger awhile; but his motivation is unclear to the observer. At the teleost level, not only are these acts more elaborate, but the father may remain to watch and to fan the eggs. A further act is added, also at the teleost level, when he remains to keep watch over the hatchlings. Similar behavior occurs among some Amphibia; *mutatis mutandis*, it is the rule among birds. A further stage comes into being when the parent (or parents) "trains" the young. The cyclostome pattern illustrates "elementary" or "nest" parentalism; egg-tending yields us "brood" parentalism; if in addition the hatchlings are cared for, it is "full" parentalism or "familial-ism"; if, further, there is training of the young, we have "complete familialism." Yet another complication occurs when the youngsters of an earlier brood help care for those of a later brood. This occurs repeatedly among birds; there are rudiments of it among some monkeys; otherwise, the only mammal in which it occurs is, apparently, man. As it represents rather a reproductive precocity which is pro-dromal—which eventually will be directed upon the individual's own offspring—and adds no effective principle to the raising of young, it needs no special name. All but the last of the above-given series is represented at the level of the teleosts.

b. We must note the progression in psychology—(I) selecting a nesting site, (II) preparing a nest, (III) courting a sex partner, are separate acts; act III has no necessitous connection with acts I and II (and in many vertebrate species, act III occurs without any acts I and II); but acts I and II are "meaningless" unless followed by act III. This observation serves to illustrate the interrelated nature of "syn-drome" and "configuration."

With the appearance of brood parentalism, the parent has devel-oped a *behavioral attitude* toward the genital product. This product actually is a new individual already; but it is not one where there can be a behavioral reciprocation or mutualism. But when at last the par-ent cares for the hatchlings, we discover also that the hatchlings orient toward the parent: There is sociopsychological reciprocation. It occurs, to be sure, between a matured and an immature psyche;

---

[16]This definition obviously is teleological, in final analysis. At this juncture, however, we are using it for no more than a practical heurism.

and the matured one is not engaged in eliciting new behavioral patterns from the immature. When we reach the level of familialism—confined to the avian and the mammalian levels of cerebral evolution—the parent engages in applying programmatically—that is, according to a segmental pattern that is synchronized with other developments—certain appropriate stimuli which are essential at particular times if innately determined psychic mechanisms are to unfold properly.

c. It is important to notice that the earliest parentalism is exercised by the male rather than the female. This continues to occur among all classes but the reptiles and the mammals. Female cooperation, and even sex-reversal of the role, begins to appear in phylogeny at the level of the fishes. A few more details of this matter will be forthcoming later; for the present, the essential points are: (1) Such parental exercise by either or both sexes can be readily shown to derive from the essential ambisexualism of the vertebrates; (2) parental care among the vertebrates is not to be identified without further ado with the female sex; it is to be defined, rather, simply as the pattern by which a vertebrate generation provides for its offspring. If this startles, it is but a reflection of the fact that the reader of these lines is a mammal—a member of one of the only two vertebrate classes where parentalism is unexceptionally and elementally a female task.

d. The progressive parentalism in the phylogeny of the vertebrates adds sequels to the original drama of the reproductive phase (the erotic one) which are nevertheless of a considerably different nature from the original. Caring for eggs and young obviously has an orientation upon an object other than one's sex partner. Among the higher vertebrates, and perhaps also among the lower, eroticism and broodliness do not come under the same hormonal dominance. But evolution of the vertebrates in terms of evolving hormonal patterns as parentalism becomes more complex, is a very significant story that seemingly is not destined to be written down in the near future. In the course of evolution, however, as the reproductive phase comes to occupy an ever-greater proportion of the time taken by one entire diphasic cycle of the biogram, it is the brooding subphase more than the erotic subphase that has been extended. Thus it comes about that mares, who are seasonally polyestrous, have a gestation period of about eleven months. Since this is followed by a period of lactation, it is tantamount to saying that this animal has come to possess no period at all in which she is free of all sex hormone dominance whatever. We shall discuss the primates later.

The Juvenile Age-Peer Group

Where species exercise nothing more than nest parentalism, the young never have contact with their parents. As they all start existence at roughly the same time, they hatch practically simultaneously. They are born, that is, as an aggregation; but they quickly develop into a congregation, wherein they begin to interstimulate. Socialization by one's age-peers is for the vertebrate the primal agency for establishing status. Later, as familialism emerges in phylogeny, orientation to the parent begins practically simultaneously with orientation to one's nest siblings; at highest levels—among birds and mammals—it sets in almost immediately after hatching or being born; and so it begins even before the more primitive orientation does. Nevertheless, this more ancient process increases as the juvenile matures, while the orientation to the parent diminishes. At the bird and mammal levels, where the young undergo a prolonged period of psychological as well as physiological dependency upon a parent, we often find the parent eventually "dismissing" the offspring by some positive act. Thenceforth the young ceases to be "offspring," the parent ceases to be "parent." Every psychologist is familiar with what happens, on the human level, when parent and offspring fail to carry this process through. Apparently there are no human societies which do not acknowledge this fact in some culturally formalized manner. This socialization by one's age-peers is destined to continue throughout the individual's lifetime. This further illustrates the principle that the familial is episodic within the larger framework of the total society (*vide ante*). We shall recall it again, when at the human level we deal with the matter of family of provenience versus family of procreation.

A SYSTEMATIC COMPARISON OF VERTEBRATE BIOGRAMS[17]

We shall survey some essential features in the biograms of successive phyletic levels of the vertebrates. Once again we remind ourselves that a comparison of extant forms can never replace comparison of extinct forms. Our handicap, moreover, is even more serious: The survivors of the classes represent in some cases dominant faunas; others, only remnant faunas which are often as atypical of their category as can be. Except for the cyclostomes, the class Agnatha is

[17]The taxonomy used here is mainly that of A. S. Romer. See his "Vertebrate Paleontology." iHs scheme is excellent, though not universally accepted; in the present situation, it is eminently usable.

extinct; only three out of six amphibian orders survive, and they are at a far remove from those that gave rise to the reptiles; similarly, only four of the sixteen orders of reptiles survive, all carnivorous, and very unlike the respective orders which gave rise to the mammals and the birds. A curious consequence is that it is possible to make speculative inferences about features of the biograms of Archosaurs from those of their avian descendants, which do not actually obtain in the reptilian orders that survive. Furthermore, we discover that birds and telerosts resemble each other strikingly in their biograms, while differing extremely in habitat and bodily form; furthermore, they represent separate branches of vertebrate evolution—by odd coincidence, their palae-ancestors were emerging from the Archosaurs and the Holostei respectively at approximately the same time, namely, the Triassic period; and this challenges an explanation.

Yet another handicap lies in the fact that we possess but fragmentary information about the embryogenesis of behavior mechanisms in the various taxonomic divisions of the vertebrates; and what we do possess is very unevenly distributed. *Per contra,* what we possess is excellent, and a lasting tribute to the insight of its discoverers.

THE AQUATIC VERTEBRATES

The earliest unmistakable vertebrates—Agnatha (Ostracoderms)—have been recovered from the Ordovician period. The earliest traces of Chondrichthyes, Crossopterygii, and Dipnoi are in the Silurian; by the Devonian they are abundant. Chondrostei occur in the Devonian; they become abundant throughout the Upper Paleozoic. The Holstei appear late in the Upper Paleozoic; they become abundant in the later Triassic; they have their heyday in the Jurassic; but by the Cretaceous they are ceding the waters to the teleosts, who originate in the Triassic and have become increasingly abundant into modern times.

Class Agnatha: Order Cyclostomata

Lampreys and hagfishes, the only surviving Agnatha, are worldwide in their distribution. In their nonreproductive phase they are marine, lacustrine, and riverine. All, including the saltwater dwellers, migrate anadromously into freshwater for the reproductive phase. The majority of the earliest migrants are male; in some species, perhaps in all, the last wave is all female.

In the spawning grounds, the males appropriate nesting sites, and by moving stones in the stream bottom they build round-to-oval nests. When the females arrive, there ensues a courting-and-copulation ritual; this induces the females to lay eggs, over which the males then milt. After the spawning, the parents, more especially the males, may linger for a short while near the nest. In many species, both parents die shortly thereafter.

The eggs hatch into free-swimming larvae (*Petromyzon: Ammocoetes*). In come species these take months, in others years, to mature. The metamorphosis from larva to adult occurs, in some freshwater forms, during their anadromous migration to the spawning grounds. The hatchlings congregate and migrate catadromously.

Several features show diagrammatically, and in as yet undifferentiated anlage-form, what in the higher vertebrates become more complex patterns:

1. Phase migration.

2. A reproductive syndrome (among higher forms, initiated by a periodic arousal of pituitary activity, and believed to be true also of the cyclostomes) which includes home-spot identification, nest building, a courting that ends in spawning (with external fertilization, however); a lingering of the parent after spawning.

3. Male initiative in the syndrome, with female complementation.

4. The young as a self-socializing age-peer group—phyletically as well as ontogenetically the earliest socializing agency. Since the elders die before the eggs hatch, there is no overlap of the generations. This makes a society equivalent to a generation, and there can be no social interreactions between individuals of different maturation levels.

(By comparison—a wasp colony consists likewise of a generation; but reproduction is occurring all the time, though restricted to one source; all the working population forms an age-peer group, even if hatched at successive times [but the age-peer group is subdivided rigidly into older and younger adults, each of which subgroups performs specific tasks]; and there are larvae and pupae. The activities of the colony center upon a reproductive ménage—a feature utterly absent from much the longer phase of the cyclostome biogram.)

Class Chondrichthyes: Order Elasmobranchii

These again are marine predators, hence dependent upon the movements of their prey; so that during their nonreproductive phase they are wide-ranging. The coenonia migrates anadromously for the reproductive phase, and the young migrate later catadromously *en masse.*

Very few genera fertilize their eggs externally; the male courting, in other words, goes over into a coitus. Some genera thereupon lay fertilized eggs; but a very large number of genera are ovoviviparous; that is, laying is delayed until the young are capable of swimming freely.

1. To the varietal range of birth methods there is no corresponding phylogenetic elaboration of bodily form: between unfertilized oviparity and viviparity there is little more than a delay in the matter of extruding.[18]

2. Coitus transforms the female into a peripatetic nesting site. Since in phylogeny all reproductive modifications are simultaneous and complementary in both sexes (it is a system and not just a single type of body form that changes—this in contrast to, say, the loss of gill slits, which are a feature present uniformly in all members, i.e., both sexes, of a species), this transfer of nest into the body of the female replaces the male syndrome of search for a nesting site and building a nest; only male competition and courting technique remain.

But the other end of the drama expands into familialism. This, as we already know, can occur whenever the parent—male or female—remains present while the hatchlings emerge. Obviously there comes into being a psychoneurological mechanism which either is stimulated to activity by the hatchlings or is activated autogenously yet synchronously.[19]

But—again as part of the sexual complementation when reproductive systems evolve—a portable nesting site within the female eliminates the possibility of male brooding and male familialism. A physiological modification in one sex correlates with a psychological modification in the other. Throughout verterbrate phylogenesis, this organic involvement between physiology and psychology is a major phenomenon.

Class Osteichthyes: Chondrostei, Holostei, Dipnoi, Crossopterygii

These orders were once very abundant in the Paleozoic, but are now a remnant fauna. We have but fragmentary observations about

[18]Naturally, there are also differences in physiological timing, presence or absence of a leathery egg capsule, etc.
[19]Or both. There is accumulating a mass of interesting findings, although their subjects are teleosts and not Elasmobranchii. See, e.g.: Baerends and Baerends, 1950; Tinbergen, 1951, p. 58f.

their life habits; such as they are, they introduce nothing beyond what we have found in the preceding forms.

Chrondrostei, Holostei, Crossopterygii migrate to spawn. Sturgeon parents remain with their eggs for a brief period before returning to the sea; the hatchlings tarry in shallow water, and gradually migrate together to the deep. The male bowfins arrive at the spawning ground first, build nests (frequently, a single male builds and cares for several), court the females with a sort of ritual; the male drives the female away after she has laid, or if she neglects to lay; he remains with the nest until after the young hatch, accompanies them when they leave, until they join up with other juveniles to form an age-peer group.

The surviving lungfishes are adapted to the alternating seasons of drought and flood of the African and South American tropics; which means that they shuttle between aestiviation and activity. In flood times, they have a period of feeding without sexual activity. There follows a period of nest building; the males remain to guard the young until they become quite active; they then resume feeding, and thus store up a reserve for the next aestivation.

The lungfishes do not represent the line whence the terrestrial vertebrates have sprung—that distinction belongs to the Crossopterygii. But they do illustrate an important generalization: Specialized adaptations of life mode are effected by animals during their non-reproductive phase; it is thus with aestivation in the present case. Nature, as it were, does not tamper with the established life mode during the process of active reproduction. Once a life mode has been remodeled during the period of reproductive quiescence, she can afford to bring the reproductive life mode into a new adjustment. The most dramatic illustration of this has been the evolution of the Amphibia and the Reptilia, as we shall see.

At the phyletic level of the Dipnoi, we encounter male brood parentalism (Lepidosiren and Protopterus).[20] At the level of the Holostei (Amia),[20] we encounter male familialism—which, as far as evidence goes, is the prevailing form of parental care among the Teleostei.

TELEOSTEI

All the foregoing vertebrate forms represent remnant faunas; at the same time, lodged within their taxonomic levels are the lines by

[20]See Wunder, 1931. *Ergebnisse der Biologie* **VII**:188.

which the dominant forms of today have emerged. The teleosts, on the other hand, are the dominant form of aquatic vertebrates today, just as the birds and the mammals share the dominion of the land. Thus they are at once numerous and multiform; but their phyletic line and that of the terrestrailized vertebrates are mutually digressive, so that the characteristic features of each in no wise are palae-ancestral to those of the other.

The significance of this for our investigation cannot be over-stressed. From the standpoint of Tetrapods, the bodily morphology of the teleosts is bizarre, both in its peculiar features-in-common and in the many extravangances of shape, such as the grotesqueries that dwell in the bathysphere; also such extremes as the sea horse, the sunfishes, and the eels. Yet the patterns of biogram are remarkably similar in both the aquatic and the terrestrial phyletic lines, despite radically different environments and bodily architectures.

This principle we have encountered already on a smaller scale; for instance, where within the same piscine Order there occur ovi-parity and viviparity and transitional variations between these, with concomitant adjustments of behavior patterns. What we are now about to encounter are the behavioral resemblances between fishes and birds, despite thoroughly dissimilar environments and bodily architectures. The details of the specific acts which they perform will, of course, relate to both the features of the environment and the bodily equipment which performs the acts; yet behind these specific and recordable phenomena there exists an overall similarity.

Moreover, the data from the teleosts are adequate for supplying us for the first time with the wide range of variation in sociopsychic behavior which can occur within a major taxonomic division, even while this behavior retains a basic, common "envelope" pattern. As undoubtedly the members of an order all stem from some common palae-ancestry, the variations in their behavioral patterns must repre-sent evolutionary modifications. Occasionally, we find it possible to reconstruct, speculatively, a plausible account of the course these have taken.

The economic importance of so many teleosts has brought about an enormous body of literature, especially with reference to their spawnings and migrations; but the very reasons for producing the literature at all are those which have made it so one-sided in the topics it has selected to deal with and the species with which it has preferred to concern itself. Of course there are also many studies that are purely biological; but the fact that the behavior of a single species, and that the differential behavior of individuals within it, is endlessly complex, has limited our knowledge thus far to but a tiny few of the enormous number of species in existence. We possess excellent detailed studies of behavioral patterns of cichlids, jewel-fish, goldfish, and especially sticklebacks—the favorite of ethological studies by N. Tinbergen.[21]

The Nonreproductive Phase

The teleost order is so vast and multiform that we may expect, and do find, a very wide range in the degree of gregariousness and solitary life habit. We need not expect that even in a large and gregarious group the individuals will be as closely spaced during the period of active feeding as they will be when migrating; in fact, as a generality, when stationed on the respective territories of their biogrammatic phases, they maintain at least some degree of dispersion; any migratory period represents an episode wherein they are at their greatest concentration, and sensitive to each other's movements.

That a moving school of herring, for instance, is a social body with a certain minimum of organization, has been observed when they advance upon a boat and suddenly become aware of it. The front rank, of course, perceives the foreign obstacle first, and reverses direction instantaneously. And an instant thereafter the entire school has reversed—undoubtedly in response to the reversals before them and surely without ever having even had the chance to perceive the obstacle. That fishes are very sensitive to small anatomical details and motions of their fellows has been documented over and over; there is a sensitive optical organization within the mesencephalon-diencephalon. In fact, for their sensitivity in social interreactions, vertebrates seem generally to rely heavily upon optical stimuli, whatever be the use they make of olfaction.

But there is no indication that dominance hierarchies become established where the group is large. On the other hand, in laboratory aquaria, where the number of individuals is kept small, dominance-subordinance has been observed very definitely.[22] Small numbers of goldfish learn the topography of their aquarium more rapidly than do single individuals, and they learn more rapidly if an already experienced "guide" is present.[23]

---

[21]1951.
[22]See particularly Noble, 1939b; Braddock, 1945.
[23]Welty, 1934.

The Reproductive Phase

Phase migration *en mass* is so prevalent among teleosts (just as it has been among the earlier forms we have considered) that it is hard to escape the conclusion that we are dealing here with a prototypic heritage. The migrations frequently, perhaps almost always, are anadromous; and if the species is saline-aquatic, the movement is to a spot of less salinity.[24]

The mere fact that herring, salmon, sardines are closely massed during their migrations is what interests those who exploit them economically; not how these masses come into being. We may surmise that, during the nonreproductive phase, the individuals were living in small groups more or less scattered, or more or less singly, yet only moderately dispersed. On the other hand, during the non-reproductive phase predator species hunt singly; yet they too tend to congregate in the reproductive phase. I would suggest that the degree of density during migration may have a positive correlation with degree of density during the phase of sexual quiescence; and that this principle might be found to hold for the other vertebrate classes as well.. During group migration vertebrates as individuals are constantly oriented more strongly toward their fellows. The locality, on the other hand, is transient at every moment; the orientation to it is molar rather than individual.

Herring, and some other species, migrate enormous distances from the feeding grounds to the breeding grounds; the fry migrate the distance in reverse—a very protracted process. Apparently the sexes do not travel as moieties; but as far as I know, no one has determined whether, at some time before final arrival, they split into the sex moieties. It seems generally true nevertheless that in a teleost coenonia it is the males who usually arrive first.

There ensues the drama which by now is beginning to be familiar to us; in certain species, notably some of the sticklebacks, the actions have been very carefully analyzed by Tinbergen; and we shall return to this matter shortly.

[24]It has been conjectured that this is a heritage from an age when the seas were less salty than they are today. On the other hand, because many fish make the transfer actually from salty to sweet water, it has been argued that the teleosts took origin from palae-ancestors who dwelt in freshwater. But an embryo developing in freshwater contains a *higher* concentration of salt than its environment does. Whichever hypothesis be favored, however, again we encounter the fact that embryos never are suited to the same environment as that in which they are destined to spend their adult lives—and there is also the possibility that heightened salinity may be an organism's self-system-adjustment (internal environment change).

Unfortunately, our records at this point, abundant though they be, are very deficient precisely where we badly need fuller data. We know about the nesting habits of only a minority of species; there is no systematic study of the habits with regard to taxonomic affinities; and when egg tending is reported without mention of hatchling tending, we do not know whether it represents the fact of the situation or merely incomplete reporting. What now follows must allow for these strictures.

The teleosts are mostly (but not universally) oviparous, with external fertilization; parentalism is almost always a male function; occasionally it is a matter of bisexual cooperation; never, apparently, unless there is viviparity, is the parentalism exclusively a female function.[25]

It is rather striking that the faunas which today represent but remnants of what anciently and primitively were dominant forms—Chondrichthyes, Holostei, Amphibia, Reptilia—include a variety of reproductive schemes; while the dominants of today represent selective narrowing upon single schemes that prevail over an entire major division: The teleosts are as just described; the birds are altogether oviparous with internal fertilization; the mammals are altogether viviparous with internal fertilization.

Some teleost species go no farther than preparing a nest, then depositing ova and spermatozoa in them; the adults apparently die not long thereafter. This holds for the salmons, who are Isospondyli and therefore rather primitive animals. The drama recalls the simplicity of the lampreys. Some other forms have advanced no farther; others show broad parentalism; still others show familialism; occasionally, there is biparental familialism. But these successive additions do not follow taxonomic affinities, nor do they correlate with level of evolutional advancement in bodily morphology.

Wunder[26] has tabulated the pertinent behavior in a select number of species from Dipnoi, Holostei, and Teleostei. He lists 22 genera from 14 teleost families. Assuming that the author's sources have reported accurately, we find the following arrangement:

Primitive taxonomic families:

Isospondyli:

Mormyridae: Male familialism

Osteoglossidae: Male familialism

---

[25]From our mammalian standpoint, the most bizarre distortion of this basic pattern occurs among some of the Hemibranchii: the Solenostomidae. Among the sea horses, the male develops a portable nest: a marsupium; into which he induces the female to lay her eggs. He tends eggs and hatchlings thereafter.

[26]*Ergebnisse der Biologie* **VII**:188. The adaptation here is ours.

Ostariophysi:
  Siluridae: Biparental familialism[27]
  Cyprinidae: Male brood parentalism
Moderately evolved taxonomic families:
  Haplomi:
    Poeciliidae: Male familialism
    Gasterosteidae: Male familialism
    Centrarchidae: Male familialism
    Percidae: Biparental familialism
Advanced taxonomic families:
  Labroidei:
    Labridae: Male brood parentalism
    Cichlidae:[28] Biparental familialism
  Scorpaenoidei:
    Gobidae: Male brood parentalism
    Cottidae: Male brood parentalism
    Cyclopteridae: Male brood parentalism
  Pediculati:
    Batrachidae:[29] Male familialism
    Blennidae: Biparental brooding

The list is, of course, too fragmentary for any purpose but to suggest the preponderance of male parentalism and its expansion to familialism, and to indicate the noncorrelation between taxonomy and scheme of parentalism. Some further remarks are appropriate. Egg tending commonly includes fanning the eggs with the pectoral fins, which creates a current that facilitates respiratory exchange.

As in all the other forms we have recorded hitherto, whenever parental care stops before the hatchlings appear, the latter develop no other orientations than those to their age-peers. But if the parent tarries until the hatching, invariably he develops an additional act to his syndrome. He no longer fans the clutch; but he prevents their straying too far, and in a variety of genera he retrieves them in his mouth.

The phenomenon confronts us with the problem of the psychogenetic extension and differentiation of behavior in phylogenesis; but to discuss it carries us far beyond the scope of the present essay. There is a hint of what is involved, in the following additional phenomena: In some cichlids (the family is one of the most evolved of

---

[27]Wunder lists only male familialism. It is known, however, that females participate
[28]Not included by Wunder.
[29]Taxonomically, better, perhaps, "quasi-Pediculati."

the teleosts), both parents care for the clutch. *Hemichromis* parents take turns guarding the eggs and the hatchlings, allowing the other to absent itself for a while. The *Tilapia* female takes up the eggs in her mouth as soon as the male has fertilized them; and they incubate *in situ*. When the youngsters are alarmed, they swarm back into her mouth. Neither the eggs nor the young induce the swallowing reaction of the parent.[30] In the face of danger, the *Cichlasoma* parent summons the youngsters by a peculiar motion, and they respond by gathering about the parent.

The young begin life as an aggregation. Very quickly there unfolds a psychoneural mechanism which is preadapted to orient toward an object that behaves "parentally"; another such mechanism develops orientations of another sort with age-peers. Both parents and offspring gradually deorient (that, at least in the male stickleback, there is a physiological accompaniment, is manifest from the fading of the red color of the abdomen), leaving the age-peer interreactivity to last a while longer.

AMPHIBIA

Of the six orders of Amphibia, only three—the Anura (Salientia), the Urodeles (Caudata), and the Apoda (Gymnophiona, Caecilians)—are extant, the other three having disappeared in Permian-Triassic times. The survivors combine peculiar bodily specializations with fish-like reproductive physiologies (amphibians and fishes are classed together as "Ichthyopsida"); yet these reproductive physiologies show a large variety of secondary modifications, so that any description must choose between brevity with unavoidable oversimplicity and amplitude with a degree of inaccuracy. We are forced to choose the former.

Amphibian Reproduction

It was primitive Embolomerous Amphibia which were palae-ancestral both to the specialized forms of today and, by a separate route, to the proto-reptiles; it was various forms of these latter who, at different times gave rise to all the subsequent forms of reptiles, to the proto-mammals and to the proto-avians. We wish—vainly—for the unbroken succession of biogrammatic transformations which accompanied the

---

[30]For sundry examples in the present discussion I am indebted to the writings of Tinbergen, particularly those of 1951 and 1953. See also Baerends and Baerends, 1950.

evolution particularly of the mammals and of the birds. On the other hand, the extant Amphibia, though but a remnant fauna, possess so wide a range of variations to the reproductive syndrome that assumably the now-extinct forms would have fallen within it.

The full significance of the amphibians' position in phylogenesis has escaped us so far because it has not been realized that they represent the transfer of the vertebrate nonreproductive phase to the land, while the reproductive phase (its biology is always the more conservative; and the reason therefore is not hard to see) remained essentially attached to the primal medium. It was the further transfer of the reproductive phase to the land which has been the evolutionary accomplishment of the reptiles.

This, of course, is a very diagrammatic statement. Even the extant Amphibia show various degrees of land adaptations for their reproductive phase. Gymnophiona lay their eggs on land, and curl up about them—reminding us of some of the snakes. So do some of the more evolved Urodeles—some Amphiumidae and Plethodontidae, and some of the Amblystomidae, who are more primitive. The Anura, of course, cannot coil about their eggs; but some frog and toad genera lay their eggs on land, with other provisions to keep them moist (some Ranidae, Bufonidae, Hylidae, Brachycephalidae). Yet other genera from these same families (as well as others) have preserved the piscine method. If some of the Embolomeri succeeded in transforming to reptiles, presumably it was because terrestrial oviposition was indeed part of their repertoire already, but the fact that some Amphibia oviposit on land demonstrates that merely doing so does not make them into reptiles. To this matter we shall return when discussing the reptiles.

A conspicuous feature of the amphibian biogram is the very frequent presence of a larval stage, with progressive metamorphosis, between egg and adult. Roughly speaking, it is a literal living-over during ontogenesis of the adaptive change from aquatic to terrestrial life mode; whereas, in reptiles, birds, and mammals, the adaptive change is undergone autogenously within a prenatal confinement; it is, so to speak, but a "symbolic" or "formal" transition, carried through in a surrogate for the aquatic environment. But among amphibians—just as among fishes—emergence from confinement may be postponed; so that some genera are ovoviviparous (some Plethodontidae, Bufonidae, Salamandridae, Brevicipitidae, Proteidae). Moreover, if the eggs are laid on the land, the larval stage is passed within them: The young are hatched more or less metamorphosed. But, just as among the fishes, ovoviviparity can occur in water. Some amphibian families—the moderately evolved Sirenidae and Proteidae, and the advanced Ty-phlomolgi (Plethodontia)—are "permanent larvae" who reproduce nonetheless (neoteny). These are cases of progressive fetalization—not primitive states.

Ovoviviparity usually requires internal fertilization. Yet here, too, is an interesting exception. In the copulation of certain Salamandrid genera, the spermatozoa are contained in a spermatophore which the female actively inserts into her cloaca.

The Amphibia lack the separate spawnings by the females and the males; as far as I know, they all copulate. Fertilization is nonetheless external in the Anura, and among the most primitive of the Caudata and in the neotenous Sirenidae. Among many Anura, the female cannot even extrude eggs without the exceedingly powerful *amplexus* of the male. (Incapacity to ovulate without the male stimulus has been encountered among the sticklebacks. It obtains also in rabbits.) As the eggs are extruded the male discharges spermatozoa upon them. In the rest of the Urodele families, fertilization is internal.

The courtship rituals of the Urodeles are varied, and from our standpoint, bizarre. The Anura sexes do not execute the complementary "dances" now familiar to us; on the other hand, the males lure the females with those prolonged and vociferous callings which are celebrated since the days of Aristophanes and were undoubtedly very generally familiar immeasurably earlier than that.

This brings us to the subject of the reproductive phase and drama themselves.

The Amphibia migrate to breeding grounds, and migrate back when the drama is concluded. There is no indication that they travel as organized schools; but their gathering appears to be one of individual congregating. Nonetheless, the males are very "touchy"—if two male toads happen to make contact, they fight, and the others in the vicinity pile into the melee.[31] Male frogs take up conspicuous stations and call. "Krafft (1911) reports a female *Nectophrynoides tornieri* quietly listening to the song of a male, and on several occasions I have found female Cricket Frogs, *Acriogryllus*, sitting in a circle with heads directed toward a calling male."[32]

We are now in possession of all the essential steps in the evolutional differentiation of a sexual psychodrama. In the cyclostomes, we have a bisexual rhythm-taking which consisted of the male "courting" the female, and even seizing her briefly. But there is no copulation: The spawnings are successive. Copulation may well be an extension

[31]Moore, p. 203.
[32]Noble, 1931, 409.

of the courting psychodrome, and differentiate yet further in proportion as nuclei and tracts in the brain, particularly in the diencephelon-mesencephalon, become assorted and defined in the course of phylogenesis. The rhythm-taking of copulation can follow one of two courses: male discharge (this is the reverse order of the piscine order, wherein the female discharges first); and synchronization of the two discharges (as in frogs), whereat fertilization is external.

Nesting habits vary highly, along with the kind of location sought for egg deposition. There are relatively few cases where the male prepares a nest and lures the female; but they do occur: Megalobatrachus, a primitive caudate (a Cryptobranchid), not only builds the nest, but is very emphatic in driving off the female once she has oviposited. Males of various *Hyla* species construct nests very carefully; although in other species the eggs are carried about in a manner soon to be described.

Nothing is more interesting, however, than the many kinds of "portable nests" which both sexes develop in sundry anuran families. The simplest device is that where the egg mass adheres to the thighs of the parent when they are extruded. Certain other species carry them on their backs—one parent may even glue them onto the other. Other parents have them attached to the abdomen. Or, there may be pits in the skin of the back; more elaborately still—once the eggs are deposited, the skin of the back may grow folds which close over them, forming a dorsal marsupium. Other genera convert the laryngeal sac into an incubation pouch—recalling the oral incubations of some cichlids.

The process may be carried over into familialism by either sex (depending, of course, upon the species). The young hatch as larvae, and attach themselves by suckers to the back of the parent. Male Phyllobates and Dendrobates (South American Brachycephalidae) actually place the tadpoles upon their backs, and transport them overland to the other body of water where they are destined to remain until as adults they undergo their reproductive phase migration back again.

The Nonreproductive Phase

There is little if any evidence that during the sexually quiescent phase an amphibian coenonia has any special organization whatever. Allee,[33] in fact, has cautioned us against assuming that status-hierarchialism

[33]1952.

is a characteristic of the vertebrates, despite its widespread occurrence, because it has never been seen in Amphibia.

For that matter, neither has it been seen in the cyclostomes and the Chondrichthyes. But this by no means closes the question. Among amphibians we do encounter at least male fighting when sexually activated, and their taking up territories. These items may be plausibly considered as a sort of behavior detritus surviving from the more complete ancestral form of the syndrome. Suggested in this merely negative way, the point of course is weak. On the other hand, musculoskeletal architecture of the Amphibia lends itself to no more than simplex and sluggish movements on land; individuals are not engaged in repeated and active interreactions; and such motions as they perform appear to be the antecedents of status contests. Moreover, it is dangerous to argue the absence of a neurological capacity from its failure of expression. For instance, toads do not of their free will plunge into water and swim; yet if tossed in, they instantly produce a complete swimming technique exactly resembling that of frogs. Latent neuromotor potentialities are exceedingly perdurable in phylogenesis. A fetal opossum, and even a human infant too young to sit up, if placed in water will swim with the undulations of a fish, using the epaxial and hypaxial musculature of the trunk—which is phylogenetically a more ancient system than that of the terrestrialized appendages.

Finally—the extant Amphibia are a remnant fauna, and specialized away from their palae-ancestral prototype. We do not know whether or not the Embolomeri engaged in status contests. Moreover, there appear to be no studies of amphibian behavior carried out by ethologists. And we must leave it at that.

REPTILIA

Of sixteen reptilian orders, only four have survived. In their Mesozoic heyday, the class included gigantic herbivores, which in turn were preyed upon by carnivores that matched them; marine forms that dominated the life of the sea; gliders and fliers; two-legged runners; vaguely mammal-like forms. All the surviving orders are carniverous; and their prey, with but few exceptions, is small. Altogether, this composes a very unsatisfactory picture of what the reptilian biogram must have been. Over against this situation is the fact that in all the more primitive bird orders it is male parentalism that prevails—a thing unknown among the extant reptiles. Since this is apparently the archetypical pattern among the lower vertebrates, it is inferable that it also existed among the extinct Archosaurs who gave rise to the birds.

But within these limits, we can find among the extant reptiles, summarily, all the rest of the repertoire in the reproductive drama: the phase migrations; male territorialism and combat; male courting by sex rituals; status contests; intrasex competition; nest building (but now confined to the female); brood parentalism; familialism.

We fail to encounter, during the nonreproductive phase, the flock maneuvers of the teleosts, birds, and mammals, although many species of reptiles congregate. But there are few situations where reptiles show rapid and sustained motion *en masse* (it occurs among aquatic snakes). It is not inconceivable that such maneuvers occurred among the now extinct Pterosauria, Ichthyosauria, Sauropterygia, Ornithischia.

The Reproductive Phase: The Reptilian Egg

All extant reptiles possess an egg evolved considerably beyond that of the most advanced amphibian. There is a drought-resisting, leathery outer shell, which nevertheless is permeable to gas exchange. Now, it is universally true that maternal physiology is constituted so as to construct an egg that is preadapted for a certain environment; and it is equally true that the egg is an organism which during its entire ontogenesis creates itself so as to exploit the environment bequeathed to it; but in the reptiles we first encounter peculiarly felicitous illustrations of the principle that at the juncture of two generations adjustment is not that of an organism to a mere environment but of two organisms which express a mutualism. For the eggshell is secreted by the mother; the embryo complements this by constructing out of its own tissues a set of special prenatal respiratory organs which it later discards; and this combination mediates between the aquatic environment within the egg and the terrestrial environment for which the hatchling must be instantly prepared. As we have seen, there are Amphibia who produce moderately drought-resisting eggs; but nothing as elaborate as this reptilian system. The hatchling reptile has a more mobile locomotory apparatus (with a correspondingly appropriate neural equipment), a more drought-resisting integument, a more highly powered circulatory-respiratory system, than the amphibian: It can wander afar.

Our habit of thinking taxonomically, and seeing the Amphibia and the Reptilia as distinct classes, may serve to trick us, when we consider the evolutionary process of the terrestrialization of a vertebrate line. Actually, on a geological scale, the transition was relatively rapid, and the gradation from embolomerous amphibian to the earliest known Cotylosauria is smooth. The time span was within the mid-Carboniferous, and of the magnitude of ten million years or so. The period is marked by no major alterations of climate. And although we have been emphasizing the distinctiveness of the two biogrammatic phases, we are not to think of the one (the nonreproductive) being definitively terrestrialized before the other commenced its adaptive alterations. We should picture, rather, a line of primitive vertebrates gradually extending their nonreproductive range ever farther inland, but returning to the waters in their reproductive phase migration. Conceivably, in the earlier stages eggs may have been laid in damp spots that dried before the embryo was ready to hatch.

Among reptiles the external fertilization of extruded eggs, whether done in a prepared nest or by way of amplexus such as obtains among the Anura, is naturally out of the question: But for coitus with internal fertilization, the reptiles would never have originated. The eggshell, of course, is added after fertilization, if at all; for some snakes and lizards are ovoviviparous. The latter method consists, as usual, of retaining the developing egg a little longer within the maternal oviduct; the advantage being that, where the climate is dry, the period of risk in desiccation is shortened. In some species, the alternative between the methods is facultative. Quite a number of lizard genera, furthermore, have developed genuine placentation; which entails true viviparity. (This raises the question, of course, as to whether the palae-ancestors of the mammals already possessed a placenta, or whether in mammals this structure is a "delayed development" along their already established line of phylogenesis.)

At all events, parentalism has become confined almost entirely to the female. With ovoviviparity and viviparity, this is readily understandable. It is less inevitable with oviparity; for, as has been said before, among the more primitive birds, brood parentalism and familialism are a paternal function. Nevertheless, no modern reptilian male remains with his mate until she lays the eggs, that he may take over. We may surmise that the deficiency resides in the cerebral organization; although not necessarily so.

The Reproductive Phase: Behavior

To observe the biogram of *Anolis carolinensis*, Greenberg and Noble[34] kept and observed for over four years a total of about 600 males and females in large enclosures.

[34]1944. Our sketch omits much valuable detail.

During the breeding season (February through August) the males fought at the slightest pretext, developed unstable dominance hierarchies; and when the spacing was adequate, they appropriated home territories, patrolled their boundaries, and otherwise tended to respect each other's properties. The females wandered over the entire territory; they fought readily when they met each other—but they also continued to do so when in the nonreproductive phase and established intrasex dominance-subordinance statuses, a thing which the males seldom did. If the females intruded into a male's territory, they were challenged; but the ritual quickly developed into that of courting and copulation. When about to ovulate, the female dug a hole and buried a single egg; she repeated the performance as the eggs ripened. She did not linger.

With the waning of the reproductive phase, the males ceased to maintain private roaming territories but only a home site; they ceased to pay agonistic attention to individuals of whatever sex.

We shall comment upon some features of this simple outline; then turn to some general, comparative comments about the reptiles in general.

Both Craig (1918) and the ethologists have drawn our attention to the course of instinctive syndromes, which start out with generalized and equivocal acts and progressively narrow down to acts of singular "purpose." The syndrome starts with *appetitive* behavior. Thus, the male Anolis' search for a territory, his choice of it, and then, with this matter settled his readiness for fighting males and courting females, comes to the fore. The *consummatory* act—copulation—is a discharge that ends the series: It does not set the stage for a next act. But as long as the pituitary gland continues to activate the endocrinal patterning of the reproductive phase, the fighting and the courting potential continues to be recharged and ready for release under the proper stimulation.

This syndromal outline is common, *mutatis mutandis,* from fishes to mammals. Among the *Anolis,* here are some of the details. If a stranger intrudes the homeowner challenges by displaying: He erects a crest, expands his dewlap, a certain black spot becomes darker. His body bobs, he advances. There is no evidence that he distinguishes sex. If his opponent responds similarly his acts intensify; whereupon so may his opponent's. The interstimulation goes over into the fighting psychodrome. If the intruder is a female, the initial behavior of the male is the same though in a less pronounced form. The ethologist presumably would explain this as due to the fact that the female lacks the strong display markings of a male and so (at first) does not stimulate as sharply. At any rate, her response is a bobbing, a peculiar nodding; whereupon the male's behavior changes. He approaches; she continues to nod; he mounts her. Greenberg and Noble judge that the bobbing nod is merely a sign of subordinance in general. The female, in her turn, seems instantly attracted, instead of angered, when a male displays his dewlap; and this serves as the first cue to her chain of responses. A male so displaying can attract a number of females, and annex them to his harem. (These females indulge in status contests.)

The difference in the two dramas clearly is not in the individual ingredients but in the formula of their synthesis—like the difference, we might say, between bread and cake.

The treatment of territory Because they were confined to enclosures—no matter how generous their jailers may have been—Greenberg and Noble's lizards had no opportunity for a phase migration in the physical sense, but they did perform psychological phase migrations. We cannot tell, of course, what they would have done if free; and their observers may possibly have demonstrated a principle inadvertently; namely, the adaptive quality (to a confined space) of a social pattern which conserves the pattern by virtue of that very quality. It is my impression that writers sometimes have failed to perceive this very profoundly significant fact; for, in comparing behavior in two kinds of animals, they seize upon the superficial contrasts as though they were absolute differences; whereas the truth of the matter must be, that they are witnessing contrastive operations of essentially the same innate equipment as that equipment deals with contrastive circumstances. We have already noted several cases of this: dominance-subordinance expressed if the group is small but not if the group is large; leadership in a small group but not in a large one; territorialism under one set of circumstances but not in another. We may add—a physical phase migration performed by some of the members of a bird flock while others perform but the psychological component; in fact, there are passerine individuals who migrate southward one winter but remain north for one or more subsequent winters. In social adaptation we have the defeat of Procrustes: The sleeper possesses the capacity to stretch and contract in keeping with a variable bed length—a profoundly significant fact of organic evolution.

It is a generalization by no means confined to the reptiles that the members of a coenonia, when not engaged in a phase migration, roam about an area of but limited radius. And within this radius, many such individuals possess home spots that have nothing to do with the reproductive phase yet which they defend.

There is a sizable literature on the subject of territorialism in vertebrates (to say nothing of that in invertebrates, especially arthropods). It is expressed by many vertebrate species, yet under such a variety of circumstances, and so inconsistently among the species and the sexes, that students have come to surmise that the term is actually being used to cover a large number of unrelated phenomena which have nothing in common except the fact that the animal somehow and at some time identifies with a chosen location.

In the cases both of a snake defending its lair in its phase of sex quiescence and a lizard defending its station during the breeding phase, we do indeed have different sets of "interests" that are being exercised; the animals being under two different endocrine tonal organizations. What is nevertheless common to both is the fact that the animal is attaching its organizational homeostases to location; it develops a locative ego involvement which lasts only as long as the endocrine tonus does. This contrasts strongly with the "meaning" of the hive to a bee; it bears rather a superficial resemblance to the lairs of arachnids.

The lizards certainly are not the most primitive of reptiles; yet in some respects the reproductive psychodrome resembles that of lower vertebrates more than do those of some of the other reptiles. We have already noted that nest building by the male has dropped out consistently with the assumption of nest building by the female *after* copulation and internal fertilization; except for this, among lizards we still find the choosing of home spot, the fights with the other males, the courting of the female. As for those reptiles which do not have this stereotype, we are left to conjecture whether they are exhibiting regressive evolution. Some turtle genera of the northern United States have been reported to have no sense of territorialism;[35] yet it is admitted that in the spring these animals wander away from their hibernating territory and return in the late fall. Among the sea-tortoises there occurs what resembles superficially a curious reversal of the phylogenetic course: The animals spend their nonreproductive phase in the sea; the females come ashore to lay and to bury their eggs inland; they return to the sea, where the males are gathered to await them; copulation takes place, but the spermatozoa are stored until the following year, when oogenesis is reactivated. In terms of the annual season, the female reproductive cycle is activated before the

[35]Cagle, 1944.

male; but we must remember that these animals dwell in very low latitudes; and in terms of the biogram of the species, the female is oogenetically many months *behind* the activation of the male, while her eroticism is activated *shortly after* that of the male—a normal vertebrate stereotype. The nonreproductive phase now takes place between insemination and ovulation in the female; the male calendar has remained conservative. That this arrangement represents evolutionally a shifting of syndromal segments is hardly to be doubted. (The mammals present numerous cases of shiftings.)

As we know, the close of the Mesozoic marked a disaster for the reptilian class. The Pleistocene appears to have brought further limitations, in that the dwellers in moderate latitudes must hibernate, and the highest latitudes exclude terrestrial poikilotherms. This cannot but distort the two-phase biogram. At the other end of the spectrum are the low-latitude reptiles who aestivate; and the distortion of the biogram resembles that of the Dipnoi. Some of the snake genera who congregate in the unfavorable season remain compionate during the favorable one,[36] the females merely retiring to ovulate. Instances of congregating by reptiles are too numerous to need documentation; but I am not aware that they have ever been studied to discover whether they possess any rudiments of social organization.

The nesting psychodrome   The most elaborate psychodrome occurs among crocodilians in various regions of the world. The mother builds a nest, furnishes it with decaying matter that furthers incubation; she covers it over and hovers nearby or lies atop it. The youngsters set up a shrill piping before they break their shells; whereupon she hastily opens up the nest, liberates the brood, and they fellow her down to the water.

If a marauder disturbs the nest of a Caiman mother before the hatchlings leave, "she attacks furiously, and sets up a bellowing which draws the neighboring adults to the spot."[37] We shall encounter these details again among birds.

AVES

The birds represent the last of the terrestrial vertebrate classes to evolve. They also represent the only surviving version of the reptilian

---

[36]Noble and Clausen, 1936.
[37]Wunder, 1934, 27f. Iguana females defend their nests of eggs furiously, ibid.

Drang nach Flucht; and no matter what their subsequent readaptations toward terrestrial or marine occupance, their bodily architecture continues to advertise this fact.

Adaptation for flight includes: homoiothermy, with very high blood temperature; reduction to an efficient minimum of the motor repertoire—the individual movements are gross, few in variety, and confined to the appendages—neck, wings, legs; one functioning ovary—along with production of a very telolecithal egg (a heritage from their reptilian ancestry).

The avian paradox comes forth in the way of life which has accompanied these physiological matters. Flight has made possible the most extensive phase migrations of all the vertebrates, a biannual exercise. The restricted repertoire of body movements is exploited into complex and varietal situations—signifying that the sensory-adjustive phase of the neuropsyche is versatile. Birds are constantly passing back and forth between atmospheric and terrestrial support—an ecologic change that is extreme as well as very sudden; moreover, they can stand very rapid changes of atmospheric pressure, when diving from a great height or ascending on the wing. Although wings have very restricted motion repertoire, their musculature undoubtedly possesses extreme proprioceptivity; the cerebellum is highly developed. This high-motion life, when compared with that of the reptile, is far more varied experientially, more highly charged emotionally, more responsive to the behavior of one's own kind (socially sensitive), and it manifests an intense concern for the offspring which, in most of the orders, enlists the activity of both parents. The high social sensitivity undoubtedly is made possible by the anosmatic brain which on the other hand possesses high visual acuity.

The reproductive syndrome is equally paradoxical. Birds are sauropsids; in gross dimensions, the reproductive physiology advances hardly at all over the reptilian: The mother merely secretes an extra, calciferous shell. The *Weiterbildungen*[38] that have made a bird out of a primitive reptile are written in minute characters within the germplasm. Coitus with internal fertilization and oviparity are heritages from that reptilian palae-ancestry; but now this large egg must be carried through the air inside the female while it is being readied for laying. Yet her mate remains with her and in various ways participates in the brooding psychodrome; in fact, among the most primitive birds, he remains the prime parent once the egg is laid.

---

[38]This technical term has been borrowed in English. "Further elaborations."

Reproductive Phase

In the north middle latitudes, we witness the final stage of the phase migration that initiates the reproductive period, and the initial stage of the phase migration to the area of the nonreproductive phase. Therefore we can judge at first hand the social complexion of the nonreproductive phase only by watching the birds who fail to participate in the second migration.

As for the first phase migration—it exhibits the vertebrate stereotype: Under pituitary activation, the males separate out from the females; fly in groups (northward) to the breeding grounds, select territory, identify it by station calling ("song," "crowing") and aerial acrobatics, fight off isosexual intruders; in some cases, they even start building nests. When the females arrive, there is courting, nest building, mating, incubating, and care of the young.

This stereotype, of course, is subject to wide deviations, too numerous to record here. Table 1-1, combined and adapted from Kendeigh and from Gregory,[39] is very informative.

Within the limits of its data, the table indicates that:

1. The Class Aves as such characteristically practices all three acts of the familial psychodrama: nest building, incubating, care of the young, including feeding.

2. Among the more primitive orders (Palaeognathae) parentalism is always a male role; in a few cases there is female supplementation, but never over the entire range of the psychodrome.

3. It is a common but not universal characteristic of the Neognathae for the sexes to share equally in all three acts.

4. Within a given order, the families tend to resemble each other in this matter; but this is only roughly so; and certain orders are characterized by a diversity among their families in the matter of sex role.

5. Incubation is always continued into care and feeding of the young.[40]

6. In some families, the male also feeds his incubating spouse. This relation is never reversed. In some cases, the male adds this to

---

[39]Kendeigh, 1952, particularly Table 51, pp. 282ff; Gregory, 1951, plate 15.1 (opposite p. 546, vol. 2).

[40]There is a strange exception to this among the megapodes (Galliformes) of New Guinea. The male builds a mound of decaying vegetable matter. The female lays eggs in the midst of this while it is being built. The male drives her away except when she is laying. When the chick hatches, the male helps it to dig its way out. But for the sex, this behavior obviously resembles what is common among the Crocodilia.

TABLE 1-1

	Nest Building	Incu- bating	Famili- alism	Male Feeds Female
PALAEOGNATHAE:				
Apterygiformes				
Apterygidae (kiwis)	M F	M	M	
Casuariformes				
Dromiceidae (emus)	. . .	M	M	
Struthioniformes				
Struthionidae (ostriches)	M	M f	M F	
Rheiformes				
Rheidae (rheas)	. . .	M	M	
Tinamiformes				
Tinamidae (tinamous)	. . .	M	M	
NEOGNATHAE:				
Aquatic birds:				
Colymbiformes:				
Colymbidae (grebes)	M F	M F	M F	
Gaviiformes				
Gaviidae (loons)	. . .	M F	M F	
Sphenisciformes				
Spheniscidae (penguins)	M F	M F	M F	
Procellariiformes				
Diomedeidae (albatrosses)	M F	M F	M F	
Procellariidae (puffins)	M F	M F	M F	
Hydrobatidae (storm-petrels)	M F	M F	M F	
Pelecanoididae (diving-petrels)	M F	M F	M F	
Pelecaniformes				
Phaëthontidae (tropic-birds)	. . .	M F	M F	*
Pelecanidae (pelicans)	. . .	M F	M F	
Sulidae (boobies)	M F	M F	M F	
Phalacrocoracidae (cormorants)	M F	M F	M F	
Anhingidae	. . .	M F	M F	
Fregatidae (frigate-birds)	M F	M F	M F	
Heron-Falcon line:				
Ciconiiformes				
Ardeidae (herons)	M F	M F	M F	
Scopidae (hammerheads)	M F	M F	M F	
Ciconiidae (storks)	M F	M F	M F	
Threskiornithidae (ibises)	M F	M F	M F	
Phoenicopteridae (flamingos)	. . .	M F	M F	
Falconiformes				
Cathartidae (vultures)	. . .	M F	M F	
Accipitridae (hawks)	m F	m F	M F	***
Falconidae (falcons)	m F	m F	M F	***
Wading and shore birds:				
Gruiformes				
Mesoenatidae	. . .	M f	M f	
Turnicidae (bustards)	M F	M	M	

TABLE 1-1 (Continued)

	Nest Building	Incubating	Familialism	Male Feeds Female
Pedionomidae (bustards)	. . .	M	M	
Gruidae (cranes)	M F	M F	M F	
Rallidae (rails)	M F	M F	M F	**
Rhynocetidae (kagus)	M F	M F	. . .	
Eurypygidae (bitterns)	M F	M F	M F	
Otidae (bustards)	. . .	F	F	
Charadriiformes				
Jacanidae	. . .	M	M	
Rostratulidae ("snipes")	. . .	M (f?)	. . .	
Haematopodidae (oyster-catchers)	. . .	M F	M F	
Charadriidae (plovers)	M F	M F	M F	
Scolopacidae (woodcocks)	. . .	M F	M F	
Recurvirostridae (avocets)	M F	M F	. . .	
Phalaropodidae (phalaropes)	M	M f	M f	
Burhinidae	. . .	M F	. . .	
Glareolidae	. . .	m F	. . .	
Stercorariidae (skuas)	. . .	M F	M F	*
Laridae (gulls)	M F	M F	M F	
Rhyncopidae (skimmers)	. . .	F	M F	
Alcidae (guillemots)	M F	M F	M F	*
Uplands and forests:				
Anseriformes				
Anhimidae (screamers)	M F	M F	. . .	
Anatidae (geese)	m F	m F	m F	
Galliformes				
Megapodidae (megapodes)	M	. . .	. . .	
Cracidae (chachalacas)	M F	F	. . .	
Tetraonidae (ruffed grouse)	F	F	m F	
Phasianidae (quail)	M F	m F	M F	
Meleagrididae (turkeys)	F	F	F	
Opisthocomidae (hoatzin)	M F	. . .	. . .	
Columbiformes				
Pteroclididae (sand grouse)	. . .	M F	. . .	
Raphidae (solitaires)	. . .	M F	. . .	
Columbidae (pigeons)	M F	M F	M F	
Cuculiformes				
Cuculidae (roadrunners)	M F	M F	M F	
Trogoniformes				
Trogonidae	M F	M F	M F	
Coraciformes				
Alcedinidae (kingfishers)	M F	M F	M F	*
Momotidae	m F	M F	M F	
Meropidae (bee eaters)	M F	M F	M F	
Coraciidae (rollers)	. . .	M F	M F	
Upupidae (hoopoes)	. . .	F	F	****

TABLE 1-1 (Continued)

	Nest Building	Incu-bating	Famili-alism	Male Feeds Female
Phoeniculidae (wood-hoopoes)	. . .	. . .	M F	
Eucerotidae (hornbills)	M F	F	M f	****
Caprimulgiformes				
Caprimulgidae (goatsuckers)	. . .	m F	M F	*
Apodiformes				
Apodidae (swifts)	M F	M F	M F	*
Trochilidae (hummingbirds)	F	F	F	*
Strigiformes				
Tytonidae (owls)	. . .	m F	M F	****
Strigidae (owls)	M F	m F	M F	****
Psittaciformes				
Psittacidae (parrots)	m F	m F	M F	****
Piciformes				
Galbulidae (jacamars)	m F	M F	M F	*
Bucconidae (puffbirds)	M F	M F	. . .	
Capitonidae (barbets)	M F	M F	M F	*
Ramphastidae (toucans)	. . .	M F	M F	
Picidae (woodpeckers)	M F	M f	M f	
Passeriformes				
Dendrocolaptidae	M F	M F	M F	
Furnariidae	M F	M F	M F	
Formicariidae	M F	M F	M F	
Cotingidae	m F	F	M F	
Pipridae	F	F	F	
Tyrannidae	m F	F	M F	*
Menuridae	F	F	F	
Alaudidae	F	m F	M F	*
Hirundinidae	M F	m F	M F	*
Oriolidae	m F	m F	m F	
Corvidae	M F	m F	m F	***
Paradisaeidae	F	m F	m F	
Paridae	M F	m F	M F	**
Sittidae	M F	F	M F	**
Certhiidae	m F	m F	M F	*
Chamaeidae	M F	M F	M F	
Timaliidae	m F	m F	m F	*
Cinclidae	m F	m F	m F	*
Troglodytidae	M F	F	M F	*
Mimidae	m F	m F	M F	
Turdidae	m F	m F	M F	*
Sylviidae	m F	m F	M F	*
Regulidae	M F	F	M F	
Muscicapidae	M F	m F	M F	**
Prunellidae	m F	m F	M F	*
Motacillidae	m F	m F	m F	*
Bombycillidae	M F	m F	M F	***

TABLE 1-1 (Continued)

	Nest Building	Incu- bating	Famili- alism	Male Feeds Female
Ptilogonatidae	M f	M F	M f	*
Artamidae	M f	M f	M F	
Laniidae	M F	m F	M F	***
Prionopidae	M F	M F	M F	
Sturnidae	M F	M F	M F	
Melithreptidae	? F	m F	M F	
Dicaedidae	m F	m F	M F	
Zosteropidae	M F	M F	M F	
Vireonidae	m F	m F	M F	
Coerebidae	m F	F	M F	
Parulidae	m F	F	M F	*
Ploceidae	M f	m F	m F	
Icteridae	F	F	m F	*
Thraupidae	m F	F	M F	**
Fringillidae	m F	m F	M F	**

Explanation of the table:
The listing follows a general trend of evolution from the more primitive to the more complex, although a mere listing obviously is limited.
For the families except those of the Passeriformes, sample forms are appended under their popular names, insofar as these families include forms having such names.
The relative involvement of the respective sexes in any of the psychodromes is indicated by capitalizing their symbols or leaving them in lower-case type.
Where no data are available, the indication is by . . . , or by a blank.
*indicates that feeding of the female by the male partner occurs.

his incubating and young-tending duties; in others, the female incubates and the male feeds her.

7. This appearance of spouse feeding by the male is scattered over the class, and therefore suggests multiple emergence. But it is striking that it is most frequently represented among the Passeriformes—the most evolved avians. This order, moreover, almost always displays biparentalism.

The sustained cooperative effort of the sexes in building the nest and caring for the young is remarkable. It far exceeds in complexity anything done by the poikilotherms. The latter, it always seems, pursue a task "single-mindedly"; a bird is moderately capable of digressing to another bit of conduct, along the road of its main pursuit. The fact that a male retains his brooding interest during the "blank" interval between fertilization and oviposition has been mentioned earlier. To the elemental feature of protection of the hatchlings the bird parents have added young-tending: They search assiduously for food (the young being hatched too immature to fend for themselves, yet without an attached yolk sac), and in many cases cleanse the nest of droppings. The parent-young relationship is not a simple one; let the reader consult the literature of ethology.

In measure as the young become fledged, if the nest is at a height above the ground the parents encourage their flying instinct to unfold itself (*"Dressur"*). This initiates the emancipation of the young from the familial pole. Some birds that nest on the ground are known to perform an equivalent of this detaching behavior.[41] This psychological break, which ends the kinship status completely, is an important step in the social maturation of both birds and mammals.

We return for a moment to male spouse feedings. Speculatively—it may have arisen partly as a premature arousal of the young-tending psychodrome; but this certainly does not dispose of the matter. The male hornbill plasters up all but a small opening to the nest, after his spouse has settled on the eggs. He then feeds her faithfully (for six weeks to four months); after the young have hatched, she relays part of this food to them. Among other genera, the female spouse may beg food successfully from her mate, by performing a prostrating flutter that resembles partly the begging technique of a youngster and partly the copulatory invitation of a receptive female.[42]

Among the colonial families, none are more remarkable than the penguins for their communal incubatings and creches. Only a part of the population may be breeding at a time; among the Emperors, there is a scramble among the idlers—male and female—to take over the incubating if a parent wishes to be relieved; and similarly, the young of the Kings are herded together in large numbers and watched by a few adults while the rest are away.[43]

Status Hierarchialism

Among gregarious birds, if the groups are not large (but they may be small subgroups within a very large colony), each sex may develop status hierarchies; in the case of female pigeons, poultry, and a few others they have been labeled "peck orders" and "peck right." Some bird genera exhibit degrees of intersex dominance. The courting sex is likely to be the dominant; and this is usually, but decidedly not

[41]See Brückner, 1933, for a classic study of familialism (Gynopaedium) in chickens.
[42]Perhaps Hursthouse's (1940, p. 122) remarkable narrative about a male little blue penguin belongs here. Whenever he returned to his nesting spouse, he brought a "garland" of some colorful plant and dropped it upon her. He ceased this after the hatchlings appeared. The female was never seen to perform in this way.
[43]For the remarkable social life of penguins, consult Wilson, 1907; Levick, 1914; Hursthouse, 1940; Richdale, 1940–1, 1949, 1951.

universally, the male. Among poultry, the male hierarchy as a whole tends to dominate the female hierarchy as a whole; moveover, if a rooster fancies a hen who is far down in her hierarchy, she immediately moves up beside him, in terms of the attitudes of her fellow hens.

It is to be noted that, wherever the male chooses a home spot, and the female accepts his courting suit, she is making an orientation first of all to the male, and so identifies herself with what starts out as his territory. Nest building and young-tending thereafter develop into an immediate focus of orientation.

It has also been established experimentally that the females of at least some birds cease to be erotic as they become broody; and these two orientations are under different hormonal presidencies.

Because birds have afforded classic opportunities for analyzing status hierarchialism which in one form or another occurs very commonly if not universally among the vertebrate classes, the present juncture is opportune for presenting it in a generalized outline:[44]

1. The stronger individual usually wins its pair contacts, but there are frequent exceptions because experience may be more important than strength. On first meeting, robust animals usually defeat those that are ill.

2. Mature animals usually dominate those less mature; thus hens dominate young chickens, and dominance based on age may continue long after the younger animals are physically superior to their elders. This rule has many exceptions, such as are furnished by the fact that newly matured canaries may dominate their fully mature associates, and half-grown kittens can keep old cats away from food.

3. In many animal groups, such as fishes, turtles, lizards, chimpanzees, the larger animals usually have higher social rank than their smaller associates. When the difference in size is not great (and sometimes when it is), the larger size does not insure dominance. White Leghorn hens also dominate hens of other breeds that are decidely heavier individuals.

4. The location of the first meeting is often important since many animals fight best in or near their home territory.

5. In strange territory, an animal accompanied by others from the home flock or horde often wins from a stranger more easily than if alone. The association of acquaintances may be more important than being within the home range.

6. Animals with young, especially females with young, tend to fight more fiercely than at other times.

7. Males usually dominate females, particularly in those species in which the male is the larger and showier sex. Often there are two rank-orders in a

[44]From Allee et al., 1949, p. 413f.

bisexual group, one for the males and another for the females, and these scarcely overlap.

8. The amount of male hormone present, within an indefinite physiological range, often increases social dominance of either sex. The sexual component of the drive for dominance in sword-tail fishes (Xiphophorus) may be distinguished from the social drive by gradual cooling; the sexual appetite was lost at 10° C., and the drive for social status continued until the water reached 6°.

9. The female consort of a dominant male tends to be accorded his social status so long as she remains near him. This can be expanded to the more general rule that in closely associated pairs of animals, the social status of both tends to be that won by the more dominant individual.

10. An ordinarily successful animal may be temporarily tired or ill and so may lose a combat that it might well be expected to win. This is a common cause of triangles of dominance in which a $>$ b $>$ c $>$ a; even the omega individual has been known to dominate the otherwise alpha hen of a flock.

11. Individuals standing high in their own social groups are more likely to dominate a stranger than are those with low social status. Winning, if repeated, tends to produce continued victories in pair contests; continued losing predisposes towards further defeats.

12. The paired reactions of animals to each other, and an old or even ill individual may continue to dominate vigorous associates long after it has lost the power to defeat them in actual combat.

13. It is hard enough to judge critically concerning psychological factors in human affairs; the difficulty is much greater with other animals, but there is much evidence of the importance of such effects in winning social status. One animal acts as though intimidated by the appearance of a stranger and gives way without fighting. In other cases, both act as if frightened; the one that recovers first usually wins. Another psychological aspect is the appearance in non-human animals of reactions toward flock mates that in man would be regarded as expressing individual antipathy or favoritism. Thus high-ranking cocks of the common domestic fowl, when in bisexual flocks, may suppress the mating behavior of some subordinate cocks and allow others to push them away from the copulating position.

14. Hereditary differences are important, as well as factors related to recent experience; for example, inbred strains of mice may differ both in aggressiveness and in fighting ability.

15. Seniority of membership in flocks of similarly aged hens shows a high correlation with high social rank.

The most certain sign of social dominance is the winning of an encounter with another individual, either by fighting or by some milder substitute. Often a series of such contacts is needed before the pair relations are definitely established; in some instances, especially between males, the defeated individual repeatedly attacks.

Defeat is often accompanied by easily observed changes in attitude. A defeated fish may drop its challenging posture of tense body and erect fins; the fish seems to hang limply in the water; it backs slowly away and then turns and flees. Many animals, among them hens, mice and boys, not infrequently emit characteristic cries when beaten. The head furnishings of defeated hens sometimes blanch, while those of the victor remain flushed. Defeated mice rear up in characteristic postures.

Other signs of low social rank include the avoidance of encounters with superiors; defeated hens move about quietly, often with head held low, or hide in out-of-the-way places or in protected niches. Animals of low rank sometimes accept or even offer to assume the female position in a copulation; monkeys and cats have this tendency.

Miscellaneous

There are several other features of the avian biogram which have already been mentioned in various connections, or which demand a further note.

Territorialism This psychodrome appears in various apparently contradictory contexts among other vertebrates as well as birds. Whatever its guise or occasion, it is an ego mobilizer. It is strongly asserted by the males of many—but by no means all—genera in the mating phase; it also may survive or appear in another context during sex quiescence. (The individual may possess a "lair.") Moreover a gregarious bird may be just as assertive of a home spot as is a solitary dweller. In some animals (e.g., the phalerope) there is a sex reversal of the nesting-courting psychodrome and its accompanying territorialism; but wherever a male bird identifies himself with territory and the female cooperates in a familialism, her orientation, as has already been mentioned, is first of all fixed upon him; as the parentalism proceeds, she apparently orients to brood.

The Kumpan We have mentioned the high social sensitivity of birds. A youngster raised without association with age-peers of his own kind may be permanently deflected from the orientations normal to his society; as Lorenz has shown in the cases of various genera.[45] Here belong also the "Kaspar Hausers."[46]

Social Organization During the Nonreproductive Phase Very little has been studied about this phase. We do not know either whether

[45]Lorenz, 1952; also, more technically, 1931, 1935. See Lorenz' discussion of "Prägung," 1937a, p. 299.
[46]Katz, 1948 or 1953; Brückner, 1933.

the intrasex hierarchies, or in how far intersex dominances, persist.[47]

Frequently—and this holds for mammalian herds also—the flock admits strangers to its membership only during the nonreproductive phase. This is consistent with the fact that the reproductive phase sees a heightened individualism.

Rhythm-Taking The prophase of migration sees birds gathering into flocks—including the breeding season's new crop—and developing a sharp sensitivity to each other's movements by way of mass maneuverings. Penguins, at this time, practice spectacular "military parade-ground" movements. How the proprioceptivities of vertebrate individuals in general are synchronized by molar social stimulations is a problem that remains unsolved.

Fish and Bird Parentalism

Fishes that spawn, and the more primitive orders of birds, present a most striking parallel of reproductive syndrome—although the birds carry theirs one important step beyond that of the fishes. The males of both classes stake out nesting territories, drive away isosexual intruders, build nests, court females, brood the eggs, protect the hatchlings. We can hardly escape the conclusion that there are somehow and somewhere within their central nervous systems similar programmatic mechanisms. Nevertheless, the bird brain is more highly organized than that of any fish; and this must somehow account for certain superiorities of syndromal behavior.

To maintain a programmatic chain of instinctive behavior in activity, there must appear the proper sequence of external stimuli—an observation we owe to both the ethologists and some of the laboratory psychophysiologists. This is what makes it possible for the male stickleback to pass smoothly from courting to spawning to expelling the female to fanning the eggs to tending the hatchlings. (Whether an extraneous stimulus can be injected into the chain is not now the question.) But among birds, the progression is not that simple. An external stimulation to programmatic behavior is indeed necessary— such as a sustaining contact of the bird's breast with the eggs which maintains its brooding interest—yet abeyance in a motivation is not equivalent to its extinction. Thus, were it not for coitus with internal fertilization, the reproductive phase of the vertebrate biogram could

[47]For a résumé of the question of dominance and territorialism, see Noble, 1939b. In *Melopsittacus undulatus*, the females dominate during nonbreeding; the males during breeding. See Masure and Allee, 1934. There are other instances of this arrangement.

not have become terrestrialized. But thereupon there must occur a time lapse before the egg is laid. Yet this temporal hiatus does not extinguish male parentalism; nor, among the females, does oviposition necessarily go over into parentalism. We are speaking here of the Paleognathae—the primitive subclass of extant birds. The male ostrich collects from his harem a nestfull of eggs, monopolizes their brooding, and is indeed an intent and effective caretaker. Now, it is as characteristic of the male bird to remain familially interested as it is for the male mammal not to be. Female familialism is added to the bird lines during the evolution of the Neognathae; the genera which lack male familialism are exceptional (a regression?).

Biparental familialism occurs among the higher teleosts, as we have noted before. But the biparental familialism of the birds develops a *complete* familialism, in which the parents "train" the young (*"Dressur"*).[48] Essentially, the process appears to be that of the parents' supplying, by their behavior, the proper stimulations for eliciting release of innate behavioral mechanisms, at the correct programmatic moment when those mechanisms have achieved the proper maturative level. It is to be remembered that this is done by a brain which possesses an elaborate corpus striatum and optic tectum but only a very rudimentary neopallium. But investigation of the point-to-point relations between neurophysiology, neural architecture, and ethology has not yet reached even an embryonic stage.

BIOGRAM, INSTINCT AND INTELLIGENCE

To find, as we do, that the teleosts exhibit among themselves a common pattern of psychodromes which varies only in its detail content; that the yet more primitive vertebrates, scanty though their data be, support the teleost findings; that the birds likewise form a recognizable common type in this respect, yet that despite their evolutionary divergence teleosts and birds have remarkably parallel biogrammatic configurations; that what we know of the Amphibia and the Reptilia (again, scanty though that material be) is consistent with these and often corroborative—all this forces us to the inference that we are dealing with patternings that are innate or instinctive and properties of verberate morphology. Nonetheless, somewhere along the line of vertebrate phylogenesis "intelligence" emerges—if by that term we mean the capacity for making judgments. But if we were to discover

[48]The process has been analyzed ingeniously by K. Lorenz. See particularly Lorenz, 1937a, b.

that, even with the possession of this capacity, animals still manifest the broad features of what appears to be this same biogrammatic configuration, we cannot but suspect that the instinctive is still as vitally operative as ever, and that intelligence does not negate it but somehow is its coadjutor. Perhaps we should think of instinct and intelligence as two psychologisms, the latter of which has emerged out of the former to render more effective the relations of the former to the *Merkwelt;* the reciprocal consequence being that the projective-associative processes of this new psychologism serve to create an enrichment of the *Merkwelt.*

This rather philosophical way of couching an idea can be converted into operations by splitting the problem in two: the psychophysiological aspects of brain mechanisms evolutionally considered, and behavior analysis particularly as practiced by the ethologists.

Basic Cerebral Architecture

Generalities 1. The vertebrate brain starts, ontogenetically and phylogenetically, as a dorsal hollow tube. Its ventral wall develops motor administration (basal plate); its dorsal wall, sensory reception (alar plate).

There is further a radical difference in the brain structuring that develops respectively anterior to and posterior to a landmark region which includes the termination of the notochord and the seat of the pituitary gland; for posterior to this landmark the brain builds up, essentially, from both alar and basal plate material;[49] anterior to it, the construction derives essentially from alar plate material alone (prosencephalon; which becomes tel- and diencephalon).[50] The mesencephalon develops as a sort of transitional region between the other two portions of the brain.

These basic facts from developmental anatomy determine the neural administration of the vertebrate bodily organization, and the nature of instinctive and intelligent psychic processes.

2. Phylogenetically and ontogenetically, they develop from the undifferentiated region of the sensory administration the adjustive mechanisms. This at once indicates that reception of an external energy by the organism is but the beginning of a digestive process which starts as a conversion of that energy into a stimulus and eventuates in its conversion into information which the organism utilizes.

[49]Rhombencephalon; which becomes met- and myelencephalon; cf. deuterencephalon of Amphioxus.
[50]cf. archencephalon of Amphioxus.

In ontogeny, the motor neurons are already sparking generalized movements of body segments before the adjustive mechanisms establish connections with them.

This separateness of the motor and sensory-adjustive mechanisms needs emphasis before integrations may be considered. For, and furthermore, in the phylogenesis of the vertebrates the two have pursued degrees of development that are considerably independent of each other. A man, a horse, and a bird in a field, for instance, are meeting the same environment, and their repertoire of motion elements is both limited and largely the same. The differences in their receptive capacities is, if anything, even less (the differences are secondary: emphasis upon olfaction or vision, color sensitivity, etc.); but the adjustive differences are enormous. From cyclostome to mammal, adjustive differences are even vaster.

The adjustive mechanisms thus appear as intercalations between the sensory and the motor components. If these were lacking, obviously the sensory stimulation could go over immediately into a local motor response. The intercalations are coordinators between the various parts of the organism, to effect an overall response. At the same time—the more uniform this general intercalary neural mass, the more generalized the coordinative response. Nevertheless the intercalation introduces a time lag between the "anticipation" and the "consummation" of the stimulus-response circuit (Sherrington). No less important than these adjustive areas of excitation are the inhibitory areas that balance and are integrated with them. These occur, expectably, in both the more primitive and more evolved brain levels. When, therefore, we encounter copulatory activity inhibited in both a male rat and a rooster we are not surprised to discover it cortically regulated in the former and not in the latter; but at the same time we are not justified in saying that the inhibitory function in the rat has "passed out of the control" of the region which homologizes with the agent in the rooster. We should not forget that a brain with a neocortex is living in a far more complex situation than a brain which lacks it; the brain is itself an agent in creating the situation; and inhibition and activation are obverse and reverse of the same coin of psychic life. A rich psyche is richly inhibitive as well as richly excitative. The rat behavior, so to speak, is a sort of "rooster-plus."

These capacities for compounding excitements and inhibitions and so delaying response result, at higher phylogenetic levels, in such complex actions as *Umweg* behavior; in man, the consummatory response can even be delayed for years—held in abeyance while other responses are made, and hierarchies of choice created. It appears to be this aspect of human conduct which has allowed some psychologists and culturologists to lose sight of the innate basis of these responses.

Excitation and inhibition are exerted not only upon effectory mechanisms of the body; the adjustive system includes a feedback servomechanism by which, we may say, the neural administration of the organism keeps track of itself. The organism is a self-balancing configuration, utilizing excitation and inhibition. The regulation is not a property of either of these components; it resides in a relationship between them—a molecule, so to speak, of which they are two of the atoms. Not only is there this differentiation, but, as certain energy paths become emphasized over others, neurons actually migrate nearer to the source of their stimulation; and they lengthen their axons "behind" them, that is, in the direction away from that stimulus, thus maintaining connections with the cells to which they relay the energy (neurobiotaxis). Nerve cell proliferations, nuclear differentiation, nerve cell migrations are the processes whereby the various adjustive mechanisms in the vertebrates have been built up; only the most conspicuous of which are the mammalian cerebral hemispheres.

These assortative cellular groupings within local portions of the brain are largely responsible for the rise of altered relationships between an organism and its environment; they are a part of the evolution which makes a different organism, one with commensurately different life functions. They account, in large measure, for differences of life mode between a bird and a mammal; but also for the differences between a salamander and a frog.

By corollary, some brain regions are evolutionarily more stable, others more labile. (For instance, the stria medullaris thalami is very stable in the vertebrate series; the telencephalic pallium has been remarkably labile.) Nonetheless, all migrations and other alterations occur within the bounds of an all-embracive architecture.[51]

3. The distinction between the motor and the sensory-adjustive provinces is cardinal to the understanding of instinct: The *Auslösende Schema*—a functional unit of the ethologists' analyses, which surely

[51] I am confident that this can be said without its committing me to the old notion of a predetermined, primordial pattern of a vertebrate neuroanatomy. That man, bird, and beast, no matter how diverse, have never ceased being vertebrates, all comparative studies continue to reaffirm.

must have its seat in the adjustive structures of neurology—is to be distinguished from the motor (behavioral) response.[52] For, if the IRM ("innate releasing mechanisms") be modified by experience, the same motor pattern is released, yet upon an altered situational object. It is equally clear that the adjustive mechanisms make it possible for a motor (behavioral) response, which originally replied to a situation wherein olfactive information predominated, subsequently to reply to a predominantly visual stimulus. This point will be illustrated later.

4. Another basic and persistent architectural feature of the vertebrate brain is a gross dichotomy of "visceral" and "somatic" mechanisms. (The two are, however, interconnected—necessarily so.) They serve to regulate the internal economy of the organism and to effect its adjustments to and exploitation of the external environment. Thus it is, for instance, that the hypothalamus contains the head ganglia of the ortho- and parasympathetic systems; the most primitive telencephalic pallium divides into somatic-olfactory (prepiriform palaeocortex) and visceral-olfactory (hippocampal archicortex) regions. These latter two regions we shall encounter on more than one occasion.

5. The "deuterencephalon" (and the spinal cord) controls adjustively the basic bodily functions; some of which are internal (circulation), others externalized (locomotion); yet others are in part both (respiration, nutrition, reproduction); and it possesses both sensory-adjustive and motor regions. The "archencephalon," on the other hand, is sensory-adjustive only; primitively and diagrammatically, it is responsible to the organism for the distance perceptivities of olfaction (chemical: telencephalon) and vision (physical: diencephalon-mesencephalon).

How these two sensory systems complement each other, and how one or the other comes to be predominant in the life mode of a class, subclass, or order, is decidely relevant to the present study; unfortunately, we must limit ourselves to the most general outlines as we proceed. One point, however, demands emphasis immediately. Among the vertebrates, the social interreactions rely more heavily upon visual than olfactory stimulations, even though both be involved. In the search for food and escape from enemies, on the other hand, olfaction predominates at the primitive phyletic levels, and predominates among many phyletically advanced forms. Succinctly—the vertebrates meet the physical environment with varying

[52]Tinbergen, 1951, p. 52.

reliance upon olfaction and vision; to meet the *ego-tu-ille environment,* the emphasis of reliance is upon vision. This can be said, without underemphasizing the roles of olfaction in the matter.

Telencephalic Pallium In all the vertebrates, the telencephalic pallium has some degree of organizing capacity. The primitive vertebrates (to judge from cyclostomes) possessed an "inverted" type, which eventually made possible the terrestrialization of forms whose *Merkwelt* was served conspicuously by olfaction, as we shall see. In cyclostomes, we may identify, primordially, a mesial region which (at the amphibian level) is identifiable as the hippocampal area (archipallium), a lateral region which correspondingly eventuates as the piriform area (paleopallium); and between them a generalized pallial area, which in the mammals expands enormously—the cortex of the cerebral hemispheres.

This pallium represents the adjustive domain of the olfactory portion of the prosencephalon. That the organ of the intellect should have been derived from this semingly improbable source, however, has an understandable history; and recent and current research suggests that it also accounts for quite a number of the emotive symptoms in certain psychosomatic disorders.[53]

We have noticed already that primitive aquatic vertebrates hunt and escape predominantly with their olfactory sense. Accordingly, olfaction is connected with the exteroceptive and proprioceptive senses in the thalamus-mesencephalon via the piriform region (olfactosomatic). But olfaction has yet another function: It acts as a general facilitating agent upon other brain processes; and this is "localized" in the hippocampal formation (olfacto-visceral).

In phylogenesis, the intermediate pallium becomes invaded by fibers from the thalamus (diencephalon). It is these which eventuate in the projective and associational fibers which connect with the neopallial cortex, and, as we might say, inject "intelligence" into a more basic psychoneurological architecture. Another important consequence of this evolution is that all the sense departments except olfaction connect with the thalamus, which in turn relays to the cortex; while olfaction connects directly.

How this operates among the phenomena we are interested in may be summarized thus: Experimental neurology indicates that, in such a syndrome as the reproductive, its component segments are medi-

[53]See MacLean, 1949.

ated by mechanisms in the brain stem (and spinal cord). But, from fish to bird and mammal, if the pallium be suitably ablated, these segments do not organize into a pattern.[54]

To the neocortex we shall return, after surveying the diencephalon (with the mesencephalon implied in appropriate spots) and the rhinencephalon.

Diencephalon 1. If it can be said at all, of an organ whose effectiveness is compounded of harmonized operations stemming from all of its regions together, that there exists a region *par excellence* of neuropsychic coordination, that region is the diencephalon.

It connects with practically all the other parts of the brain. Somatic and visceral sensations are brought into dynamic relationship. Some but not all of its information it relays to the cerebral hemispheres, where the information is projected upon the cortex.

Its hypothalamic portion heads up the para- and orthosympathetic systems, and adjusts their balance, thereby exerting a control over the visceral forces which are the organized energy sources of instinct. It transmits its tensions to the somatic nervous system, and thereby activates an appetitive toward food or sex. Its fiber connections are rich—notably, with the rhinencephalic olfactory mechanism, with the optic mechanism, with various parts of the diencephalon itself, with the pituitary gland. Phylogenetically, it has been considered to be "primarily a precipitate within the olfactory system in a region from which central autonomic structures developed. It became a primitive center for olfactory-visceral correlation."[55]

During phylogenesis, as vertebrate forms have become more encephalized by developing the telencephalic pallial mechanisms, the emotive driving power of the hypothalamus has been brought under adjustive controls. *En revanche*—those very adjustive controls in their turn do not escape the influence of the hypothalamus. The instinctual, in other words, does not cease to exist; it comes, rather, to share its administration with a younger descendant in the psychic dynasty.

The vertebrates which lack the neopallial development of the mammals are quite capable of carrying through the entire biogrammatic complex; and the mammals add no basic features to the biogram. We might say that lower vertebrates possess diencephalic integration but without first passing their information through a neocortical analysis. The diencephalic integration is not thereby lost after the

[54]Cf. Beach, 1942.
[55]Grinker, 1939, p. 43.

mammals interject their neopallial refinements into the total behavior complex.

Three distinctly different kinds of cases may serve to illustrate the operations of the brain stem during waking where the cerebral hemispheres are not involved, though they belong to the neural systems involved.

1. W. R. Hess and his collaborators, by electrical stimulations of very definite and localized spots in the cat hypothalamus, have induced the animal to run through the psychodromal chain of preparing itself for sleep and finally succumbing.[56] (2) Female rats who have suffered experimental cortical ablations, but with intact brain stems, remain capable of executing the elements of the maternal psychodrome, but these are unorganized and desultory.[57] (3) "Nielsen and Sedgwick reported the case of an anencephalic infant who lived 85 days and showed arousal and sucking responses and contentment at coddling, cried at rough handling, and otherwise expressed instincts and emotions. In this case there was no active neural tissue anterior to the midbrain. Evidently, therefore, the reactions were accomplished by no higher integrating mechanism than that available in the brain stem."[58]

2. The system which intergrates the responsive action of the animal is called by Penfield the "centrencephalic" system. This is situated, in all probability, in the reticular system that stretches from the corpus striatum of the diencephalon posteriorad, and in the intralaminar system of the thalmus (diencephalon). To this system the cerebral cortex (particularly, the memory mechanism of the temporal lobe) feeds its data for integration into the total response of the organism.[59]

"(The thalamus)," says Walker,[60] "is the mediator to which all stimuli from the outside world congregate and become modified and distributed to subcortical or cortical centers so that the individual may make adequate adjustments to the constantly changing environment. The thalamus thus holds the secret of much that goes on within the cerebral cortex."

3. Although "consciousness" should properly be considered an

[56]Hess calls it the *"Schlafsyndrom."* See Hess, 1943, 1944, 1954. Similar experiments have been performed by a number of workers.
[57]Beach, 1937.
[58]Remarks by Dr. James O'Leary, *in re* Jasper, Ajmone-Marsan, Stoll, 1952, p. 170.
[59]Cf. Penfield, 1952; Penfield, 1954; Penfield and Jasper, 1954; Jasper, Ajmone-Marsan, Stoll, 1952. These studies are very instructive on the function of the brain stem in normal and pathological behavior.
[60]1938, p. 277. See also 1937, p. 259.

organizational state rather than an entity having a seat, still the regions of the brain contribute to it differentially; yet if there is one particularly essential region of the brain that is indispensable, it is an area lying about the third ventricle in the diencephalon. This contrasts sharply with the cerebral hemispheres, which may be injured or subjected to ablations without the loss of consciousness. On the human level, of course, "consciousness" does not occur without the *content* supplied to it from the cerebral cortex; but this does not allow us to deny a noncorticate consciousness to the vertebrates who lack the conspicuous mammalian feature. (But "self-consciousness" is quite another question—placing on a further secondary, derivative analytic plane; for undoubtedly it constitutes a *Weiterbildung*.)

At the human level, the implications of these matters to psychoanalysis are inescapable; and Schiller[61] has remarked, "The cortex is apparently reserved for the conscious parts of the ego; the basal ganglia and brain stem, for what is unconscious in the ego and for the id."

The Rhinencephalon It was indicated earlier that the primitive, aquatic vertebrates organized their *Merkwelt* mainly about two senses, each being represented by a major segment of the prechordal brain ("archencephalon"): the olfactory possessing the telencephalon, the optic possessing the diencephalon. Further, each of these segments contained adjustive mechanisms associated with the senses. We can cast the phylogenesis from that point on in the shape of an issue: Which of these sensory-adjustive domains should be capable of evolving the most elaborate psychic mechanisms?

The teleosts exploited the potentialities of the visual domain: The tectum opticum of their midbrain is elaborate, it is in close communication with the hardly less elaborate diencephalic corpus striatum. The forebrain, on the other hand, is of the everted type, with a correspondingly thin pallium (which is not the homologue of that of the inverted type). In the *Merkwelt* of the teleost, vision dominates both its food quest and avoidance of enemies, and its social interreactions.[63]

But the terrestrial vertebrates represent the continued evolution of a vertebrate line having an inverted forebrain, and one in which it was the adjustive mechanisms of the olfactory domain which eventually produced the cerebral cortex. The result is the peculiarly

[61]1952, p. 204.
[63]It should need no elaboration either here or elsewhere, that "dominant" (etc.) sense does not connote any exclusivism

elaborated rhinencephalon, or limbic lobe, which MacLean in a brilliant analytic survey names the "visceral brain."[64] Primarily telencephalic, it includes differentiated features of the diencephalon and mesencephalon. It includes the hippocampal formation, which, embedded (in primates) within the temporal lobe, mediates between the yet more archaic portions of the olfactory brain and the neocortical part of the temporal lobe. The latter, in turn, is the seat of the elaborated memory mechanisms. The rhinencephalon is extensively connected with the hypothalamus in contrast to the neopallial cortex, which lacks such direct connections.

Much of what is known about the limbic lobe comes from clinical experience with epilepsies. There occur "dreamy states"—mental diplopias—anxieties, rages, a sense of smelling, tasting, etc.; mastication; emotive experiences all indicating hippocampal, amygdaloid, and other involvements. The mechanisms seem to be relevant to the oral-anal and the sexual dependencies and drives uncovered by psychoanalysis.

"The relationships and alleged functions of the rhinencephalon," says MacLean, ". . . indicate that though our intellectual functions are carried on in the newest and most highly developed part of the brain, our affective behaviour continues to be dominated by a relatively crude and primitive system. This situation provides a clue to understanding the difference between what we 'feel' and what we 'know.'[65]

There is no other portion of the brain that is so graphic an illustration of how and where the instinctive meets the intellectual in a human psychic process than that right here. In as insightful a paper as has appeared on our subject in the present decade, Kubie says:[66]

What has become increasingly evident in more recent work is the fact that this ancient brain [i.e., the rhinencephalon; whence have been derived the archipallium, the paleopallium, and the mesopallium—E.W.C.]—much of which lies in the depth of the temporal lobe, with its dreamy states of psychomotor epilepsy and its body-memories—has extensive relationships with both the neopallium and the hypothalamus. As MacLean points out, this part of the primitive forebrain lies in the basal-mesial portion of the temporal lobe with direct connections to the hypothalamus, becoming thereby a crossroads or association for both *internal* and *external* perceptions arising from the eye, the ear, the body wall, the apertures, the genitals, and viscera. Smell reaches it directly. Here then, within the temporal lobe and its connections, is the crossroads where the "I" and the "non-I" poles

[64]1949.
[65]Op. cit., p. 351
[66]1953c, p. 31f.

of the symbol meet. It is impossible to overestimate the importance of this fact that the temporal lobe complex constitutes the mechanism for integrating the past and the present, the phylogenetically and ontogenetically old and new, and at the same time the external and internal environments of the central nervous system. It is through the temporal lobe and its connections that the "gut" component of memory enters into our psychological processes and the symbol acquires its dual poles of reference. Thus in the temporal lobe and its deeper primitive connections is the mechanism for the coordination and integration of all of the data which link us to the world of experience, both extero- and interoceptive. It is by means of this temporal lobe complex operating through a bipolar symbolic system that we are able both to project and introject. It makes of the temporal lobe and its intricate bilateral and autonomic connections, which MacLean has called the "visceral brain," the central nervous organ which can mediate the translation into somatic disturbances of those tensions which are generated on the level of psychological experience. It might even be called the psychosomatic organ.

The Cortex Again   Even a brief review of the nature of the mammalian neocortex is far beyond our present scope; nor should it be really necessary: its residual equipotentialities over against its functional localizations; its subcortical as distinct from its cortical functionings; its centrifugal and centripetal relations with various parts of the basic brain, as well as the limits of those relationships; how it affects as well as how it is affected by, those various parts; the data from neurosurgery, experimental ablations, electroencephalography; and so forth. Phylogenetically, it expresses that general vertebrate tendency to refine, by analysis and synthesis, the adjustive aspect of its neurological treatment of environmental energies, as that tendency is expressed in the telencephalon.

Suppose a complex electronic calculator housed in a building. Were we to decide that our machine could deliver more complex results if somewhere we could interpolate a large number of analyzing circuits, we might construct a housing annex, run a large bundle of wirings out from our machine, sort them in the annex by spreading them out and interconnecting them endlessly with relays; let these include mechanisms for storage of past information (as electronic machines do); then, let some of the operations in our main machine be detoured into the annex apparatus; at last, when the operations occurring in the annex are fed back into the main machine, the latter incorporates them into its final results.[67]

[67]In drawing the analogy, I am not intending to reduce the operations of the brain to the level of electronic calculators; I wish only to suggest the position of the cerebral hemispheres in relation to the basic brain. There is a rather common mis-

The cortex, in other words, possesses localized areas to which information is projected from the basic brain. With this spread out, there is space for infinitely detailed associative connections between points in these areas.

To bring this into relation with our subject—the behavior patterns of primitive vertebrates represent undifferentiated totalities; those of the higher are just as total, but they are compounded by the addition of differentiated ingredients.

A shark apparently moves in a *Merkwelt* of olfactive-gustatory-visual-reverberative-visceral stimuli which reinforce each other; there is no reason to believe that it can act selectively by virtue of one of these stimulations as against the others. On the other hand, Lorenz[68] reports that a jewel-fish father who had retrieved in his mouth one of his young, encountered some food on his way back to the nest, which he snapped up. He paused, then ejected food and offspring, recaptured and swallowed the tidbit, retrieved the youngster, and resumed his journey. The same writer[69] reports that he was attacked by his otherwise friendly daws when his black bathing trunks showed from his pocket: The black-in-possession-of-a-figure could not be discriminated from a predator-grasping-a-daw. The bird's highly elaborated corpus striatum but rudimentary (perhaps even retrogressive) neopallium allows it a receptivity to details-in-configuration with, however, but limited discriminatory analytic ability within that configuration. A chimpanzee, when confronted with an automatic feeding machine requiring a certain kind of chip as coin but not others, discovers for himself which chips are "genuine coin," and then spends a great deal of time and effort in acquiring a supply of them for future use. A human can choose between buying liquor now and paying for an education next year.

INSTINCT

In this article (which after all is intended as a survey and abstract) it is beyond our scope to review the status of modern concepts of instinct; and it should be unnecessary. But something has to be said, since convergence is occurring between psychoanalysis, ethology, and experimental neurology; and this progression is of the utmost im-

---

conception that the cerebral hemispheres are sitting on top of the brain, and that they dictate to it.
[68]1952, p. 37f.
[69]Op. cit. p. 141 seq.

portance to anthropology.[70] Freud's own thought on the nature of instinct underwent, as we know, a considerable development between his "Instincts and Their Vicissitudes" (1915) and his "Outline of Psychoanalysis" (1940). For the purposes of the present essay, it will suffice to summarize that an instinct, according to Freud, is characterized thus: Its energy source lies within the organism; it is durative, that is, it is not a temporary confluence of psychic energy; it cannot be evaded or destroyed, no matter what the attempt at its suppression. Freud's conceptions of the role of the nervous system and the way by which motor responses become transmitted phylogenetically, have not stood up as well as this summary characterization, which was then postulated as deriving from those conceptions.

Latterly, Kubie has produced a homeostatic implementation of Freud's view that "a classification of instincts must rest upon a physiologic rather than a psychologic basis" and that "instincts represent the demand which the body makes on the mental apparatus."[71] Thus:

All instincts consist of a) the direct or indirect expression of biochemical body processes, through b) inherited yet modifiable networks of neuronal synaptic patterns, which c) are molded in turn by superimposed, compulsive and phobic mechanisms. These are seen to operate in normal psychology as in psychopathology. The relative roles of the three components of instinctual activity vary in differnt instincts and in diffrent species.

Therefore it is impossible to make any absolute distinction between Instinct and Drive ("Trieb"). The differences are quantitative rather than qualitative, and are due to the different roles played by the components mentioned above.

In many of the instinctual processes the biochemical source of energy is converted into behavior through deprivation; because deprivation synchronizes the continuous asynchronous flux which in states of rest goes on in body tissues. The biochemical processes, however, are linked to warning mechanisms, which under ordinary circumstances come into play before any actual tissue deprivation occurs. Therefore in higher animals instinctual patterns are triggered off by warning mechanisms rather than by tissue hungers.

Therefore on the psychologic level, instinctual aims and objects are also built around the warning mechanism.[72]

[70]For a very informative and comprehensive review of instinct in man, which brings together psychoanalytical and ethological theory, see Fletcher, 1957.

[71]Kubie, 1948, p. 29. The paraphrasing of Freud's view is Kubie's. Precisely how the symbolizing processes of man become involved with the instinctive processes, is, I believe, a key problem to the understanding of the emergence of Homo out of the pre-hominid Primates.

[72]Kubie, 1948, p. 29a.

A bird newly arrived on the breeding grounds begins its psycho-drama with a rather unfocalized behavior, one that strikes us as rambling. Craig (1918) termed it "appetitive behavior." The conduct pursues a course which progressively narrows down upon a final "consummatory act"; and this, in the parlance of today, discharges a tension so that homeostasis is effected. A neurophysiological para-phrase of this drama is another statement of Kubie's.[73]

[In the organs of the body which have instinctual function—they have direct apertural connection with the external world, and serve for swallowing, excretion, genital functioning—] ". . . the patterns of instinctual behavior are always *initiated* as somatomuscular activity under the guidance of the voluntary nervous system, but end up as almost purely autonomic action. As each individual instinctual act gets under way, there is a gradual increase in the participation of autonomic function until finally, at the critical point, the autonomic nervous system takes off on an independent jet-propelled flight of its own. One sees this most clearly in swallowing, urinating, defecating, and of course, in sex; but it is true in subtler ways in every instinc-tual act."

This statement, to be sure, did not have in mind the scope of instinctual patterns which in this essay we have brought together as hierarchies of syndromes and finally a biogram. The syndromes, how-ever, have been the subject of study by the ethologists, of course from the particular standpoint that they occupy.[74] The ethologists, for instance, find that in making an instinctive response animals react not to every physical stimulus that they are able to perceive, but to certain specific "sign stimuli," often configurative, according to the physio-logical states in which they find themselves at the time. The reaction is viewed as being "released" by an internal, poised mechanism ("innate releasing mechanism"—already mentioned). The releasing stimulus, moreover, often acts also as a directive upon the response, as well as a mere releaser of it. In the neonate, the response as well as its orientation may be less focally directed than it eventually be-comes under the operation of maturative processes; and it may be-come a part of a hierarchy of appetitive-consummatory acts, which are becoming defined and organized. During ontogenesis, the innate mechanisms, being still labile and malleable, may receive a *Prägung*, as already indicated. This normal elicitation or this distortion of an innate, maturing mechanism clearly is not the same thing as "con-

[73]1953d, p. 3b.
[74]See Tinbergen, 1942, 1948, 1951. For his exploitation of Craig's system, see 1951, pp. 104–107.

ditioning" mechanisms that operate where ontogenesis has already been completed.

The present essay seeks to go a step farther than the consideration of discrete syndromes of behavior, such as the so-called "reproductive instinct" which Tinbergen has dissected.[75] The phyletic comparisons that we are making seem to indicate that even these blocks of behavior belong to a larger whole. The indication is that the vertebrate form possesses a total behavioral as well as a total physical architecture.

SYMBOL

Although we may not deny altogether to some, at least, of the Alloprimates a rudimentary capacity for symbolizing, this function in "fully developed" form is as unique to man as is speech. Indeed, since speech itself is a form of symbolopoea, the power to speak must have developed apace with the power to symbolize (or only a step behind it), during the evolution of the pre- and protohominids.

We are still a long way from understanding the cerebral mechanics of language—which means not only controlled articulations and interspersed interruptions (silences) but their linkages with memories and abstractive activity. At least six areas of the human cortex on the lateral aspect of the dominant hemisphere, when stimulated electrically, can produce one or another form of aphasia; two of these areas, on either hemisphere, produce vocalizations. Two of the areas of aphasic arrest lie close to the memory cortex of the temporal lobe. Electrostimulation of the temporal lobe raises to consciousness, far more vividly than in a mere recollective evocation, a picture of past events or scenes; so vividly, indeed, that they seem actually to be occurring, even while the patient is conscious of the fact that he is where he really is.[76] The frontal lobes are essential to foresight and future planning. All of this says, in most informal language, that the capacity to utter intelligent speech and to symbolize in general, demands a patterned cooperation between differentiable areas of the brain; that those areas just mentioned undoubtedly are involved more particularly, as well as an indefinite number of other regions of the brain. And incidentally, all these cortical regions occur in the apes, although quantitatively far less so than in man. In onto-

---

[75]1951, pp. 102–104.
[76]Cf. Penfield, 1952; also Penfield and associates.

genesis, moreover, the cortical areas myelinate programmatically, and not simultaneously; roughly, the order corresponds to a phylogenesis, though not perfectly. And we do not even know but that the programmatic order in which the myelinizations occur may have something to do with man's uniquely successful "phylogenetic attempt" at developing speech.

Nevertheless, we cannot get away from the hypothesis that the power to symbolize and to speak is a function of the whole brain, or at least an indefinitely large part of it; and this means that the archaic brain too must be involved in the formula. In the *rapprochements* that are currently taking place between psychoanalysis and neurosurgery, there are indications that that is the case. In a very significant paper, Kubie[77] says, in part:

There is the symbolic function by means of which in thought and speech we represent abstractions from experience. Here the term "symbolic function" is coextensive with all higher psychological functions, and especially with concept formation.

There is the symbolic function with which we are all familiar in figures of speech, metaphors, slang, poetry, obscenities, puns, jokes, and so forth. Here the concept behind the symbol is translated into some other mode of expression. . . . This use of the symbolizing capacity of the human psychic apparatus characterizes that type of function which Freud called *preconscious* or the *descriptive unconscious*. It reaches its most systematic development of course in the intuitive processes of the creative artist and the scientist.

Finally, there is the more limited psychoanalytic use of the term "symbolic function" where the symbol is a manifest representation of an unconscious latent idea. Here the link between the symbol and what it represents has become inaccessible to conscious inspection.

. . . It is important to recognize the continuity of these three kinds of symbolic function: since it is because of this continuity that every symbol is a multivalent tool. That is to say that simultaneously on conscious, preconscious, and/or unconscious levels every direct or indirect representation of any conceptual process will in all circumstances, if in varying proportions, be literal, allegorical, and also "symbolic" in the dreamlike or psychoanalytic sense. Consequently, in actual daily use symbols are simultaneously charged with meaning in all three ways and on all three levels. This makes of every symbol a chord with a potentiality of at least nine simultaneous overtones. . . .

The capacity to make abstractions from disparate, concrete experiences and to represent those abstractions by various symbolic devices is the *sine qua non* of man's highest psychological and spiritual qualities. Without this

[77]Kubie, 1953b, pp. 67 seq., *passim*. See also Kubie, 1956.

capacity, it would be impossible for man to have any psychological processes more complex than the sensory afterimages of prior experiences. . . . His ability to isolate fragments of his experiences and to represent them separately makes it possible subsequently to synthesize new psychological concepts out of fragments of earlier sensory events. . . . In their early developmental phases our concepts are vague, broad, and overlapping; but . . . with maturation, they gradually become more discrete and distinct. The same steps are observed in the evolution of the symbolic representations of concepts: i.e., in the drawings of children and in their acquisition of language. . . . Early in its formative process every concept and its symbolic representatives develop two points of reference, one internal with respect to the boundaires of the body, and one external. This dual anchorage of every symbol in the constellation "I" and in the constellation "Non-I" is inherent in the process by which we acquire knowledge and by which we orient ourselves both to ourselves and to the outer world. It is also a key to an understanding of the process by which psychological tensions and experiences can acquire somatic representation. These later complications . . . only serve to accentuate this function of the symbolic process as a bridge between the inner and outer world. One consequence . . . is that the differentiation of the "I" from the "Non-I" is always relative and never absolute. . . .

. . . These considerations have a firm grounding in physiological and anatomical facts. . . . Every symbol has simultaneous poles of reference to the "I" and to the "Non-I" worlds: the "I" having its origins in the proprioceptive percepts of the body, and the "Non-I" in exteroceptive percepts of the outer world. Thus the symbolic process is itself the bridge between the "I" and the "Non-I" on both a perceptual and a conceptual level. For this bipolar (or multipolar?) reference of all symbols on the psychological levels, there is also a neuroanatomical and neurophysiological basis through their bipolar (or multipolar?) representation in the central nervous system. In its full development this anatomical and physiological basis for the bipolarity of the symbolic process may be as uniquely characteristic of the human brain as is the symbolic process for human psychology. The body-roots of the "I" component of the symbol have their central representation in the more primitive archipallial cortex and its association systems. This links the "I" component of the symbolic process to visceral functions, through the automatic tie-up of the archipallium, with direct expression via the effector system of the hypothalamus, and finally through its special relation to the olfactory system. In this way, the "nose-brain" constitutes a link between the archipallium or visceral brain (Mac-Lean) and the neopallium, the latter with its primary relation to distance receptors and their specific and highly differentiated association systems. Anatomically and physiologically, therefore, as well as psychologically, olfaction is an intermediate link between the bodily pole and the outer pole of the symbol (i.e. between the "I" and the "Non-I"). These relationships parallel the evolution of the nonosmatic, primate life from osmatic lower forms.[78]

The foregoing leaps over our review of mammalian and primate biograms, to human phenomena. There is no promise in sight that the technique of psychoanalysis and neurosurgery will ever unearth the minds of the lower mammals as they are doing in the case of the human mind. And here we have the reverse of what obtains usually, where the nonhuman sheds light upon the human; for the present investigations upon the human suggest that we are probing the infrahuman via the instrumentality of the human.

MAMMALIA[79]

1. The earliest, and very rare, mammalian remains are found in the Upper Triassic formations of North America, South Africa, and Europe. The wide distributional range compensates, in a way, for the rarity: it indicates that the proto-Mammalia must have existed long before that. Of the five subclasses, two (Allotheria and Trituberculata) are extinct; two (Prototheria and Didelphia) are rare or locally confined; the dominant subclass is that of the Placentalia, whose earliest finds date from the Upper Cretaceous. Of a total of 25 placental orders, only 14 are extant. As a class the Mammalia have been panecumenical only since the early Tertiary period. Their deployment and adaptive radiation have been thorough: In habitat they are marine, amphibious, subterranean, fossorial, ambulatory, cursorial, rectigrade, arboreal, and volant. Unlike the birds, in which as a general rule the members of any given order all occupy very similar habitats, a mammalian order may contain representatives adapted to a rather wide variety of environments (Carnivora, Perissodactyla, Artiodactyla, Rodentia, Primates).

[78]Kubie adds to this passage a footnote (p. 75) that reproduces a personal communication from Dr. MacLean, to the effect that "archipallial" is perhaps too narrow a term, since paleopallium and mesocortex should be included; they being well represented in all mammals. He suggests the more inclusive term "primitive cortex," which avoids cytoarchitectural misconceptions.

[79]There exists a plethora of literature on the social organization of various mammalian species. Most of it, quite expectably, concerns certain single features; there are relatively few comprehensive studies of the sociality of species. A number of primate species have continued to receive a great deal of attention. For a general survey of mammalian sociality, having a mode of attack quite different from the present paper, see the excellent discussion of Hediger (1952). For an excellent field study of the biogram of a mammalian species, consult Darling, 1946 (1937).

Birds and mammals both are characterized by activity sustained through homoiothermy. The variety of beaks and feet among birds testify to the range of motor patterns exhibited by the birds as a class, but also to the narrowness of that range per order, family, or genus. We have seen, moreover, that the cerebral architecture of the bird permits a given genus to exploit that motor capacity beyond anything found in a reptile. The mammals both resemble and differ from the birds in this matter. They emerged from a different reptilian organization at a different moment of geological time (a slightly earlier one). With few if any exceptions they have retained or further developed a greater degree of motor versatility; in this matter they match the birds with their variety of pedal and dental morphologies; and coupled with this, they have elaborated the neopallial hemispheres.[80]

The Mammalian Version of the Vertebrate Biogram

The mammalian biogram preserves the features of the vertebrate biogram, thus:

1. It is diphasic, at least psychologically; but modified in ways that will be explained. There is phase migration, psychological always, but often areal as well.

2. The social cohesive is status determination, which under requisite circumstances develops status hierarchies. Small groups manifest leadership-followership.

3. Ambisexualism moderates the sex-determinism especially in the reproductive phase (e.g., homosexuality).

4. There is intrasex competition during the reproductive period, and social moieties based on sex.

5. Territorialism is expressed under circumstances analogous to those among the other vertebrates.

6. Commonly, the males take the initiative in the reproductive syndrome: They fight among themselves, court the females with ritual. The "stamping-ground" is all that remains of the ancient homespot claiming and nest building.

7. There is complete familialism; although for physiological reasons already noted, the role is exercised almost solely by the female.

8. The young become a self-socializing group in measure as they deorient from the parental polarity.

[80]This is the way the mammalian class has worked out. The lowliest mammals undoubtedly were far less intelligent than modern birds; and this is substantiated by the brains of extant monotremes and the simpler didelphs, and aiso of certain Eutheria.

A Note on the Configurative Nature of the Mammalian System

The neopallium furnishes the mammals with a superlative psycho-neurological adjustive capacity. The versatility of the motor repertoire lags far behind the adjustive—as is the case also among the other vertebrates; still, it is the most versatile in the entire subphylum. The combination permits an enormous variety of psychodromal details, yet the biogram itself is not thereby disintegrated.

This is consistent with what we have already encountered. The *Merkwelt* of the mammal is rich, not because its environment is richer than that of the other vertebrates, but because it can project analytically and associate synthetically beyond what the others can do. The organism creates its own *Merkwelt;* nonetheless, the body continues to make the same demands upon its mental apparatus. We may appraise it, without too much risk of error, as being such that the psychodromal trait differences among the various kinds of mammals are the concessions which the vertebrate biogram has made to feet and teeth.

And also to viviparity-plus-lactation. This is a complex evolved by the organism's own internal environment; and there is no known physical environment, past or present, which by way of natural selection could bring about its origination. To suggest that a configurative mutation of multiple genes explains it, does no more than indicate the mechanics by which the change may be brought about. We may as well admit that some principle of configurative evolution still remains to be discovered. The mammalian configuration of viviparity-plus-lactation, moreover, is as at home in Arctic seas as it is in the tropical rain forest; even though secondary differences that relate to the character of the particular environment do occur, such as the time of year when oestrus takes place.

Mammalian viviparity and lactation have evolved together; and neither would be thinkable without the other. It is not merely a matter of a programmatic drama within the maternal physiology; it involves a corresponding organismal adjustment by the embryo. There exists an ecological complex, in which the internal environment of the maternal organism becomes the external environment of the embryo; and the embryo exercises a reflex influence upon the maternal environment.

These remarks are being made to emphasize a configurative complexity which no atomistic evolutionary accounts are adequate to explain. The point is, that the mammalian configuration has required such a complicated set of lock-and-key adjustments among "unrelated" portions of the body which are "meaningless" unless taken together, that we are forced to examine them integratively. Both the mammalian configuration as an evolute out of the reptilian, and the variations that make up that configuration, must be viewed in this light.

Therefore it becomes valuable for us to examine in a little more detail the congeries of features throughout the mammalian body which are the ingredients of the distinctively mammalian organization; and we shall examine the anatomy of the gestation-lactation complex, because it is particularly involved in what we are studying.

The specialized segment of the Müllerian ducts known as the uterus is an environment wherein an organism-in-process is engaged in pre-adapting itself for emancipation from that environment and introduction to quite a different one; but this demands in turn, within the harborer, the presidency of a luteinizing hormone. This presidency, however, is in its turn a subdrama within a yet larger endocrine drama. Another mutualism that integrates into the whole is the placenta—a structure which maternal uterus and embryo create together out of their own tissues. When birth occurs, another maternal endocrine presidency supervenes—that of lactogen. These hormones, to be sure, are more ancient than the mammalian class. The point is, that evolution is commonly discussed in terms of adaptations to an external environment; here we are encountering adjustive evolution within and among the parts of the internal environment which is solely that of the organism itself. That there is a common master gland, the pituitary, merely pushes the problem a step farther back.

This is only the biochemical aspect. On the anatomical side, there is a set of evolutive modifications, first seen in the Mesozoic era, which together are what the statisticians would call an "improbable" state. For it involves the cranial myotome within the province of the VIII (acoustic) and the VII (facial) cranial nerves, the dermal bones associated with the branchial arch in the province of the third division of the V (trigeminal) cranial nerve, and a local specialization on ventral thorax and abdomen of sebaceous glandular tissue under the control of the thoracic autonomic nervous system.

To translate this into evolutive phenomena: While the embryo develops a suctorial apparatus from parts of the branchial arch system, the parent develops thoracic succulatory glands. The one mechanism is "meaningless" without the other. The suctorial apparatus is the facial musculature, particularly the lips under governance of the facial nerve; with it goes a simplification of the mandible—a loss of bones and acquisition of a new hinge on the remaining dentary. The "lost" bones meanwhile transfer to the acoustic mechanism. The rather informal secretion of teeth—in the province of the V cranial nerve—among the reptiles is formalized into a milk and a permanent dentition, the eruption of which is synchronized with the regression of the suctorial instinct.

It is in terms of such concomitances that we must also view the detailed changes that eventuate in the mammalian version of the vertebrate biogram. Gestation and lactation together take time; we must expect the duration of the reproductive phase to encroach upon that of the nonreproductive phase. Yet this by no means extinguishes the complex of interests that throughout the vertebrate tradition have been seen to occur phasewise: Their diagrammatic distinctiveness is diminished; they tend to become concurrent.

The Reproductive Phase

1. This is an appropriate place for raising the problem of seasonal agency in hormonal activation, particularly of the reproductive syndrome. That seasonal daylight affects the sex cycle of birds and of mammals is sufficiently familiar as to need no documentation here. The seasonal periodicity of domesticated mammals eventually becomes reversed if the animals be transferred to the Southern Hemisphere. It is also probable that domestication itself has altered the sexual rhythms of a number of them (although how much of this is due to genetic selection and how much to environmental influences remains unclarified). But it is equally significant that environmental forces do not produce exactly the same effects at the same time upon all varieties of mammals: The body has its autogenous factors. Nor are the sex-activating hormones absolute tyrants. Quite as certainly as administration of testosterone to a castrated rooster or chimpanzee will induce male behavior, so certainly can sexual behavior be inhibited completely by a psychological stimulus—even in a physiologically normal rooster. (If a flock contains a champion rooster, he can so affect another male whose dominance drive is weak that the latter will not mount a receptive hen even in the absence of the dominant male.) The propensity for copulating survives loss of potency, even in man.

The point of the moment is simply this. It is a far cry from the forthright simplicity of the vertebrate reproductive syndrome as expressed by cyclostomes, to its psychophysiological complexity at the level of the mammals. For this reason, it might indeed be difficult for us to perceive the diphasic biogram at all as it obtains among the mammals, but for our previous examination of the other vertebrate classes. Mammalian gestation is an elaborate and energy-consuming process as compared with egg laying. In many mammals, the period of gestation has been lengthened to well over half the year—among horses it lasts eleven months, among elephants almost two years. In tiny mammals, the trend is in the other direction: *Mus musculus* has an oestrus cycle of three to nine days the year round. In either direction, we find an encroachment of the time allotment of the reproductive phase upon that of the nonreproductive phase, until there have evolved mammalian genera who appear to have erased the diphasic character of the biogram completely, by virtue of their always being at some point in their reproductive cycle.

The appearance nevertheless is spurious. For the oestrus cycle itself emphasizes periods of sex activity and sex quiescence. And we can have no doubt that both elephant and mouse exhibit *Weiterbildungen* from the primitive, diphasic biogram; for the latter still persists among many mammals, especially the more primitive ones. The *Weiterbildungen* are further cases of that organismal autonomy, that failure of environmental determinism, which was mentioned above. The persistence of the diphasic situation shows up best in the psychological aspects. For the animals continue to have reproductive and nonreproductive foci of interests, and when the one set is active the other tends to be inhibited. (Animals do not feed and copulate simultaneously.)[81]

2. For parent birds, incubation is followed by foraging for solid food, for the youngsters have engineered parental change of behavior by actively hatching. The mammalian fetus, on the other hand, is passive; it is the parent who engineers the emergence by coordinating autonomic and voluntary nervous processes. Thereupon a new and purely autonomic process is injected: milk secretion, with an urge in the mother to be suckled and in the youngster to suckle (a "psychological trophallaxis"). We have noted already that in the bird, the erotic and the broody psychodromes typically do not mix but are successive. While it seems that in the females of many (though not all) mammalian genera eroticism is in abeyance during pregnancy, it may gradually reappear during lactation, depending upon the genus in question (rabbits, deer, monkeys, apes, humans). Interests of the reproductive and nonreproductive phases, as first identified in the lower vertebrates, thus tend to run more or less concurrently among the different mammalian genera.

[81]The reproductive schedules of mammals are hopelessly beyond the scope of the present paper. For a comprehensive survey, see Asdell, 1946. For a comprehensive survey of the relationships between endocrines, neurophysiology, and behavior among the vertebrates, see Beach, 1948.

The nature of this arrangement is simplest in mammals who still undergo an annual periodicity yet possess a lengthy gestation period; for instance, various genera of deer. *Cervus elaphus,* for instance, breeds during the early fall, gives birth in late spring; the young suckles until the following late spring—even after the next fawn has been born. The young stag leaves the maternal herd when it is about three years old; the young hind remains. The sexual part of the reproductive cycle is indeed periodic annually; but the lactation period completely fills up the otherwise nonreproductive phase. During the nonsexual period, the sexes live as separate moieties; the female moiety—composed of adult hinds and their youngsters—feeds and even plays frolicsome games.

Such facts as these compel us to reconsider the very definition of a diphasic biogram with which we began; and we realize now that we have been using adults only as our frame of reference. Have we been justified? This was simple to do, when we started with the cyclostomes, where the reproductive activity practically ceases after the eggs and sperm have been shed. We have realized that a new chapter had been appended when we passed from nest parentalism to a brood-parentalism; and it is this appended chapter that has gradually encroached upon the time allotment of the period when there is erotic quiescence. But actually, when we confront a society which is exercising familialism, there are three kinds of societies all active concurrently: (1) the social interreactions of the adults, (2) the last chapter of the reproductive phase, which is care of the young by the parents, and (3) the incipient society of the new and still immature age group, which is certainly in no reproductive phase at all. And not only among mammals but even among some species of birds, we find a further complication. For some of our songbirds breed twice in a summer's season; and the second installment of hatchlings arrives before the first has completely deoriented from its parents. Whereupon we may discover the older offspring exercising precociously a parentalism many months before they develop the erotic: they help their parents take care of the younger brood. We do not find the equivalent of this among the mammals for the obvious reason that no older sibling is capable of suckling its younger sibling; nevertheless, among red deer and other mammals where the new sibling is born before the older one deorients, there develops a play-companionship that is within the family circle—and in which incidentally, the mother too may join.[82]

[82]There are among some alloprimates (e.g., macaques) sporadic and fragmentary "broad parentalisms" by older yet immature female siblings exercised upon their infant siblings (to say nothing of similar performances by small human sisters).

In sum, it is plausible to conclude that the *psychological* facies of the two biogrammatic phases survives even among those mammals where the discrete *chronological* facies have lost their identity through physiological extensions and encroachments upon the period of the nonreproductive phase.

Sex and Family

The peculiar mammalian physiological pattern of coitus–uterine gestation-lactation has its psychological corollary: The female always possesses a double reproductive orientation: an erotic orientation toward a male partner and a broody orientation toward her offspring; while the male possesses but one: an erotic toward a female partner. Hence the monopoly of familialism by the female sex.

This does indeed simplify the male psychodrome in one obvious direction; it complicates it rather unexpectedly in another. At least, wherever the coenonia lives gregariously during the phase of sexual quiescence, the males compose a protective rampart not only about the young but about the females also. Protection of the young against intruders is a parental role among other vertebrate classes; what is interpretable as transferral of male parentalism upon his spouse occurs among many birds; but in no other class do we encounter the rampart psychodrome which suggests a compounding of territorialism and parentalism turned into a kind of social generalization. Males act only as a body in protecting a group as a whole; in a variety of cases individual males have been seen to protect an individual youngster at imminent risk to themselves. However, the reports are too desultory to allow us any generalization.[83]

The single reproductive orientation of the male and the double orientation of the female is the cardinal fact of mammalian familialism. The structure of human familialism cannot be grasped until this mammalian fact has first been comprehended thoroughly.

Is the well-nigh universal absence of parental behavior in the male due to an absence of the requisite psychodromal mechanisms in his neurologic constitution? This is very unlikely. Both castration and experimental injection with female hormone bring out in them behavior

[83]Male monkeys and chimpanzees have been definitely documented as retrieving a youngster of their band when it was exposed to an aggressive danger. There are tales of elephants doing likewise; although I am uncertain as to their authenticity. Hediger declares categorically that during rutting season a buck deer dashes to the rescue of a fawn that emits distress cries; and that by imitating these cries hunters (who mistakenly believe they are imitating a mating call of the hind) are successful in luring the bucks to their doom. See Hediger, 1952, p. 304.

patterns that are otherwise permanently latent.[84] Moreover, like other vertebrates, the mammal is sexually ambivalent; both sexes possess lactogenic mammae, which are sensitive to hormonal stimulation. Homosexual behavior is common to both sexes, in at least a wide variety of genera.

We have already noted that neuromotor patterns exist in latent form among vertebrates who normally never express them; as, for instance, in the swimming toad, opossum, or human neonate. The loss of limbs elicits in mammals compensatory motor coordinations. A dog or a pig minus the use of hind limbs walks on its front ones; a dog that loses its homolateral limbs runs on the remaining contralateral pair.[85] These, of course, have no replicas in phylogenesis; on the other hand, if a dog loses his front limbs, he immediately takes to hopping, kangaroo-fashion. In all such cases, the behavior is spontaneous and autodidactic. A dog with limbs intact learns with difficulty, and only under human incitement, to walk on his hind limbs. It is as though the loss of a front pair of limbs destroyed also a psychic block.

The relevance of such observations (they are but samplings) to the question of male parentalism in mammals lies in their possible elucidation of the male parentalisms that occur (if but sporadically) among apes and finally in man. They suggest latencies in the neurological mechanism that appear only under some kind of extraordinary stimulation. There are a few instances of the male parental psychodrome in other mammalian orders. Occasionally, the fox and the wolf males remain with the females they have impregnated until after the pups are born. When at last the latter have been weaned. the male brings home to them disabled prey, for them to worry and kill.[86] The core of the matter lies in those cases where a male and a female prolong their companionship until after she has delivered. What transpires, apparently, is that the male first tolerates that unaccountable appurtenance of the female, the adnexa which seem to be part of her "context"; eventually he develops some degree of direct social response to it.[87]

It is, of course, nothing new that familial attitude in adult humans of both sexes ranges from intense interest to utter indifference. It is

[84]To revert, for a moment, to the situation in birds—a male turkey-cock, who normally never incubates eggs, if tied down upon a clutch for a while, will spontaneously return to incubate them after being released. The brooding stimulation comes from contact of the breast with the eggs (Taibell, 1928).

[85]Cf. Katz, 1955 (1948), p. 132f.

[86]Sometimes, moreover, a male mammal (particularly, a dog) "adopts" a youngster.

[87]For the situation among the alloprimates, see later.

equally familiar that maternal attachment, taking the species as a whole, is a far more durable bond than is paternal attachment. The mammalian heritage undoubtedly underlies the innumerable cultural devices which *Homo sapiens* has produced to cope with it; it also underlies the difference between incest involving the mother and incest involving the father. Were man a member of the class Aves, the cultural superstructure erected upon the innate familial fundament undoubtedly would be a very different thing.

The Juveniles

1. The ontogeny of offspring, no matter of what animal phylum, is a history of an emancipation from a progenitor. Among cyclostomes, the history is brief: emancipation comes essentially at the zygote stage. Emancipation is delayed, in measure as parentalism evolves into familialism. In mammals, the delay is long and complex.

First, there is a physiological intimacy of mother and embryo, wherein the embryo possesses an environment composed of its own extraembryonic membranes plus a maternal housing, with nutritional and excretory facilities. During this time, there occurs a degree of psychologic development we are only beginning to appreciate. The first emancipation is the event of birth, with exposure to stimuli from the external world. There is an important difference between the intrauterine environment and that of the external world: Embryonic development is in synchrony with the maternal environment; the neuropsychic mechanisms are not forced to cope with emergencies. The external world, on the other hand, does not merely feed stimuli to the infant in measure with its capacity to cope with them: The infant's neuropsychic capacities, so to speak, are "behind schedule." Maternal care now becomes a new, a psychological uterus; but one in which the factor of psychologic response from the infant is suddenly very weighty. Even feeding is not automatic or passive, via an umbilical cord; but the infant must suckle actively. It is not a one-way arrangement, however: Suckling by the infant is also a physiological and a psychological need of the mother. This "psychological trophallaxis" is inestimably important in mammalian maturation.

The next step in emancipation of the young is that of weaning— again a physiological event but with psychological implications. The last such step occurs when the young, either of its own accord, or through expulsion by the parent, is set completely loose so that it no longer will behave toward a parent as though she were a parent. In the entire process, the physiological aspect of the trophallactic configuration diminishes earlier than the psychological aspect. The juvenile's schedule of maturation is inducing him to deorient from his parental focus, while he is becoming increasingly responsive to the actions of his age mates—which are actions and rhythms like his own. These represent the phyletically older socialization processes, albeit they supervene later in ontogenesis.

The foregoing stresses the peculiar complexity in the mammalian physiology of ontogenesis; but it presents only one facet of the story. The other facet is the psychology of ontogenesis—rendered far more complex than that of any other vertebrate, by virtue of the unique neopallial development.

The learning process is not the same during the time of growth of a brain as it is after that brain has completed its growth. Beside this, the learning process in a brain that lacks (normally) a neopallium —as in the case of birds—by virtue of that very fact cannot be the same as that in a brain which possesses a neopallium. Nonetheless, experimental observation indicates that there are also remarkable resemblances in the learning behavior of birds and mammals. A cerebral common denominator is indicated as being in the brain stem. In the present connection, the point is that in the psyche of neonates of both birds and mammals there exists a "critical period" which permanently sets the youngster's orientation to parent. Lorenz[88] has analyzed the phenomenon with critical insight among birds; an analogous phenomenon is attested among mammals, insofar as they have been studied.

Deprivation of contact between mother and newborn has effects upon the latter which may be permanently crippling socially. Both birds and mammals, if taken from their parents and brought up as pets by humans, become attached to the latter, ofttimes even to the point where they become incapable of ever adjusting themselves to their own kind.[89]

A mammalian parent, if she (and also he, in the case of man) establishes a behavioral mutualism with her offspring, permits the youngster to initiate personal liberties with her which she resents from a

[88]1935; 1952, p. 129ff. See also Tinbergen, 1953, p. 110ff. and his reference to Heinroth, ibid.

[89]Students of such phenomena warn against a too-ready application to animals in the wild state of what transpires in domesticated forms and in laboratory subjects. Still, the phenomena now in question occur among such a variety of genera and under such different life conditions that their innate genuineness can hardly be doubted, whatever the peculiarities of guise they may assume. At any rate, consult: Blauvelt, 1955, 1956; Schneirla's remarks, in Soulairac, 1952, pp. 96, 102; Murie, 1944; Scott, 1945, 1950; Tinklepaugh and Hartman, 1940; Yerkes and Tomlin, 1935; Spitz, 1945, 1946. For a review of mother-infant behavioral mutualism, see Beach, 1951, p. 423ff.

strange youngster. (This bears a resemblance, to be sure, to the in-tolerance of strange youngsters exhibited by fishes and birds.) The resentment is not present initially; so that a strange neonate is adopted as readily as the neonate also adopts; the acceptive-aversive discrim-ination is a somewhat subsequent maturation.

Probably all mammalian youngsters play. The nature of play has never been completely elucidated. Here we shall attempt only the minimum of observations. It is a rhythm-taking among actors whose rhythms are commensurate. It resembles the adult behavior of the species, yet recalls the progression of other developmental processes; for these start out, as we know, more or less generalized and random, and only gradually become precise and analytic. Group play among juveniles is the embryogenesis of socialization, in which the members of the group mutually stimulate their maturing neuropsychic processes. "Conditioning" takes place; but it differs from the training admin-istered by an experienced individual, in that it is unintentional. Play not only has less precise configurations than the adult actions which it presages, but it is always comparatively incomplete: playfighting lacks the deadliness and the emotional charge of adult fighting; play-coitus never consummates. Play resembles fetal intrauterine move-ments, in that it too betrays the presence of kinetic energies within the emergent neurophysiological patterns of the organism. But those energies belong to the sensory-adjustive side of the neuropsyche quite as much as they do to the motor side; and the only animals that play are such as possess a high measure of the former. This seems to limit playing to the Aves and the Mammalia.

I would suggest that only animal species that can play are animals which also display curiosity.

The Sociality of Mammals

Since taxonomic affinity presupposes a common palae-ancestry at some point in phylogenesis, and a subsequent genetic differentiation, presumably the life modes of extant related forms owe their differ-ences to developmental alterations. To a considerable extent all Carni-vora, for instance, do indeed show a certain resemblance in this re-gard; the biograms of all artiodactyls bear a certain "artiodactyl" complexion; and so on. But in terms of the gross components of the biograms, the number of possible variations is so limited that, as species differentiate, their departures from a prototype lead them in directions that converge, at least in superficial resemblances, toward species belonging to utterly different orders. Thus it comes about that classifications of mateship, such as that of Alverdes (1935), cut across taxonomic classifications. For instance, in the breeding-season kangaroos, some Cervidae, Pinnipedia, equines, baboons (the "season" among the latter, of course, is permanent) the males collect harems and fight off intruders. On the one hand this suggests affinity with a now-familiar general vertebrate pattern; on the other—the superficial resemblance between these instances tends to dissolve as soon as we pursue them back to the antecedent situations out of which they arose. For kangaroos evidently live the year around in small bisexual herds; in breeding season, a champion male monopolizes the females as much as he can; but those beyond his capacity attach themselves to the other males; and the result, apparently, is a number of permanent splinter groups or herds. Some Cervidae, on the other hand, spend their nonreproductive phase as small groups of separate sex moieties; at rutting season, the male individually seeks out the female herds. There are the usual male sex fights; but actually the winning males do not establish dominance over harems; instead they are temporary guests and fellow travelers in a female herd whose leader remains the alpha-hind. Wild onager stallions take over the domination by "bullying" the females. So we have convenient illustrations of the differences that may exist among closely related forms in Antonius' study of equines (1937). He summarizes thus (p. 287):

1. True horses: A definite herding under leadership and ward of the strongest stallion; a marked threat pose by the stallion; absence of a "breedy mien"[90] in the mare; no noteworthy "drive" by the mare.

2. Onager: Herd formed under leadership of a mare; the adult stallion joins the herd only during oestrus; he keeps it together, defends it against rivals. The stallion lacks a threat pose. The mare shows a breedy mien, but apparently there is no "drive" before being covered.

3. Ass: Herd formed under leadership of a jenny; the adult jack consorts with the jenny only during oestrus; he does not keep the herd together. The jack does not strike a threat pose; the breedy mien is very pronounced; there is an impetuous "drive" before the covering.

4. Steppe zebra: Herds of various sizes are formed by a stallion (sometimes a pairing?); no pronounced threat pose by the stallion; some breedy mien on the part of the mare.

5. Mountain zebra: Formation of small troups (leadership?); the stallion apparently attached but loosely to the herd. Threat pose

---

[90]"Rossigkeitsgesicht." There is no accepted English equivalent.

occurs, grounded in the very peculiar combat pattern. A very marked breedy mien on the part of the mare. Apparently no "drive."

6. Grévy zebra: Formation of small troups (leadership?); the stallion but loosely attached. No threat pose; very marked breedy mien; the "drive" less impetuous than in the ass.

Even without any attempt at analysis, it appears obvious that all these patterns are variants upon some basic theme; and this leaves both the basic theme and the variations to be identified and appraised.

Another case is the gregariousness of the Primate band and that of artiodactyls who maintain a bisexual herd at all times. The primate band is sexually active the year around, the artiodactyl herd shows the familiar diphasic alternation. The primate band, in other words, is manifesting the gregariousness of the rutting season simultaneously with that of a phase of sexual quiescence. Since the artiodactyl herd holds together even without the stimulation from a sex tonus, the mechanisms of the two cases of gregariousness are not equivalent.

From these samples it is evident that there is a social difference between a harem and a female society possessing a male consort, even if we must appraise this as a secondary matter—one that reflects the relative strength of dominance drives in the two sexes. Coitus, to be sure, requires a temporary submission of the female; but there is a difference between a solicitation that subordinates, a willing acceptance of an imposed subordination, and submission against the

TABLE 1-2 The Life Modes of Some Mammalian Individuals

Nonreproductive Phase	Reproductive Phase		
	I *Bisexual Pairs*	*II* *Moieties Reunited* *Somehow*	*III* *Bisexual Herd* *Continuous*
A. Solitary	Many felines		
B. Bisexual pairs	Rhinoceroses?		
C. Sex moieties	Cetacea?	Various Artiodactyls Pinnipedia H[a]	
D. Semi-moiety: female sex grouped male sex tending to solitude		Various Artiodactyls Perissodactyls H	
E. Bisexual herd	Rodents Lagomorphs		Perissodactyls H Primates H Rodents Lagomorphs

[a] H indicates that some of the species collect harems.

will. We find a resemblance that cuts across orders, from horse to kangaroo, simply because the respective cases reflect the capability of the males for actualizing their dominance drives.[91]

We may obtain a rough idea of the permutations among mammals as a class, if we first arrange separately the life modes during the reproductive phase and those during the nonreproductive; then note what change, if any, takes place as the phases alternate. Table 1-2 is illustrative only, and it ignores the important point just made; namely, the factor of dominance drive.

THE "DIPHASIC BIOGRAM" IN THE PRIMATE COENONIA

The Reproductive Province

Until we possess comprehensive—and *accurate*—information about the many and undoubtedly varied primate societies, all generalizations must be highly tentative. It is equally clear, nonetheless, that some degree of generalization must be attempted now.[92]

The primates are but one of the polyoestrous mammalion orders; and, like these orders, they include genera that breed seasonally, others the year around yet with fluctuation of sex activity, and still others in which the fluctuation may have disappeared. It needs to be emphasized here that animals in captivity are not reliable indicators of the natural physiological cycle; and that the unresolved controversy over the pristine, "natural" condition of man is a reflex of the fact that, in this matter (regardless of what may be the situation in other matters) culture has acted as a "self-captivity."

Sex Relations   The menstrual cycle is beyond doubt a specialization of the mammalian oestral cycle, which, roughly speaking, is the symptomatics of the alternating and successive presidencies of estrogens and progesterone; the menstrual cycle reflecting a further microana-

---

[91]Dominance drive and sexual drive are considered by a number of students to be separable phenomena, as far down as the fish level. As the one drive certainly occurs without the other, there is substance in the claim; but once this is recognized, there remains the other fact that both drives very frequently occur in one and the same act; and this in its turn demands explaining.

[92]Outstanding are the studies of Bingham, Carpenter, Hediger, Kummer, Nissen, Yerkes, Zuckerman. See the bibliography. The psychological studies by Maslow on the status contests in experimental primates (which he extended even to human females) are excellent and highly useful within their frame of operation; but captive animals do not organize a fully functioning society.

tomical evolution.[93] It is definitively identifiable as such only when we reach the level of the monkeys. Concomitantly over the course of primate phylogenesis, the number of offspring per gestation is reduced to a norm of one.

The reproductive syndrome of any (vertebrate) species always is a matter of bisexual complementation; so here the unremitting succession of menstrual cycles in the female is matched by a sexual constancy in the male. In other words, the primate pituitary is always secreting gonadotrophic hormones.

Consequently, the neurologic mechanisms are never without some tonus due to sex hormones. And, since in this respect all individuals actually are ambisexual, we have, already in the alloprimates, the groundwork laid for the discoveries of Sigmund Freud; for the berdaches and the prostitutes of both human sexes; and also for the masculinity of Shakespeare's poetry and of Beethoven's symphonies, and the womanliness of Mme. Schumann-Heink's singing.

The primate female when in heat seeks the offices of a male; we term this, in a technical sense and therefore quite without judgmental or moralistic overtones, "seduction." However, this behavior certainly is not peculiarly primate.[94] At the same time, the female in heat is particularly interesting to the male. It appears to be true that, if the male/female ratio is such that there is always an adequate supply of females in heat, males tend to ignore the females who are not erotic at the moment.

But this is not "sexual promiscuity" in the sense usually applied to domesticated dogs. Domesticated dogs are not a society: They are an artificially fractured coenonia. Caged monkeys certainly are not a normal society. There is a difference between the chaos of a broken-down coenonia and the regularism that underlies the sexual informality of one that is functioning. So we prefer to observe primates under natural conditions as far as possible. Several female macaques, in heat simultaneously, may indeed compete for the favors of one and the same male. The harems collected by male baboons in a zoological garden, however,[95] cannot be taken as typical of a species. The harems and the sex jealousy of these animals seem to have been elicited by the confinement of space and the excessively unbalanced male/female ratio of individuals.[96] In other words, their evidence is unreliable.

[93]Note the simplex piriform uterus; mode of zygote implantation; decidua.
[94]For a description of its course in the red deer of Scotland, consult Darling, 1946 (1937), p. 177f.
[95]Cf. Zuckermann, 1932.
[96]Prof. Sherwood Washburn, in a personal communication, tells me that he was struck by the absence of male sex jealousy among wild baboons in South Africa.

Heterosexual liaisons may last over one menstrual cycle or may be prolonged over an indefinite number (*Kumpan*-ship). Liaisons thus may possess the character of temporary monogamies—seriatim polygamies (not unlike the situation in Euro-American civilization). The point to emphasize here is that there can be no stereotypical arrangement, no "normal condition" describable for a primate society in these matters; the pattern of heterosexual relationships is not an independent variable, but a function of group size, sex ratio, population density with respect to territorial area, adequacy of forage (with psychological "sense of well-being"). Social behavior, in brief, is contextual.

If a male and a female chimpanzee consort for a prolonged period, the female has the opportunity for exhibiting a capacity which illustrates both the constant readiness of sex tonus in Primates and rank status in heterosexual pairs. The male is more likely to be the dominant, and therefore to secure most of the tidbits fed into the cage by the keeper. The female, even though not in an erotic condition, will present herself sexually, as a bribe for a share of the tidbit.[97] Students of the behavior term this, technically, "prostitution."

Parental Behavior

The literature on alloprimates reports quite a number of instances where male monkeys and apes assume parental responsibilities; unfortunately, most of them are highly suspect of faulty observation or interpretation. The rarity of instances is itself significant; but so, of course, is an authentic case even if it be rare. Bingham observed a heterosexual pair of captive chimpanzees who had produced an infant. The mother nursed, carried, and sheltered her, while the father participated not at all. When at last, however, the tiny girl began scrambling about, he initiated a gentle though sporadic "dandling," and later induced her to frolic.[98]

Such accounts of the family and group living of wild apes as we have are few and nothing more than travelers' accounts.[99] Yerkes and Yerkes[100] quote from several of these; however, to supplement what

[97]It recalls the female bird begging her male consort to feed her.
[98]Bingham, 1927. His details are well worth consulting. The kind of actions engaged in by the respective parents were distinctive and, by comparison with those of humans, very much in character with what human fathers and mothers frequently do, respectively.
[99]Footnote, 1969: This, happily, is no longer quite true. But ten years ago we lacked the reports of Jane Goodall.
[100]1929, pp. 432, 439f. For their summary appraisal of primate social life, see op. cit. pp. 566ff.

has been cited from Bingham, it seems more useful to adduce a passage from R. M. Yerkes' description of a captive chimpanzee family:[101]

During early acquaintance of the consorts the male sometimes was rough and hostile towards his female; she protective, timid, never defensive. Later mutual friendliness developed and the male was consistently gentle and considerate toward this particular female. Finally, during the period of familial relations and subsequently, manifestations of affection and devotion, particularly by the male, were observed. Mutual grooming was common, as well as physical attentions which may be designated as petting.

Sexual intercourse was not observed during the gestational period, nor during lactation to the date of separation of mother and infant from the father. At this time, nearly four months after parturition, the female sexual cycle, with its characteristic features of menstrual bleeding, genital swelling, and ovulation, had not been reestablished.

The male was an interested, passive observer of the parturitional process and of the newly born infant. He in no way interfered with, or aided in, maternal care, but instead was gentle, friendly, and cooperative toward the member of his family. The mother was continuously protective of infant and self, trusting neither her consort nor human males who approached her and her charge. The male seemingly accepted this attiude as a matter of course and without sign of resentment. Familial relations, like the relations of the consorts prior to the birth of the infant, appeared to be favorable to the health and contentment of the parents and to the development of the infant. We eventually characterized them as natural and normal. It is our surmise that this particular family, save in its limitation to a single female and a single offspring, more nearly represents the typical familial relations of the species in freedom than does any other of the descriptions available in the literature.

While it may be seriously questioned that any single family can stand for the species—the individual personalities of chimpanzees are varied and each is peculiar to itself—there can be no doubt that the kind of relations here described does occur at the chimpanzee level of primate phylogenesis, whatever its frequency or rarity.

The rapidity of the menstrual cycles results in monkey and ape families of a mother plus more than one youngster, each at a different age level of development. (This clearly is but a version of the mammalian familial stereotype.) The mother-offspring relationship necessarily is different for each—which must demand a certain psychic versatility in a parent, such as need not be present where she does not have to deal with more than one level of maturity at any one

[101]Yerkes, 1936, p. 369.

period. The primate "polypaedium" is not the same as the canine or feline litter.

The females being, as a group, at all stages of their menstrual cycle at all times of the year, and the males being erotic all that time, the youngsters at all times span the entire growth period of the species. This complicates the age-peer phenomenon, but certainly does not eliminate it. Chimpanzee youngsters, for instance, form up into very boisterous gangs.

The childhood of the ape is a prolonged period—part of that retardation process we have already come to associate with the enlarging cerebral hemispheres in phylogenesis. This allows very many repeated interactions with a mother; and at the human level (as we shall notice again) this produces lasting attachments with a mother, which somehow have to be transmuted if the psychological deorientation which is characteristic of mammals is to take place. In man, this produces also the social effect termed kinship. If there is even a trace of such a situation among apes, we have no evidence of it. But at least we have the physiological setting for the human development already laid at the ape level.

The Nonreproductive Province

There appear to be no primate coenoniae that are other than gregarious—in spite of the lone individuals that are encountered—although the bands of some species are much larger than those of others. Ape bands are smaller than monkey bands.[102]

Because sexuality is constantly present as an ingredient of psyche among the primates, we have seen that the primate coenonia knows no actual period of sexual inactivity. Nonetheless, there remain the contrasting polarities of interest: those centering about reproduction and those centering about food—and whatever else the alert primate mind finds interesting.

Macaques and howlers of both sexes are rovers, straying away from their bands; but apparently the males are much more so than females. In band movements, the males tend to set the direction and the females to follow along with their youngsters. Fights between bands

---

[102]This generalization is, to be sure, debatable. Gorilla and chimpanzee "families" are encountered in the wild; yet apparently these smaller units reassemble in the evening, and even when dispersd in small groups, they apparently keep in touch. At the human level, we would not call a society any the less a group because the individuals disperse during the day. That apes should scatter diurnally over a larger territory than monkeys might be due to the difference in the amounts of feeding needed for such different-sized bodies.

occur between the males of an invading and of a defending band. (The actual fighting is preceded by a great deal of bluffing and threatening, which may prove to be sufficient for its purpose.)

Monkeys are capable of acting in concert in a variety of situations, although whether this ever becomes planned teamwork is not clear.

There is no evedince that any alloprimates ever develop administrative organization: Dominance-status does not go over into chieftainship; nor does a son succeed his father.

There is one feature in the province of food-getting which perhaps is an anlage of what on the human level eventuates in the fusion of extrafamilial and familial interests—a fusion which surely is at the root of man's culturized biogram. This feature has already been mentioned elsewhere in another connection; The female chimpanzee "prostitutes" to obtain the favor of a tidbit from her male consort.

Outside of the birds, we have not found one adult giving something to another.[103] But between the birds and the chimpanzee there is a big difference. In the case of birds, the feeding psychodrome is part of raising a brood, and therefore it belongs to the familialism psychodrome. But in the primate the act is entirely fortuitous. It belongs to *Kumpan*-ship. When, however, a male brings into this *Kumpan*-ship a value object obtained outside the familial orbit, and an exchange between male and female is effected, we have an anlage of what in man becomes the familialization of the male. This is a key factor in that integration of the extrafamilial (nonreproductive phase) with the familial (reproductive phase) which finally produced the humanness of human society. To this we shall return.

Status Contest and Hierarchialism

Status—the cohesive of vertebrate society—becomes so prominent a behavioral force in primates, that it demands special notice. And it has indeed received much analysis from a number of students.[104]

In the primate groups, the males form a characteristically mammalian rampart. Moreover, together they control the motion patterns of the entire group. (The degree of control varies among species; possibly a size discrepancy between males and females is a factor, but if so, it is but one of many.) Intrasex status hierarchies are more or less strongly developed, and seem always to be present. Status

[103]However, compare Hediger, 1952, pp. 318f.
[104]Notably, Carpenter, 1942a,b; Crawford, 1940; Maslow and associates, 1936–1942; Nowlis, 1941; Yerkes, 1939, 1940; Zuckermann, 1932.

begins to be defined (in macaques, at all events) during the social play of childhood, and the social conditioning of the maturative period produces lasting effects.

Sex is very much involved with dominance-subordinance status and behavior; but the involvement is too complex and paradoxical for more than brief registry of some features here. Maslow, for instance, claims that sex behavior can be aroused by two separable motivations (even though they can occur simultaneously): sheer desire for sexual satisfaction, and a will to dominate a subordinate of either sex; so that the latter motivation may occur between isosexual as well as heterosexual pairs ("displacement activities"?) Furthermore, dominance *drive* does not assure that the individual will achieve dominance *status*. (Even on the monkey level, observers have noted, this failure can have its effect on personality.)

The actual conduct of a dominant monkey (in a captive group) has been analyzed into features such as the following:[105]

The dominant animal typically:
1. Preempts all or most of the limited food supply;
2. Frequently mounts the subordinate animal, regardless of the gender of either the mounting or mounted animal;
3. Is rarely or never thus mounted by the subordinate animal;
4. Frequently bullies the subordinate animal, but
5. Is almost never thus bullied by the subordinate animal;
6. Initiates most of the fighting that occurs in the pair;
7. *Never* cringes under aggression;
8. Is rarely passive under aggression;
9. Almost never flees from the subordinate animal;
10. Is likely to be more active than his subordinate partner (?);
11. Is likely to do more grooming than his subordinate partner;
12. Is likely to initiate more play than his subordinate partner.

And further:[106]

The behavior syndrome characteristic of the subordinate animal is as follows: he gets little or none of a limited food supply; he responds to aggression by passivity, flight, and less often by fighting back; he rarely exhibits any aggressive behavior; he plays the female role in mounting behavior, whether male or female; and generally behaves with deference to the drives of his more dominant partner.

The female may be dominant over other females or over males, and, when she is dominant, her behavior differs in no observable way from that of the dominant male unless she comes into heat.

[105]Maslow and Flanzbaum, 1936, p. 306.
[106]Maslow, 1936, p. 276.

. . . Evidence . . . seems to indicate that the assumption of the female role by a dominant female (due to coming into heat) leads to loss of dominance.

Dominance seems to be less marked in young than in older monkeys.

A dominant animal was found in every group studied (with the possible exception of one).

The dominance hierarchy may be temporarily abrogated during periods of intense play.

A new animal introduced into a group will assume his status in the dominance hierarchy of the group in a very short time.

The behavior called "prostitution" behavior by Kempf seems to be better interpreted as behavior motivated by the dominance drive, and is thus best thought of as subordination behavior rather than sexual behavior.

While dominance status is usually fairly permanent, it was observed to change in a few cases for assignable causes.

In a group or pair, the largest animal will almost certainly assume the role of dominant overlord, if he is much larger than the other animals. If, however, the difference in size is not very great, smaller animals may become dominant.

Now some observations by Yerkes:[107]

Every individual appears to be by nature either dominant or subordinate. Either sex may be dominant over the other. The larger, older, and more experienced individual ordinarily has the advantage.

The dominance-subordination patterns of response are dependent primarily on traits of physique (size, strength, endurance) and of psychobiological constitution (temper, courage, assurance, persistence).

Dominance-subordination is not a constant relation. It fluctuates or even changes in sign with the sexual status of the female and with such events of daily life as disagreements, contests, or quarrels over food, shelter, possessions, social privilege.

The male if dominant grants privilege to, or is dominated by, the female when she is in oestrus, whereas if subordinate to her he may achieve privilege to the extent of priority of response when she is sexually receptive.

Pairs of mature females exhibit dominance-subordination relationships as do males. Ordinarily the naturally dominant individual, if in oestrus, grants privilege to her subordinate companion, whereas the subordinate, in oestrus, may achieve privilege and act as if temporarily in control.

Associated female chimpanzees may exhibit homosexual behavior which closely simulates the heterosexual. But whereas in many other mammals the female in oestrus commonly mounts a companion of like sex, the chimpanzee in these circumstances is mounted.

[107]Yerkes, 1939b, p. 134f.

The mating behavior of chimpanzees may be initiated by either sex, and its form and consummation seems to depend in many cases as much on the one sex as on the other. The prevalent statement that sexual initiative and control rest with the male is erroneous.

Sexual perversions are exhibited. Examples are: masturbation and hyper-sexuality by either sex, rape by the male; frigidity and prostitution by the female. The terms are used objectively to designate patterns of behavior and have no reference to purpose or intent.

Finally, Maslow[108] has some striking remarks about the psychological similarities and differences between monkey and man:

> The most important common conclusion for the two groups, human and infrahuman, is that dominance is a more potent determiner of, or is more closely related to, sexual behavior than is sexual drive. In both groups, sexuality may be used as a power weapon in the Adlerian sense. One form of homosexuality may be explained in the same way as in the monkey. This is also true for one aspect of sadism-masochism, which were found to go together in the human being as they did in the macacus. In human beings, as also in monkeys and apes, sexual position was found to have definite psychological significance. In both groups it was found necessary to treat as separate, sexuality and reproduction. Both groups are relatively free from sexual cyclicity, the human group even more than the infra-human. This relative freedom from cyclicity in the human being is certainly more com-plex than in the infra-human, for cultural factors are certainly involved as well as biological differences.
>
> The chief difference we wish to point out between the sexuality and dominance of animals and humans is that dominance, and consequently sexual behavior, is determined in the monkey almost wholly by social posi-tion. While it was found to be true that there were individual differences in what may be called by analogy dominance-feeling, still this was a minor factor as compared with dominance status. What this means essentially is that practically all determination and inhibition of behavior in the monkey is due to external, immediately-present social forces (the presence of other animals). In the human being, we have a tremendous expansion of the importance of *internalization* of these social forces, so dominance-feeling becomes far more important and dominance-status far less important in determining attiudes and behaviors in the sexual sphere. We can rate most human beings in our society as generally bold or timid; but for the monkey, we are forced in almost all cases to specify the particular social situation in which he is at the moment. There are human beings who are inhibited in the presence of practically all of their peers, but there exist few such monkeys and these are products of exceptional circumstances.

[108]1942, p. 292f.

MAN

Preview

This, stated synoptically, is the biogram of genus *Homo:*

It is a variant of the vertebrate biogram: Social metabolism shows two polarizations—those of familial and nonfamilial or extrafamilial interests respectively. The social cohesive is one of (experientially determined) statuses. There are juvenile age-peer groups.

It possesses a complete familialism characteristic of mammals; it is maternal. Consistently with the order to which it belongs, namely, it is one of those which live gregariously at all times, the males form a rampart about the females and young.

The male possesses but one primary reproductive interest orientation: erotic toward the female. The female possesses two: erotic toward the male, broody toward her young.

The human familialism is of the (mamalian) primate variety by virtue of the unremitting polyoestrous-menstrual cycle plus male sexual constancy. The cerebral development is typically primate[109] and is developed during a prolonged period of immaturity.

But, though possessing a characteristically primate brain, the cerebral development is the positive extreme of the primate range; so that its symbol-making powers are vastly superior to those of the nearest extant ape. This, and the familialization of the male, together form the basis of distinction between alloprimate and human sociality.

Statuses become symbolized, and so institutionalized.

Family status is part of this definition.

Male familialization integrates the interests of the familial and extrafamilial fields or polarities.

The extrafamilial field proves to be psychically exploitable so that it comes to outrank by far the familial field in the complexity of its interactions.

A psychoecology develops commensurately, in which the universe itself is grasped in the form of symbolizations.

Delayed Maturation of Intelligence

Delayed maturation as the facilitating factor in the phylogenesis and ontogenesis of man's unique intelligence is by now a cliché of

[109]In another connection, the author has attempted to demonstrate that the human cerebration is not aberrant, but is what should be normally expectable for a primate of this size. This suggests that the chimpanzee is a "phyletic microcephal." We may consider the human cerebrology as exemplifying in the fullest what the primate type of cerebrology is capable of producing. Cf. Count, 1947.

anthropology; however, certain aspects of the maturation of psyche affect our argument, hence they may be set down briefly.

The human cerebral development is a *Weiterbildung* of the primate type. Cellular multiplication in the brain ceases very early in infancy, myelination of cortical areas proceeds differentially during early childhood, full ponderal size is reached in early adulthood, but some other changes continue throughout life. In the human cortex, the sensory projection areas are widely separated by interpolated "association" areas. During growth and maturation, there occurs a type of learning that ceases to obtain after achievement of adulthood: Primary learning may be regarded as "the period of establishing a first environmental control over the association areas, and so indirectly, over behavior."[110] First learning is slower in mammals characterized by advanced cortical evolution than in the lowlier genera; as the former reach maturity, they possess a relatively larger and more differentiated body of projection-association nervous matter—especially association —and thus a greater capacity for learning complex relationships for conceptualizing. Simple relationships, on the other hand, are grasped by both lower and higher genera with about equal rapidity. Increase of experience facilitates the learning of whatever degree of relationships any genus is capable of mastering: The animal learns to learn.

We may now refer back to what has already been said about symbol. Between some prehominid level and that of *Homo,* a primate phyletic line has developed a capacity for multivalent symbolizing; and it is hard to believe that this is not somehow an integral part of the same process which has made it possible for man to live simultaneously in the past, the present, and the future: to do a thing now in the light of a remembered past event for the sake of a future value. Man, as Korzybski has said, is a "time-binder."

The frontal lobes, it is now known, function in organizing planned, purposeful conduct: They are, we might say, the "organ of judgment."[111] But back of the judgmental functioning of the frontal lobes lie the analyses of experience to which the mechanisms of the temporal lobes have contributed so finely.

Status in Human Society

As among other vertebrates, the cohesive of human society is status. But man does not necessarily relinquish one status when acquiring

---

[110]Hebb, 1949, p. 125.
[111]It seems reasonable to consider them as an agent in the erection of the super-ego. It is interesting to notice that, in apes and monkeys, the frontal lobes compose relatively about as much of the total hemispheres as in man.

another. He is the only animal known which can embody multiple status at one time. But the interests of the several statuses do not lend themselves effortlessly to a harmonious symbiosis. Man is often faced with the problem of accommodating the interests of several statuses within one action; and if he does not succeed, he develops personality conflicts, even neuroses. We may term the persistence of psychological effects from a former status into the period when a later status has presumably become dominant, a "reverberance."

Statuses, furthermore, undergo further evolution. They become social generalizations. In a monkey society, the fact that this infant belongs to this female is hardly of concern to any one but the pair; in human society, everybody's behavior becomes everybody's business. And this kind of phenomenon is the anlage of public opinion. In human society, furthermore, statuses themselves obtain status.

Social generalizations seem never to occur without appropriate symbolizations. The status of sonship, of fatherhood, becomes an *eidolon*. This is not an intellectualization in primitive man, but a quite pragmatic conception: Sonship is as sonship does, and vice versa. Statuses become part of the mores. Homination has included the emergence of multivalent symbols and multiple statuses. This is an interesting juxtaposition.

Nor does *Homo* stop with concentrating multiple eidolons within one person. Statuses, after all, are geminal. They involve reciprocation: Sonship and parenthood are an obverse and reverse; there can be no commanders without the commanded. This reciprocative character of statuses permits the development of group statuses. The geminal status of sonship-parenthood inplies such status in another family; the status of "family" is a group status recognized by the society. A family is nonexistent except as it is composed of a number of individuals, and among these individuals there must be a minimum number of different statuses that have no meaning except as components of family (the male and female parents, and the offspring-siblings.)

Familialism

It must be evident that, when these processes occur within the orbit of the familial polarity, they formalize family relationships. This is all the more possible because the formative years in man are so prolonged. There is a great deal of opportunity for *Prägung* and conditioning by a mother where time and highly associative-adjustive brain are conjunctive. The psychological weaning process indeed never becomes complete: The man and the woman still remain the son and daughter of their mothers, even though they have also become a husband and a wife. To have at once the multiple status of son, husband, and father defines the double orientation to a family of provenience and a family of procreation. And if the son or daughter remains in the household of the mother, his or her son or daughter is immediately in the position of filial descent only one step farther removed. And there is no other vertebrate beside man in whom the status of a kinship persists after adulthood is reached.

It is important to note that these statuses are social, not biological matters, since when they arose among the protohominids they could not have been constituted on grounds other than behavioral relationships. The biological antecedent—that of parturition—is what supplies a setting for the development of status; and later, in proportion as humans rationalize their behavior, the parturitive act is given value and so becomes a reinforcement of the status; but the biological fact itself is not the core of the status. Even among modern sophisticates, a child can be adopted and receive full social status as son or daughter. Among some extant primitive societies, moreover, the emphasis in treatment of a child is not upon its biological derivation from a particular woman but upon its identification as filial relation to a group of sisters: They are all its "mothers," even though the actual biological connection is also quite well recognized.

The most significant single process that has produced the human family out of the alloprimate has been the familialization of the male. From what has just been said, we are prepared to see this as a social and not a biological process. Recognition of biological paternity does not enter the picture at all. For one thing, realization that male injection of semen is the indispensable cause for a parturition nine months later is quite a feat of intellectual engineering, and to this day seems but imperfectly grasped—in some rare cases even not grasped at all—by some primitive groups of *Homo sapiens*. In the next place, the act of coitus is not given the weight among primitives that it receives in more institutionalized societies. An Eskimo who has been absent for two years and whose wife, on his return, presents him with a six-month-old baby, may be quite pleased. An East African prefers to marry a woman who has already demonstrated, premaritally and from other consortings, that she is fertile. Primitives readily adopt children, and sometimes even exchange them. Sex jealousy among primitives is not socially structured in the way it is in Occidential societies.

The status of husband most plausibly seems to have arisen out of those protracted associations between a male and a female which we have already noted to be frequent among alloprimates; with the male then acquiring a social interaction with the female's offspring by, so to speak, passing around the mother. This association among alloprimates does occur, but only after the youngster has begun to disengage itself from the maternal embrace. Certainly we need give no consideration whatever to the romantic notion that the human male came to assume a protective responsibility toward the increasing helplessness of the female for whose pregnancy he was responsible.

Already it has been mentioned that, when such protracted associations occur, the male is certain to bring home at some time the fruits of his activities outside the familial orbit. We are thinking now of the pre- and the protohominid societies, in which incipient symbolopea and technologies were emerging. There is no reason why we should not assume that these developments ran concurrently, since they do not seem to be confined to different calibers of cerebral development. But symbolopoea and technology are not confined to one sex or the other; and protracted association of the sexes inevitably effects association of their symbols, technologies, and the fruits of both. The division of labor in a society on the basis of sex is quite presumably the oldest specialization in technology; it certainly is a universal today. But again it is the environmental circumstances under which a society labors that determine which particular techniques shall be attached to which sex. This is part of the sex-status eidolon of any particular society.

But with the emergence of culture, we have a striking reversal in the relative social complexity of the reproductive and nonreproductive biogrammatic phase. Among the cultureless lower vertebrates, the more complicated interrelationships and social structuring lay amidst the reproductive syndromes. At the human level, we find an amalgamation of interests from the familial orbit and from the area outside that orbit. Here the fact that primally and primarily the male mammal has but one reproductive orientation while the female mammal has two, affects their relative interest activities. For the female (and we are speculating upon the proto-hominids, but considering also primitive *Homo sapiens*) centers much of her technical activity about her brood interests; the male, on the other hand, continues to roam peripherally. And here we find male (secret) societies; hunting and other venturesome parties; male communal recognition that new members to their status have appeared out or the juvenile age group (rites de passage); chieftainships; sorcerers. These regularize status contests and hierarchialism; they not only effect a cooperative pooling of skills and resources, but also bring into cultural harness that traditional tendency for males to establish territories and fight each other to a point of truce where each recognizes the other's boundaries. All this makes of the nonreproductive interest sphere by far the larger and more complex of the two biogrammatic phases. Man's familialism tends to adjust itself to the larger structure of his society rather than vice versa.

Familialism and Incest

Incest with its taboo is the negative side to the definition of human familialism. It is quite as integral as the positive side, and the two are related.

It is a semantic misfortune that three distinct phenomena—sex relations between mother and son, between father and daughter, between brother and sister—should be blanketed under the same term merely for the reason that they all belong within the familial sphere. Moreover, the three discrete phenomena are the heterosexual trio within a larger frame; another two being isosexual: the social relations between brothers and those between sisters. A sixth relationship—that of husband and wife—makes quite another category.

We shall remark upon these three incests separately.

a. Mother-son incest: Zuckerman (1932, pp. 272ff) notes that immature primates develop sexual attractions toward their mother. This is at least consistent with the doctrine of Freud. It is well known that human children, even infants, possess an embryonic sex life. As for the mother, nipples are in some way an erogenous zone. However, we shall not pursue this analysis here. We may note that the embryonic nature of a child's sexuality cannot be other than inadequate for satisfying the sexuality of an adult—in the present case, his mother. The "rhythms," as we may say, are incommensurate.

The mammary syndrome—a bipersonal one—is a psychological trophallaxis. Once it has been experienced it appears to be inhibitory to a sexual mutualism between the same individuals. Her son is the only male whom a woman has suckled. He is nonetheless a male with whom she has intimate contact, long after she has weaned him. In infrahuman mammals, supposably, the sexual mutualism can occur with freedom only if and as the mammary trophallaxis is erased. In man, there is reverberance: Maternalism-sonship does not extinguish even in adulthood. Whether reverberance exists at all in apes, we do not as yet know.

Hypothetically, mother-son incest should therefore never occur; yet in actuality, it occurs, although we cannot say how frequently. Incest-with-taboo—the taboo is part of the definition of incest—arises out of psychic conflicts within two persons. On the part of the mother, the erotic and the broody orientations become converged (nystagmatically!) upon one love object. The son, on the other hand, is undergoing the mammalian maturative process of deorienting from parent. His conflict too involves this deorientation from his earliest erotic target. We are all familiar with the psychological inconsistencies wherein a woman treats her husband in a motherly way, or sees her son as a sort of replication of her father; a husband uses his wife as a mother substitute; a woman refuses to marry because no man recreates the image of her father; a son can find no woman the equal of his mother. These are forms of psychic aberration which occur in our own society; the same psychoneurologic mechanisms exist also among primitives, whatever be their external expressions.

b. Between father and daughter there is no mammary trophallaxis. The daughter and father first build up an adult-immature relationship. As the daughter becomes nubile, an erotic attitude on the part of either toward the other is quite capable of developing. There is one positive barrier: the mother. In the female intrasex status contest, she is the dominant. Erotic interest between father and daughter means potentially a "harem"; in this case the rival female is also one upon whom mother once exercised her brood orientation. There is reverberance.

As between these foregoing two forms in incest, it is hardly to be doubted that father-daughter occurs far more frequently.

c. Opportunity for coitus between brother and sister is practically omnipresent. It also lacks the reverberance from earlier statuses that is present in the two preceding forms. The taboo, moreover, though very widespread, is far from universal, and even today there are societies where it is condoned if not approved. In the first two forms, which are transgenerational, one parent-and-spouse stands as a barrier to the relationship. In the case of brother and sister, there is no injured third party; but instead both parents stand against it.[112] That human social groups treat intersibling incest sternly suggests that it would be frequent otherwise.

From these relationships we derive one of our definitions of the human type of family. It is a group within which the principals are expected to engage in coitus, while to all others it is forbidden. The

---

[112]Among juvenile play groups, at any rate if they are primates, desultory erotic acts occur frequently and spontaneously. It is not an implausible speculation that these may occur between human brothers and sisters, if they play together.

arrangement probably did not spring into existence full-blown; it must have evolved as part of the general development of status eidolon. It is society that creates the definition, and society is antecedent to the family.

The evolution of the status of child—its position in the social group —undoubtedly is a complex story, and one that we shall not undertake here. The status of child received its definition in measure as the family became defined. But it is to be noted that the definition of incest is one feature of the definition. For in a society, especially a primitive one, the child is identifiable in terms of what individuals may not ever have coitus with him or her. An adult individual may never have coitus with a member of his or her family of provenience. On the other hand, coitus is expected, even mandatory, in his or her family of procreation; which means the spouse only.

This allows plenty of latitude for polygamy, polyandry, brother-right, joint family, extramarital coitus, which are subjects of a derivative nature.

Another subject which is relevant here, but on which we have but scanty data, is that of homosexuality within the family; between father and son, mother and daughter, brother and brother, and sister and sister. These, however, introduce the whole question of homosexuality; and the family is not an institution of which these factors are a part of its minimum definition; therefore we may safely omit their further discussion in this study.

Concluding Remarks

From our entire discussion of vertebrate sociality, it should be clear that:

1. Societies did not take form by a confederation of families, since the family is a stable group defined as such by society;

2. The family represents the organization of society's reproductive mood; hence

3. The family polarizes only a portion of the repertoire of a society's interests;

4. It conforms to the society rather than vice versa, and therefore reshapes and readjusts itself as the society alters;

5. Nowhere does it possess within itself the complexities that exceed (or equal) those outside itself. For the number of statuses possible within a family is strictly limited; on the other hand, the human capacity for symbolopoea and the capacity for developing status eidolons and group statuses outside the family orbit have no visible limits.

The essential point, however, to which our essay has tried to give reasonable substance, is this: There is a vertebrate biogram that is genetically founded; it is an aspect of the total vertebrate form or configuration, and therefore inalienable, however modifiable secondarily. Man differs from the other vertebrates—to state it more norrowly, from the alloprimates—not in lack of conformity to the biogrammatic framework, but *in the particularly rich content that he has fitted into it.* The content shows the effect of symbolopoetic action upon more basic neuropsychic mechanisms—yet without disrupting those mechanisms. "Instincts" are as vital and as powerful as in any other vertebrate; but during phylogenesis something further has been inserted—yet not *ex ante nihilo.* This is a very different thing from the old view that "intelligence" and "learning" have superseded archaic "instinct." It says, instead, that there has not been a loss and a compensatory substitution, but an addition that in no wise has diminished something already very anciently present. This is the scheme whereby man's psyche has become the most powerful in all organic nature.

It is hoped that this survey will have contributed toward a common systematic ground for the social and the biological sciences which are exploring man; toward a future anthropology of the whole.

SUMMARY

We have been searching for a social configuration of the entire vertebrate subphylum—including man—starting from the premise that a common neurophysiological architecture should expectably result in some common pattern of *modus vivendi.* Such a pattern, at any level in the vertebrate subphylum, and for any species or individual of the subphylum, we have termed a *biogram.*

We believe that the search, though very far from complete, has revealed a vertebrate biogram that is as characteristic of the vertebrate gestalt or form as is that of any social insect taxonomic category.

The vertebrates appear to have possessed their social biogram while they still were primitively aquatic. The biogram survived transferral to the land, in measure as the vertebrate line became terrestrialized. It has evolved *pari passu* with the rest of the vertebrate organic form, because it is part of that form.

The vertebrate biogram is diphasic: a reproductive phase and a nonreproductive. Each is under a distinctive hormonal presidency. The presidency activated innate neuropsychic mechanisms. For each phase, the vertebrates perform a migration, which may be an actual movement from one region of the world to another; but whether or no, there is always a "psychological migration."

Vertebrate individuals are all fundamentally ambisexual; so that all possess the entire behavioral repertoire *(in potentu)* of their respective species, sex differentia of behavior being elicited by the respective sex-hormonal patterns.

Among lower vertebrates, the more complex and intensive inter-individual reactions take place during the reproductive phase. This relativity is reversed at least at the human level *(vide infra)*.

From the Agnatha to the Mammalia and Aves, the reproductive drama evolves an increasingly complex series of acts, *pari passu* with the cerebral evolution and other physiological *Weiterbildungen*. Thus, from a primitive level of a simple "nest-and-egg parentalism" (Agnatha), the drama evolves through "brood-parentalism," "full parentalism" to the "complete familialism" of birds and mammals. Contrary to common belief, among the vertebrates it is the males, not the females, who primitively are the more "parental." Female parentalism is the later evolute.

Phylogenetically, the earliest socialization agency is the juvenile age group. Socialization by the parents is phylogenetically the later evolute; but when once established, it becomes ontogentically the earlier.

The emergence of neopallial cerebral hemispheres in the mammals has enriched behavior; but it in no wise has destroyed the vertebrate biogrammatic configuration. "Intelligence," etc. in no wise negates the innate, "instinctive" base, upon which the enriched behavior has been erected. This leads us to reappraise the functional significance of the cerebral hemispheres; for, among the lower vertebrates which lack them, the total biogram is no less carried through than in the highest vertebrates.

The specifically human expression of the vertebrate biogram shows its phylogenetic derivation from out of the alloprimate, which in turn is an evolute of the mammalian, and the latter in turn of the reptilian. Without losing any of the innate grounding that it shares with its lower relatives, the human biogram is richer by virtue of those cerebral mechanisms which have made symbolopoea possible. Hence, on the side of social organization, we have:

The power to symbolize leading to social generalizations (e.g., "eidolons");

The familialization of the male, which has two essential consequences: (1) a biparental familialism, which has a different composition from that found in birds, and is not duplicated among the other mammals; (2) an integration of the interests developed primarily in the nonreproductive field, with the interests developed (primarily by the female) about the familial polarity.

Human familialism includes status definitions for both parents and young, and these definitions include, *en revers*, definition of incest-and-its-taboo.

Familialism, at any vertebrate level, is seen to be a particular *mood* of society, within which only some of the interests of the society may be polarized. However, it is only at the human level that skills and symbol are developed most intensively, and the widest range of statuses and interindividual reactions occurs. As a result, behavior outside of the reproductive polarity is far and away more complex than that within the polarity. This is the reverse of the situation found among all other vertebrates. At the same time, it is at the human level where the interests of both the biogrammatic phases are brought into mutual relation and support. Nevertheless, because of the preponderance of the nonreproductive activities, it is the familial patterning that follows where the extrafamilial patterning leads—much more than vice versa.

It is hoped that the foregoing attempt at integrating the findings of zoology, ethology, psychology (including psychoanalysis), neurology (including experimental neurology and neurosurgery), biological and social anthropology, will contribute toward an anthropology of the whole.

A SELECTED BIBLIOGRAPHY

Adrian, E. D. 1947. "The Physical Background of Perception." Oxford University Press, Oxford.

Allee, W. C. 1936. Analytical studies of group behavior in birds. *Wilson Bull.* **48**:145–151.

———. 1938. "The Social Life of Animals." W. W. Norton, New York.

———. 1952. Dominance and hierarchy in societies of vertebrates. See: Colloques, 157–183.

———, A. E. Emerson, O. Park, Th. Park, and K. P. Schmidt, 1949. "Principles of Animal Ecology." Ch. 23, 24. W. P. Saunders, Philadelphia.

Allen, E., C. A. Danforth, and E. A. Doisey, 1939. "Sex and Internal Secretions." Williams & Wilkins, Baltimore.

Allesch, G. J. v. 1937. Die Beziehungen zwischen tierpsychologischen und menschen-psychologischen Tatbestanden. *Z. f. Tierpsych.* **I**: 128–139.

Alverdes, F. 1927. "Social Life in the Animal World." Harcourt, Brace, New York.

———. 1935. The behavior of mammalian herds and packs. See: Murchison, ed.

Antonius, O. 1937. Über Herdenbildung und Paarungseigentümlichkeiten der Einhufer. *Z. f. Tierpsych.* **I**: 259–289.

————. 1938. Nachtrag zu dem Aufsatz, Über Herdenbildung und Paarungseigentüm-lichkeiten der Einhufer. Z. f. Tierpsych. **2:**115–117.

Aronson, L. R., and G. K. Noble. 1945. The sexual behavior of Anura. 2. Neural mechanisms controlling mating in the male leopard frog Rana pipiens. Bull. Amer. Mus. Nat. Hist. **86:**87–139.

Asdell, S. A. 1946. "Patterns of Mammalian Reproduction." Comstock Publishing Co., Ithaca, N. Y.

Baerends, G. P. 1952. Les sociétés et les familles de poissons. See: Colloques, 207–221.

————, and J. M. Baerends. 1950. An introduction to the study of the ethology of Cichlid fishes. Behaviour, Supplement I: 1–242.

Beach, F. A., Jr. 1937. The neural basis of innate behavior. I. J. Compar. Psychol. **24:**393–440.

————. 1938. The neural basis of innate behavior. II. J. Genet. Psychol. **53:**108–148.

————. 1942. Central nervous mechanisms involved in the reproductive behavior of vertebrates. Psychol. Bull. **39:**200–226.

————. 1947a. A review of physiological and psychological studies of sexual behavior in mammals. Physiol. Rev. **27:**240–307.

————. 1947b. Evolutionary changes in the physiological control of mating behavior in mammals. Psychol. Rev. **54:**297–315.

————. 1948. "Hormones and Behavior." Paul B. Hoeber, New York.

————. 1951. Instinctive behavior: reproductive activities. See: Stevens, ed. Ch. 12.

————. 1953. Animal research and psychiatric theory. Psychosom. Med. **15:**374–389.

————. 1955. Ontogeny and living systems. See: Schaffner, ed. 1955. 9–74.

Bierens de Haan, J. A. 1937. Über den Begriff des Instinktes in der Tierpsychologie. Folia Biotheoret, ser. B. **2:**1–16.

————. 1947. Animal psychology and the science of animal behavior. Behaviour **I:**71–80.

Bingham, H. 1927. Parental play of chimpanzees. J. Mammal. **8:**77–89.

————. 1932. Gorillas in a native habitat. Carnegie Inst. Wash. Pub. #426.

Blauvelt, H. 1955. Dynamics of the mother-newborn relationship in goats. See: Schaffner, ed. 1955. 221–258.

————. 1956. Neonate-mother relationship in goat and man. See: Schaffner, ed. 1956. 94–140.

v. Bonin, G. 1952. Notes on cortical evolution. Amer. Med. Ass. Arch. Neurol. Psychiat. **67:**135–144.

Bourlière, F. 1952a. Classification et caractéristiques des principaux types de groupe-ments sociaux chez les vertébrés sauvages. See: Colloques, 71–81.

————. 1952b. Le territorialisme dans l'organisation sociale des vertébrés. See: Colloques, 199–207.

Bowlby, J. 1953. Critical phases in the development of social responses in man. "New Biology #14," 25–32. Penguin Books, New York.

Braddock, J. C. 1945. Some aspects of the dominance-subordination relationship in the fish Platypoecilus maculatus. Physiol. Zool. **18:**176–194.

Breder, C. M., Jr., and R. F. Nigrelli. 1935. The influence of temperature and other factors on the winter aggregations of the sunfish, Lepomis auritus, with critical re-marks on the social behavior of fishes. Ecology **16:**33–47.

Brückner, G. H. 1933. Untersuchungen zur Tierpsychologie, insbesondere zur Auflö-sung der Familie. Z. f. Psychol. **128:**1–110.

Bullough, W. S. 1951. "Vertebrate Sexual Cycles." Methuen's Monographs on Bio-logical Subjects. Wiley, New York.

Cagle, F. R. 1944. Home range, homing behavior and migration in turtles. Misc. Pub. Mus. Zool. Univ. Michigan #61.

Carmichael, L., ed. 1946. "Manual of Child Psychology." Wiley, New York.

————. 1946a. The onset and early development of behavior. See preceding, 43–166.

Carpenter, C. R. 1934. A field study of the behavior and social relations of howling monkeys. Compar. Psychol. Monog. **10:**2.

————. 1935. Behavior of red spider monkeys in Panama. *J. Mammal.* **16**:171–180.

————. 1940. A field study in Siam of the behavior and social relations of the gibbon (*Hylobates lar*). *Compar. Psychol. Monog.* **16**:5.

————. 1942a. Sexual behavior of free ranging rhesus monkeys (*Macaca mulatta*). *J. Compar. Psychol.* **33**:113–162.

————. 1942b. Characteristics of social behavior in nonhuman Primates. *Trans. N. Y. Acad. Sci.* **II**:248–258.

————. 1952. Social behavior of non-human Primates. See: Colloques, 227–247.

Chadwick, C. S. 1941. Further observations on the water drive in *Triturus viridescens*. *J. Exp. Zool.* **86**:175–187.

Clark, G., and H. G. Birch. 1945. Hormonal modifications of sexual behavior. *Psychosom. Med.* **7**:321–329.

Clark, W. E. LeGros. 1932. The structure and connections of the thalamus. *Brain* **55**:406–470.

Cobb, S. 1952. On the nature and locus of mind. *Arch. Neurol. Psychiat.* **67**:172–177.

Coghill, G. E. 1929. "Anatomy and the Problem of Behavior." Macmillan Co., New York, and Cambridge University Press, Cambridge.

Collias, N. E. 1944. Aggressive behavior among vertebrate animals. *Physiol. Zool.* **17**:83–123.

————. 1950. Social life and the individual among vertebrate animals. *Ann. N. Y. Acad. Sci.* **51**:1074–1092.

————. 1951. Problems and principles of animal sociology. See: Stone, ed.

————, and C. Southwick. 1952. A field study of population density and social organization in howling monkeys. *Proc. Amer. Philos. Soc.* **96**:143–156.

Colloques Internationaux du Centre National de la Recherche Scientifique. XXXIV. Structure et Physiologie de la Société Animale. Paris, 1952.

Count, E. W. 1947. Brain and body weight in man: their antecedents in growth and evolution. *Ann. N. Y. Acad. Sci.* **46**:993–1122.

————. 1958. The biological basis of human sociality. *Amer. Anthropologist* **6**:1049–1085.

Craig, W. 1918. Appetites and aversions as constituents of instincts. *Biol. Bull. Marine Biol. Lab. Woods Hole, Mass.* **34**:91–107.

Crawford, M. P. 1937. The cooperative solving of problems by young chimpanzees. *Compar. Psychol. Monog.* **14**:2.

————. 1940. The relation between social dominance and the menstrual cycle in female chimpanzees. *J. Comp. Psychol.*, **30**:483–513.

————. 1952. Social life in Ungulates. See: Colloques, 221–227.

Davis, D. D. 1936. Courtship and mating behavior in snakes. *Zool. Ser. Field Mus. Nat. Hist.* **20**:257–290.

Dempsey, E. W. 1951. Homeostasis. See: Stevens, ed. Ch. 6.

Dennis, W. 1941. Infant development under conditions of restricted practice and minimum social stimulation. *Genet. Psychol. Monog.* **23**:143–189.

Drever, J. 1955. The concept of early learning. *Trans. N. Y. Acad. Sci.* **17**:463–469.

v. Eickstedt, E. 1936. Ganzheitsanthropologie. *Z. f. Rassenk.* **3**:109.

Emerson, A. E. 1952. The supraorganismic aspects of society. See: Colloques, 333–353.

Evans, L. T. 1936. A study of a social hierarchy in the lizard, *Anolis carolinensis*. *J. Genet. Psychol.* **48**:88–111.

————. 1955. Group processes in the lower vertebrates. See Schaffner, ed. 1955. 258–289.

Fischel, W. 1927. Beiträge zur Soziologie des Haushuhns. *Biol. Zentralblatt* **47**:678–695.

————. 1937. Die Affektäusserungen und das Gefühlsleben der Tiere in wissenschaflicher Beurteilung. *Z. f. Tierpsych.* **1**:66–77.

————. 1938. Affekt, Gedächtnis und Leistung bei Wirbeltieren. *Z. f. Tierpsych.* **2**:198–220.

Fletcher, R. 1957. "Instinct in Man." International Universities Press, New York.
Ford, C. S., and F. A. Beach. 1951. "Patterns of Sexual Behavior." Paul B. Hoeber, New York.
Friedmann, H. 1935. Bird societies. See: Murchison, ed. Ch. 5.
Galt, W. E. 1947. Sex behavior in primates. *Ann. N. Y. Acad. Sci.* **47**:617–634.
Gavan, J. A., ed. 1955. "The Non-human Primates and Human Evolution." Wayne University Press, Detroit, Michigan.
Gesell, A. L. 1945. "The Embryology of Behavior." Harper & Bros., New York.
————. 1948. "Studies in Child Development." Harper & Bros., New York.
————. 1949. Human infancy and the ontogenesis of behavior. *Amer. Scientist* **37**:529–553.
Goldstein, K. 1939. "The Organism." American Book Co., New York.
Greenberg, B. 1943. Social behavior of the western banded Gecko *Coleonyx variegatus* Baird. *Physiol. Zool.* **16**:110–122.
————. 1947. Some relations between territory, social hierarchy, and leadership in the green sunfish *(Lepomis cyanellus). Physiol. Zool.* **20**:267–299.
————, and G. K. Noble. 1944. Social behavior of the American chameleon *(Anolis carolinensis* Voigt). *Physiol. Zool.* **17**:392–439.
Gregory, W. K. 1951. "Evolution Emerging." 2 vols. Macmillan, New York.
Grinker, R. R. 1939. Hypothalamic functions in psychosomatic interrelations. *Psychosom. Med.* **1**:19–47.
Halstead, W. C. 1947, "Brain and Intelligence." University of Chicago Press, Chicago.
Hartman, C. G. 1945. The mating of mammals. *Ann. N. Y. Acad. Sci.* **46**:23–44.
Hebb, D. O. 1949. "The Organization of Behavior." Wiley, New York.
Hediger, H. 1952. Beiträge zur Säugetier-Soziologie. See: Colloques, 297–323.
Herrick, C. J. 1929. Anatomical patterns and behavior patterns. *Physiol. Zool.* **2**:439–448.
————. 1948. "The Brain of the Tiger Salamander." University of Chicago Press, Chicago.
————. 1956. "The Evolution of Human Nature." University of Texas Press, Austin, Tex.
Hess, W. R. 1943. Das Zwischenhirn als Koordinationsorgan. *Helvet. Physiol. Acta* **I**:549–565.
————. 1944. Das Schlafsyndrom als Folge dienzephaler Reizung. *Helvet. Physiol. et Pharmacol. Acta* **2**:305–344.
————. 1954. The diencephalic sleep center. In: "Brain Mechanisms and Consciousness. A Symposium." Chas. C. Thomas Co., Springfield, Ill.
Hilzheimer, M. Die Wanderungen der Säugetiere. *Ergebnisse der Biol.* **V**:219–289.
v. Holst, E. 1937. Vom Wesen der Ordnung im Zentralnervensystem. *Naturwiss.* **25**:625–631; 641–647.
Houssay, B. A. 1949. Hypophyseal functions in the toad *Bufo arenarum* Hensel. *Quart. Rev. Biol.* **24**:1–27.
Howard, H. E. 1920. "Territory in Bird Life." John Murray, London.
Hursthouse, E. W. 1940. Notes on the breeding of the little blue penguin. *The Emu* **40**:121–123.
Huxley, J. S. 1914. The Courtship-habits of the great crested grebe *(Podiceps cristatus). Proc. Zool. Soc. London*, pp. 491–562. (There is no further numeral reference.)
Ingram, W. R. 1939. The hypothalamus: A review of the experimental data. *Psychosom. Med.* **1**:48–91.
Jacobsen, C. F. 1936. Studies of cerebral function in primates. *Compar. Psychol. Monog.* 13, ser. #63.
Jasper, H. C., Ajmone-Marsan, and J. Stoll. 1952. Corticofugal projections to the brain stem. *Arch. Neurol. Psychiat.* **67**:155–171.
Jaynes, J. 1957. Imprinting: the interaction of learned and innate behavior. *J. Compar. Abnorm. Psychol.* **49**:201–206; **50**:6–10.

Jeffress, L. A., ed. 1951. "Cerebral Mechanisms in Behavior." Wiley, New York.
Kappers, C. U. Ariëns. 1947. "Anatomie comparée du système nerveux." De Erven F. Bohn, Haarlem.
———, G. C. Huber, and E. C. Crosby. 1936. "The Comparative Anatomy of the Nervous System of Vertebrates, Including Man." 2 vols. Macmillan, New York.
Kardiner, A. 1939. "The Individual and His Society." Columbia University Press, New York.
———. 1945. "The Psychological Frontiers of Society." Columbia University Press, New York.
Katz, D. 1926. Sozialpsychologie der Vögel. Ergebnisse der Biol. I:447–478.
———. 1948. "Tiere und Menschen."
———. 1953. "Animals and Men." (Translation of the foregoing.) Penguin Books, New York.
Kendeigh, S. C. 1952. "Parental Care and Its Evolution in Birds." Illinois Biological Monog. XXII. University of Illinois Press, Urbana.
Kennedy, C. H. 1927. The exoskeleton as a factor in limiting and directing the evolution of insects. J. Morphol. Physiol. 44:268–312.
Klüver, H. 1951. Functional differences between the occipital and temporal lobes. See: Jeffress, ed. 1951. 147–199.
———, and P. C. Bucy. 1939. Preliminary analysis of functions of the temporal lobes in monkeys. Arch. Neurol. Psychiat. 42:979–1000.
Köhler, W. 1925. "The Mentality of Apes." Harcourt, Brace, New York.
Kubie, L. S. 1948. Instincts and homeostasis. Psychosom. Med. 10:15–30.
———. 1953a. The central representation of the symbolic process in psychosomatic disorders. Psychosom Med. 15:1–7.
———. 1953b. Distortion of the symbolic process in neurosis and psychosis. J. Amer. Psychoanal. Assn. I:59–86.
———. 1953c. Some implications for psychoanalysis of modern concepts of the organization of the brain. Psychanalyt. Quart. 22:21–52.
———. 1956. Influence of symbolic processes on the role of instincts in human behavior. Psychosom. Med. 18:189–208.
Kummer, H. 1957. "Soziales Verhalten einer Mantelpavian-Gruppe." Hans Huber, Bern U. Stuttgart.
Lashley, K. S. 1929. "Brain Mechanisms and Intelligence." University of Chicago Press, Chicago.
———. 1938a. The thalamus and emotion. Psychol. Rev. 45:42–61.
———. 1938b. Experimental analysis of instinctive behavior. Psychol. Rev. 45:445–471.
———. 1947. Structural variation in the nervous system in relation to behavior. Psychol. Rev. 54:325–334.
———. 1949. Persistent problems in the evolution of mind. Quart. Rev. Biol. 24:28–42.
———. 1951. The problem of serial order in behavior. See: Jeffress, ed. 112–136.
Laven, H. 1940. Beiträge zur Biologie des Sandregenpfeifers (Charadrius histicula). J. f. Ornithologie 88:183–288.
Lehrman, D. S. 1955. The perception of animal behavior. See: Schaffner, ed. 1955. 259–267.
Levick, G. M. 1914. "Antarctic Penguins." J. Heinemann, London.
Loewe, C. H., Jr. 1948. Territorial behavior in snakes and the so-called courtship dance. Herpetologia 4:129–135.
Lorenz, K. 1931. Beiträge zur Ethologie der Corviden. J. Ornithol. 79:67–120.
———. 1935. Der Kumpan in der Umwelt des Vogels. J. f. Ornithol. 83:137–213; 289–413.
———. 1937a. Über die Bildung des Instinktbegriffs. Naturwiss. 25:289–300; 307–318; 324–331.
———. 1937a. Über den Begriff der Instinkthandlung. Folia Biotheoret. Ser. B. 2:17–50.

——. 1952. "King Solomon's Ring." Methuen, London.

——. 1953/1955. Über angeborene Instinkformeln beim Menschen. Z. f. menschliche Vererbungs- und Konstitutionslehre **32**:385–389.

——. 1955. Morphology and behavior patterns in closely allied species. See: Schaffner, ed. 1955. 168–220.

McGraw, M. B. 1946. Maturation of behavior. See: Carmichael, ed. Ch. 7.

MacLean, P. D. 1949. Psychosomatic disease and the visceral brain. Psychosom. Med. **11**:338–353.

——. 1954. The limbic system and its hippocampal formation. J. Neurosurgery **11**:29–44.

Magoun, H. W. 1952. An ascending reticular activating system in the brain stem. Arch. Neurol. Psychiat. **67**:145–154.

Malinowski, B. 1929. "The Sexual Life of Savages." Halcyon House, New York.

Maslow, A. H. 1936. The role of dominance in the social and sexual behavior of infra-human primates. J. Genet. Psychol. **48**:261–277; 310–338; **49**:161–198.

——. 1937. Dominance-feeling, behavior, and status. Psychol. Rev. **44**:404–429.

——. 1939. Dominance-feeling, personality, and social behavior in women. J. Soc. Psychol. **10**: 3–39.

——. 1940. Dominance-quality and social behavior in infra-human primates. J. Soc. Psychol. **11**:313–324.

——. 1942. Self-esteem (dominance-feeling) and sexuality in women. J. Soc. Psychol. **16**:259–294.

——, and S. Flanzbaum. 1936. The role of dominance in the social and sexual behavior of infra-human primates. J. Genet. Psychol. **48**:278–309.

Masure, R. H., and W. C. Allee. 1934. Flock organzation of the shell parakeet Melopsittacus undulatus Shaw. Ecology **15**:338–398.

Mead, M. 1947. On the implications for anthropology of the Gesell-Ilg approach to maturation. Amer. Anthropologist **49**:69–77.

Meek, A. 1916. "The Migrations of Fish." Edward Arnold, London.

Moore, H. J. 1954. Some observations on the migration of the toad (Bufo bufo bufo). Brit. J. Herpetol. **1**:194–224.

Morely, D. W. 1953. "The Ant World." Penguin Books, New York.

Morgan, C. T. 1951. The psychophysiology of learning. See: Stevens, ed. Ch. 20.

Murchison, C., ed. 1935. "A Handbook of Social Psychology." Clark University Press, Worcester, Mass.

Murchison, C. 1935a. The experimental measurement of a social hierarchy in Gallus domesticus. I. J. Gen. Psychol. **12**:3–39.

——. 1935b. II. J. Soc. Psychol. **6**:3–30.

——. 1935c. III. J. Genet. Psychol. **46**:76–102.

——. 1935d. IV. J. Gen. Psychol. **12**:296–312.

——, C.M. Pomeret, and M. X. Zarrow. 1935. V. J. Soc. Psychol. **6**:172–181.

Murie, A. 1944. The wolves of Mt. McKinley. U.S. Dept. Interior Fauna Series #5 Washington, D.C.

Nalbandov, A. W., and L. E. Card. 1945. Endocrine identification of the broody genotype of cocks. J. Hered. **36**:35–39.

Nice, M. 1941. The role of territory in bird life. Amer. Midland Naturalist **26**:441–487.

Nissen, H. W. 1931. A field study of the chimpanzee. Compar. Psychol. Monog. **8**:1.

——. 1951. Phylogenetic comparison. See: Stevens, ed. Ch. 11.

——. 1955. Problems of mental evolution in Primates. See: Gavan, ed.

Noble, G. K. 1931. "The Biology of the Amphibia." McGraw-Hill, New York.

——. 1939a. The experimental animal from the naturalist's point of view. Amer. Naturalist **73**:113–126.

——. 1939b. The role of dominance in the social life of birds. Auk **56**:263–273.

——, and L. R. Aronson. 1942. The sexual behavior of Anura. I. Bull. Amer. Mus. Nat. Hist. **80**:127–142.

————, and H. T. Bradley. 1933. The mating behavior of lizards. *Ann. N. Y. Acad. Sci.* **35**:25–100.

————, and Clausen. 1936. The aggregative behavior of *Storeria deKayi* and other snakes. *Ecol. Monogr.* 269–316.

————, and B. Curtis. 1939. The social behavior of the jewel fish, *Hemichromis bimaculatus* Gill. *Bull. Amer. Mus. Nat. Hist.* **76**:1–46.

————, K. F. Kumpf, and V. N. Billings. 1938. Induction of brooding behavior in the jewel fish. *Endocrinology* **23**:353–359.

————, and M. Wurm. 1943. The social behavior of the laughing gull. *Ann. N. Y. Acad. Sci.* **45**:179–220.

————, and A. Zitrin. 1942. Induction of mating behavior in male and female chicks following injection of sex hormones. *Proc. Soc. Exp. Biol. Med.* **30**:327–334.

Nowlis, V. 1941. Companionship preference and dominance in the social interaction of young chimpanzees. *Compar. Psychol. Monog.* #17.

Odum, E. P. 1942. Annual cycle of the black-capped chickadee. *Auk* **59**:499–531.

Papez, J. W. 1937a. The brain considered as an organ. *Amer. J. Psychol.* **49**:217–232.

————. 1937b. A proposed mechanism of emotion. *Arch. Neurol. Psychiat.* **38**:725–743.

————. 1944. Structures and mechanisms underlying the cerebral functions. *Amer. J. Psychol.* **57**:291–316.

Parr, A. E. 1927. A contribution to the theoretical analysis of the schooling behavior of fishes. *Occasional Papers, Bingham Oceanographic Collection* **1**:1–32.

————. 1931. Sex dimorphism and schooling behavior among fishes. *Amer. Naturalist* **65**:173–180.

ter Pelwijk, J. J., and N. Tinbergen. 1937. Eine reizbiologische Analyse einiger Verhaltensweisen von *Gasterosteus aculeatus* L. *Z. f. Tierpsych.* **1**:193–300.

Penfield, W. 1952. Memory mechanisms. *Arch. Neurol. Psychiat.* **67**:178–198.

————, and H. Jasper. 1954." Epilepsy and the Functional Anatomy of the Human Brain." Little, Brown Co., Boston.

————, and Rasmussen. 1950. "The Cerebral Cortex of Man." Macmillan, New York.

Peters, H. 1937. Experimentelle Untersuchungen über die Brutpflege von Haplochromis multicolor, einem maulbrütenden Knochenfisch. *Z. f. Tierpsych.* **1**:201–218.

Pickwell, G. B. 1931. The prairie horned lark. *Trans. Acad. Sci. St. Louis,* **XXVII**. St. Louis, Missouri.

Pool, J. L. 1954. The visceral brain of man. *J. Neurosurgery* **11**:45–63.

Richdale, L. E. 1940–41. A brief summary of the history of the yellow-eyed penguin. *The Emu* **40**:265–287.

————. 1949. A study of a group of penguins of known age. *Biol. Monog.* #1. Dunedin, N. Z.

————. 1951. "Sexual Behavior in Penguins." University of Kansas Press, Lawrence.

Riddle, O. 1941. Endocrine aspects of the physiology of reproduction. *Ann. Rev. Physiol.* **3**:573–616.

Rogers, F. T. 1922a. Studies of the brain stem. VI. An experimental study of the corpus striatum of the pigeon as related to various instinctive types of behavior. *J. Compar. Neurol.* **35**:21–59.

————. 1922b. A note on the excitable areas of the cerebral hemispheres of the pigeon. ibid. 61–65.

Roheim, G. 1950. "Psychoanalysis and Anthropology." International Universities Press, New York.

Romer, A. S. 1933 seq. "Vertebrate Paleontology." University of Chicago Press, Chicago.

Schaffner, B., ed. 1955. "Group Processes I." Josiah Macy, Jr. Foundation, New York.

————. 1956. "Group Processes II." Josiah Macy, Jr. Foundation, New York.

Schelderup-Ebbe, Th. 1922. Beiträge zur Sozialpsychologie des Haushuhns. *Z. f. Psychol.* **88**:225–264.

————. 1924. Zur Sozialpsychologie der Vögel. *Z. f. Psychol.* **96**:36–84.

———. 1935. Social behavior of birds. See: Murchison, ed. Ch. 20.
Scheuring, L. Die Wanderunger der Fische. *Ergbrisse der Biolo.* **V**:405–691; **VI**:4–304.
Schiller, F. 1952: Consciousness reconsidered. *Arch. Neurol. Psychiat.* **67**:199–227.
Schneirla, T. C. 1946. Problems in the biopsychology of social organization. *J. Abnorm. Soc. Psychol.* **41**:385–402.
Scott, J.P. 1958. Animal Behavior. University of Chicago Press, Chicago,
———, and M. V. Marston. 1950. Critical periods affecting the development of normal and maladjustive social behavior in puppies. *J. Genet. Psychol.* **77**:25–60.
Scott, J. W. 1942. Mating behavior of the sage grouse. *Auk.* **59**:477–498.
———. 1945. Social behavior, organization and leadership in a small flock of domestic sheep. *Compar. Psychol. Monog.* **18**:1–29.
Shaw, C. E. 1948. The male combat "dance" of some Crotalid snakes. *Herpetologia* **4**:137–145.
Sheps, J. G. The nuclear configuration and cortical connections of the human thalamus. *J. Compar. Neurol.* **83**:1–56.
Sherrington, C. S. 1947–1952: "The Integrative Action of the Nervous System." Yale University Press, New Haven.
Shoemaker, H. H. 1930a. Social hierarchy in flocks of the canary. *Auk.* **56**:381–406.
———. 1939b. Effect of testosterone propionate on behavior of the female canary. *Proc. Soc. Exp. Biol. Med.* **41**:299–302.
Sladen, W. J. L. 1956. Social structure among penguins. See: Schaffuer, ed. 1956. 28–93.
Smith, W. J., and S. Rose, 1952. The social behavior of vertebrates: A review of the literature 1939–1950. *Psychol. Bull.* **49**:598–627.
Soulairac, A. 1952a. L'effet de groupe dans le comportement sexuel du rat mâle. See: Colloques, 91–99.
———. 1952b. Etude experimentale du comportement en groupe du rat blanc. ibid., 99–103.
Southern, H. N. 1948. Sexual and aggressive behavior in the wild rabbit. *Behaviour* **1**:173–194.
Spencer, C. C. 1943. Notes on the life history of Rocky Moutain bighorn sheep on the Tarryall Mountains of Colorado. *J. Mammal.* **24**:1–11.
Sperry, R. W. 1951. Mechanisms of neural maturation. See: Stevens, ed. Ch. 7.
Spitz, R. A. 1945. Hospitalism. In: "The Psychoanalytic Study of the Child," pp. 53–72. International Universities Press, New York.
———. 1946. Hospitalism: a follow-up report. In: "The Psychoanalytic Study of the Child," pp. 113–117. International Universities Press, New York.
Spurway, H. 1953. Territory and evolution in sticklebacks. In: "New Biology #14," pp. 33–43. Penguin Books, New York.
Stebbins, R. C. 1944. Field note on a lizard, the mountain swift, with special reference to territorial behavior. *Ecology* **25**:233ff.
Steiner, A. Neuere Untersuchungen über die Arbeitsteilung bei Insektenstaaten. *Ergebnisse der Biol.* **X**:156–176.
Stevens, S. S., ed. 1951. "Handbook of Experimental Psychology." Wiley, New York.
Stieve, H. 1950. Der Ovarialzyklus vom Standpunkt der vergleichenden Anatomie. *Naturwiss.* **38**:8–13, 33–38.
Stone, C. F. 1925a. The effects of cerebral destruction on the sexual behavior of rabbits. I. *Amer. J. Physiol.* **71**:430–435.
———. 1925b. II. ibid. **72**:372–385.
———. 1926 III. *J. Compar. Psychol.* **6**:435–448.
———, ed. 1951: "Comparative Psychology." Prentice-Hall, Englewood Cliffs, N. J.
Strauss, E. 1938a. Vergleichende Beobachtungen über Verhaltensweisen von Rabenvögeln. *Z. f. Tierpsych.* **2**:145–172.
———. 1938b. Versuche an gefangenen Rabenvögeln. *Z. f. Tierpsych.* **2**:172–197.
Taibell, A. 1928. Risveglio artificiale di istinti tipicamente femminili nei maschi di taluni uccelli. *Soc. Nat. Matem. Modena* **7**:93–102.

Thomson, A. L. 1926. "Problems of Bird Migration." H. F. & G. Witherby, London.

Thomson, J. A. 1923. "The Biology of Birds." Macmillan, New York.

Tinbergen, N. 1942. An objectivistic study of the innate behavior of animals. *Bibliothec. Biotheoret.* **1**:39–98.

——. 1948. Social releasers and the experimental method required for their study. *Wilson Bull.* **60**:6–51.

——. 1951. "The Study of Instinct." Oxford University Press, New York.

——. 1953a. "Social Behaviour in Animals." Methuen, London.

——. 1953b. Fighting and threat in animals. In: "New Biology" #14:9–24. Penguin Books, New York.

——. 1955. Psychology and ethology as supplementary parts of a science of behavior. See: Schaffner, ed. 1955. 75–167.

——, and J. J. A. van Iersel. 1947. "Displacement reactions" in the three-spined stickleback. *Behaviour* **1**:56–63.

——, and D. J. Kuenen. 1939. Über die auslösenden und die richtunggebenden Reizsituationen der Sperrbewegungen von jungen Drosseln. *Z. f. Tierpsych.* **3**: 37–60.

Tinklepaugh, O. L., and G. G. Hartman. 1940. Behavior and maternal care of the newborn monkey. *J. Genet. Psychol.* **40**:257–286.

Toncray, J. E., and W. J. S. Krief. 1946. The nuclei of the human thalamus. *J. Compar. Neurol.* **85**:421–459.

Tracy, H. C. 1926. The development of motility and behavior in the toadfish. *J. Compar. Neurol.* **40**:253–369.

Uexküll, J. v. 1909. "Umwelt and Innewelt der Tiere." Julius Springer, Berlin.

——. 1926. "Theoretical Biology." Kegan Paul, Trench, Trübner, London.

——. 1938. Tier und Umwelt. *Z. f. Tierpsych.* **2**:101–114.

——, and G. Kriszat. 1934. "Striefzüge durch die Umwelten von Tieren und Menschen." Julius Springer, Berlin.

Uhrich, J. 1938. The social hierarchy in albino mice. *J. Compar. Psychol.* **25**:373–413.

Wachs, H. Die Wanderungen der Vögel. *Ergebnisse der Biol.* **1**:479–637.

Walker, A. E. 1937. The thalamus in relation to the cerebral cortex. *J. Ment. Dis.* **85**:249–261.

——. 1938. "The Primate Thalamus." University of Chicago Press, Chicago.

Warren, E. R. 1927. "The Beaver," Williams and Wilkins Co., Baltimore.

Weber, H. 1937. Zur neueren Entwicklung der Umweltlehre J. v. Uexkülls. *Naturwiss.* **25**:97–104.

Weiss, P. 1928. Erregungsspezifität und Erregungsresonanz. *Ergebnisse der Biol.* **3**: 1–227.

——. 1941. Self-differentiation of the basic patterns of coordination. *Compar. Psychol. Monog.* **17**:1.

Welty, J. C. 1934. Experiments in group behavior of fishes. *Physiol. Zool.* **7**:85–128.

Wheeler, W. M. 1923. "Social Life Among the Insects." Harcourt, Brace, New York.

——. 1928. "The Social Insects." Harcourt, Brace, New York.

Whitman, C. O. 1919. "The Behavior of Pigeons." Carnegie Institute of Washington, Washington, D. C.

Wilson, E. A. 1907. Aves. In: "National Antartic Expedition 1901–1904. Natural History. II: Zoology." The British Museum, London.

Wislocki, G. B. 1929. On the placentation of primates, with a consideration of the phylogeny of the placenta. *Carnegie Inst. Contrib. Embryol.* **20**: #3.

Wunder, W. 1931. Brutpflege und Nestbau bei Fischen. *Ergebnisse der Biol.* **VII**:118–192.

——. Nestbau und Brutpflege bei Amphibien. *Ergebnisse der Biol.* **VIII**:180–220.

——. Nestbau und Brutpflege bei Reptilien. *Ergebnisse der Biol.* **X**:1–36.

Yerkes, R. M. 1936. A chimpanzee family. *J. Genet. Psychol.* **48**:362–370.

——. 1939a. The life history and personality of the chimpanzee. *Amer. Naturalist* **73**:97–112.

——. 1939b. Social dominance and sexual status in the chimpanzee. *Quart. Rev. Biol.* **14:**115–136.

——. 1939c. Sexual behavior in the chimpanzee. *Human Biol.* **11:**78–111.

——. 1940a. Social behavior of chimpanzees: dominance between mates in relation to sexual status. *J. Compar. Psychol.* **30:**147–186.

——. 1940b. The relation between social dominance and the menstrual cycle in female chimpanzees. *J. Compar. Psychol.* **30:**483–513.

——, and M. I. Tomlin. 1935. Mother-infant relations in chimpanzees. *J. Compar. Psychol.* **20:**321–358.

——, and A. W. Yerkes. 1929. "The Great Apes." Yale University Press, New Haven.

Zuckerman, S. 1932. "The Social Life of Monkeys and Apes." Harcourt, Brace, New York.

——. 1933. "Functional Affinities of Man, Monkeys, and Apes." Harcourt, Brace, New York.

2 The Lactation Complex*

A Phylogenetic Consideration of the Mammalian Mother Offspring/Symbiosis, with Special Reference to Man

---
I

An earlier essay, published in *Homo,* submitted a thesis under the concept of "biogram." It asserted that the life mode of any animal kind possesses a configuration, a pattern, a gestalt, which is an integral expression of its bodily morphology; that this biogram can be generalized taxonomically, so that we may speak of a vertebrate, a mammalian, a primate, a human (sub) system. It was claimed that, although this represents a function of the total organization of the animal's morphology, it is grasped best from studies of behavior and of central nervous system (CNS) in juxtaposition (although the present position of these sciences does not permit any one-to-one correlations). In measure as evolution continues, furthermore, the biogram increases its complexity of detail and richness of behavioral content; yet its schema—first laid down when the vertebrates were in their formative stage of phylogenesis—is in no wise disrupted:Biogrammatically as well as architectonically, vertebrates remain vertebrates; and this holds for man as genuinely as for any and all others; so that his culturized life mode remains consistently within the biogrammatic con-

*From *Homo* **XVIII**:38–54, 1967. Partially adapted from a lecture delivered before the Faculty of Anatomy, San Francisco Medical Center, February 20, 1962. The research was under subsidy of the National Institute of Mental Health.

straints—and also is a reification of its potentialities under a set of given circumstances.

The inquiry which eventually reached this conclusion began and ended in anthropology (the term being taken here in its American sense); for it continued into psychology and sociality the quest that began in the nineteenth century with comparative anatomy: What is man's place in nature? Between the initial and final points, however, the inquiry was an induction chiefly from the data of comparative morphology and of ethology; although, of course, not exclusively so. With the concept formalized, a hypothesis was deduced and applied to man.[1]

The inquiry began in 1951; it was presented to various academic audiences during the ensuing years; eventually, two divergent lines developed—albeit they must at some point reconverge: a theoretical and a substantive one.

The theoretical direction is being followed elsewhere. Suffice it here that the biogram concept owes much of its theory to the ideas of v. Uexküll and v. Bertalanffy, and that it is being pushed into domains of information theory, cybernetics, general systems theory.

The substantive direction has led to special studies of two phenomena or sets of processes which have weighed heavily in anthropogenesis: the mother/offspring symbiosis and the speech function: the "lactation complex" and "phasia." It is not necessary to claim for these a position of exclusive preeminence before appreciating the urgency of their exploration.

Each of them, in other words, is a seizable universe of discourse; each may be treated as a subsystem of biogram-as-system; each suggests an account of its evolutionary synthesis from rudiments which obtain at a lower phyletic level and which we may consider to have been anlagen for the eventual development of each complex. We are not hereby propounding any orthogenetic hypothesis. All that is involved is our hindsight: We trace evolution backwards, from the definitive complexity at the human end; had we existed, in some disembodied state, when reptiles were life's most advanced organization, we could never have predicted from their features the immensely involved relations between mammalian mother and her young.

This essay will not pursue the phasia problem;[2] only that of the lactation complex. The studies of both are holistic: They cut across

[1]Count, 1958–9. See also 1958; for a brief, nontechnical presentation, see 1964–5.
[2]For a preliminary paper, see Count (1962), 1964.

the technical disciplines of comparative morphology and behavior. For these fragment the reality of animal organization. They do indeed afford detailed *Kleinarbeit* which are the indispensable analytic precursors of syntheses. But we are also aware that with such procedure a Heisenberg principle sets in: A dissection into (arbitrary) constituents destroys the very crucial information that we are ultimately seeking: the relationships that constitute organization.

The study of the lactation complex has its intrinsic value; nevertheless, it is submitted herewith as a pilot study—as suggestive of direction for research of the future.[3]

One final statement of position, before we launch our exploration. The mother/offspring relationship is one of ecology: The mother is the environment of the offspring originally mechanical and physiological, with psychological dimensions supravening in measure as the mechanical and physiological retire. Unlike the *Umwelt* of physical nature, however, both of the principals share a common information code, which they express nonidentically, yet reciprocatively, cybernetically. The *social* dimension of behavior may be defined as that part of any animal's behavior which is elicited only by virtue of the sharing of a common, appropriate code. The code is innate—written into the DNA of the species to which the individuals belong. Whatever experiential component an organism—man included—may write into its behavior remains a function of whatever is already written into its DNA formulation.

Coghill (1929a) once described succinctly the course of ontogenesis: "The behavior from the beginning expands throughout the growing normal animal as a perfectly integrated unit, whereas partial patterns arise within the total patterns and, by a process of individuation, acquire secondarily varying degrees of independence. . . . Complexity of behavior is not derived by progressive integration of more and more originally discrete units." Today we hardly question this. He was speaking of ontogenesis, but it is equally applicable to phylogenesis; and on both counts it is cardinal to our account of the "lacation complex."

May we follow this procedure:

1. A phylogenetic review of the evolution of the suctorial and the mammary apparatuses.

2. A juxtaposed account of phylogenesis of behavior.

---

[3]This paper is preliminary to a monograph now in formation.

3. Some comments on the mother/infant tie in mammals, based chiefly on goat and rhesus investigations.

4. Some suggestions on the fate of the lactation complex as ontogensis advances beyond it.

II

Placentation

For reasons that will appear in due course, we cannot do justice to the lactation complex without a note on the progress that precedes it.

In the Eutheria, lactation takes up where placentation leaves off. Monotremes suckle their young, but they have no placenta; they deliver encapsulated embryos in an advanced state—I cannot help calling this a "pseudo-oviparity." Although it is no longer held that the monotremes are ancestral to the placentals, this physiological behavior is conveniently considered as transitional between reptilian and definitively mammalian schemes.

I cannot pretend competence in evaluating the phyletic position of the monotremes; but there are some facts that get in the way of the appraisal mentioned. (1) the earliest known fossils of the monotremes are much younger than those of marsupials and placentals; (2) yolk sac and allantois placentas, in ranging degrees of complexity, occur rather widely among extant reptiles, particularly the lizards. This order alone ranges from oviparity through ovovivparity to placental viviparty, without thereby entailing other correlative phylogenetic complexities. Modern ecologic-geographic distribution of the lizards suggests that placentation happens to be the lizards' answer to cold-dry climates of high altitudes (Weekes, 1935). This at least is consistent with speculations on the generic "explosion" of the mammals with the extinction of the giant reptiles at the close of the Cretaceous period.

Perhaps, then, the replilian ancestors of the mammals—the therapsids—were already placentals. We may, if we choose, balance this against the monotremes, and speculate as to which came first: placentation or lactation. Its only pertinence to our topic that I can see is, what it would imply about the hormonal sequence that programs mammalian ontogenesis: estrogens, progesterones, luteinizing hormones, prolactin. The hormones themselves are of wider and of more ancient occurrence than the mammals. Prolactin induces other segments of the reproductive-behavioral syndrome in other verte-brates—for instance, salamanders. Only in mammals does it operate upon the integumentary specializations which produce milk.

The Integumentary Muscle Sheet

One transformation that leads from reptile to mammal is that of the integument—highly complex, as of course we know. The two features which concern us are: the emergence of the integumentary muscle sheet, and the emergence of the sebum-sweat-hair complex. The latter will be deferred for the present.

The muscular sheet is most diagrammatic in the monotremes, and there is no reason to believe that here, at any rate, these little beasts are not prototypical. The sheet simply envelops the trunk from snout to anus; the fibers tend to decussate in the midventral line; under-standably, they are sphincters about orifices, mouth and cloaca: the marsupial margins of the didelphs; in the latter they also form the *compressor mammae*—which is worth noting. Aside from anomalous relics, they persist in man as oral and anal sphincters, and as the platysma, which, noteworthily, tenses degulutition.

Most remarkably, the facial portion of the sheet, which in the Eutheria undergoes differential refinement to become the mimetic muscles, is visceral muscle and is motorized by the VII cranial nerve; while the rest of it, beginning with the sphincter colli *sive* platysma, is of somatic derivation and is postcranially innervated.

Were this a paper on the origin of the mammals and their biogram, instead of a focus on the lactation complex, we would now be launched on the entire course by which the mammalian scheme emerged out of a reptilian. The transformation of a stiff, scaly integu-ment into the flexible and motile one of the mammals, with its new secretions, undoubtedly is primarily a homoiothermal mechanism that functions in postuterine life, and is not an embryologic adaptation. Oblique considerations lead us to suppose that this transformation was occurring at the same time that transformations in the gill arch region were going beyond what took place when the reptiles emerged out of amphibians; and also gestative-parturitive elaborations. We could not leave the subject without considering the limb-and-trunk developments that reflect a more active and refined set of motions; and a host of other topics. They all point to a life mode that exploited energy in novel ways—despite the fact that the pallium of the earliest mammals who have left evidence shows little advance over the reptil-ian. If our scale be that of individuals with life spans, the evolutionary change was slow; on the geological timescale, it was rapid. It occurred during a portion of the Triassic period.

Transformation of the Reptilian Jaws into the Mammalian Type

The mammals are derived from the reptilian subclass Synapsida—more closely, the order Therapsida. The latter occurred as early as the Middle Permian; they diversified and continued into the Triassic; by the Mid-Jurassic, if not before, some stem of these had become definitely mammals. The transition still needs much filling in of detail, but the outline is well established.

We are familiar with one of the most striking particular cases of evolutionary transformation on record: the detachment of the more proximal elements of the reptilian jaws and their transfer to the otic mechanisms. The quadrate of the skull base becomes the incus, the articulare the malleus, the angulare the tympanic ring. (I recall my despair and patience when, as one of Professor Camp's graduate students on the Berkeley campus, I was trying to help resolve the fate of the goniale—in vain. It was a wholesome experience.) The reptilian jaw articulation is now the malleus/incus interface. (The reptilian columella almost certainly homologizes with the stapes; this was in contact with the quadrate, so that even in the therapsids the columella-quadrate-articulare may have served otic function before secession from the jaw mechanism.) The distal mandibular element—the dentary—developed a new articulation with the squamosal; the masticatory muscles—innervated by the motor component of the V cranial nerve—shifted insertions and the vectors of the jaw closure acquired new axes. (The VIII and VII cranial nerves together innervate one of the primal somites—that of the hyoid arch system; the malleus and incus belong to the mandibular arch system.)[4]

I fail to see any advantage, in adult life, to all this remodeling of the jaws, but that may be only my ignorance. At the same time, the VII nerve and its superficial muscular lamina have extended their territory, and have overridden that of the V nerve, until they extend well forward of the territory of the masticatory muscles, and close down about the rostral portion of the snout. And this rather startling peculiarity forms the main suctorial feature of the infant mammal, and actually has very little primary utility subsequently. Perhaps this

---

[4]The gill-arch system begins its anisometric transformations among the pre-Selachians; the most drastic changes are those effected by the amphibians; the mammalian, however, is a *Weiterbildung* which began in primitive reptiles; it was not performed by the pre-avians.

is at first a little hard to believe—we are so used to the impression that either an organ is sloughed off when it is outgrown, as the extra-embryonic membranes, or else, if it survives, its utility is vindicated in the adult. The notion of an apparatus developed in connection with a temporary function of early postnatal life that survives the period of that *ad hoc* usefulness, may not seem quite entertainable. Yet it is this insertion of a transitory life mode—lactation—between gestation and nutritional autonomy, that is the improbable process; and an *ad hoc* suctorial apparatus is no more anomalous than an *ad hoc* mammary apparatus. Both of them survive their primary functions and acquire a tissue of secondary functions or significance whose persistence does not depend upon the exercise of the primary function.

Was the facial nerve enlarging its province while the middle ear was forming? An involved anatomical argument could, I believe, make this probable. There is also an oblique indication that this must have been so. The mammalian basic dental morphology is that of incisors, canines, and molars, and this is established fairly early in the therapsids —before the jaw elements are sloughed off. What is more significant is that the earliest truly mammalian jaws also have the single-row dental arcade instead of the less formalized reptilian pattern, and this implies formalization of the reptilian deciduous property into that of the impermanent-permanent succession which is a property of the mammals. At all events, delay in tooth eruption goes with injection of the lactation complex into the ontogenetic course; and this is an instance of paedomorphosis.

In the eutherian mammals, the facial sphincter sheet has undergone the further individuation into the mimetic muscles; and such refinement inevitably has for its behavioral concomitant some further functional exercise. Beyond this point, we can only guess; yet some guessing may be interesting. The early-Tertiary mammals had neopallia well beyond the reptilian but still very far inferior to those of the later Tertiary; yet their skull shapes are congenial to mimetic muscle reconstructions. In modern mammals, mimetic muscles are used for communication. Perhaps in phylogenetic course, this was the next general function to which these muscles were put. Their development is most versatile in the higher primates—the suborder Simia; the superlative instance being *Homo*. This is not all. The primate mandible is fused into one arch; the upper lips are also fused, completing the orbicularis oris. In those mammalian orders where the lips are thus sutured, they are protusible: e.g., perissodactyls, edentates, as well as primates. Additionally, the primate muzzle has retreated, and the lips are long; they can be erected outward, in deviant plane from the surface of the bone over which they are draped. Monkeys, apes and man can purse and can kiss—and they do. May I further suggest—*obiter*—that we have just reviewed incidentally some antecedents and prerequisites for the articulatory end of speech.

III

The Evolution of Vertebrate Parentalism

We are now, so to say, about to put the complex to work; and a summary sketch of the evolution of parentalism in the vertebrates will help.

1. *Agnatha*   The male chooses a nest site, prepares it, induces the female to lay eggs in the nest, then milts. Both parents abandon the clutch. The youngsters, on hatching, collect into an age-peer group, by coalescence of the sibling groups.

2. *Teleosts*   There is behavioral variety with taxonomic diversification; but at least frequently the male chooses nest site, builds the nest, induces the female to lay eggs, then milts; but now he may remain to protect, and also to fan the water about the eggs. The hatchlings orient to him and he shepherds them. There is some biparentalism, and occasionally female parentalism alone. Age-peer groups form up essentially as in the Agnatha.

3. *Amphibians*   A great variety of nesting, courting, mating procedures; yet essentially all the preceding features occur, but shaped to the amphibian anatomy.

In both fishes and amphibians we see a primitive familialism injected into, or elaborated upon, hatchling-to-age-peer sequence. Which means that we already have, in an epiphenomenal way, the principle in operation which at a later phyletic stage interjects the lactation complex.

4. *Reptiles*   By a pragmatic definition, reptiles are those vertebrates who succeeded in transferring the reproductive phase of the biogram onto the land, thus completing the terrestrialization begun by the Amphibia, who had so transferred the nonreproductive phase. Now, among aquatic vertebrates there is scattering occurrence of the male treating the female as a nest—which she is, in a peripatetic way. But this internal fertilization is an indispensible prerequisite for carrying out reproduction on the land. In the nature of the case, now, whether oviparous or viviparous, the female has the "inside track" for parental

caring. She builds her nest, apparently, under stimulus of the incubation within her. She tends the laid eggs. The hatchlings orient to her.

5. The parentalism of *birds* is basically very much that of oviparous
reptiles who care for eggs and brood. Yet strikingly, among the more
primitive orders it again is the male who is the only or at least the
principal caretaker. The most evolved orders practice biparentalism;
exclusively maternal parentalism is rather exceptional. But to the reptilian base birds have added active feeding of the young by the parent,
and a "training" of the young. From fishes to reptiles we encounter
"elementary" familialism; in birds we have "complete" familialism.

6. Among the *placental mammals,* the definition of family is
mother-plus-offspring. We must forgo at this time accounting for the
male nonparticipation. To the bird parents' active feeding of their
nestlings, the mammals can counterpose lactation. But whereas feeding nestlings entails a very heavy behavior burden, in lactation physiology removes much of the burden from behavior.

Mammals, like birds, have evolved "training" of the young.

One fact has great portent for subsequent development of the
young. From fishes to mammals and birds, the brood diminishes
drastically in number of individuals, until in the Simia it is commonly
down to one. Among fishes, the socialization of the age-peer group
begins with the numerous group siblings—although the genetic relationship has no social significance. Among the Simia, age-peer group
socialization can begin only when the youngster begins to deorient
from parent. The simian parent (monkey, ape, human) may of course
be bonded with several youngsters at one time; but they are not of
the same age, so that we have but a quasi-age-peer group among the
siblings. This, however, is partially effective: Contrast the capacity for
social adjustment to age peers of the only child and the large-family
child.

Parentalism As Ecology

Let me now stress some points of theory:

1. *Adaptive radiation* represents the way in which the *adult* vertebrates have taken advantage of environmental-ecological diversity. To
this obverse there is a reverse:

Evolution of parentalism presents a congeries of devices that en-
sures ever more and more to the period of the vertebrate individual's
immaturity an environment having a minimum randomness; for the
organism's adaptive range is still narrow and undifferentiated.

And correspondingly;

2. Vertebrate ontogenesis begins (as, for that matter, does that of every other animal) as a sheerly physiological relationship with a very undisturbed environment; introduced at some later graduation are psychological modalities; commensurately, physiological modalities become less immediately related to the environment. The organism *graduates* its encounter with vicissitude.

3. The lactation complex is injected, ontogenetically and phylogenetically, into this adaptive continuum.

Paedomorphosis occurs widely in nature, as organismal adaptation to natural environment. Now we have a parental organism promoting it in offspring. And it is a tissue of psychophysiological interplay.

Again let us delve down among the reptiles.

Reptilian Maternalism

Alligator Almost three decades ago, E. A. McIlhenny (1935) produced a very competent naturalist's description of the alligator's life history.

During the period of incubation, there was no material added to the nest, but on days when it did not rain, the old alligator would crawl over the top of the nest and liberally wet it by voiding water through her vent. . . . On very hot, dry days the wetting was done twice a day. After a hard rain she would crawl on top of the nest and drag her body over it, thus slicking the surface. Towards the end of the eighth week . . . I could plainly hear the young ones grunting in the nest, and knew they must be hatching, but as the mother had not opened the nest, I did not disturb it. . . . I knew the young would not come out of the nest until she had removed the top six or eight inches. . . . The old one, after crawling a couple of times around her nest . . . went back to the water at the end of the path, keeping in sight of the nest. . . . When the young begin hatching, they make the fact known to their mother by a shrill, grunting sound. The old alligator then removes with her mouth the packed-down material covering the hatching little ones, so that they crawl out of the nest and join her.

Later on he says:

. . . The old alligator was crawling around the nest making low grunts, sounding very much like a large pig, and the young could be heard answering. She slowly went down her path to the water grunting every little while. On reaching the water, she turned keeping her head on land towards the nest, but with most of her body in the water. At 11:30 the first of the young pushed through the loose top covering and it was quickly followed by the others; all of them ran in a most lively way to the mother who kept her position and continued to grunt. Her little ones took to the water alongside her and she slowly backed out of sight into the rushes with them on each side following.

McIlhenny fed the mother raw meat every few days; she would come for it but she never brought her young with her. One month after the hatching, he sought out her lair. She was sunning herself with her youngsters. "She gave a few low grunts and all the young ones slid off the banks and disappeared under water." "The young after hatching stay with their mother until the next spring."

An Oviparous Lizard   Some oviparous lizards merely deposit their eggs in an appropriate dugout; others tend them, giving behavioral complementation to the nest's ecological inadequacies. In this case they may turn them over regularly and lick them clean. Llewellyn Evans (1959) states that Halver (1931) found that if the eggs of a non-tending *Lacerta* be turned over, the vascular system of the embryo risks injury. If the eggs of the tending *Eumeces* not be turned over, there is a high mortality rate (Fitch, 1954). Note in each case the nature of the maternal and offspring adaptations. The egg-tending lizard, by the way, also voids water over the nest on hot, dry days.

Evans (1959) has recorded a motion picture study of maternal behavior of the lizard, *Eumeces obsoletus,* and these items are selected from the companion article:

As hatching sets on, the mother passes from egg to egg repeatedly. As the youngster breaks the shell, she applies pressure to him with her head, body, or feet; rolls or rubs him so that with each stimulation he struggles farther out of his membrane envelope. She moves about, nosing the empty shells also. The whole process takes but minutes. For a number of days thereafter, Evans' mother lizard continued to lick her youngsters, particularly their cloacae. He customarily fed her mealworms and beef liver. Before the hatchlings, she had snapped them up immediately. With the youngsters moving about her, even though she had opened her jaws to snap, if one of them seized at the morsel she merely closed her jaws and permitted the robbery. The interruption and change of response was instantaneous.

An Ovoviviparous Lizard   R. B. Cowles (1944) has reported parturition in an ovoviviparous lizard thus:

The actual expulsion of the fetus requires about one minute from its first appearance until separation from the parents. . . . Prior to birth the female appears somewhat more restive than normal. This period of unrest may begin some twenty or twenty-five minutes prior to giving birth to the young, and involves many backward movements and a licking of the mouth, and also of the spectacle of the eye. . . . The first reliable symptom of parturition "birth pains" appears to be an elevation of the femora to a nearly vertical position, so that they assume a marked "V" posture. This elevation of the legs may be repeated several times, and probably indicates the stretching of the pelvic and associated muscles. Just prior to birth the legs are maintained in this position for as much as three minutes, but they are lowered just before the expulsive movements become evident.

During actual birth the legs are returned to the normal position and support the body and vent well above the ground. As this time the body of the parent is strongly flexed, so that the snout almost touches the vent. In this position the fetus, with its enveloping membrane, is partially protruded. When the membranes appear the mother grasps the fetal envelope in her teeth and rips it open. This action seems to activate the young. In any event, the violent struggles that follow release the tail and hind legs of the fetus. The young are extruded tail, or rather breech, foremost, and back down. Thus the aimless grasping movements of the hind limbs and the thrashing of the tail result in engaging these members about the base of the parent's tail. If the young pauses in its struggle, the mother may, and usually does, nip the young on the exposed flank and leg. This appears to act as a stimulant and the young thrash violently and by their contortions extricate themselves from the parental cloaca. As they touch the ground they right themselves and run to a distance of two or three inches.

Since the young leave the fetal membranes within the cloaca, these must be extracted; the parent grasps the protruding membranes in her mouth, gradually draws them out and swallows them. After removing the egg case and its contained liquids, she licks up any droplets of fluid that may have fallen to the ground, and resumes a normal position. This entire procedure from the moment the fetal membranes appear at the opening of the cloaca and all visible traces of birth have been removed, requires about two minutes.

Notes in Comment on Parentalism As Ecology   1. All this is carried through by a CNS lacking the mammalian neopallial cerebral hemispheres.

2. A principle of wide application among vertebrates is illustrated: psychophysiological complementation. Surveying vertebrate phylogeny, one has the impression, so to speak, of physiology and psychology relieving each other of burdens (or, if you prefer, of "passing the buck" to each other!). Let me illustrate this principle further:

Shallow water fishes build nests and deposit their germ cells in them. The deep sea fishes are believed to have been derived from shallow water forms. The nest-building syndrome is suppressed, male courting culminates in his treating the female as a nest, and the male incubating vigil has no outlet. Incubation may be prolonged to a viviparity; whereupon the hatchlings orient to that nearest big, moving thing—their mother. (The most bizarre instance of this, is that of the sea horse: The male induces the female to lay her eggs in *his* portable nest, a sort of marsupium; so that *he* tends the clutch.)

Various toads, male or female, develop pouches in their dorsal integument, from which the hatchlings emerge. (The terrestrialization of the nonreproductive biogram phase but not the reproductive one, by the amphibians, is underlined by the Brazilian tree frogs. The father tends his tadpoles; then, when they have reached the appropriate stage of maturation, he picks them up and transports them overland to the place where they will live thereafter—until they too are ready to return to the breeding territory for the reproductive phase.)

The mammals will illustrate the principle further. Here the female has transferred to pure physiology all the egg-tending behavior of her earliest reptilian ancestress (or, rather, her therapsid ancestresses probably did it for her, should our earlier speculation be valid—that the therapsids were placentals.)

There is a corollary. From nature observations and from hormonal experimentation, the behavioral repertoire of the species has been found to reside in the CNS, irrespective of sex. Consequently, we discover that over the vertebrate phylum a behavior segment can be taken over by one sex and correspondingly retired in the other—or be activated in both sexes; in which cases there very frequently develop mutual complementations—a kind of "teamwork." There seems to be no vertebrate species that does not express sex complementation.

The corollary has yet wider application. Species possess latent behavior reserves that would never be discovered under normal life-circumstance. Of course, the laboratory psychologists could not function were this not so; but it has other instancing. As when, for instance, a turkey cock can be induced to incubate eggs; or a toad, placed in an inescapably fluid environment "reverting" to a frog-like behavior, and coming to prefer it. However, this aspect must be set aside, once its relevance to our subject is recognized. And:

3. Starting with oviparity, the embryo constructs out of its own body tissue *ad hoc* organs, unfortunately termed "extra-embryonic" membranes, which mediate it with the environment. Its protection is an artifact supplied in one way or another by the parent (compare the Anamniota and the Amniota).

With ovoviviparity, the parent provides complementarily mechanical protection by way of its own body, and physiologically provides for gas exchange and water conservation. Excretion is no great problem.

With placement, all these "luxuries" are maintained; but now the embryo's "extra-embryonic" organs interreact with the mother-environment. The parent supplies nutrients on a demand basis, instead of one packaged provisioning at the outset; and there is also "excretory service."

The overlay, or interjection, of the lactation complex continues by sequel the biochemical bond in its metabolic aspect. But it enlists voluntary innervation and muscle tonus, which absolutely requires a behavioral mutualism of mother and infant. Here are the anlagen of "training."

And to this principle also there is a corollary. In ontogenesis behavior and somatic readiness are not perfectly synchronized; one may be viable before the other; one may extinguish before the other; in phylogenesis the organization of the one may survive the disappearance of the other. Consider:

Penguin males fight chest to chest, flailing each other appallingly with their flipper-wings. Immature penguins adopt the stance, and flail away with flippers still too short to reach. Under provocation, penguins have been seen to execute incipient and ineffectual flight movements. Physiological sex viability may be attained without its prompting copulation, in a variety of animals; *per contra*—sex hormone injection into sexual immatures can elicit from the CNS the full-dress behavior.

Eventual extinction of actual lactation process does not necessarily entail extinction of a whole mass of behavior that was mobilized about it. Survivals of such ingredients from an earlier ontogenetic state into a later one I have termed "reverberances."

Evolution of the Mammae

We are at last in position to discuss the mammae.

It is a familiar thing that they are a local *Weiterbildung* from the sebum-hair-sweat histomorphology, and that their innervation is thoracic-sympathetic. We can afford to forgo further review of this. In the stem mammals, perhaps they were functional in both sexes; and this would invite speculation as to the respective parent roles in those ancestors, and also on the lactogen problem.

Now, what is their function/meaning in the mother/infant mutualism?

Mention has been made of the fact that the marsupial mother possesses compressores mammae as part of her muscular integument, so that she actively cooperates in the transfer of milk. The marsupial neonate is, by comparison with placentals, the least developed and most premature of all the infants of the mammalian class; so that the maternal behavior complements or compensates for the fetal structural and functional inadequacy to meet its environment. (And I cannot resist temptation to suggest, in keeping with some previous remarks, that although in the placentals the compressor mammae is gone, the urge or impulse to use it may have survived—even in man. At least there is the negative case of cows *withholding* milk delivery under emotional disturbance.)

We come now to the most striking aspect of the complex. There is no anatomical relevance between pharyngeal-pouch derivatives—the suctorial apparatus—and the thoracic integument elaboration—the mammae. Not merely in their developments respectively from un-related bodily structures, but in their respective innervations from the CNS and the autonomic chain. For their activations are asynchronic in any one individual but synchronic cross-individually, the two (con-specific) individuals being at diametrically different developmental stages of their biograms. Yet it is unimaginable how the one feature could have evolved without the other. Of one thing about this very peculiar situation we may be sure: The whole complex evolved during the process and course whereby a zygote-as-organism and its harbor-ing (maternal) organism cooperated in an effort to achieve an eventual independence of each other. We have here a case of *dyadic* or *geminal* evolution, a *socioanatomic* or—better—a *sociomorphologic* evolution.

We are familiar with the principle among some of the orders of insects: to some extent among the Coleoptera, but more thoroughly among Isoptera and Hymenoptera. That is to say, we are well ac-quainted with the phenomena in a descriptive way—including physio-logical and biochemical factors—but we still do not possess a plausible explanation for the causative mechanisms in their phylogenesis. Verte-brates, on the other hand, clearly are constructed on very different lines; the only sociomorphologic specialization that comes readily to hand is that of sex dimorphism. But as for reciprocations between morphologic structuring and behavioral structuring (such as have been hinted at in this essay)—if there exist any serious studies of such, with inductions that lead to a deductive hypothesis, I am unacquainted with them. For instance: the properties of the embryonic vascular system in *Lacerta* species, which are complemented by the maternal behavior in turning them over periodically or neglecting to do so. Nature is replete with such cases. And we can rationalize them by stating that they have survival value, which of course is no explanation at all. Biological science simply has not come to grips with the phenomena of geminal evolution and of psychophysiological complementation as a problem of phylogenesis.

However, these remarks are becoming digressive; albeit, I believe, the digression is desirable and even necessary. The holistic approach bases on the premise that in phylogenesis it is not traits that evolve but systems that make novel adjustments.

And now we are done with the anatomic base of our account. Henceforth, we are concerned with behavior. We can advance with the better assurance, because we have recognized that behavioral accounts which are not backed by biological relata are by that much insecure.

Mammalian Mother/Offspring Mutualism: Parturitive and Postpartum

Directly, I shall sketch a tolerable minimum of items in the maternal/offspring relations of goats, at the time when they are established postpartum; preliminarily, a note about *"Prägung"* or "imprinting."

From experiments on fishes, mammals, birds—especially birds—it appears that the young emerges triggered to attach itself dependently upon whatever object satisfies its immediate need. (Note that we are leaving "need" undefined at this time.) Duration of "openmindedness" (forgive my using this word!) varies with animal kind—from but a few seconds (in some birds) to some longer period; but once that period is over, the question is closed: The deprived infant will remain a psychic orphan (this term again is mine, for good or ill)—he may become deflected upon a surrogate from the normal object of attachment: He has much of his further social development predetermined accordingly. For he is unalterably "trapped" (now I am using Harlow's term) by a foster, surrogate, or real parent. This, roughly stated, is a *"Prägung"* or "imprinting."

What external stimuli effect this orientation and closed attachment? This, clearly, depends first of all on what kinds of receptivity the animal has in viable form at the time that the process can occur. Vertebrates notably operate on a basis of cue redundancy; visual, tactile, olfactory, acoustic stimuli are variously prepotent, according to the developmental pattern of the particular genus or species in question. Thus, a large, moving object close by is cue to, say, a neonate artiodactyl, whose vision is already active; an oppossum or a monkey clings to an immediately available large, soft, rough surface. Infant calls and appropriate call responses characterize at least some of the Bovidae. (It seems to me that they occur among artiodactyls that live as a herd, but do not occur among those who tend to be solitary—as, for instance, a deer—at time of birth.) By way of neurophysiological parenthesis—the various kinds of stimuli all seem to be equally capable of activating the limbic system: We cannot, therefore, expect to account for these differences in effective stimulus by localizing them in the limbic system.

A corollary of the *Prägung* modality is *"Dressur"*—"training." In the normal parent/offspring relationship, the parent supplies appropriate stimuli which elicit expression of now viable innate capability. For instance, parent birds urging their fledglings to try flight; a chimpanzee mother coaxing her infant to locomote. I would like to include the rather rapid change in the human infant who, sometime after its eighth month, passes from phasic idiocy to phasic attempt.

I would now invite your consideration of certain details of mother/ neonate relationship of goats, and then to certain features in the behavior of infant rhesus. This arbitrary selection of subjects derives from the systematic investigations being carried on by Helen Blauvelt[5] at the Cornell University Behavior Farm Laboratory, and the experiments of Harry Harlow and associates in the Psychology Department of the University of Wisconsin.

Goats Immediately upon delivery, the mother goat ordinarily turns to lick the kid—she sees, smells, feels, tastes it. She bleats in response to the kid's bleating; her bleating stimulates the kid to bleat. The kid struggles to her—the specific or prepotent stimulus being, apparently, vaguely her size and proximity. It nibbles along, wagging its tail, and eventually finds the mother's teat. She meanwhile responds to its activity by licking along its body; so that when at last it reaches the teat, she is licking its anal region; and this holds the kid in place. If this process of effecting the mutual lock-and-key pattern is interrupted, the animals have to start over again and run through the program.

This raises several speculative points. The licking may stimulate the respiratory center; the anal licking may stimulate the suctorial instinct (a point that should interest the psychoanalysts) and reminds us of the lizard.

What happens if the mother does not have the opportunity to lick her kid immediately after birth? The answer of experiment at Cornell is that even with a separation of but a few minutes, when reunited

[5]These authors have read and published extensively. I am indebted to their papers, but it is not practicable to include herewith extensive bibliographies. See, for instance, Blauvelt (1954), 1955; Harlow, 1960.

with her offspring she treats it as a stranger. Conversely, in the absence of a mother, the newborn kid still orients toward some large,
stationary object, such as a retaining wall. This, I think, is well worth
noting, in view of the many striking cases of analogous kind which
the ethologists have recorded in birds (and also fishes); and it will
come home shortly, when we consider Harlow's monkeys.

An additional observation: In a group of advanced-gravid goats,
the rhythmic cries of any newborn kid will elicit bleating responses
from the rest. Yet ordinarily, a nursing mother will not permit strange
kids to suck her.

Space does not allow a fuller treatment of other very striking facts
which experiments in deprivation have brought out at Cornell; yet
one more item must be registered. Twenty-four mother goats were
immediately separated from their newborn kids for an hour. This
disturbed and delayed mutual adjustment, which, however, was eventually accomplished. Yet, "2 months later these mothers were observed to nurse their own kids less and alien kids more" than was the
case with a group of controls. And somewhere in this whole treatment
I must add that, while there has been no room anywhere to indicate
that "mother" and "young" are at best but statistical norms in these
behavior phenomena, and that each term encompasses individuals
as so many variables, the fact of this matter remains in the back of
the mind. Other interesting variables are those of circumstance: e.g.,
the rare birth of twins, the yet rarer of triplets; and the strategic
situation wherein a mother may be induced to adopt an orphan.

Rhesus Harlow exploits a combination of techniques from the behavior laboratory and the ethologist's situations. His base of departure
is a pair of mother substitutes—two cylindrical wire frames, one
covered with terry cloth, the other equipped with nipples and milk.
The value difference to the infant is always consistently significant:
He visits the nipples when hungry, but spends much time cuddling
upon the terry cloth. When suddenly terrorized it is to the terry cloth
that he scampers and cuddles; a few moments later, using "her" as a
point d'appui he sallies quite boldly to the frightening effigy, in-
vestigates it with mouth as well as hands, and tears it to pieces. When
not hungry, he may hug the terry cloth and suck a finger.

Two infants placed together and brought up without a mother will
hug each other intensely; the bond continues powerfully, apparently
is self-reinforcing; at the age when youngsters normally are ready
for mutual, social advances, these are unresponsive—they are social
idiots. In field experiments, if the mother is removed, twins will cling

to each other; when she returns, they break apart and seek her. In Harlow's laboratory, if the terry cloth was taken away (for laundering), the youngster immediately fell into a strong anxiety state.

A striking thing developed as these youngsters advanced toward sex maturity. They did not respond to sex overtures from socially normal monkeys.

Interesting and significant in many ways as Harlow's ingenious experiments are—and I fully appreciate them—to the naturalistically minded student, one to whom the ethologist's ideal is congenial, the experimenters seem but to delude themselves that they are holding a maximum of variables constant while allowing a minimum possible number to vary. What really has happened is that most of the relevant situation has been destroyed, not held constant; so that the free variables have, figuratively speaking, a paraplegic quality about them.

For the surrogate mothers are inert. They initiate nothing, they do not alternate encouragements and restraints. Never is the youngster clasped, never is he carried about suspended under her torso by his own hands. She does not stimulate his proprioceptive needs; her body does not "give" with his changes of posture. Very importantly, there is no exchange of noises—even on the first day of life, the infant puckers his lips to vocalize, but this receives no reinforcement from a maternal response; by-and-by he ceases—which is what happens with the kid under analogous circumstances. The experiments seem to have been devised in disregard of cue redundancy. Much more, in fact, is happening or failing to happen than what the bare surface of the experiment shows cognizance of. It were an injustice not to add that Harlow would readily admit this; he could with justice respond "que faire?" The fact, nevertheless, is that no one has yet devised a scheme whereby the whole situation can be retained yet held constant while permitting but one factor to vary. No wonder that nature's time bomb revealed, later on, the accumulative deficit. Apparently unintentionally, Harlow had demonstrated that satisfying the merely physiological needs of food and warmth of an infant is not enough.

And the fact that a newborn opossum, kid, calf, foal, kitten, puppy very quickly explore for a teat still does not prove at all that hunger is its first need or urge. No mammal ingests—no neonate sucks—unless it is first secure. This is demonstrable in natural situations and experimentally. In those mammals whose infants cling, attachment to nipple is sought and maintained even when there is no lactation-sucking. And even after being weaned, the rhesus youngster scrambles to the nipple if disturbed; if all that has been said, beginning with the alligator, is valid indication, the newly emerged immediately seeks a new point of reference in exchange for what has just been lost. This condition seems implicit, even when it is not realized, in the studies of "territorialism" of adult vertebrates. From the viewpoint of the present study, "territorialism" is one form of the organization of this more basic and primal urge to a point of reference as it works out in the matured individual.

And finally, it is unjustifiable to assume that even milk ingestion is but a satisfaction of a physiological deficit. Food ingestion may indeed also be a way of promoting the sense of security. In the newborn, sense of security may well come from an ectodermal and an endodermal stimulation together. Here we do well to recall Coghill's words about individuation out of undifferentiated patterns in ontogeny. Even in adult humans—may not effect of security from food ingestion continue to obtain?

Orality as a Case of Paedomorphosis

At the outset of this section, let me stress that by "orality" I have no particular psychoanalytic interpretation in mind. The oral zone definitely is investigative at least in members of the reptile, bird, and mammal classes; but birds with their beaks certainly have traveled very far away from mammals with their cartilaginous noses (itself a paedomorphism) and muscular lips—in fact, at this point the birds seem to me much less reptilian than the mammals are—whose noses and tongues are also investigative (in varying pattern and degree, by orders). I am quite convinced that oral investigation has a complex mass of affective connotations; at all events, the psychoanalysts have put the finger upon a very profound and involved matter. But I have no desire to bring forward any elaborated theory that outruns the kind of facts that this paper offers.

A mother lizard nuzzles her new hatchling. Quite probably this has an olfactive modality; but we cannot ignore the possibility that it also involves a tactile sensivity in the premaxillary skin. The *motivation* therefor, and its satisfaction, are of course beyond our ken. That it stimulates the hatchling and promotes the incipient mother/offspring bond is entirely reasonable to suppose.

This does not entirely cover the situation. In reptiles the tongue also is investigative; in fact, its operation in the lizard is interlarded with the nuzzling. As in mammals and birds, the intrinsic and extrinsic tongue is built up of anlagen innervated by the post-hypophyseal (the deuteroencephalic) cranial nerves: V, VII, IX, X, XI, XII.

The premaxillary integument of the mammal assumably is basically homologous with the reptilian; and certainly mammals nuzzle in no essential way distinguishable from that of the lizard. But under that dermis the mammals have extended a sheet of musculature innervated by the facial nerve; in the monotremes, as already noted, this is clearly part of the sheet that covers the entire trunk; and posterior to the facial-nerve spread, postcranial nerves take over. Here, then, is an obvious muscular continuum; its evolutionary origination may indeed represent a homoiothermal mechanism unit. But the nuclei of the VII cranial and the spinal nerves remain situated in different parts of the CNS; surely this has significance in the further differential evolution of the use of facial and postcranial integumentary muscle.

Speculatively, perhaps this *Weiterbildung* which is part of the mammals' definition may already have been appearing in the therapsids of the Permian-Triassic periods—contemporaneously, that is, with the conversion of the angulare-articulare-quadrate into tympanic ring-malleus-incus and the fixating of the mammal-like dentition formula. Now, while we are not ready to admit that with respect to absence of placentation the monotremes represent the transition from reptiles to mammals, it is not in fact an arbitrary loading of the dice to estimate that with regard to the integumentary muscle sheet, the monotremes probably do reflect the primal therapsid-to-mammal homoiothermal evolution. So, on the ventral surface of the body, in both males and females, there is a bare area where the edges of the integumentary muscle sheet fail to meet and decussate and the mammary glands develop; and there is sphincteric action of the sheet in the facial region under activation by the VII cranial nerve; and a separate sphincteric action of the circummammary region of the sheet (the sphincter mammae) under activation by thoracic sympathetic nerves.[6] Each of these is normally stimulated to action by mutual contact of the respective anatomical regions. This is diagnostically mammalian.

This piece of orality is inserted into the pattern already extant in the reptiles, and we must consider it a case of neoteny, like extra-embryonic membranes in their turn; an *ad hoc* adaptive mechanism produced by the larval stage of the organism and unrepresented in any ancestral adult form.

The organism is free to discard its "extra-embryonic" membranes when there is changeover from an enclosed, "manufactured" environment to the unenclosed, "raw" world; but in the case of a neoteny that functions only *after* introduction to this raw world, it is irrevoc-

[6]Perhaps there is significance for the mother/infant suctorial complex to be read out of the fact that any autonomic outflow of a VII cranial is parasympathetic while that of a thoracic is orthosympathetic.

ably too late to slough it off. The problem of the growing organism, when at last it is "through" with the mechanism—here, specifically, the suctorial apparatus—is how further to dispose of it.

Meanwhile, the reptilian investigative function of the oral region has not been lost; the suctorial lip-pursing is an adjunct. The primates are one of those mammalian orders, however, who possess a raphe (cf. perissodactyls and edentates). The Simia moreover all have progressed toward muzzle orthognathism (the muzzle of the Cynocephali has developed a secondary protrusion, which does not affect our statement). This combination facilitates a labial protrusive capacity that is unique. In the newborn primate, investigative and suctorial-lactative motivations appear to be undifferentiated—as already pointed out—which is consistent with other embryogenetic generalizations. The investigative strengthens as the infant primate develops reactivity toward the "raw" world; the suctorial-lactative recedes with deorientation from the mother; but it never disappears, and with sex maturation it compounds its intricacy. Kissing is but one form of the oral-sexual exploration found in monkeys, apes, man.

IV. DISMEMBERMENT OF THE COMPLEX

I have used the original, primary function and eventual usage of the facial neuromusculature to hint what may happen in the course of individual mammalian maturation. When the suctorial activity itself is outgrown, the musculature never again has so concentrated, so "single-minded" and vital a role. It differentiates, diversifies its activities, and these are caught up in other patterns; rodents, carnivores, proboscids, perissodactyls, primates exploit it in communication. Primates—with their fused mandible and upper lip—and Proboscidea—with their strange naso-oral extension—use it for exploration; and primates, as we have noted, extend the oral exploratory to include sexual stimulation. But the suctorial capacity will remain latent in primates and perissodactyls, however different be the later occasions for its exercise. And it is not unthinkable that even in those orders who show no occasion for its later use it has but retired in limbo.

The other feature of this matter is that the dismemberment may not be perfectly synchronized in mother and infant; weaning may actually have to be initiated by the mother; at least in man, the lactation impulse may continue in some measure to *reverberate* into adulthood. Whether this occurs in other mammals as well, of course we still have no way of finding out. Yet it is not without significance, perhaps, that there are adult carnivors who accept the offer of a bowl of milk; even though they negotiate it as a liquid surface, like a pool of water. Some monkeys, on the other hand, apply a modified suctorial technique to the routine drinking of water: they slurp it up. And certainly water drinking in both perissodactyls (horses) and artiodactyls (cattle) is a scarcely modified suctorial technique.

From all of the foregoing, is there not the suggestion that maturation does not proceed so much by extinction of activities which are replaced by others, as by dismemberment of patterns and reassignment of their parts to new assemblages? What is seen so concretely in the fate of the suctorial apparatus—may this not transpire also in behavioral syndromes?

May we leave the subject at this point. What transpires during later childhood, during adolescence, yes, during the rest of a lifetime, is "reverberance." The subject now becomes the property of psychoanalysts, genetic psychologists, researchers into mental health. Among these are anthropologists who make cross-cultural comparisons.[7]

Every item in what we have been considering has its human relevance. Nonetheless, not a single element of man's biogrammatic heritage has our remarkable species left unculturized. Obviously, we cannot leave this dimension out of consideration. But neither can this dimension be correctly understood without the insight gained from understanding all of the foregoing—birth, for instance. In many societies, the parturient squats, and gravity is a midwife; the fall seems to shock the fetus into muscle tonus—a thing which happens in other mammals. The recipes for cleaning the infant; for stimulating his orality by blowing into his mouth, etc. Even anal stimulation, to get the fetus to breathe. The conventions surrounding lactation. The contact-access between mother and infant; its disturbance or non-disturbance by other ministrant individuals. Procedures which instigate deprivation, frustration, or do not do so. The circumstances by which weaning is timed—for good or ill.

Thus, whereas in our culture a mother comes to the psychiatrist with guilt disturbances because she does not feel the attachment for her infant that she "ought" to feel, this may conceivably have roots not in her innate capacities, but in her not having participated consciously in its birth, in cleaning it promptly, but in having it presented to her,

[7]It has been encouraging to discover that the views arrived at in the foregoing discussion have so many points of agreement with those presented by Bowlby, 1958. Benedek, 1952 stresses the fact that far too little attention has been devoted to the maternal side of this mutualism. Such neglect could not occur under a holistic contemplation.

done up in unfamiliar wrappings by a stranger. On such a matter, I cannot pretend to any authority, however likely it may seem from extra-human comparisons. But "guilt" reaction is a developed property of personality shaped by a culture—such as ours—in which "guilt" is part of its value structuring; and this is an outcome of the particular culture's history. Every culture has its own patterning of the personality deficit which we vaguely term "inadequacy." There is nothing unreasonable about the notion of guilty sense of inadequacy being a product of deprivation of experience in exercising innate capabilities.

Am I at last in position to be permitted a bystander's observation? You will not take it, I am sure, as a criticism of the procedures followed by the therapists involved, but as a bioanthropologist's mental note about a biological situation.

Mother-and-infant goats are not the only pairs who, if interrupted by an intruder while trying to establish their lock-and-key mutualism, have to start from the beginning or develop permanent pattern deficits. When a woman lands in the psychiatrist's office while her baby goes under observation at the pediatrician's this bystander cannot help thinking that the situation that needs watching is somehow gone; and that a page of biogram—of peculiar ecology—has been torn down the middle and respective halves handed to these two very competent yet dreadfully handicapped rescuers to read.

The cultural involvements of mental as well as physical health are now receiving systematic attention on a scale that reaches out into many diverse cultures. It is an energetic field, anthropologists are participating actively, but the exploitation has no more than begun.

SUMMARY

The notion of "biogram," introduced in earlier issues of *Homo,* has undergone further developments both theoretically and substantively. In this essay, a substantive study is made of a particular segment of the mammalian biogram: the complex set of vectors which defines the reciprocal relationship between maternal parent and offspring peri- or postnatally. The vectors range from anatomical systems to mutual psychological dependence—matters which are well known; yet a holistic view seeks to demonstrate that none of them is adequately intelligible except in terms of the configuration they compose. They could not have evolved from premammalian anlagen except integratively or as a system, not only in terms of what must have taken place within an individual organism, but what took place reciprocally between two organisms: Evolution of maternal mechanisms was concomitant with evolution of corresponding fetal mechanisms: a geminal or dyadic evolution. Biological science has not accustomed itself to giving evolutional accounts in such terms.

The exploration of biogram began as an anthropological problem. But the bulk of research concerns a wider systematic range; it is used as background for studies of man. The mammalian mother/offspring symbiosis has been one of the profoundest agents in the homination process. This is witnessed by persistent effects in shaping "normal" and "abnormal" behavior throughout an individual's lifetime. Implicitly, all cultures come to terms with it adaptively.

But clearly, before this may be discussed, the conversation must first pass back to the disciplines represented here. I have no doubt that in the years just ahead there will be more such conversations, between the biological and the social scientists, the pure explorers, and the therapists both remedial and preventive-constructive.

REFERENCES

Benedek, Th. 1952. "Psychosexual Functions in Women." New York.

Blauvelt, H. 1954, 1955. Dynamics of the mother-newborn relationship in goats. pp. 221–258. In: "Group Processes. Transactions of the First Conference." New York.

Bowlby, J. 1958. The nature of the child's tie to his mother. *Internat. J. Psychoanal.* **39**:350–373.

Bresslau, E. 1920. "The Mammary Apparatus of the Mammalia." London.

Coghill, G. E. 1929a. The early development of behavior in Amblystoma and in Man. *Arch. Neurol. Psychiat.* **21**:989–1009.

————. 1929b. "Anatomy and the Problems of Behavior." Cambridge.

Count, E. W. 1958. The biological basis of human sociality. *Amer. Anthropologist* **60**: 1049–1085.

————. 1958-59. Eine biologische Entwicklungsgeschichte der menschlichen Sozialität. Versuch einer vergleichenden Wirbeltiersoziologie mit besonderer Berücksichtigung des Menschen. *Homo* **9**:129–146; **10**:1–35, 65–92.

————. 1962, 1964. Phasia: On the phylogenesis of speech. A bioanthropological contribution. *Proc. IX Internat. Congr. Linguists, Cambridge.* The Hague.

————. 1964–65. Whence mankind? *The Key Reporter* **30**:(2)2–8.

————. 1966–67. Animal communication and man-science: An essay in perspective. In: "Communicative Behavior in Animals." Bloomington.

Cowles, R. B. 1944. Parturition in the Yuccaa night lizard (*Xanthusia vigilis*). *Copeia* **2**:98–100.

Evans, L. 1959. A motion picture study of the lizard, *Eumeces obsoletus* Baird and Girard. *Copeia* **2**:103–110.

Harlow, H. F. 1960. Affectional behavior in the infant monkey. pp. 307–358. In: "The Central Nervous System and Behavior. Transactions of the Third Conference." New York.

McIlhenny, G. E. 1935. "The Alligator's Life History." Boston.

Weekes, H. C. 1935. A review of placentation among reptiles with particular regard to the function and evolution of the placenta. *Proc. Zool. Soc. London* **42**:625–645.

3 A Note on Incest and the Origins of Human Familialism*

RECAPITULATION OF A THESIS

In earlier papers the concept of the "biogram" has been presented (Count, 1958, 1958/9): The life mode of any animal represents the externalized functionings of its morphology. It is a configuration; it can be grasped systematically. It is taxonomic; it evolves as a feature of a total morphologic evolution.

The inquiry which eventuated in those papers began with an anthropological question: Since man's physical constitution is that of a vertebrate-mammal-primate (pace further taxonomic refinement), should not also his life mode be consistently such, and a reflection of this fact? The inductive answer was a definite yes.[1] The logical consequence should be that man's sociocultural uniquenesses are a configured elaboration within a regular biological fundament. Certainly there never could have been a break in life mode during the period (whatever its length) when the bodies of some primates were being transformed toward humanness (whatever that be).

If the biogram be valid, then it is amenable to treatment as a system, in a technical sense of this term; thereupon, for operational purposes,

*From Homo, XVIII:2, 78–84, 1967.
[1]These essays were abbreviations out of a mass of research which it was purposed to convert into a book.

subsystems may be abstracted, and these reduced in their turn to sub-subsystems. The procedure is arbitrary, but operationally permissible; nonetheless, information is lost wherever interrelations are therewith truncated.

Two particular subsystems have been receiving closer study: (1) the parentalism of vertebrates-mammals-primates-man; (2) the speech function of man ("phasia"). They afford excellent test cases for the biogram concept. *Ad* (1): Parentalism is coeval with the origin of the vertebrates, and hence is a formative participant in their evolution; it has undergone a most striking elaboration during phylogenesis. *Ad* (2): In diametric contrast, "phasia" is unique to man, and an extremely late emergence; yet however elaborated as a part of the homination process, somewhere and somehow its *Anlagen* must reside in man's nonhuman ancestry, and presumably they have counterparts in extant alloprimates (primates other than man).

Both of these lines of development undoubtedly are rooted in the constitution of the central nervous system (CNS)—not to mention any other morphological features; and indeed, if behavior be the externalized functionings of a morphology, then it is feasible and useful to view all behavior as but the presenting symptoms of CNS processes or functioning mechanisms.

INTRODUCING THE TOPIC OF THIS NOTE

An aspect of parentalism, as it becomes elaborated into familialism, has been treated recently (Count, 1967). This note submits another aspect—this time as part of the development which eventuated in the "familialisation of the male" (see 1958, 1958/9). It offers to a wider circle of colleagues a set of matrices which already have been favorably considered by some colleagues and graduate students when in seminar the subject has been that of the origins of the human family.

These matrices represent logical considerations; not a speculation upon the sequence within the process whereby Pliocene-Pleistocene protohominids turned *Homo*. The matrices intend to bring out the status definitions which had to be resolved somehow, in the *Weiterbildung* that eventuated in the humanized primate familialism.

Field work has been supplying science with the details of alloprimate familialism. Human familialism we know. The 1958 and 1958/9 essays suggested the psychological vectors which prompted the attitudes that define incest. But to carry their argument further is a task for psychologists, not anthropologists. (Yet this author had hoped that the suggestions would constitute an invitation to some collaboration between interested anthropologists and psychologists.)

Primates are autoerotic, homosexual, heterosexual; any one individual can be all three. From ape to man (whatever holds for lower primates) the reproductive system has evolved hardly at all; nor indeed has the brain—except for the powerful increase in the capacity of the cerebral hemispheres to process information. Human sexuality, then, relative to that of alloprimates, reflects this vastly more powerful processing capacity interrelating with a not-much-different "visceral" brain and a quasi-identical reproductive mechanism.

Something about the elaboration of brain mechanisms is being said in other essays; here, they would carry us too far afield. But, for the sake of perspective, we should take note that the mammals as a whole have not diversified their reproductive systems remarkably since they at last became a vertebrate class in their own right, while indeed their brains have gone on to remarkable development during the Tertiary period; presumably their behaviors have undergone commensurate elaborations, but we have only fragmentary evidence. Such comparisons are, to be sure, matters of relativity; among the primates —an order remarkably prone to variability—man's reproductive system is, as already said, quasi-identical to that of an alloprimate while his brain power is exceedingly superior.

The quasi-identity of the respective reproductive systems is worth recording, since it is less well realized by nonspecialists. The primate uterus is simplex, piriform, with deciduate placenta and the implicated fact of menstruation; the penis is pendulous, capable of being manipulated. There is one pair of pectorally situated mammae. About the only distinctively human feature are the labia majora, and correspondingly the human perineum lacks the periodic swelling that advertises oestrus in the female alloprimate. These labia are best understood as principally a feature of the adaptive remodeling of the pelvis-perineum in the acquisition of orthogradation; they do not materially alter the sexual pattern itself. On the other hand, the orthogradational remodeling has raised the frequency of ventroventral copulation from its relatively low incidence in alloprimates to its quasi-universality in man.

Summarily, we encounter the all-pervading evolutionary principle of interplay between "conservative" and "progressive" mechanisms. And it is systems, not traits, that evolve, cybernetically. If we realize the force of this truth, we avoid the pitfalls of some pseudoproblems; we do not, for instance, assign the role of cause to some "progressive" features, and to "conservatisms" the position of being material for the former to work upon. And we become receptive to the idea that human familialism evolved in integral association with the organic procedures indicated.

It all becomes more vivid when we realize that autoerotcism, homosexualism, "sexual aberrations" are of mammalian incidence, and not confined to primates, whatever their explanation.[2] However, primates are rather distinctive (although not unique) in that their sex hormones are active the year around; so that their nervous systems are perpetually under these hormonal tonuses; they cannot but behave accordingly.

There is a further and fundamental mammalian consideration. The males possess but one sex orientation: an erotic toward an (adult) female; females possess two: an erotic toward an (adult) male and a broody toward (immature) offspring; and these orientations are constrained to adjust their mutual incompatibilities. The sex differences are hormonal; they do not reside in the respective nervous systems.

It is this kind of animal which eventually evolved the human familial group. The constituent individuals were and are, potentially and/or actually, in varying degrees, successively, simultaneously, heterosexual, homosexual, autoerotic, capable of sexual *bizarreries*. Incest is not an isolated phenomenon or problem, but an aspect of a far wider and more complicated problem or phenomenon.

Whence the rationale of the matrices.

The essays of 1958 and 1959 proposed that the humanization of a primate familialism was effected by:

1. The *Weiterbildung* of "status":

Status is the cohesive of vertebrate sociality in general. In alloprimates, it is already very complex. In man, statuses themselves achieve status; several are held simultaneously, and thereby are liable to generating incompatibilities.

	MS	FS
G_1	M. G_1	F. G_1
G_2	M. G_2	F. G_2

LEGEND:
MS   Male sex
FS   Female sex
G_1 First generation
G_2 Second generation

Formula: $2S \times 2G \rightarrow 4SG$; i. e.,   2 sexes covering 2 generations result in 4 inequivalent individuals

Matrix I

[2]To this writer, about as "bizarre" a case to witness was that of a spayed bitch who seized a small kitten, assumed a straddle and executed "vacuum" pelvic thrusts—the couple being very discrepant in size.

2. The lengthening, durative association of a male sex partner with a female (whom he has unknowingly fecundated), and the consequent pooling of their skills and interests—in measure as these elaborated from protohominid to *Homo*. The essays have termed this the "familialisation of the male." It must nevertheless not escape us that the males of an alloprimate group exercise a general-supervisory role and a "diffuse parentalism," and apply this *ad hoc* to an individual. In other words, the anlagen of a full-blown parentalism exist at the alloprimate level.

	$H(M. G_1)$	$W(F. G_1)$	$B(M. G_2)$	$S(F. G_2)$
$F(M. G_1)$	X			
$M(F. G_1)$		X		
$S(M. G_2)$			X	
$D(F. G_2)$				X

LEGEND:
Horizontal:

H	Husband
W	Wife
B	Brother
S	Sister

Vertical:

F	Father
M	Mother
S	Son
D	Daughter

Formula: $(N_1) \supset (2 N_s)$; i. e., implies twice the number of statuses; a given number of individuals where N_1 is number of individuals, N_s is number of statuses

Matrix II

3. Child-ness becomes a status. It is a derivative status, as will be indicated later.

We must be clear as to what the matrices can and cannot do. They represent logical categories, not sequential evolutionary process. The latter we shall never recover, any more than we ever shall *in re* the emergence of the human speech function ("phasia"). Nevertheless, minimally the statuses of four kinds of individuals have had to become defined: husband-father, wife-mother, son-brother, daughter-sister; they exist, moreover, universally at the *Homo* level, and not at all at the primate level.[3]

Matrix I:

The minimum basic human familialism requires 2 sexes and 2 generations; giving 4 inequivalent individuals.

Matrices II, III:

[3]Except for some anlagen; a pseudo-exception. Mother-son relations persist to some extent in alloprimates. The best documentation of this fact comes from the observations of Dr. Donald S. Sade. In a full-scale account of incest, they could not be left out. But their consideration would not add to the matrix presentation.

This passes to the social dimension. Each individual incorporates two *simultaneous* statuses; each status being a moiety of a dyad. Thus the individuals are

I. Husband-father
II. Wife-mother
III. Son-brother
IV. Daughter-sister

and the dyads are

A. Husband-wife
B. Father-offspring (but two offspring sexes)
C. Mother-offspring (but two offspring sexes)
D. Brother-sister

that is, each moiety defines and is defined by the other. Dyads A and D are isogenerational; dyads B and C are transgenerational. The simultaneous statuses I–IV ("simultaneous" implies that their definitions are not mutually independent and that they occur in the respective cases within one and the same individual) involve an individual in transgenerational transactions. This defines them.

The capacity of human individuals to hold plural statuses simultaneously; the definitions of statuses as social generalizations; the property of human statuses of possessing status in their turn (e.g., "husband" dominates "wife," "son" is subordinate to "father," "husband-father" carries prestige value in public council)—these features can become sources of intrapersonal conflicts, even neuroses. It is a reasonable speculation that, in evolutionary course, the status resolutions indicated in various ways by the cells of the matrices "just grew." At any rate, the sets hint that all the statuses somehow are codes that have become formalized out of groups in which all sexualisms listed earlier were either latent or active.

	M. G_1	F. G_1	M. G_2	F. G_2
M. G_1		H : W	F : S	F : D
F. G_1			M : S	M : D
M. G_2				B : S

LEGEND:

H : W	Husband-wife
F : S	Father-son
F : D	Father-daughter
M : S	Mother-son
M : D	Mother-daughter
B : S	Brother-sister

Formula: $\dfrac{N(N-1)}{2}$

Matrix III

Matrix IV:

This casts the simultaneous statuses I–IV in terms of those possible

sexualisms. The posibilities cover, in 4 inequivalent individuals,
4 autoeroticisms
2. transgenerational homosexualisms
4 heterosexualisms, categorized into
    1 isogenerational, and licit
    2 transgenerational, and illicit
    1 isogenerational, illicit

	H-F	W-M	S-B	D-S
H-F	autoerotic	+	homosexual	—
W-M		autoerotic	—	homosexual
S-B			autoerotic	—
D-S				autoerotic

LEGEND:
H-F	Husband-father
W-M	Wife-mother
S-B	Son-brother
D-S	Daughter-sister

Sociosexual formula: $\dfrac{N^2-N}{2}$ where N = number of individuals

Sexual formula: $\dfrac{N^2+N}{2}$

Matrix IV

Matrix V:
Because Matrix IV neglects isogenerational homosexualisms, two extra heterosexual siblings are added. The cells now have become self-explanatory.

Matrices IV and V state that only one heterosexualism is licit, and it is expected (or even required, in extant societies). It occurs between the only two adults of the group. The licit constraint, then, is itself a feature of ascriptive-achieved status; and, we understand, the status is a paraphrase of social attitude. Now, whether the society be allo-primate or human, it is "managed" by adults. Child-ness (in human society) is a status by reference to adults; part of its definition is nega-tive: Children are incapable of serious sexualism. Incest recognizes a status incongruity.

The psychological constraints outlined in the earlier essays led to the prediction that the weakest incest taboo and the one most fre-quently defied, is the intersibling; while the strongest is that of mother-son. Now, heterosexual play between young children, in ex-tant primitive societies, may be frowned upon by adults, yet also treated indulgently; but tolerated, expected, encouraged among sub-adults of different families while emphatically forbidden between siblings of any age. The matrix analysis does not touch upon the question of why, even after a brother and sister have reached adult status and definition, they still may not cohabit—at any rate, in extant societies. I have no satisfactory explanation to suggest. Against the fact that now they have achieved adult status, I can only counter that human statuses have become durative—once a brother and sister, always a brother and sister.

So much for the heterosexual constraints. Have the homosexual and the autoerotic propensities weighed at all in the definition of human family? They surely continued to occur.

Since autoeroticism is not social, there seems no way that it could have applied directly. With homosexualism, the answer is less easy. Would, for instance, father-son homosexualism compete against husband-wife heterosexualism? At any rate, homosexual taboos lack the stringency that adheres to incest taboos. Evidently homosexualism is not the threat to status definitions which have schematized human familialism.

Anthropologists are very familiar with the cross-cultural variety of attitude patterns toward extrafamilial heterosexualisms along with the quasi-unanimity against incest.[4] And it has long been understood that the strength of a taboo is an index of the strength of the propensity to commit the act that has generated the sanction. Equally interesting is the ambiguity of social attitudes, in a long-range dimension, toward

	H-F	W-M	$(S-B)_1$	$(S-B)_2$	$(D-S)_1$	$(D-S)_2$
H-F	autoerotic	+	homosexual		+	
W-M		autoerotic	+		homosexual	
$(S-B)_1$			autoerotic	homosexual	+	
$(S-B)_2$				autoerotic	+	
$(D-S)_1$					autoerotic	homosexual
$(D-S)_2$						autoerotic

Sociosexual formula: $\dfrac{N^2 - N}{2}$

Sexual formula: $\dfrac{N^2 + N}{2}$

Matrix V

[4]Also, with the rationalizations where incest is or has been indulged or even prescribed, continuously or on some ritual occasion. These cases are proving to be more numerous as information accumulates. But they remain rare.

adultery and fornication, for the attitudes may fluctuate with social changes. Familial structure is very sensitive to social change outside its bounds, and changes accordingly—yet incest taboos hold steady. Under biogrammatic perspective, this is intelligible: The primary group which incorporates familialism has its own particular set of antecedents: The interindividual-intrafamilial tensions are precultural, subcultural, noncultural. Once given the emergence of humanized status and statuses, incest-and-taboo plus encouragement toward extrafamilial discharges of sexuality is the only possible resolution of a dilemma; it is one coin with two sides. Yet the dilemma, like the Devil, is always with us. It seems to me that this statement is more informative than one which recognizes only that the taboo is directed against the strong potential of a certain practice. For the latter way of stating it sees but one side of the resolution. What seems more accurate, is *simultaneous taboo and redirection; together* these measures cope practically with the incompatibility of two statuses in one individual transacting with two statuses simultaneously in another. The existence of this "polyploidy" is recognized by primitives, whether explicitly or in unconscious, unformulated ways. At all events, we need not wait until the day when humanity discovered that a male fecundates a female before we look for the origins of the incest attitude. And perhaps the unconscious, unformulated attitude is vaguely as old as the Australopithecines or the Pithecanthropines.

And this note dares go no farther. The matrices are mechanical and logical; they have no more than a degree of heuristic value. The human relations they process are altogether too earthy, their irrational components are too powerful for man's struggling rationality to adjust to with more than an uneasy success. This tohu-bohu cannot be boxed into a matrix.

SUMMARY

As a certain primate phylum underwent humanization during the later Tertiary and earlier Quaternary, there was a *Weiterbildung* of its status definitions; among them, the "familialization" of the male and "child-ness." Individually, primates are autoerotic, homosexual, heterosexual concurrently. A series of matrices erected on these sociopsychological features indicates that incest definition has resolved practically a logical incompatibility inherent in sexual activity between certain statuses.

BIBLIOGRAPHY

Count, E. W. 1958. The biological basis of human sociality, *Amer. Anthropologist* **60:** 1049–1085.

———. 1958–59. Eine biologische Entwicklungsgeschichte der menschlichen Sozialität. Versuch einer vergleichenden Wirbeltiersoziologie mit besonderer Berücksichtigung des Menschen. *Homo* **9:**129–146; **10:**1–35, 65–92.

———. 1967. The lactation complex. *Homo* **18:**38–54.

4 *Animal Communication in Man-Science*

*An Essay in Perspective**

*From "Approaches to Animal Communication," Thomas A. Sebeok and Alexandra Ramsay, eds. Mouton & Co., The Hague, 1969.

SOME STATEMENTS OF POSITION[1]

Animal Communication: Its Relevance to a Man-Science

To be an animal is to communicate; it is a property of being an animal. Humans are animals. They communicate. How far do the features of animal communication apply to them? What is the humanness of their communication? Man's phyletic ancestry having been non-

The author wishes to thank the Department of Sociology and Anthropology of Tulane University, and particularly Prof. Arden King.
[1]This essay continues the author's research into the problem of the phylogenesis of phasia—the human speech function seen as a neurophysiological process. Phasia was conceptualized as a subsystem of the biogram; its first presentation was at the IX International Congress of Linguists, Cambridge, Mass., 1962. In its turn, biogram, the life mode of an animal kind or of any taxonomic level or category, is taken to be the externalized expression of the organism holistically conceived. The inquiry began, in 1951, as an examination into the processes whereby humanization presumably occurred to (Tertiary-Quaternary) primates. It was constrained to introduce to an anthropological problem the thinking of certain other disciplines, particularly neuropsychology and ethology—both of which were at that time alien territory to anthropologists. The theme was presented to a variety of academic audiences during ensuing years; the first publications appeared in 1958, 1959–9 (see Bibliography). The

human, how did a human communication develop from a nonhuman one?

A man-science must take cognizance of these scientific and philosophical questions of which anthropology has taken but a limited view. The Wenner-Gren symposium on animal communication, and this monograph which has followed from it, move in the direction of an enlarged anthropology. Actually, there are two anthropologies; one biological, the other sociocultural. They share an object of study, but their orientations remain within the biological and social sciences, respectively. The philosophical asumption of biological anthropology is that of any and all other organic sciences which underwent the Darwinian revolution: Man the animal is accounted for as a variant of a more comprehensive norm; his distinctiveness is explained *in continuo* from this base. Sociocultural anthropology did not participate in, nor did it undergo, the revolution (in spite of the fact that all anthropologists assume the operation of organic evolution): Its frame of reference remains the human phenomenon, and all accountings operate within this closed system. In sociocultural anthropology, the discontinuity between the life mode of man and the life modes of other animals is assumed for practical reasons, and the accidents of paleontology reinforce this attitude, since there exist today no super-apes or quasi-humans. Evolution, then, for sociocultural anthropology, acquires an entirely different meaning from that of organic evolution. It now means the cultural elaborations which *Homo sapiens* has undergone since the time when his intelligence capacity reached a plane at which it could be treated as a constant. The semantic non-identity does no harm, as long as the term—"evolution"—is defined in any case, and as long as it is not used in two utterly different senses within the same set of statements. Unfortunately, this stricture is not always observed.

Evolution of culture in the original, organic sense took place as a part of the same transformational process which eventuated in *Homo* from some alloprimate matrix. Both language and culture are axioms of *Homo*. This has been established empirically. Confusion begins when

---

term biogram was coined before the writer had encountered ethogram; it should be rather obvious that the terms are mutually congenial.

The term "speech" is employed herein informally, as it is in the vernacular. "Language" is used if it has been used by others whose material is under discussion. Other neologisms occurring in this essay: Symbolopoesis, the neuropsychological activity which produces symbols. Symbolopoea, a product of this process. The term is used when it is undesirable to attach it to a neurological connotation. Alloprimates, any primates other than man.

one attempts to imagine a *Homo* who, *post facto,* developed language and/or culture. Futility compounds confusion when there is speculation as to whether a tool-using Australopithecine could also have had a (proto-) language.

Linguistics is the most fully developed of the social-anthropological sciences. Operating within the closed system of *Homo sapiens* behavior, it has developed the heuristic schema of phoneme-morpheme-syntax which gives logical structure to the empirical findings from all human speech codes. This indeed suggests something about the mentation of *Homo sapiens*. At the same time it corresponds neither to the ontogenesis, nor to the pathologic disintegrations of speech, and it suggests nothing to speculation about the phylogenesis of speech.

Perhaps the attempt to open up a closed system of anthropology, to search for the anlagen of speech, man's most telling distinction and that which separates him from other vertebrates, could have come only from linguists. If linguists succeed in their exploration, sociocultural anthropology will begin a translation to the plane now occupied by biological science. A conjunction of thought between the two anthropologies is much to be desired.

Hockett and Sebeok have confronted both anthropologists and students of animal behavior with the proposition that the communication systems of animals and men hint at the possession of common aspects; logical features which may or may not be due to similar mechanisms at work (Hockett, 1960); or behavioral segments such as the ethologists identify which may be no more than analogous, or again may have their rationale in some homology (Sebeok, 1962). Hockett seems to say, "Human communication possesses a certain set of logical properties; some of these, likewise, seem to be represented in the communication systems of arthropods, as well as of vertebrates; others do not, and the presence or absence does not appear to be capricious. Can this be verified to a point where we may uncover clues which account for the evolution of human distinctions?" Sebeok seems to say, "Human speech is a pattern of behavior, and behavioral patterns are the study of ethology. Can we effect some synthesis between semeiotics and ethology such that the emergence of human speech may be treated, so to say, as an especially elaborate case of ethologic evolution?" The difference between the two is more a matter of tactics than strategy, since both target upon the same philosophical problem. Both, moreover, show the influence, in different ways, of information theory. We have, indeed, moved far in our philosophy since the sterile days of bowwow, dingdong, poohpooh;

I am inclined to the surmisal that only since the advent of systems theory and holistic approach have we come to possess instruments powerful enough to penetrate the riddle of man's capacity to speak.

The Queries of Animals

That animals communicate is a more basic topic than *how* they do so. On the one hand, communicating is a particular case in the more general category of the transfer of information. On the other, among animals, the modality is a question of what organs have been evolved to handle information, and of the coordination of these organs for communication.

We may say that animals set information in motion because they query their environment. Here we are using query in a sense that includes warnings, challenges, and commands; since, when these effect a change in the behavior of another, the change is reported back to the querier.

Inductively now, we shall distinguish seven situational categories of motion in information.

1. An electric current is passed normal to a surface containing iron filings, and a design is effected. There has been information input. The source of the information is irrelevant; the location of the source is relevant. The iron filings sought no information; their role was passive. To continue the current adds no new information; to withdraw it does not destroy the design. It is not hard to imagine more complicated cases of this general nature.

2. The release of sperm or eggs (by various marine invertebrates) includes release of heterosex cells by a conspecific organism. This case is immeasurably more complex than the preceding. Two very complex probabilistic systems, possessing a common informational code, must simultaneously (or nearly so) be in a state wherein the code operates; that is, they must be in phase. We are now treating the systems themselves as though together they were a code, and separately the moieties of a coupling. Sperm and eggs are not biological identities. Sperm extrusion does not, in the simplest case, induce sperm extrusion from another source; it induces egg extrusion. Here the source of the instruction (the query, the initiating message) is relevant and unique, in the sense that only the conspecific sperm induce ovulation. (That ovulation may be artificially and experimentally induced is beside the point.)

3. A yucca plant opens its flowers at nighttime when the yucca moths are active (The case is borrowed from Frings and Frings, 1964:

3–4). This category resembles 2, but now the two related systems—yucca and moth—are utterly different; their origin is not from a common genetic coding. Rather, there has been a "phylogenetic learning," a systems adaptation of each to the other. There is synchrony, and the information sources are reciprocally relevant.

4. A marine vertebrate or a bat emits sonic energy (a signal). The return is an echo from any object. Here the code is one-sided. The echo surface is unaltered, it does not participate, as in cases 2 and 3. Yet the texture of the surface alters the sonar, and this alteration becomes information when it impinges upon the animal's acoustic organ. The information has ridden the energy alteration and has acquired surprise value. The coding, both in output and input, has been an exclusive property of the querier.

5. The members of a shoal of fish or a flock of migrating geese emit, individually, beeps or honks. Surmisably, there are echoes from the surfaces of the rest of the group, in which case there is resemblance to 4. But undoubtedly the case is more complex. The query may now be a combination of "Keep your distance" and "What is my position?" In case 4, the feedback was confined to the querier; in case 5, the signals result in all individuals involved maintaining an optimum balance of distance and propinquity. This is a cohesive of sociality. It does not appear that one beep or honk comes in response to one particular other.

6. A female locust or frog heads for the source of a male's chirp. She is not emitting a sonic query herself; yet she is in a receptive state whereby her total behavior is a query. The extent of the male's querying is left open to discussion, as in the question of surprise value. The interchange resembles 5, but the very definition of information must now be reconsidered. The two organisms are conspecific (cf. 2 and 5) which, by definition, connotes a code in common. Yet only the male is capable of emitting a sonic message: The female can receive, but she cannot emit it. There is no sonic dialogue. On the part of the male, there probably is a cybernetic behavior. On the part of the female, there is a different cybernetic behavior: She targets upon the source.

We shall term any reciprocating, mutually complementing behavior a dialogue. The ritual which follows the meeting of the male and the female fits the term; what preceded it was a prodromon. A dialogue always is asymmetric; in the present case, the prodromon is extremely so.

7. A male and a female stickleback encounter, and a ritual ensues. A jackass calls; a jenny responds with a call. Both cases resemble con-

siderably case 6. But the approach of the female stickleback began with the migration of females long before they could have received messages from males. Is there a point in the approach when an odor from the males narrows the appetitive upon target? The male's first information of the female is via sight, and the gestalt only later includes an identification of the female as distinct from another male.

In the case of the donkey, while both systems have a set which is prodromal, the targeting is guided from the very outset by a shared call code which both exercise, but asymmetrically. Dialogue begins at a distance: Identification begins there, via sonic information; then sight is drawn in. This does not duplicate the order of the stickleback case. Nor, in the case of the donkey, is the modality sequence confined to but one possibility. The perceptive-cognitive build-up is not dependent upon a stimulus sequence. This does not exhaust the complexities of the several situations.

At times, any gathering of information has been termed a case of communication; so that perhaps all seven situational categories would come under this term. This emphasizes certain obvious common features, neglecting differences. It may have some value, but for us the disadvantages preponderate. Communication *proprement dit* will be confined in this essay to dialogue between conspecifics.

Semeiotics[2]

Animal messages are honest; that is, the information conveys meaning. Signals are ridden by semantic content. The feature analysis of semeion has been done by Sebeok with lucid economy (Sebeok, 1962; Sebeok, 1967). That feature which he appraises as a major, if chaotic, topic context I am inclined to consider the capstone of the whole question of animal communication (Sebeok, 1965:1012; see also Shannon and Weaver, 1949: 117, both on grounds of systems theory, and on grounds of brain mechanism. The writer, elsewhere, has developed the notion of the biogram. To him, communication is one of its skeletal parts. Since the biogram is a holistic notion, he finds himself no longer capable of thinking about information processing by animals other than as a contextual exercise.).

Questions of context compel us to ask those of cue redundance, of fluid definition of noise, of gestalt, in a wider sense than that of stricter definitions. Consider the following illustration from ethology.

[2]The spelling is better etymology than semiotics, and it avoids the ambiguity of semi-. Semi-otics would be nonsense. "Semeiotica," moreover, is the original spelling. See Locke, "An Essay Concerning Human Understanding."

A herring gull nestling pecks at the food in its parent's bill. The red spot on the bill serves to target the behavior; in the absence of the spot the nestling will peck, although less readily or certainly. A female gull solicits sexual attention from her mate by the "please feed me" signal which in chicks has but hunger-sema back of it. The male may or may not "read the message" appropriately; he may respond by feeding her, and she may accept. Other cues added to the pattern may reduce the ambiguity. Yet the sema has not been altered from the original, initial situation of the nestling. What has been added serves as a synonym supplement; it just fills out the message.

There is a curious analogy in the case of a Chinese reading aloud to his fellows from a newspaper. The ideographs are unequivocal; they may be translated into phones which are their exact equivalents. But the Chinese language contains a very large percentage of phones (morphemes) which are loaded with a large repertoire (thesaurus) of utterly unrelated *semata*. Consequently, when the ideographed message is converted into phonic code, the reader inserts by improvisation synonymous morphemes of quite different phonetic composition. This obviously narrows down the choice of interpretation from which the listener must select in order to understand what the ideographs are conveying to the reader. Redundancy, noise, degrees of freedom of choice, context, are not definable exclusively in terms of message-as-sent, but must include message-as-received. Context, in fact, must underlie the psychology of sensory habituation.

If I can read lips, and also can hear you, the movement of your lips is a disturbance to me, a "noise." I must compel myself not to watch your lips. If, however, you are almost or totally inaudible, then commensurately your lip movements convey to me the information via a supplementary modality, as the primary modality loses information value to me. (Occasional selectivity is a known property even among invertebrates.) If you and I are both watching a third person, what to me is noise may be information to you.

"[One aspect of] the whole-parts problem," says Prosser (1965:368), is that "qualitative differences and informational bridges between levels of complexity of organization, have scarcely been approached by information theory."

Information Ecology and the Three Environments

Bartlett (quoted in Bruner, 1957: 346) has spoken of an organism's "effort after meaning." In "Design for a Brain," Ashby (1960) develops a definition of adaptation in terms of maintenance by a (living) system of its essential variables within optimal physiological limits so that it achieves an "ultrastability from having organized its own purpose through a learning process." Wiener (1950; 1954: 38) has appraised this as "one of the great philosophical contributions of the present day."

Ashby shows the trial-and-error procedure of an organism to be a necessity of such a machine, but his appraisal of the procedure is radically different from that made by some psychologists. For the latter, the experimental animal is trying for success; hence a failure is rated zero. Trial-and-error thus is "merely a second-rate way of getting to success" (1960: 83). Whereas it follows from Ashby's hypotheses that the trials are the necessary, and indeed the only possible, method for gathering information indispensable to adaptation.

It seems to me that here is the foundation of an information ecology, in contradistinction to an energetics ecology. The latter is the kind which possesses the name, "ecology": It concerns the ways in which organisms cope with the energies of the physical ambience—whether in exploiting them for metabolic maintenance or in developing protections against them. An energetics ecology expresses the same mentation which conceived economics as the distributional treatment of resources, which normally are scarce relative to demand; an approach consistent with the idea of energy conservation.

But *how* an organism exploits its environment is a problem in *meaning* and a functional description of its own organization. Adaptation has quite another definition under an information ecology, from that under an energetics ecology. Sociality and communication promise more under the former than under the latter.

We can also look at the ecology of a vertebrate organism in terms of the following three environments:

1. The organism queries information from its physical surroundings by means of its sensory receptors. (Cf. situational categories 2, 3, 4.)

2. The organism has an internal environment (a self-environment), mediated informationally by traffic of the autonomic system with the brainstem (particularly, the hypothalamus).

3. The organism's conspecific fellows constitute its social environment. (Cf. situational categories 5, 6, 7.) Since these are obviously located in the same spatial-temporal ambience as itself, necessarily it uses the same sensory modalities as in 1 to cope with this environment. Yet clearly, environment 3 is distinct from environment 1. In 3, there is a shared code, with feedback in both moieties.

In ontogenesis, the organism faces the problem of organizing a space-time from the three environments concurrently; and thereby it achieves an I/not-I orientation. The mediating mechanism is chiefly the CNS. Communication as a capability becomes definitive as a feature of this ontogenetic, maturative process. In this connection, there exist among vertebrates (whatever be the case among invertebrates) morphological complexes which are at once anatomical-physiological-biochemical-psychological requiring that they all be studied as holistic systems. In a separate study, I have examined the lactation complex of mammals wherein an adult (maternal) individual possesses a set of parts and an infant (offspring) individual possesses an utterly irrelevant set, and neither subsystem makes sense except as the complement of the other (Count, 1967). This constitutes a case of geminal evolution, which, to my knowledge, is a phenomenal category that biology has not yet tried to cope with. Sociality, too, is a matter of anatomy.

The Behavioral and the Functional Approach to a Purposeful Mechanism

The information theorist and the communication engineer are free to focus their interest upon the structure of message, the signal, and the efficiency of its transmission. The focal interest of the student of the organism is upon the "machine" (in Ashby's sense) which emits and/ or receives messages. What to the one group of students is instrumental, to the other is final, and vice versa.

But the students of the organism are of two kinds—the students of behavior and the students of the organism, *proprement dit*. Both the behaviorists and the informationists (if the suffering reader will indulge these opportunistic labels) treat the machine as a black box— though for different reasons. The students of organism in the narrower sense are busy prying into the black box. In this essay, they are the neurologists of whatever specialty.

Given any object, relatively abstracted from its surroundings for study, the behavioristic approach consists in the examination of the output of the object and of the relations of this output to the input. . . . [It] omits the specific structure and the intrinsic organization of the object. This omission is fundamental because on it is based the distinction ·between the behavioristic and the alternative functional method of study. In a functional analysis, as opposed to a behavioristic approach, the main goal is the intrinsic organization of the entity studied, its structure and its properties; the relations between the object and the surroundings are relatively incidental. . . . While the behavioristic analysis of machines and living organisms is largely uniform, their functional study reveals deep differences.
(Rosenblueth, Wiener, and Bigelow, 1943:18, 22. Slight rephrasing, without changes of meaning. Hereinafter, RWB).

The contrasts between the constitutions of artifactual and organismal machines—their functional difference—are stated very succinctly by RWB (see their article). If, now, we take only the organism, we find that RWB's principle still holds as between them. The female locust and the female frog, say (see the sixth situation category of information), show a behavioral but not a functional resemblance. To be sure, both operate as colloids, ionically (by contrast with artifactual machines, which operate electronically and as metals); and both exploit the fundamentals of neuron and neuronal circuitry. But arthropod and vertebrate organize these fundamentals in radically different schemata.

Accordingly, we now have a principle. The greater the behavioral resemblances (say, between insects and vertebrates) we may spot, the grosser they are; and therewith the less pertinent are the data from a (comparative) neurophysiology or neuropsychology. That is, behavioral and functional approaches are not congruent. *Per contra,* when we operate at the micro-level where performances of neurons and neuronal circuits again make comparisons between arthropods and vertebrates pertinent, the data from a comparative behavior study vanish from all relevance. By contrast, this does not obtain if the comparisons are between, say, fishes and birds; here, behavioral and neurological "homologies" are a valid subject of discourse, and how the one is related to the other a part of the validity.

This in no wise makes of insect and vertebrate communication two mutually irrelevant subjects—quite the contrary, for reasons which should be clear from all the foregoing. If there is such a thing as a biological discipline at all, then communication of animals is one of its integral facets.

But if we are to consider animal communication a valid topic of discourse, we shall not pass far beyond the merely descriptive stage until we have come to terms with the nonidentities of "analogy" and "homology."

This must be spelled out before we proceed farther. The electrophysiology of insect and vertebrate neurons operates on the same principles. The significance of reverberating circuits to problems of memory and learning has transfer value from the one animal organization to the other. But their respective exploitations of projection and of interconnection design in their arrangements of nervous mechanisms differ. Both an ommatidial eye and a lens-and-retina eye analyze photic frequencies, but the insect eye cannot tell the insect brain what the vertebrate eye tells the vertebrate brain. No more, presumably, would either brain know what to do with the information coming from the eye of the other. Where do the respective semantic loads begin? What, moreover, in neurophysiological terms, *are* the respective semantic loads? Neuron transmission is an activity of relative potential changes in potassium and sodium ions; what is the microphysiology of *semeion*?

But the problem changes some of its character when we are confronted with the hunting or the fleeing behaviors of shark, hawk, lion, and human. Here, the fundamental cytoarchitectonics have recognizable similarities which are accountable only on the basis of phylogeny. Neither logical inference nor such empirical results as are available from histology, electrostimulation, neuropharmacology, would support the notion that from shark to man the information processings have radically altered within homologous structuring. This has no meaning when the comparison is between insect and vertebrate— nonetheless, a hawk possesses a basal ganglion elaborated out of and beyond the anlagen which obtained in the reptilian ancestry of birds; a cat possesses a limbic lobe and a neocortex elaborated out of some other parts of the brain of its infra-mammalian ancestry. Each of these two elaborations performs its respective analyses; however, these do not supplant those of more primitive levels which persist within the total brain. They but carry the analyses into further refinements. In the vertebrate brain, the several evolutional levels continue to play back to each other. This is the way the vertebrates compound their information processings and organize their behavior. It is simply erroneous, and careless science, to speak of a "higher level" as having somehow unsurped the control function of a "lower level"—as for example is done when it is indicated that the lateral geniculate nuclei do the final processing in the frog's brain, while in mammals the final processing "has been taken over" by the striate area of the neocortex. The mammalian lateral geniculate nuclei are quite as active in the total performance as in any frog. It is very important for the comprehension of even the most abstruse of human intellectual process that cytoarchitectonically the hippocampus of man is very comparable to that of a mouse, and continues to perform accordingly. It is a principle within the theory of systems that an identical "result" may be arrived at via an indeterminable number of different processings. This is "equifinality" (Bertalanffy, 1950). Therefore, as we note the alarm calls of a bird and of a monkey, they may be indeed comparable as *behavioral equifinality;* but *functionally* they are messages with only a partial comparability.

There should be no need for the remark that behavior analysis is a much finer and informative thing than the preceding notes might seem to imply; ethology has amply demonstrated this. But behavior is to neurology what a topographic map is to a stratigraphic map. The contours of the former cut across those of the latter. Yet the first is very largely determined by what the second implies. One might push the analogy a step farther, and say that the surficial agents that have operated upon the topography are to the stratigraphy as the experiential is to the innate in the production of the behavior quotient. The point is that no matter how finely divided our behavioral analyses, every isolate is the resultant of a compounded activity of neurophysiological mechanisms, and the patterns of the activity remain incongruent with the patterns of the behavior.

The symposium which generated this monograph devoted its major efforts to animal communication from the behavioral approach (the exception was Moulton). While due cognizance of this must be taken, this essay will attempt to insert the counterweight of the functional approach.

The behavioral approach starts with an output and moves on to infer its input value to a receiver—as evidenced from the output which the latter produces in due course. The functional approach centers upon the organism-as-system as a processor of information. Input now becomes the starting point, output the final point; but what transpires in between holds the center of interest. Since behavior is but the externalized component of a total organism involvement, it constitutes but the presenting symptoms of neurophysiological process. To informationalist and behaviorist, communication is an output-input channel with a black box at each end. To functionalist it is an organism-as-system in the center with an input on one side and an output on the other. The focus is the black box. This characterizes the attitude of the present essay. The key orientation becomes the continuum of perception-cognition.

SOME POSTULATES. A REVIEW

The focal study of an information ecology is that of a teleologic machine seeking information and which thereby adapts—of which study, the macula (so to say) is, by what mechanisms and computations the organism copes with information. The following postulates are submitted toward an information ecology (the list is not exhaustive):

1. Brain mechanism represents an exceedingly complex probabilistic system (Beer, 1959, 1960).

2. The system is but a subsystem of organism-as-system. Organism-

as-system, in turn, is a subsystem or moiety of the coupling, organism-environment.

3. Three environments have a reality (external, internal, and social, as described earlier), yet the organism interrelates them. How it does so is subsumable under the analysis of space-time. An information ecology begins here.

4. Organisms quest for information; paraphrased, they exert effort after meaning. Matters of "learning" begin here (Wiener, 1954: 38).

5. The organism does not merely quest to extinguish tension; it also accepts tension as a positive experience (Goldstein, 1947: 222, 223).

6. Information may be said to "ride" energy. Sema "rides" information. Organismal messages are honest.

7. The physical environment does not communicate. This is a corollary or a converse of 4.

8. "Behavior" constitutes the presenting symptoms of neurophysiological processes.

9. Whatever be true of the animal kingdom in general, vertebrates seek information via several modalities which connect with physical and chemical properties of the universe, respectively and severally. Problems of configuration, cue redundancy, space-time analysis begin here.

10. Behavioral and functional approaches are mutually incongruent. This insures that neither is adequate for dealing with the complete phenomenon of animal communication. The key problem and strategy for a science of animal communication is how the one phenomenon is produced by the other.

A Matrix

On the strength of these postulates, we shall convert the three environments and the two ecologic disciplines into a matrix (the theoretical implications of which are being developed in another study):

ECOLOGIES	ENVIRONMENTS		
	A Physical surroundings	B Organism's internality	C Social surroundings
E: Energetics	EA	EB	EC
I: Information	IA	IB	IC

The matrix embraces the entire phenomenon of organism-related-to-environment. Any cell actually is or may be the frame of a discipline; e.g., what is normally understood as the discipline of ecology is placed in EA; that of physiology, in EB; psychology in IA and in IC. (For the significance of IB, see Maslow, 1966). To pursue an analogy, the cells resemble a morphemics of a metalanguage concerning organism-environment (*Merkwelt/Wirkwelt*); but their syntax extends vertically, horizontally, diagonally, as joins of the cells. The scheme is synholic. The object language which is the target of our metalanguage represents the activity itself of the organism. This means that the behavior of the organism—internality and externalization—is treated as being a grammar or a language of organism. Both "behavioral" and "functional" approaches are amenable to the scheme, but expectably, they obtain different results. By hypothesis of the very scheme itself, the results cannot but be relevant to each other; but how remains a fundamental problem for a future science.

Meanwhile, colloquia between students of behavior and students of the CNS are proceeding, and they are probing toward an answer. But they are two neighbors leaning over their fence and chatting purposefully, though not in intersection. Is it too much to hope that the diagram of metalanguage may open the way to a common stroll?

TOWARD A NEUROPSYCHOLOGY OF VERTEBRATE COMMUNICATION

General Considerations

"As P. W. Bridgman pointed out some years ago, if nature appears to be mathematical, it may be due to our insistence upon asking questions that we can and will answer only in mathematical terms" (Frank, 1948: 190).

"To Sir James Jeans's contention that the physical universe is constructed on mathematical lines, an equally competent mathematical physicist, Sir Arthur Eddington, replies, 'The mathematics is not there till we put it there'" (Herrick, 1956: 30).

Perceiving: the Neurological Course

The brains of animals and men are neither digital nor analog computers, although experimentally it is convenient to treat functionings *as if* they were the one or the other. The all-or-none firing of a neu-

ron permits a digital application. However, given a nerve fiber con-
ducting nondecrementally on this principle, there is evidence that at
the terminal segments of axons, the excitation is transformed from
all-or-none to graded activity, or the reverse, such that a train of
specific all-or-none impulses is transmuted into a relatively steady
state, and vice versa. This can only mean that the process in nervous
tissue most immediately employed in the regulation of activity of
body organs is of the graded and potentially continuous type rather
than of the impulsive and discontinuous type.

The chief physiological business of the nervous system is transacted in
graded-response elements which are dendrites or dendrite-like sensory
terminals; and it is these which initiate and pattern the axonic pulses into
coded messages. It is on the basis of all this that neurons have entered into
labile patterns of relationships. What we do, mentally or physically, is
probably to express the state of excitability of the graded response tissue
that initiates impulses in axonal conductors. This is what we do physiologically; one may some time hope to infer from this what we do subjec-
tively.

(Bishop, 1956: 380, 396)

As an input passes from more peripheral to more central neurons,
response becomes out of phase with the frequency of the original
stimulus pulse; so that

. . . one is drawn to the view that the distribution of excitation and inhibition among the fibers of the central pathways may be a crucial factor in
getting the message through. . . . Some of these transformations may well
be from "space into time"; in other words, primary receiving neurons scattered over an area may converge on a synapse and an increase in the
number of them receiving the stimulus . . . may be signaled in the post-
synaptic neurons by such signs as: decrease in latency, increase in rate of
firing, or number of discharges per stimulus. . . . The nervous system has
several other very potent mechanisms for introducing more information
into the centrally directed pathways, and one of these is feedback from
the cortex. . . . A descending, inhibitory influence may play a role in
"editing" the flow of information by acting to suppress some of the input
from the periphery of the receptive field and thereby producing an effective
inhibitory surround to the main focus.

(Brazier, 1964: 1426f.; see also the section on the reticular formation in
the present article.)

Today's model of perception by the CNS is quite different from the
stimulus-response, associational, or reflex-arc model of an earlier day.
"There is de-emphasis on transmission across synaptic segments and a
shift to emphasis on integration and autogenic activity—a model in-

cluding complex networks with the capacity to hold up and alter the characteristics of impulses transmitted to them, and with the capacity to initiate activity that is transmitted elsewhere to effect control of afferent impulses traveling to the cortex and efferent impulses traveling away from it" (Bruner, 1957: 356).

The vertebrate brain is unique among brains, in that it has solved the problem of penetration and perfusion by bloodstream fluids (von Bonin, 1950: 20) and has exploited the "interconnection" system of neural circuits; the insects exploit the "projection" system. (This acute observation is Vowles': See Thorpe and Zangwill, 1961. Nonetheless the vertebrates exploit the "projection" system in a strategic combination with the "interconnection" system.) It is the interconnection principle which affords the vertebrates—in measure as they exploit it— their capacity for fine-grained analysis and the permutations of information indicated in the preceding quotations.

Universals and Purpose

"What is most characteristic of perceptual representation is that it is categorical in nature, better described in the language of set theory and Boolean algebra than any other. An input is allocated to a class of objects and achieves its identity thereby" (Bruner, 1957: 343a).

How the particulars which are the actual inputs to a sensory receptor eventuate in a response to a universal; for example, recognition of shapes regardless of size (even sharks can do this) has been given a mathematiconeurologic rationalization by Pitts and McCulloch (1947) in a study that is a landmark. Neuronal loops composing reverberatory circuits and sharing some neurons between them, permit impulses entering them to endure and participate in responses at a later time when another particular is introduced. "One no longer seeks merely an individual response to the individual stimulus, (the system) can respond to a category. And now it has been emancipated in space by the discovery of moving fields of direct current potentials, making possible the use of other parts of the brain than those directly served by the specific incoming nerve pathway. An object seen with one eye is recognized by the other. A system learned through one sensory system is recognized by another. The tune that is read from the score can be recognized by the ear" (Brazier, 1952: 547).

It seems to me that the problem of equivalence . . . is essentially the problem of how an organism processes a stimulus ensemble, what features of input it is responding to. . . . Almost invariably, as both Adrian and Lashley have suggested, stimulus information is processed in terms of *relationships* either in a spatial array or in a temporay array, and it seems highly likely that spatial relations are translated into temporal ones in the nervous system—given the requirement of time for scanning a spatially extended field. What this suggests, then, is that the equivalence of stimulus events is a function of certain invariances in relationship in a temporally extended neural excitation; certain patterns of change in excitation define equivalence. . . . Undoubtedly, some of the equivalence coding in the perceptual constancies is innate, some learned.

(Bruner, 1957: 351 f., 353)

The capacity for organizing universals from particulars, then, is inherent in such circuitry, and it must obtain far down in phylogenesis. Now we may return to the characterization of an organism as a purposeful machine.

RWB, in their binary scheme of behavior hierarchy, recognize extrapolative, or predictive, feedback-purposeful-behavior at the level applying to a cat starting to pursue a mouse; as the cat merely predicts the path of the mouse, it is prediction of the first order. To cast a missile at a moving target requires prediction of two paths—a second-order prediction. Now,

Predictive behavior requires the orientation of at least two coordinates, a temporal and at least one spatial axis. Prediction will be more effective and flexible, however, if the behaving object can respond to changes in more than one spatial coordinate. The sensory receptors of an organism, or the corresponding elements of a machine therefore may limit the predictive behavior. Thus, a bloodhound *follows* a trail, that is, it does not show any predictive behavior in trailing because a chemical olfactory input reports only spatial information: distance, as indicated by intensity. The external charges capable of affecting auditory, or, even better, visual receptors, permit more accurate spatial localization; hence the possibility of more effective reactions when the input affects those receptors.

. . . It is probable that limitations of internal organization, particularly of the organization of the central nervous system, determine the complexity of predictive behavior which a mammal may attain. Thus is it likely that the nervous system of a rat or dog is such that it does not permit the integration of input and output necessary for the performance of a predictive reaction of the third or fourth order. Indeed, it is possible that one of the features of the discontinuity of behavior observable when comparing humans with other high mammals may lie in that the other mammals are limited to predictive behavior of a low order, whereas man may be capable potentially of quite high orders of prediction.

(Rosenbleuth, Wiener and Bigelow, 1943: 21)

"Prediction" and "extrapolation," of course, must be understood within the context of the authors' title—of a system so organized that it seeks information as an adaptive (goal-directed) procedure. It seems a valid inference that the authors are translating what we commonly mean by abstractive, conceptualizing capacity into cybernetic idiom. Science is not yet in a position to bridge these considerations and those of the neurologies; yet how close it is getting may be judged from what, later on, we shall be saying about brain mechanisms and their successive phylogeneses, and the presenting symptoms of the dysphasias.

We are now in a position to speculate about the respective advantages and limitations of the different modalities whereby organisms obtain their information. How an organism arranges the relative weighting of the several modalities—sight, hearing, smell, touch—as it organizes its space-time, is a subject awaiting formalization in an information ecology. Hockett's design features of language (1960) might well be reconsidered under the scheme propounded by RWB. And why the phonic-acoustic channel should have proved the most promising for animal communication should not be hard to see. No communication channel, nor indeed all of them combined, is coextensive with the information which resides potentially within an organism; the phonic-acoustic, however, has permitted the evolution of a high order of predictive behavior. The optic channel also has proved to have high information value; but the two channels certainly are not coextensive in their possibilities. It is not an anomaly that man has developed not only speech, but the graphic arts, as a mode of communication. (That music begins to speak, when speech itself falls silent, is another, though related, question.)

The evolution of the tetrapods, it has been remarked, has witnessed a struggle for dominance between olfaction and vision, with vision winning out (in the primates, at any rate). It is a curious, but by no means unaccountable, paradox that the cerebral hemispheres are elaborations from the primitive telencephalon—the division of the brain stem primitively dealing with olfactive processing—even while the sense modality itself has not retained the prime position it enjoys in pelagic life; as for audition, in few vertebrates is it the prime sense, yet its phylogenesis has involved structural elaborations among the tetrapods that have been far more complex than what either olfaction or vision have experienced.

Coding

From this point on, we shall cease to include in our discussion all but phonic-acoustic communications; although, when we are considering the animal's organization of its space-time—which cannot be left out of the reckoning—it will be impossible to treat that organizing as if it were the product of but this one sensory modality.

When a discussion of animal communication starts, it is conventional—and indeed logical—to treat it as an output. A behaviorist would, in fact, find it awkward to do otherwise. And it is theoretically sound; for information, as it travels, can never increase but it can suffer decrement, and noise can be introduced.

But we have begun the other way. An information ecology is concerned first with the organism's effort after meaning. As students of organism, we are concerned primarily, not secondarily, with the semeion of message. When an organism utters, it is saying something. What it is saying expresses its space-time organizing. What the utterance means to the auditor is a function in turn of its space-time organizing. The system which is capable of an utterance output is a system to which some other individual's output generates an input. What goes on inside the organism is nodal.

All the foregoing is the rationale for the attempt to comprehend communication first from what happens to an input. Here is where the coding begins.

Perception itself is but the initial point of the continuum that processes information. It is valid to say that coding is what happens all along the pathways whereby the impulse reaches successive points.

Fortunately for the economy of our discussion, it is no longer necessary to prove that it is the organism itself which determines what shall constitute information. Light energy has not compelled the retina into existence. Light waves shorter and longer than the visual range strike the retina, but do not induce (visual) information. The capacity to distinguish between wavelengths (red, green) is something the organism has done to itself.

In a remarkable paper, John Dewey (1896) set forth the inadequacies of a stimulus-response psychology; and in an equally remarkable little book, F. A. Hayek (1952) demonstrates that sensory perception already is interpretation. This is now substantiated by neurophysiological experiment; for example, electrode recordings from the organ of Corti of the cat show that this structure gates the inputs after conditioning or learning; habituation begins at the periphery. The most penetrating analysis of this subject known to me is Lettvin, Maturana, McCulloch, Pitts: "What the Frog's Eye Tells the Frog's Brain" (1959). (See also the discussion in the *First Conference on Brain and Behavior;* particularly, pp. 396, 402, 404. There is corroboration from the direction of ethology—admirably summarized by Marler and by Barlow—see their contributions in Thrope and Zangwill, 1961. A superb summary of our subject will be found in McCulloch, 1948: 265–267.)

In brief, representation is categorical immediately, and in terms of relationships. Bruner proposes that

> . . . information loss in perception can be viewed as the result of successive summations at stations along the different pathways, that this summation is likely statistical in its characteristics, that the sampling of lower-order units that summate to fire higher order units is biased by a gating or programming of way stations along the pathway controlled by more central mechanisms, and that the resultant in perception is a biased summary of the external stimulating environment. . . . When neural integration has progressed to a certain level, the organization achieved appears to be able to generate mental content of its own.

> (1957: 348 f.)

CNS and Behavior

The sketchings of the CNS mechanisms that will follow are to be read only in context. They are intended only to suggest that scientific consideration of communication in animals can no longer dispense with what the neurological specialties have to contribute.

The Reticular Formation

"No account of intellectual processes and their relation to the brain can be taken seriously today when [the brain stem arousal system] is omitted from the reckoning" (Hebb, 1959:267). The reticular formation(s) have recruited extensive study since Moruzzi and Magoun, 1949. (See also Jasper, 1949, in the same issue; discussions of the formations in the 1st and 3rd Conferences on the Cenral Nervous System and Behavior, passim; Magoun, 1963 is an excellent review of the present state of knowledge.) Histologically, it is such a loose network, and superficially its cells appear relatively so simplex that its pervasive functions have been missed until recent years. It is fundamentally involved in relating environments A and B; it alerts and inhibits, is a controlling factor in emotional affection, in conditioning, and in processing information into memory (see Magoun, 1963). The information comes from its electrography: Something is known also about the biochemistry involved, including DNA. Here is a "nonspecific" mechanism without which the "specific" ones cannot operate. Its presence in the thalamus is of particular interest to us, since this essay would emphasize that phasial processes are very much of a trafficking between thalamus and cerebral cortex—and not really understandable in terms of cortex alone. Contemporaneously with the "breakthrough" that revealed the importance of the brainstem arousal system, Penfield, on the basis of neurosurgical explorations, was postulating a "centrencephalic system," a functional and not a structural entity, which he localized in a general way in the thalamus, where gatings and integrations involving activities of the rest of the body occur, and which stood in intimate reciprocation with the cortex—a kind of central dispatch office, from which the cerebral cortex received selected information which it processed and reported back. It happens that he localized the functions where the thalamic nuclei and the thalamic portion of the brain stem and arousal system occur.

There is no marked evolution of the reticular formation from the lower to the higher vertebrates, although with the development of cerebral hemispheres in the mammals, one is not surprised that there should be more of it at this level. At all events, what takes place in the cortex of man represents by no means an "emancipation" from the control of whatever goes on in this primitive formation. "I shall venture," remarks Yakovlev (1958:293), "that it is from this primordial neuronal swamp that human thought arose like a sinful orchid."

Thalamocortical Traffic[3]

Structurally, the thalamus is very complex; none of it is indispensable. By contrast, the matter of the cerebral hemispheres is remarkably homogeneous; a surprising amount of it is dispensable.

The cerebral cortex, ontogenetically and phylogenetically, represents a huge proliferation and migration of cells within the endbrain—the telencephalon—primitively, the (anterior) portion of the brain stem which receives and processes olfactive information. This function never is lost in phylogenesis even when the olfactory sense regresses or even practically disappears.

The thalamus is lodged in the between-brain, the diencephalon; it receives and processes information from practically all regions or systems of the body; which means, in one way or another, the rest of the CNS; it issues instructions conversely. Essentially, the thalamocortical traffic represents its relations particularly with endbrain portions of the CNS. It is not erroneous to say that how the cerebral cortex operates is to a very large extent a matter of how it interrelates with the thalamus, from which its inputs are exclusively obtained.

[3]The term is intended to include both centripetal and centrifugal pathways.

(Unfortunately, most of what is known about thalamocortical traffic comes from experiments upon macaques and chimpanzees—clinical material has not been subjected to the systematic analyses for which it holds forth promise.)

Some of the thalamic nuclei contain synapses with pathways to and from other parts of the brain stem—"intrinsic" nuclei. It is to be understood that the extrinsic nuclei also traffic with the cerebral cortex.

The extrinsic nuclei traffic with those areas of cerebral cortex which are already present in the most primitive mammals, and which have been long identified with the end processes of perception—visual, auditory, kinaesthetic cortex—and with locomotory activation. The intrinsic nuclei have increased phylogenetically with the expansions of the "supralimbic" cortex (discussed below).

The thalamic projections to and from the cortex are constructed essentially on the "projection" principle (see above); it is the cortico-cortical traffic which represents an emphasis on the "interconnection" principle. It is to be understood that these are diagrammatic simplifications.

The thalamus screens much of the information it receives from ever passing to the cortex. Since the thalamus receives information from all quarters, it is very much involved in organizing a holistic response. What instructions it converts into communicated information thus represent a selected segment of an entire response. It would seem that the very rationale of the cerebral hemispheres is that they compute differently from thalamic computations; the cortex, it seems, has a far greater digital capacity. But, how the thalamus computes is even less understood than how the cortex does it. This heightens our interest in the differences as well as similarities of phasial dysfunctionings when the lesions occur, respectively, in cortex or in thalamic nuclei (see below). (A classic account of the thalamus and its cortical relations is that of Walker, 1938. The most succinct review of thalamocortical traffic I know, is that of Rose and Woolsey, 1949—despite the accumulation of new data since that paper.)

The Limbic System

(Structurally and functionally, this system is an extremely complex affair; although what shall be included under its definition has not remained invariant, in this survey we shall not encounter difficulties.)

It is essentially an elaboration of the telencephalic roof (in consonance with what has been said in the preceding section); the primordia are present at least at the amphibian level. Pribram and

Kruger (1954) distinguish in it three morphological systems: (1) connecting directly with the olfactory bulb; (2) connecting with (1), but not with the bulb; (3) connecting with (2), but not with (1). System 2 is connected with the hypothalamus; system 3, with the thalamus, and with neocortical regions. Each of the systems is partly, though not altogether, cortical. The various features are not hard to homologize among the mammals; strikingly enough, there is not much elaboration from the primitive to the most evolved of the mammals, including man. It is not therefore surprising that experimental stimulations and resections of particular features in rats, cats, and monkeys should be followed by rather comparable behavior defects, and that these should be instructive when lesions in man are involved. It seems a valid statement that, while the hypothalamus, with its visceral connections, is much responsible for body tonus, it is the cortices of the limbic system which make possible those feelings or awarenesses which we call "emotion."

Experimental "sham rage" (and other emotive behaviors) in cats, of course, have been familiar for years. In man rage, terror, anxiety, the "dreamy state" *(déjà vu)*, and epileptic automatisms occur.

Since the landmark study by Klüver and Bucy (1939) it has become established that the hippocampus (plus uncus, amygdala) is essential to learning the *signal value* of a source of information. Monkeys so ablated were hyperaesthetic to objects brought into view; they conveyed them indiscriminately to their mouths, where oral aesthesis induced food to be eaten and other objects rejected. "The objects . . . had a value only as stimuli-agents and were without meaning as stimuli-signals" (Yakovlev, 1958: 403). And there was no learning: If the rejected object was perceived again a few moments later, it was treated as before. (The ablations included a portion of the temporal lobes, which are operative in the involvements of memory.)

We are not as yet dealing with how limbic system and neocortex interrelate. The hippocampus seems to be fit for

. . . the role of a universal analyzer of non-specific stimuli-signals of all those events which are predictable from long phyletic experience: signals of water, food, air to breathe, space to live in, of mate in season, of days and nights, of seasons and tides. Without such a universal analyzer of 'broadcast' signals of universal and perennial event, the differentiation of conditioned responses to messages with specified addresses—visual, acoustic, somesthetic, cenesthetic—signaling events predictable only from a short-term ontogenetic experience would not be possible.

(Yakovlev, 1958: 403)

"In primitive forms" says MacLean,

the visceral brain [i.e., the limbic system] provides the highest correlation center for ordering the effective behavior of the animal in such basic drives as obtaining and assimilating food, fleeing from or orally disposing of an enemy, reproducing, and so forth. From anatomic and physiologic considerations . . . it might be inferred that the visceral brain continues to subserve such functions in higher forms, including man.

Psychiatrists have characterized certain psychopathic behaviors as "primitive," "infantile"

. . . probably because so much of the information obtained from these patients has to do with material which in a Freudian sense is assigned to the oral and oral-anal-level. . . . These oral factors have been related to rage, hostility, fear, insecurity, resentment, grief, and a variety of other emotional states. In certain circumstances, for example, eating food may be the symbolic representation of psychological phenomena as diverse as (1) the hostile desire to eradicate an inimical person, (2) the need for love, (3) fear of some deprivation or punishment, (4) the grief of separation, etc. . . . Visceral feelings are blended or fused with what the individual sees, hears, or otherwise senses, in such a way that the outside world is often experienced and dealt with as though it were incorporated. Thus the child looking at a leaf may say, "it tastes green."

(MacLean, 1949: 344)

What we are pointing toward should begin to be discernible. What we are calling phasia—man's speech function—is nothing if not a symbolopoeic process; and "symbol" is not so simplistically identifiable as sign-versus-symbol discourses would have it. The roots of phasia reach down into the primitive, visceral brain.

There is much still to be said about this. One of those things will bring us back to phasia as an organizer of space-time in man. Neuronographically, the posterior part of the hippocampal formation (within system 2) is but one synapse removed from the part of the neocortex which, later on, we shall find active in space-time analysis and in the forming of word symbol. (Roughly, Wernicke's area: temporoparieto-occipital cortex—"supralimbic lobe"). Kubie, who has explored the brain mechanisms in search of their implications to psychoanalysis, has said:

Here, then, within the temporal lobe and its connections, is the cross roads where the "I" and the "non-I" pole of the symbol meet. . . . The temporal lobe complex constitutes the mechanism for integrating the past and the present, the phylogenetically and ontogenetically old and new, and at the same time the external and internal environments of the central nervous system. It is through the temporal lobe and its connections that the "gut" component of memory enters into our psychological processes and the symbol acquires its dual poles of reference. Thus in the temporal lobe and its deeper primitive connections is the mechanism for the coordination and integration of all the data which link us to the world of experience, both extero- and interoceptive.

(Kubie, 1953a: 31).

One last appraisal before we pass to the matter of the neocortex: "But regardless of any scanning and sweep mechanism that may exist," says MacLean,

the cortical cytoarchitecture of the hippocampal formation indicates that it would have little efficiency as an analyzer compared with the neocortex. . . . The cortex of the hippocampal formation has a similar architecture throughout its entire length and presents the same general picture in all mammals from mouse to man. On the basis of these observations one might infer that the hippocampal system could hardly deal with information in more than a crude way, and was possibly too primitive a brain to analyze language. Yet it might have the capacity to participate in a non-verbal type of symbolism. This would have significant implications as far as symbolism affects the emotional life of the individual. One might imagine, for example, that though the visceral brain could never aspire to conceive the color red in terms of a three-letter word or as a specific wave-length of light, it could associate the colour symbolically with such diverse things as blood, fainting, fighting, flowers, etc. Therefore if the visceral brain were the kind of brain that could tie up symbolically a number of unrelated phenomena, and at the same time lack the analyzing ability of the word-brain to make a nice discrimination of their differences, it is possible to conceive how it might become foolishly involved in a variety of ridiculous correlations leading to phobias, obsessive-compulsive behavior, etc. Lacking the help and control of the neocortex, its impressions would be discharged without modification into the hypothalamus and lower centers. Considered in the light of Freudian psychology, the visceral brain would have many of the attributes of the unconscious id. One might argue, however, *that the visceral brain is not at all unconscious (possibly not even in certain stages of sleep), but rather eludes the grasp of the intellect because its animalistic and primitive structure makes it impossible to communicate in verbal terms.* Perhaps it were more proper to say, therefore, it is an animalistic and illiterate brain.

(MacLean, 1949: 348)

Those who are interested in the dichotomy "iconic" and "arbitrary" may wish to consider these matters of limbic system and its neocortical connections. We shall return to these connections after some observations on the neocortex, particularly its "supralimbic lobe."

The Neocortex

We are using the term neocortex, since most of our discussion is confined to the gray matter of the (more embracive) neopallium.

This element of brain receives its input exclusively from the thalamus. In the most primitive mammals, the neocortex is confined essentially to areas of "primary perception" analyses: visual ("occipital"), auditory ("acoustico-temporal"), somesthetic ("post-rolandic"), and of somatomotor ("pre-rolandic"). How these areas interconnect, what the behavior output they organize in consequence, remains, as far as I know, a *terra incognita*. They presumably traffic with "extrinsic" nuclear elements of the thalamus; I do not know when and where in mammalian phylogenesis the "intrinsic" thalamic nuclei begin to develop their weighty role.

What should be remarked, at this juncture, is that we do not find man to be the most highly evolved with respect to this "primary perception" cortex. The striate cortex (visual), in *ascending* order of laminar complexity, runs man-and-apes–monkeys–tarsius (von Bonin, 1942: 426).

The Supralimbic Lobe and Its Relations

This label is, I believe, original with Yakovlev, who thus designates those neocortical areas which, under old terminology, would correspond essentially to an "association" cortex. It is particularly developed, but from slight to superlative degree, in monkeys, apes, and man. It consists of (1) a frontal area, approximately what lies anterior to the precentral gyrus and Brodmann 6; and (2) a temporo-parieto-occipital area, approximately Brodmann 19, 7, 39, 37, 20, 21, 22, 32, 38, 36. Some of this cortex traffics with the intrinsic thalamic nuclei; some of it—particularly the temporal area and the areas most remote from contiguity with the limbic lobe—does not traffic with the thalamus but traffics corticocortically. The thalamocortical traffic operates essentially on the projection principle: the a-thalamic cortex, essentially on the interconnection principle. Attention has already been drawn to the enormous indeterminism that this makes possible in information processing. Cytoarchitectonically, the neocortex is the most elaborate and intricate of all tissues—with its (conventionally) six strata, which obtain throughout, yet which vary in relative thickness and in certain statistical features of the cellular populations from one region to another. These microanatomical variations and the gross, overall homogeneity of the hemispheral masses undoubtedly account together for the fine-grained and highly improbable physiological events of which this material is capable. From another angle, we have a neocortex operating integratedly under a triad system: Some of it receives instructions from thalamic cell masses which have edited information which to them is input from extrathalamic sources; some of it receives instructions from thalamic cell masses which are not thus bound to inputs from exterior sources; some of it is not bound to an input from the thalamus at all. And the triad system operates *intra se* interconnectively. Some of the information passes between thalamus and neocortex via synapses in the limbic (and also the striatum); some of it bypasses the limbic lobe.

And here we may remind ourselves that under the schema of Rosenblueth, Wiener, Bigelow (see above), the carnivora may be capable of a second-order extrapolation, but only some primates and particularly man may be capable of higher-order extrapolation. "There is a mode of learning which permits an apparently unlimited freedom of choice of what one may learn. This is learning by abstraction from the concrete reality of stimuli, of the *symbols* of reality. In the case of man these symbols of the conditioning signals are language and words as ideas, in the sense of the Greek word *logos* or the second system of signals in Pavlovian sense. The supralimbic lobe is the probable substratum of this learning" (Yakolev, 1958:405).

It is a long-known fact—at least since Dubois' studies, published first in 1897, on relative sizes of brain and body in closely related animals such as small and giant Felidae—that with increase of volumes the ratio of brain to body decreases, due to the failure of the white matter to keep pace; the gray matter therefore folds in on itself, producing the gyrencephalic character of the larger brain, by contrast with the lissencephalic character of the small brain.

G. von Bonin draws attention to the fact that this results in more room for the corticocortical pathways relative to the expanse of the gray layer, in the small, lissencephalic brain as compared with the large, gyrencephalic one; and indeed there is evidence for this—for example, in the opercular region ("Broca's area") the macaque shows seven known pathways and the chimpanzee only four. And he remarks that

Wiener [1948] has pointed out the danger of "jamming" the available pathways which may threaten when the cortex becomes large and the connections do not increase proportionately. It may, perhaps with equal justification, be pointed out that too many connections may lead to mutual interference, so that in the end nothing is left but a loud background noise. This may well be the situation in lower forms. Only when signals come in clearly however, can they be reacted upon selectively. There may be an optimum of connections, and it may be that this optimum is established in the human brain.
(von Bonin, 1952: 143)

This speculation indeed provokes thought. At the same time, we should add that the white-to-gray ratio might also be an optimum for a brain like the macaque's—given that amount of gray. And in this connection, it is worth remarking that among the primates, the chimpanzee may represent something of a "microcephal" and man more nearly a "normal" in brain size, for primates of that body magnitude (von Bonin, 1952:138n. I also suggested this, in 1947).

And we may gain a perspective upon a comparison of chimpanzee and man by remarking that man's brain contains about 2^{33} neurons. Allowing an approximate equality of cell size and density for the chimpanzee, the brain volume suggests a neuron count of about 2^{31}. Were the chimpanzee to gestate for nine months instead of seven, there would be time enough for the two extra mitoses to bring it up to human size.

This suggests, for one thing, that if our Australopithecoid ancestry possessed a brain volume approximating that of a chimpanzee, in the late Tertiary, an additional two mitotic divisions over a period of some centimillennia would really not suggest that the human capacity is the product of an "explosion of brains" under a terrific "selective pressure," as appears to be a current view of the matter. But, given the interconnection principle operating within the neopallium, the difference between chimpanzee and human mentation delivery would be covered by this difference.

And, for another thing, since human microcephals can learn the basics of speech, while the chimpanzee cannot, it suggests that ratios of white to gray may be one factor that helps account for it. We shall return to this topic later.

Both faradic and strychninization experiments upon the cortex demonstrate more localized effects in man than in chimpanzee, and in chimpanzee than in macaque. A variety of experimental cortical insults to the rat brain may not seriously impair relearning of a skill; the impairment in chimpanzee may require a longer recovery; in man, the impairment may be compensated only partially or hardly at all. We shall not enter upon the microanatomic features. There are statistical differences in the sizes of some of the cortical cells between man and monkey. These are inevitably oversimplified statements, bordering on the intolerable; there are paradoxes which are not being even mentioned; their excuse is that they indicate a differentiation process which has progressed farthest in man; that the process has numerous vectors which summate as a system. The factors relate as products, not additively. But—what are the templates behind any summations we may undertake?

Suppose we exploit for a moment the view that an organism constitutes a self-environment—the environment B of our earlier scheme.

Then it likewise is a system in the sense of system theory. We are then ready to consider every evolutionary "innovation" as something to which the antecedent system must itself learn to adjust. The mammalian CHs thus constitute an extra element of situation with which the brain stem has had to cope. Without relinquishing its ancient role and title, it has adjusted to coping with a wider range of probabilities; paraphrased, the additional relations produce a total system that is more complexly probabilistic than before.

Conversely, no new emergence such as that of the supralimbic lobation could conceivably be anything different: At any time whatever its physiological state or whatever (putatively) its phylogenetic level, it could only have been adjustively related to the older mechanism or subsystems.

When a cortical lesion or experimental ablation is followed by degeneration of the fibers by which the cell gray trafficked with the thalamus, obviously something of the thalamic complex or subsystem is destroyed, because the traffic relationship constituted the goal orientation of the cells involved.

This view makes it easier to understand, I think, what happens when a cortical lesion or insult or dysfunction results in a behavior deficit or aberration. The system for which we are accepting Ashby's definition of a machine (or Rosenblueth, Wiener, Bigelow's characterization of a feedback-purposeful behavior system) continues to cope with the situation as before—but the situation has been changed.

Limbic and Supralimbic Systems

We have made passing references to relations between limbic system and neocortex. We may now bring this material in line with some final appraisals of the whole matter.

The limbic cortex is strongly related to the hypothalamus, which . . . is concerned with "all sorts of visceral and metabolic processes" that in their totality enable the organism to appreciate itself as a unified being.
(MacLean, 1954: 41)
Feelings and emotions provide us with the connecting bridge between our internal and external world. In other words, it is such experience that assures us of the reality of ourselves and the environment around us. . . . There are clinical and experimental indications that without structures comprising the limbic system we would be like disembodied spirits.
(MacLean, 1958: 619)
Here presumably is a primitive part of the brain that integrates and interprets experience in a language of feeling, not in the language of symbolic thought.

. . . In the light of the affinities of the limbic cortex generally to the type that mediates the sense of smell, might one not infer that the limbic system as a whole interprets experience largely in terms of quality and intensity? . . . Phylogenetically, it is not until the great elaboration of the supragranular layers of the cortex associated with the sense of sight, hearing and touch, that one finds a cortical screen portraying a picture that can be dealt with coldly, abstractly, in terms of symbolic language. The senses of sight, hearing, and touch allow an easy interchange of symbolic language.

(MacLean, 1955: 120)

Most of the "old" cortex is contained in the limbic lobe. The faithful reduplication of this cortex throughout the phylogeny of the mammals contrasts with the rapid evolution and growth of the neocortex around it. It has been suggested that the neocortex, in contrast to the limbic cortex, might be likened to an expanding numerator, representing in phylogeny the growth of intellectual functions.

One might think of the cerebral cortex as being to the cerebrum what a television screen is to a television set or what a radar screen is to a pilot. Presumably it represents Nature's attempt to give to the organism as clear a picture as possible for making a successful adaptation to the environment. Basically Nature has experimented with three types of cortex, or to use the language of our analogy, three types of screens. They may be appropriately referred to as the archicortex, mesocortex and neocortex. . . . The limbic cortex is structurally primitive compared with the neocortex. Radarwise or televisionwise, it therefore might be expected not to present as clear a picture of the environment as the neocortex. Second, it shows essentially the same degree of development and organization throughout the mammalian series. This would suggest that it functions at an animalistic level in both animal and man. Finally . . . the limbic cortex, in contrast to the neocortex, has strong reciprocating pathways with the hypothalamus and other ancient structures of the brain stem. This means that there is a strong projection of the visceral as well as the exteroceptive senses onto the old cortical screen. Presumably in an effort to obtain a clearer and better picture for the purposes of adapting to the external environment, Nature fashions the new screen so that it largely portrays what is transpiring in the external world. Finally a point is reached with man where a picture can be represented by word symbols alone. . . .

. . . We might think of the old cortex, the old screen, as giving a muddied picture of the internal and external environment in terms of emotional feelings; whereas the evolving neocortex provides an ever clearer picture in the form of discriminative thought. But here the analogy ends, because the cortical screens are presumed to play back on a common cone within the brain stem. Through such reciprocity of action, one could visualize a mechanism whereby emotion might facilitate or paralyze thought, or by which thought might generate or control emotion.

(MacLean, 1958 *passim.*)

There is a celebrated parable by MacLean which appropriately winds up this discussion:

One might imagine that the neopallium and the limbic system function together and proceed through the world like a man on a horse. Both horse and man are very much alive to each other and their environment yet communication between them is limited. Both derive information and act upon it in a different way. At times the horse may shy or balk for reasons at first inexplicable to his rider. But the patient and sympathetic horseman will try to find out and understand what it is that causes the panic and train the beast to overcome them. . . .

(MacLean, 1955: 121)

THE HUMANIZING OF A VERTEBRATE PHONIC COMMUNICATION

A Note on Terminology

Clinical terms for functional disorders are *ad hoc,* for they apply to presenting symptoms and syndromes. This accounts for much of the fact that the terms are unstandardized. So there are aphemia (Broca's own term), aphasia (the term which happened to receive wider favor), agnosia, alexia, agraphia, apraxia, autotopagnosia, astereognosis, etc.

If we are to use clinical evidence of pathologies, we must use its terms. Yet a better etymology and semanticity would serve scientific discussions better. The writer has used "phasia" to denote the speech function considered as neuropsychological process. It would be useful, I believe, if we were to use stereognosia, autostereognosia, topognosia as the "normal" characteristics of mentation, and their malfunctions with the dys-prefix and the privative a- to indicate an absence of the function: stereo-dysgnosis, stereo-agnosis. As it now stands astereognosis literally means a knowledge of not-space. The existing nonstandardization shows in auto-topagnosia and astereognosis. But perhaps the suggestion comes too late.

The suggested regularizing would permit us to place the dysfunction in terms of some variables of a system which have exceeded the normal limits of the phase-space which define the stability of the system. This would conform to Ashby's cybernetic definitions (1960: see particularly Chs. 4, 5).

A Conceptual Note

It is tantamount to impossible for humans to communicate voluntarily without "symbol." This essay must use "symbolopoesis," "symbolopoea"—yet leave "symbol" undefined, and use the latter term opportunistically, as used by whichever authorities are being exploited. "Symbol" will not mean the same thing to a psychoanalyst as to a neuropsychologist. But I doubt if the discussion will be clouded thereby.

The neurological evidence suggests that what students of a variety of specialties—particularly anthropologists who concern themselves with the phenomenon—call a "symbol," is but some culmination at the unmistakably human level of a continuum. Anthropologists have not been noteworthily successful in determining the nature of "symbol." This writer, on the other hand, believes he sees a continuous evolution in the gradual acquisition by mammals of those successive scanning screens—archepallium, mesopallium, neopallium—which MacLean has characterized (see the earlier quotations), and this writer would add the expansion of the supralimbic lobe. Symbolization therefore is supposable as a matter of a continuous (qualitative) degree.

And this appears to be borne out from behavioral tests upon alloprimates, particularly upon apes. That is, alloprimates possess various degrees of symbolopoesis, various capacities for symbolopoea. But this topic would overextend the present essay.

In any event, the dichotomy of "sign" and "symbol" is unhelpful; and I believe it has actually handicapped our analyses. And from the standpoint of a neuropsychology, neither does an "iconic" "arbitrary" dichotomy have much heuristic value. Illustratively: The 'arbitrariness" of a linguistic symbol is genuine enough—but probably your limbic lobe is continuing to treat it iconically all the time, and your supralimbic system probably would not be having its chance to display its "arbitrary" menu in your dining room were your limbic system not busy in the kitchen!

The ontogenetic achievement of symbolopoeic capacity likewise is a continuum; it needs no demonstration here that it has degrees of power and refinement which differ between a two-year-old, a twelve-year-old, an eighteen-year-old. Yet the practical limitations of our psychological testings, which have to be taken between specified time intervals, show developmental processes in a step-wise outline, from which we must interpolate in order to obtain a smoothed curve of development. But *just what does happen* which effects the smooth emergence of the later condition out of the earlier one?

THE ORGANIZATION OF SPACE-TIME

The call system of an animal (here we shall include phasia) is a function of its analysis of space-time.

This is a conclusion, not an assumed premise, despite its position here. We shall build up to it, before building upon it.

A base has already been attempted (see above under perceiving and coding). There the points were made that analysis of environment begins with the peripheral receptors, which instantly commence the process of converting input into information; that perception-cognition are but arbitrary placements along a continuum wherein the information continues to be lost or eliminated—a procedure which seems necessarily to accompany progressive integration and summative representation; that introduction of information into any next editing locus is paraphrasable as a parameter introduced into neuronal circuits; that this sets up the mechanism whereby particulars are edited into universals, and provision is made for conversion back and forth of space-time.

Several cardinal mechanisms have been sketched (see CNS and Behavior, above), to suggest stages in this editorial process as performed by vertebrates. The interplay of activities, which we may attempt to grasp by our opportunistic employment of digital and computer techniques, has been stressed. And we have refused to entertain any notion that the human peculiarity termed phasia contains entities which lie outside this schema.

We have tried to show that such are the neurological undergirdings of an information ecology. We shall now proceed to reduce an information ecology, in terms of this undergirding, to the organization of space-time by the vertebrate which results in its developing the polarities of "ego" and "not-ego"—a psychological paraphrase of the distinction, as well as of the relationships between an organism and its environment.

What an animal communicates is an edited selection from what, to it, is space-time. Pre-ethological insight into this fundamental of animal organization is to be credited to J. von Uexküll, in his development of the scheme of *Merkwelt: Wirkwelt* within the animal's *Umwelt*. Retrospectively, we may see this as the early gestation of an information ecology. Ethology has its being in the behavioral approach to this ecology—and ethology's indebtedness to von Uexküll is quite specifically recognized (Lorenz, 1935). But the resolution of the same reality in terms of organization of space-time comes via the functional approach of neuropsychology.

There is good experimental evidence for the statement that the organization of an *Umwelt,* the organization of a space-time, begins peripherally in the receptor organs. Informally, we may note that a sleeper—human and other mammal (cat or dog)—may remain unaroused by certain strong stimuli yet be aroused by another one of far less intensity. The phenomenon has received verification experimentally as well, from electrode recordings from the organ of Corti of cats who have become habituated by controlled conditioning (Galambos, 1959:384 and *passim*). The optics of space analysis by the eye itself recently has been set forth summarily by Ogle (1962). The sensory processes are innate, but their capabilities for stabilizing spatiality can be educed only experientially. In this matter, there have existed for some time experimental results from young chimpanzees.

How an animal organizes its space-time, is, incipiently, a function of what relation and respective reliance it places upon the several sensory modalities it commands. The *Umwelt* of an insect possessing ommatidia but no acoustic sense obviously cannot be that of one possessing the vertebrate retina and an organ of Corti—with all due allowance to the principle of stimulus variability with perceptual constancy and the contrastive systems of CNS organization based on projection and interconnection principles. The *Umwelt* of a microsmatic, optically versatile primate and that of macrosmatic, dull-visioned dog begin their differences at their receptors. Yet the receptivity of the receptors is not a constant, as habituation experiments and ethological observation have demonstrated.

"In space-time as a pattern of psycho-organismal mentation," Coghill (1938; *passim*) has remarked: "mentation . . . conforms to neither space nor time. . . . It is true that mentation requires time, and is presumably always asociated with organs that are spatial and that function in time. . . . Movement, in the development of the individual, is primary. . . . That is, motility precedes sensitivity in embryonic development. . . . Space-time is, then, a total pattern of mentation; and space and time are partial patterns arising within it."

Coghill appears to have been groping toward something tangible in neuropsychological terms: and C. J. Herrick, impressed, has tried to bring it closer to tangibility; he paraphrases Coghill thus:

. . . the analytic functions, which are primarily concerned with adjustments of the organism to its environment must of necessity be oriented in space and time with the body of the organism as a fixed point of reference. The integrative processes on the contrary, are wholly internal to the body and some of the laws of their action are relativistic rather than inflexibly bound to dimensions that can be measured in absolute units of space and time. The analysis of sensory and motor processes must be made (consciously or unconsciously) in terms of spatial and temporal relations that can be numerically expressed. Integration combines the products of this analysis in a constructive process in which space and time may not be separately individuated but retain a primordial unity as space-time defined relativistically and in parameters different from those of Newtonian mechanics.

(Herrick, 1956: 273)

It is the belief of this writer that the symbolic process which externalizes in speech and also in the arts, is the exemplification of this evolution *par excellence*.

We shall now occupy ourselves with some clinical evidence of the disturbances in space-time apprehension (analysis) and phasial codification. It is to be understood that this is not a review of the entire field; the intention is to indicate the character, the limitations, and the potentialities of this kind of evidence for a comprehension of the symbolic process in man which effects his mode of communication.

THE CLINICAL PICTURE OF APHASIA AND ITS HEMISPHERAL CORRELATES

The most obvious characteristics of disruption in phasia have shown up when a person simply loses ability, either partially or totally, to talk. Yet continuing ability to comprehend, to think creatively, has been recognized since antiquity.

A patient may be unable to utter any word at all, though he try desperately to do so; yet he comprehends anything said to him and can converse by writing. Yet sometimes after failing in his attempt to speak, he may involuntarily burst forth with the utterance, under emotional stress, then be unable to repeat. Or, utterance may be reduced to but several phones, used in response to any proposition. Again, the phonemicizing survives, but the phonemes are serialized neologistically—a jargon which conveys no meaning to the auditor. Yet again, a syntax may survive, but with neologisms standing in the places of primary semantic—like "Twas brillig and the slithy toves. . . ." Or vocabulary may survive, with syntax collapsing: "The good is old from Good God using to these ladies." (Alajouanine's example, 1956· 23. For an excellent historical review of aphasia as a clinical problem, see Ombredane, 1951.)

These phenomena may appear variously in a patient—in part, as symptomatic of the progression or regression of the affection.

While this is far from adequate coverage of the differences, it should suggest that speech disorders may range from inability to articulate what may yet be an unimpaired intellectual process, to some impairment of intellectual process, unaccompanied by impairment of articulation of morphemes.

In his essay of 1956, Alajouanine concludes that the disorders polarize around two kinds—"Broca's" and "Wernicke's." The former, to put it simplistically, represents failure in motorizing; the latter, disturbances in what we may term here the organization of a completed ideation.

These onomatic labels suggest the respective involvements of Broca's and Wernicke's areas.

Naturally, speech disorders are behavioral defects, and their recognition as such has an indeterminate past; attributing them to local malperformances of brain, however, dates from Gall's phrenology (although the brain as seat of mental functions goes back a century earlier); demonstration of cause-effect relation between a tangible lesion of a hemisphere and specifiable deficits of speech is to be credited to Broca. Although Broca's specific attribution is no longer tenable, differential diagnostics of speech disorders in association with cortical lesions have developed full clinical and scientific stature since that day.

The clinician must take his tumors and gunshots where he finds them; the "seat" of an epilepsy must be searched for; and although a localizable brain damage may be the agent, this is often not the case: There may be malfunctioning without identifiable structural defect. It is within the last four decades that electroencephalography has developed into the powerful exploratory tool that it is now; and, understandably, its principle goes back to demonstrations that a slight electric impulse applied to the exposed surface of a dog brain results in definable muscular movements.

The problem of brain study, then, has been one of organizing regularities out of random evidence. Controlled, experimental insult to the brains of nonhumans has developed approximately during the same era that has produced encephalography. Other techniques are more recent—those of a neuropharmacology and deep electrode probings. Expectably, the behavioral aspect of speech disorders has induced a corpus of psychological test batteries. And scientists from these diverse fields are today seeking to effect some common unifying principles. But I doubt if any one would say that this has been achieved as yet.

Some features have become fairly clear.

Speech disorders are no more and no less attributable to localizable regions of brain than any other behavioral dysfunction.

Neither a normal nor a pathological behavior is to be attributed to a specific region of brain, even when lesion or experimental insult results in specific behavioral defects. When the human brain is exposed during operation, and it is explored with the electrode in appropriate spots—if the patient has been talking it will render him mute; if he has been silent, a touch to the vocalizing cortex will induce him to utter sound. But no electric disturbance ever induces speech—or any other learned behavior. The excitation of memory from areas of the temporal lobe is exceptional, and not relevant here. We are not surprised, then, when a lesion of the parieto-temporal cortex and a lesion of the pulvinar—which are respectively the cortical and the thalamic ends of a thalamocortical traffic—produce similar, yet not identical, pathologic behavior (see also below).

And there are no cortical regions dealing with speech as an entity. Injuries to some cortical regions cause no observable speech disorders. Injuries to others cause this or that kind of phasial deficiency, but always as features intermingled with other behavioral deficiencies. But there are other symptoms which continue to defy even this degree of localizing. We may say only that the local insult to the brain has interrupted the normal patterning of activity of a system at that strategic point.

Not any of the deficiencies, moreover, can be pinpointed to circumscribed areas (of cortex). There are places which (under electrostimulation) produce a pronounced reaction, with a fade-out surrounding them (and a fade-in of some other kind of behavior). Some of the cortex the neurosurgeon finds expendable; other regions he is extremely reluctant to touch.

These few informal remarks must suffice. We may apply them, and recall also what has been said about the phylogenetic distinction between the "primary perception" cortices and primary motor cortex—acoustic, visual, somaesthetic; pre-rolandic motor—occurring also in the primitive mammals; and the supralimbic ("associational" in an old terminology) which they do not possess.

From his studies of German World War II battle casualties Conrad

(1954. Conrad is explicitly indebted to Hughlings Jackson) has schematized the aphasias in terms of gestalt psychology, and associates them with cortical regions about as thoroughly as can at present be done. We shall combine with this some other, generally known evidence. (This continues to be an exposé, not an interpretation by the writer; and of course it has been somewhat diagrammatized.) The quotations from Conrad are his statements of the normal processes, which are disrupted by the relevant pathologies.

1. The patient hears you speaking, but complains of its being a gibberish (like some unfamiliar, foreign language). This is pure word-deafness (Conrad does not distinguish here between word-sound-deafness and word-deafness), which involves the region of the auditory cortex of the temporal lobe. But he can himself speak coherently.

Conrad: "Verbal gestalts in the process of perception of the auditory gestalt."

2, 3. The patient hears your words, as words, yet cannot attach a meaning to them, nor handle syntax, either yours, or his own. ("Name-deafness" and "paragrammatism.") Now more supralimbic cortex is involved, especially, more temporo-parietal.

Conrad: "Verbal gestalts in process of perception of the content of meaning, out of the auditory gestalts (sensory aphasia)" and "Verbal gestalts in the process of the voluntary evocation of names (amnestic aphasia)."

These 3 (or 2) may be considered as on the side of phasia where propositions are decodified or formulated. The next two involve the stage where words are chosen and syntaxis occurs, and fed seriatim into the motorizing mechanism. Now it is the pre-rolandic rather than the post-rolandic cortex (of the preceding cases) which is involved: the primary (motor cortex [Brodmann 4—area pyramidalis], the transitional cortex [Brodmann 6, with its several subdivisions], and "Broca's area" (Brodmann 44, at any rate). Here it is impossible to separate out the next two cases topographically, yet they differ symptomatically.

4. "Broca's aphasia." The patient cannot speak, yet by substituting his arms (gesture) he evidences that he can "propositionize." (He mày yet vocalize restrictedly.)

Conrad: "Verbal gestalts in process of verbalization out of the preverbal."

5. In pure word-muteness, the patient cannot pronounce words; phonemes are lost, some still pronounceable phoneme may be substituted, "speech" becomes "thick," slowed. This involves a more restricted cortical area than case 4—particularly, Brodmann 44 (a part of the original "Broca's area").

I have arranged these in a functional sequence that will readily be noticed by the reader. It is not without its significance that, concomitantly, we start and end with restricted cortical areas which approximate areas of earliest neocortical phylogenesis, and in between these the cortical involvement broadens out and also moves into supralimbic cortex, then narrows down again as the program is delivered over to the executing cortex.

It is considerations such as these which led to Alajouanine's (1956) polarizing the aphasias as "Broca's" and "Wernicke's." However, for the presentation in this essay, the writer takes the responsibility. Nor is Alajouanine's terminology that of Conrad, and there are others also. But the writer is confident that he has done no violence to the phenomena themselves, which are well-known, nor injustice to his authorities.

For simplicity's sake, and because of the difference in the modality, nothing has been said about visual-cortex involvement. It remains nevertheless to remark on disturbances of the reading and the writing function.

Incapacity to actually write or print letters (agraphia) expectably goes with pre-rolandic involvement, particularly, a Brodmann 6–8 area in the medial frontal gyrus; while an incapacity to recognize letters (alexia) and therefore to read, involves a somewhat restricted parieto-occipital cortex. Here we are dealing with symbols of symbols.

But the full force of all this, and the way in which different features of the phasial process are inextricable from features of certain other behavioral processes, can be had only from a confrontation with actual cases. We shall adduce a few, by quoting directly from authors; and this should help us appreciate the force of the experimental results obtained from ablations on the brains of macaques.

But first, a remark on dysphasias involving the thalamus. It is noteworthy that the articulatory, motorizing defects, the "verbalizing," are associated with phylogenetically older neocortex (Brodmann 6, 4) which traffics with an extrinsic thalamic nucleus (the anterolateral) while ideational malfunctions are associated with supralimbic cortex (Brodmann 39, 40, 21, 22, and contiguities) which traffics with intrinsic thalamic nuclei (posterior lateral and pulvinar).

It should not surprise us, therefore, if thalamic lesions produce speech derangements that resemble those of the cortex they traffic with, even if the cortex be not affected. Although I am reporting such cases from the statements of clinicians themselves, the latter would insist that often the final clinching proof is not possible to obtain; so that the demonstration should be evaluated as having but a high degree of probability in that there may be some accompanying involvements. Thus, Penfield and Roberts report a case of a small hemorrhagic lesion on the pulvinar in the dominant hemisphere without involvement of the cortex.

He had severe aphasia. When the disability began to improve, he showed perseveration; he misnamed profusely, and was unaware of his errors. When shown a pair of scissors, he said, "That is a subscriber." Then he added, "That is an African." A little later he said, "Well, an African knife." When asked if he knew how to use it, he said, "No." But he took up the scissors and used them appropriately. When shown a comb, he said, "That is a symbol." He spelled out the word symbol, correctly. Then he made a gesture as though to comb his hair.

(Penfield and Roberts, 1959: 215)

THE BODY SCHEMA IN MAN

From their studies of patients who developed incapacity to perceive and identify parts of their own bodies, difficulty in grasping the relations of objects in space or an unawareness of them—even an impregnable unawareness that there was anything the matter with them —clinicians have entertained the concept of the "body schema" (there are also synonyms)—the spatial "image" of the body which all normal individuals achieve experientially-maturationally in early postnatal ontogenesis. It is rooted in sensory experience; proprioception, which of course is cybernetic; and is and remains largely an unconscious matter. Its disorders are "topagnosia," "autotopagnosia."

And the symbolic process is very much involved in the disturbances. It follows that an important strategic and tactical question is that of body schema in alloprimates—granting immediately that its putative disturbances cannot be accompanied by phasial disruptions.

Eventually, we shall review some of the experimental findings by Denny-Brown and his asociates, from macaques. There is interesting evidence on chimpanzees scattered through the literature, some of it more explicit than other. (Here, the writings of Ladygina-Kohts are a gold mine. See also references to Yerkes and to Riesen.)

Suffice it here to indicate some informal evidence. A chimpanzee makes a categorical identification of human eyes with his own: He will place your spectacles over his own; use a handkerchief to his nose, grasp a cigarette as "humanly" as he can, use a straw to suck up a soft drink after seeing you do it, feed a baby with a spoon after studying human performance. For the present, we may leave the matter thus.

The relevances between space-time analysis, body-schema apprehension, and phasia can be grasped only from detailed description; hence the necessity for the following series of passages.

In the development of the individual, the distinction between the body and all external objects is the foundation upon which the distinction between self and not-self is based, however complex and intellectualized this distinction may ultimately become. Psychologically, therefore, it is to be expected that any serious disturbance of the psychological mechanisms underlying awareness of the body and its relations with external space must seriously undermine the foundations of the personality, apart from any other effects upon mental functioning which may be independently produced by the lesion.

(Brain, 1961: 171)

The world which is external to the boundaries of the body is perceived by means of our exteroceptive sensory apparatus and through those proprioceptors by which we recognize the external parts and implements of our body, such as our limbs, faces, distance receptors, and organs of communication. This is the original "non-I" world, even though it gradually comes to include some elements of the body image. At the same time there is an internal world which is rooted originally in the dimmer, less sharply localized and less clearly discriminated subjective sensations from the body. This is the "I" world of internal somatic sensations, mediated by enteroceptive and deeper proprioceptive experiences.

It is not necessary here to trace the changing content of these two worlds or their areas of overlap; but it is possible to demonstrate that every conceptual unit is rooted in both the "I" and "non-I" worlds. Indeed, it may be that every conceptual unit may have at least a triple linkage, in the "I," the "non-I," and an intermediate world. In this way the symbol itself may constitute the bridge between these alternative and often simultaneous channels for the expression of internal tensions. In other words, it is the symbolic process, with its multipolar conscious, preconscious, and unconscious linkages, which provides us with projective pathways for language and distance imagery at the one end, and introjective pathways for somatic dysfunction at the other.

. . . all new units of external experience must enter into the evolving psychic life by hitching onto that which is already present. Thus the earliest learning builds on intrabodily experience, and the expanding knowledge of the external world relates itself automatically to those bodily impressions which have already been experienced internally. The multipolar anchorage of concepts and symbols is represented in the games, songs, and dreams of childhood, and is carried over into the dreams and symptom-structures of adult life. It is this which gives to the symbolic process its bridging functions;

and no matter what metaphorical term we use to describe it, whether we speak of it as internalization and externalization, as introjection, incorporation, identification, or projection, without the multiple anchorage of the symbolic process none of these familiar transmutations of experience could take place at all. This remains true whether the transmutations take place consciously or unconsciously, on a purely psychological level or with the body involvements of the psychosomatic process.

(Kubie, 1953a: 4, 5)

. . . Birkmeyer (1951) regarded the idea of space as being built up of concentric space-shells *(Raumschalen),* of which the innermost is constituted by the subject's own body. This shell is ontogenetically the earliest, and is the one which is most generously endowed with sensory material. Beyond lies the area of grasp, or of touch *(Greifschale),* and beyond that, the area of vision *(Sehschale).* Within each shell, the constituent sensory qualities are fused by means of a faculty of orientation. With each space-shell the subject commands different ranges of freedom. Boundaries between the various spaceshells are not absolutely rigid. Each different type of orientation is liable to its own patterns of dysfunction in cases of cerebral affection. Orientation in the outmost (visual) shell is regarded as most vulnerable since only one sensory system is concerned. . . . But at a later stage still, it may seem as though the frontiers between personal and extrapersonal space become less sharp. This is the *Ich-Lähmung* of psychiatry, where there is an illusory fusion ("oneness") with the environment. Ego blends with non-ego. This may show itself by the patient confusing his own limbs with those of the examiner, or *vice versa.* . . . Particularly is this likely to happen when the examiner holds one of the patient's limbs; the patient may then imagine that the examiner's hand is his; or that his own leg is part of the examiner. . . .

(Critchley, 1953: 333, 335)

"Unilateral neglect" constitutes one of the earliest and most characteristic manifestations of an expanding lesion within the parietal lobe. . . . The "neglect" as affecting motor function comprises a poverty of movement, and deliberate willed actions are not impaired in strength. It is important to note that at this early stage the patient is not "paralysed" or afflicted with motor weakness. The patient does not use the affected hand, even in asymmetrical bimanual activities, unless his attention is specifically directed to that side, and also unless the bimanual activity otherwise becomes obviously incommoded. . . . [Tests] illustrate a failure on the patient's part to utilize both limbs except to specific command—as if the limbs on one side were occupying a lower level in the hierarchy of personal awareness. In other circumstances, however, both arms (or legs) will be employed naturally as in such a bimanual activity as holding a golf-club or a spade, or operating the keyboard of a typewriter. . . .

Somewhat later, however, the clinical picture may change. On the one hand, the patient may develop an actual motor weakness in the limb which hitherto has been merely neglected. . . . On the other hand, there may still be no trace of motor weakness, but other clinical troubles, mental as well as physical, may well be developing, as the expanding lesion increases. The patient may cease to pay heed to one half of his anatomy, to attend to its hygiene and cleanliness. The pathological degree of neglect may even extend to the inanimate coverings of the body over the affected half. . . . (Yet oddly,) "reflexive" movements (that is movements directed towards one's own person) are more readily carried out over the opposite half. . . . The right side of the body and the right arm are largely attended to by the left hand. If unilateral neglect exists, the right half of the body will now be dealt with by the right hand, but the patient will fail in right hand–left body performances. . . .

(Critchley, 1953: 226 ff.)

. . . The behaviour of the ambulatory patient with visual agnosia is often characteristic. He enters a room cautiously and looks around in a peering fashion, with his head craned forwards and his eyes turning from one side to the other. He obviously does not fixate normally upon any object. If his gaze fastens upon one point in space, or if it turns in the direction from which an auditory signal proceeds, he does not readily deviate his eyes towards any fresh stimulus. Should his eyes come to rest upon the leg of a table, he does not follow it upwards and thence over the surface of the table-top. Sometimes the patient slowly moves his head from side to side as he walks, in a manner reminiscent of the "blindisms" or motor mannerisms of the peripherally blinded.

Should the patient be questioned as to the subjective state of his vision, he may assert that it is adequate. He will rarely admit, at this stage at any rate, that his environment is foggy or misty, that objects are blurred in outline, or devoid of colour or sharpness of contour; or that things around him seem to be in movement, or distorted in shape. But if he is instructed to look at a particular object in front of him and to name it, he will often put up a characteristic performance. He will find difficulty in sighting the object and will probably look beyond it, or above it, or to one side. Or he will peer at it with his eyes deviated far to one side, gazing out of the corners of his eyes. At this point, he may project his difficulty by blaming his spectacles. He may proclaim he cannot see clearly without his glasses. When these are found, and have been put on, he may say that they are his old pair which he has outgrown; or his newest pair to which he has not yet become accustomed. Even more characteristic is a trick of taking off one pair of glasses, putting on another, and then taking these off. Also very typical is the habit whereby the patient holds up one hand before his eyes, as if shading them from the sun, or cutting out some of the illumination. When the hand is posed in this manner his head turns from one side to another in a searching and bewildered fashion. When asked why he shades his eyes, he may reply that it "helps his vision." No doubt this maneuver assists by cutting down the number of distracting visual objects in the environment.

The patient is now ready to try and name the object before him. At first, this may be difficult or impossible. The patient may make some attempt at describing the physical properties and with that assistance proceed to identify the object in a hesitating, unsure fashion. The next object may, however, be recognized promptly and accurately, but thereafter, further errors occur. Occasionally, after an object has been eventually identified, subsequent objects may receive the same appellation. This defect may be an aphasic one, i.e. a verbal perseveration. Less often, it is an actual visual perseveration. . . .

When the object looked at is a large one, e.g. a movable trolley, the patient may slowly identify parts of the object (wheels, leg, blanket, handle) without recognizing the trolley as a whole. This corresponds in the three-dimensional sphere with the simultanagnosis of two-dimensional pictorial representations. The term is, of course, a misnomer, for the process is not necessarily a "simultaneous" one, but may consist in a synthesis or building-up of details so as to form a logical whole.

(Critchley, 1953: 290ff.)

. . . The disorders resulting from parietal lobe lesion can be separated into two main groups: (1) the true agnosias, including all difficulties in identification that involve both sides of space and person from a unilateral lesion. The agnosias are clearly perceptual disturbances, related to difficulty in classification and naming, and of manipulating the symbol of a particular class of percept in the mind. They can be traced to a disorder of symbolism, a loss of the currency (engrams) of the mental usage of ideas of letters, parts of the body, or spatial relationships. The defect has to be ascertained by speech, by writing or by drawing. It is associated with variable degrees of secondary change in behavior. (2) The second group we have called amorphosynthesis, coining a word to express a type of disorder affecting a lower level of perception. Amorphosynthesis is manifested by disorder of behavior, is one-sided from a unilateral lesion, and though it may affect the ability to manipulate the symbolic aspects of the categories of perception involved, it is not necessarily associated with any difficulty in identification of classes of objects, parts of body, or places.

In the present discussion we shall consider chiefly the more purely behavioral disturbances which we have called amorphosynthesis. In this disorder though the manifestations are unilateral, it is apparent that there is always some generalization of disturbance. For example, the patient who has shown some difficulty in putting the affected arm into a jacket also shows a defect in shaving or arranging the hair on the affected side. If he makes errors in turning to right or to left, the errors are to the affected side. The disorder of behavior may be relatively limited to behavior directed by visual or tactile stereognostic or proprioceptive sensation, but within one of these categories affects all behavior in some degree, and commonly all categories in some degree. To an extent that is difficult to define, the whole personality of these patients is also altered, a change that is variously described as indifference or "more withdrawn."

Negative Reactions and "avoiding." . . . In various degrees [the patient] has difficulty in perceiving his own disability, and hence it is the disorder in his behavior that draws attention to his illness and not a subjective sense of altered perception. The type of denial of visual loss . . . is paralleled by the patient's failure of comprehension of his speech disorder in the parietal lobe type of jargon-aphasia, by his absence of awareness of the disorder of dressing and toilet, of avoiding reactions, and denial of hemiplegia, and probably also in the so-called "asymbolia of pain."

. . . The ultimate degree of loss identification of parts of the body would appear to be disorientation of person, and not denial of limbs or of disability. . . .

If, therefore, we regard amorphosynthesis as primarily a defect in behavior, we note that it presents two general features. The first is a general indifference to external events, which may have to do with the affected side of person and extrapersonal space, and a failure of natural corresponding motor reactions. Secondly, there is a more specific withdrawal from some events, particularly those that normally have some degree of unpleasant or surprising connotation. Thus the hand is withdrawn from any new stimulus by an extension of fingers, hyperextension of the wrist and flexion at proximal joints such as to remove the limb from the stimulus. . . . This reaction, which we have called the "avoiding reaction," is as common in patients with parietal lesions as its opposite, instinctive grasping and palpation, is a frontal lobe disorder. Also, as with the altered behavior in frontal lesions, the patient is unaware of these responses and is embarrassed if his attention is drawn to them. This withdrawal from a tactile stimulus is associated with other types of negative reactions in the affected side. The patient looks away from the examiner when the latter appears on the affected side and may deny his presence or may relate him to the sound side. . . .

Some degree of avoiding reaction is associated with all forms of parietal apraxia, but it is often difficult to decide to what degree visual stimuli or tactile stimuli initiate the reaction. . . .

For example, we have recently seen a woman 66 years of age who exhibited marked visual inattention to the right side, extinction of tactile painful and visual stimuli on that side when paired with a corresponding stimulus on the opposite side. The onset of the illness four months earlier had been in the form of a sudden appearance of completely incoherent speech, with right hemianopia and inability to read. The "hemianopia" (failure of reaction to any stimulus in the right visual field) had rapidly cleared in the first week, but the disturbance of speech and reading remained. The patient, however, was now able to carry on a completely intelligible conversation on the telephone, yet still lapsed into incoherent jargon when face to face with another person, somewhat less so with her eyes covered by dark glasses. She could read silently to herself when undisturbed, yet was unable to do so in the presence of another, and spoke only garbled jargon when asked to read aloud. She denied that any of her performance was defective.

In more specific performances such as in writing these inconsistencies may be very remarkable.

For example, H. H., a 59-year-old hypertensive, left-handed man suffered a sudden onset of confused behavior without weakness in the limbs. He denied any disability but failed to cover the left side of his body in dressing, and ignored all objects and events to his left side. There were astereognosis and loss of position sense in the left limbs. Pin prick and touch were felt in the left side but showed prolonged extinction by concurrent stimulation of the right side. The left hand was held almost constantly in an extended posture, and a touch elicited a marked avoiding reaction in it with levitation. A similar touch in the palm of the right hand induced grasping. In addition there was a left inattention visual field defect, and he failed to recognize objects on the left side in a multiple object picture. There was finger agnosia on both sides and inability to calculate. He was extremely apraxic in attempting to strike a match or comb his hair with his left hand, though he could use a comb correctly in his right hand. In childhood he had learned to write with his right hand. When he attempted to write, however, he picked up the pencil naturally and appeared to write with a flourish, pausing naturally for punctuation and seemed fully satisfied with the result, which was simply a series of meaningless strokes. He refused to believe that he had not written down what he was asked.

(Denny-Brown and Chambers, 1958: 36ff., condensed)

BODY SCHEMA IN AN ALLOPRIMATE: SOME EXPERIMENTAL EVIDENCE

A very great deal of indirect evidence about this is scattered through the literature on neuropsychological and psychological experiments upon chimpanzees and upon macaques. Earlier (see above: "The Body Schema in Man"), informal mention was made of the chimpanzee case. Here, we shall consider some of the results from temporo-parietal ablations upon macaques performed by Denny-Brown and his associates. These investigators have ablated systematically the neo-cortex of macaques, and compared the resulting behavior deficits with the clinically experienced human dysfunctions. Since macaques possess no degree of phasia, the human difficulties related to the manipulation of symbols cannot be matched. Yet these difficulties in man are accompanied by other behavioral changes in varying degree; so that a "lower level of perception" remains comparable. For such as these, the researchers have coined the term "amorphosynthesis." (Brain [1961: 165] has questioned it as a neuropsychological hypothesis; but this is not involved in the context of our presentation.)

Posterior parietal area. Unilateral ablation of the posterior half of the parietal lobe was followed by an attention hemianopia to the opposite side. The animal did not reach out to place the opposite limbs on a surface, or to prehend an object approaching him on that side, but if the object approached him from the side of the lesion, and then came near enough on the opposite side, he reached to place or grasp. The opposite limbs were used for climbing and support. When the examiner was present, the animal always sat at the back of the cage in the corner on the side of the lesion, and when approached backed along the shelf and climbed down with back to the examiner in the manner already described for total parietal extirpation. He was nervous and restless with any form of stimulation, backing away from the stimulus. When the hand opposite the lesion was touched, he withdrew it with overextended fingers. He failed to abduct the affected limbs to cling to a broad surface such as the body of the examiner. In an examining chair a touch of the hand or foot induced an avoiding reaction. Reaction to pinprick was natural except that withdrawal was increased in amplitude and the fingers persisted in extension posture. If pricking was continued, a pawing movement developed, and this then continued for many seconds after cessation of the stimulus. There was no blink to threat from the opposite side.

When such a posterior parietal lesion was made *bilateral,* the behavior of the animal was greatly altered. The animal was frequently found climbing on the wire ceiling of his cage, but would usually retreat to a corner of the cage and make agitated restless movements as if to push himself further into the corner as another monkey or the examiner approached. If he came to the examiner for food, he approached backwards or upside down on the wire of the ceiling. At first he could not find food in his cage, and if given some banana ate some but soon dropped it and lost it. He was extremely nervous, fixing his eyes on the examiner and seemingly oblivious of all else. He would bite at a pin or stick only when they touched him. If grasped by one foot he would struggle violently but not attack the hand that held him. A touch on a limb while he looked at the examiner would elicit an impatient pawing movement, or if the foot was touched, a repeated dancing flexion on the leg or of both lower limbs. When a stick approached him in the cage, he tended to turn away and get off his shelf backwards. In the first two weeks he appeared not to see an object approaching him if his eyes were fixed on the examiner, and this was noticeable at times for a much longer period. Yet his limbs made a small flexion movement ("visual avoiding") if an object passed close to them. If suddenly startled in this way, he jumped violently forwards colliding with wall or cage wire. Touch of a limb in the examining chair evoked only mild withdrawal (tactile avoiding). When held up close to a vertical pole or to the examiner's body, he made no attempt to abduct the limbs to clasp such an object before he touched it. Exploratory movements then began, ending in a clumsy walking movement without adequate abduction. He would walk over, or sit in, a dish of food and only later discover its contents by touch and smell. Tactile placing was present, but visual placing remained absent, and the above nervous uncertain behavior remained constant for the longest survival (5 months). No abnormal catatonic fixation of posture was observed.

Orientation and Recognition. . . . . The striking feature of the temporal lobectomized animal is that in spite of excellent vision, the reaction to persons and threats no longer includes appropriate fear, and is replaced by a repetitive compulsive examination of all objects with frequent appeal to smell and taste for identification. The resemblance to agnosia resulting from parieto-occipital lesions in man was noted by Klüver and Bucy. Yet it is clear in our own experiments that the animal without temporal lobes can occasionally react appropriately to the examiner, can recognize objects by vision, and is certainly not lacking in the emotion of fear and its consequent swing to aggression. The stimulus, however, requires to be more intense.

The animal with severe bilateral ablation also uses smell and taste to assist identification but seldom eats in the presence of the investigator. After more extensive bilateral parieto-occipital ablation food is found by smell. Oral behavior in the form of biting new objects that touch or approach the animal becomes prominent. Olfactory and mouthing behavior are thus prominent with or without the temporal lobes and in each case exhibit the residual activity of fronto-insular cortex.

The physiological degree of disturbance of recognition of events in the person and in the environment in man following parietal lesion that we have called amorphosynthesis indicates a failure of the process of recognition that is more evident in behavior than in response to direct question. The failure of recognition of objects or persons by touch or vision alone, with ability to identify the object by means of another sense (astereognosis, agnosia for persons), is also manifest as a behavioral defect but is the more apparent to the patient because of the ability to make identification by the other sense. In the monkey the loss of social behavior and particularly in visuomotor response to other monkeys following large lesions, as in the parietal preparation, or the temporal preparation, is constant and fixed, so that for these animals these classes of objects and persons appear to cease to exist.

In man large lesions of comparable size are associated with failure to react to the opposite side. The head and eyes are deviated to the side of the lesion. If the parietal or parieto-occipital region is chiefly involved, the affected side is denied. In large frontal and temporal lesions, the affected side receives no attention, but denial is not present.

As a result of parietal ablation in monkeys, the change in behavior is such as to indicate that all stimuli are now reacted to as unpleasant ones formerly were. Alternatively the unpleasant features of every stimulus now elicit an unopposed response. At first it might appear that this feature overshadows an associated loss of any reaction to many types of stimulus. Yet in time crude placing reactions returned, and the animal could recognize his own cage by vision. Faulty estimations of place and distance were consistently in terms of underestimation, suggesting the operation of opposing negative factors. The remaining temporal lobe endows the organism with general withdrawal reactions to bright light, and intense directed avoiding responses to moving visual stimuli, but not positive identification of them. Patients with some parietal types of visual agnosia are commonly anxious and tense, and are thrown into sudden panic and confusion by a moving visual stimulus, e.g., seeing a vehicle in the street pass across their line of vision. As a result of bilateral lesions in man, difficulty in perception in terms of geometric features of objects and interrelationship of objects can occur. . . . More often the defect is apparent only in perception of such symbolic features as the shape of numerals or of letters, or the sequence of word sounds. The commonest type of defect is the interruption of perceptual pattern by the perseveration of some poorly differentiated perceptual image. In this sense, symbolic interpretation could be acting as a sensitive indicator of minor degrees of loss of spatial orientation.

Commonly in man parietal lesions are associated with unawareness or denial of disability. This peculiar feature, so evident in jargon-aphasia, in cortical blindness, and in some cases of large unilateral lesion affecting more particularly somatic sensation, implies an inability to comprehend current performance in speech, vision, or somatic sensation, respectively. It is a type of defect different from the disturbance of perception based on perseveration. It is as if the part of mind relating to the particular function in question did not exist. Absence of recognition might not appear to be compatible with an avoiding response, for the latter implies that some kind of receptiveness exists. If, however, it is recognized that in all types of parietal lesion the patient is unaware of his avoiding response, it becomes possible that the avoiding response as an unconscious release phenomenon is interfering with the process of perception. The results of extensive parieto-occipital and temporo-occipital cortical ablations in monkeys described here show that much of the symptomatology of parietal lobe lesions is due to unopposed activity of temporal lobe mechanisms, and *vice versa*. The symptomatology that is manifest with bilateral symmetrical lesions is present after unilateral lesion in milder degree on the contralateral side. In general it is the adversive "avoiding" reactions peculiar to the limbic and closely related cortex that counteract the exploratory functions of the rolandic and particularly the parietal cortex. In this the tactile avoiding reactions of the cingulate region (and related parts of areas 6 and 8 of Brodmann) and the visual avoiding reactions of the temporal lobe are most important. The high development of positive stereotactic behavior in monkey and man appears to underlie the great expansion of neocortex, displacing much of the less developed discriminative avoiding mechanisms to the medial surface in the course of evolution.

(Denny-Brown and Chambers, 1958: 55 ff., 108–111, condensed.)

ONTOGENETIC REMARKS

In view of the facts that the neocortical cytoarchitecture of the human (as well as alloprimate) brain is remarkably homogeneous overall, so that, intracortically, the regional differences are matters of histologic relativity—that is, a matter of relative quantities in cell number, density, size, etc.; and that Nature locates lesions in an arbitrary manner—it is only to be expected that every clinical case should have its uniqueness, and the sorting out of common denominators should have produced a variety of categorizings and nomenclatures. For any behavior is syndromal; speech itself is an *ad hoc* syndrome, and never is produced by cortical regions which abandon all other activity while they concentrate their efforts for the moment, upon this exclusive program.

Electroencephalography, applied exploratorily in clinical treatment of the epilepsies, and the faradic mappings of the exposed human cortex, have combined with the eloquence of the lesions to give us some notion of how Nature has built speech. The edifice does not resemble the linguistic analyses; and behavioral study is to the neurophysiological substrate as a topographic map is to a geological one.

From all the evidence that has been sketched in this survey, some features of that primate phonic communication which we term human speech do seem to emerge.

It is not some unaccountable *nova;* instead, its components are as if alloprimate endeavors at space-time analysis and synthesis had been driven to further refinement. Progressive refining has been a feature of the evolution of brain from primitive to advanced mammals (to say nothing here of what had taken place from fish to reptile). The refinement has not been on the perceptive-cognitive side only; for it can be documented even to the splitting up of muscular sheets in the distal portions of the limbs in primitive mammals, so that a greater refinement and variety of motions become possible in more evolved mammals. Although even the best of mammals cannot match the versatility of the avian syrinx, at least we can expect that the phonic thesaurus of a monkey will far exceed that of a shrew in any dimension.

What the pre-rolandic (the frontal) and the post-rolandic (temporoparieto-occipital) supralimbic cortex are engaged in doing in an alloprimate, they continue to do in the human primate, only more so. And it appears that, from the knowing of universals to the gestalting of the nontemporal, nonspatial symbol, there is no break, although in places along the continuum the evidence is thin.

In formulating a fully viable symbolic gestalt, we assemble from a vorgestalt to a preverbal gestalt, and pass it hence to verbalization— the phonated verbal gestalt. It is a continuous process, of course, an appetitive generality which focuses down to a consummative specificity, a kind of directed Markov process if you will. Crudely stated, it is as though Wernicke's area assembles a gestalt and instructs Broca's area. It is an instructional matter at every point along the procedure, and the instructions can go wrong at any point; the behavior symptoms that result will be characteristic.

Extensive and increasingly effective research is revealing how this gestalting capacity matures, particularly in man's earlier years. And again it is evident that, were we to confine our attention only to those segments of behavior which are matters of speaking, we should lose a large proportion of the available information; for how a child teaches himself to speak, in his cultural milieu—his environment C— vividly demonstrates that it is part of the effort after meaning whereby he organizes his space-time.

The reason this perceptive-cognitive organizing can pass over to a programmed utterance is that, in man, phonation has a representation in the lower pre-rolandic cortex considerably beyond that in alloprimates, and that corespondingly there is a lowered threshold of impulse. The crying at birth, the lalia of two or three months later, the eventual echolalia about a half-year yet later, are indications of this. But there are preadaptions already building up *in utero:* The human brain differs from the ape *ab initio,* in measure as the DNA instructions differ.

The perception-cognition which eventuates in the gestalting of speech, and which we have associated with parietal cortex, is not correlated in some *pari passu* way with the organization of a verbal utterance. This already has been indicated by the distinguishability between a "Wernicke" and a "Broca" aphasia. There is the very familiar fact that deaf mutes in no wise are impaired on the perception-cognition side of phasial assembling. There is the equally significant fact that infants comprehend speech precociously in comparison with their capacity to mobilize it themselves. And chimpanzees raised in human homes (there have been several different cases of this) certainly learn to comprehend spoken commands while they do not seem to be even aware of their own lack of motivation toward attempting to utter any. Decades ago, Ladygina-Kohts taught chimpanzees to read simple words. Chimpanzees are capable of an order of prediction which induces them to collect chips for a later use in a "chimpomat."

It is amply evident that the capacity for perception-cognition and the capacity or motivation for converting the results of its exercise into a phonal coding that adequately reflects it, are two quite different matters. This is difficult at best, even at the highest human level; and even at the chimpanzee level it is very obvious that the animal's power of phonal coding bears no comparison at all with its capacity for conceptualizing.

It is equally certain that the human readiness to vocalize already has undergone development even *in utero* which is unmatched by any other animal. The human birth cry is as unique as it is spectacular; it has never been adequately accounted for. We may dismiss the rationalizations which point out its useful effects in clearing the respiratory tract etc.: They beg all the questions. Nor are "outrage" and "inferiority" as accountings any more helpful.

A neonate chimpanzee, if electrostimulated in the inferior pre-rolandic area, is fully capable of suckling lip motions, but does not vocalize. In fact, there are almost no cases of vocalizings being electroinduced in any other *adult* than man.

These electrostimulations suggest a lowered threshold of excitability of inferior pre-rolandic cortex. I doubt if neurophysiologists and psychologists would consider this a satisfactory explanation. The emotive roles of hippocampus and of reticular system, in man as well as other animals, suggest further some intensification in the interractions of all these.

There ensues, in the human infant, at about two to three months, the well-known period of *lalia,* which often seems an expression of well-being; and the sounds are highly varied as well as formidably difficult for an adult to try imitating. This occurs in deaf babies as well; but it ceases earlier than in normals—presumably because of no self-reinforcement (feedback).

Some weeks or months later, melodic imitations of human talk begin; at about nine months we may expect a more definable echolalia. The first "words" are interpreted as such by a parent; but their semantics are more general propositions. (The developmental behavior, the developmental psychology, which eventuates as phasia has a large literature which needs no citations here. For current approaches in the U.S., see particularly Lenneberg, 1964. At the time of writing this essay, Lenneberg's "Biological Foundations of Language" (1967) had not yet appeared. The writer is also indebted to studies by Luria.)

Thenceforth, the young child progresses analytically and synthetically; the capacity for ever higher levels of abstractions expands programmatically; and it is very unlikely that it is saltatory, as might be inferred from the character of many psychological test batteries and their data. Whatever be the nature of the correlation cortex in the parieto-temporo-occipital area reaches its definitive cytoarchitectonics in the prepubertal period; and abstractive capacity seems not to be completed earlier.

That phonated verbalization and conceptual gestalting play back to each other is also well evidenced. This phenomenon has never been elicted in chimpanzees.

This whole program in man commences with preadaptive developments *in utero*. We may presume that DNA codings begin writing instructions into templates as early as that; so that it is not really an anomaly that even a microcephalic can achieve a rudimentary speech —because it is human, and not ape. The passing remark is worthwhile in that the developmental behavior of phonation in nonhumans remains a science for the future; yet what fragments are known do not, I believe, encourage us to look for the emergence of phasia as an opening up of a closed system of cries by a process of segmentation and haplologic recombinations.

REMARKS ON ONTOGENESIS RELATIVE TO PHYLOGENESIS

From their studies of mongoloid as well as normal children, Lenneberg, Nichols, and Rosenberger (1964: 134) see the language learning process as one

in which general principles are learned, or rules are acquired, which can then at once be applied to a whole set of conditions. This is a fundamentally different process from one in which individual items are learned and then added to a stock of other items. Such item-by-item learning is not the main characteristic of language acquisition—not even in the expansion of vocabulary. . . . Naming of objects is based on a general principle of naming which, once acquired, lays the entire foundation of symbolization. . . . "Stockpiling" of lexical terms must wait until the basic principle is established.

And Lenneberg draws our attention to the fact that children develop the capacity for speech much earlier than they mature their capacity for the higher intellectual processes; and indeed that feebleminded individuals and nanocephals develop a genuine speech capacity. (Some of these brains may be volumetrically smaller than ape brains.)

If, then, we speculate about the time and the course of·the phylogenesis of phasia, then, with Lenneberg, we may believe that speaking may be older than the higher intellectual processes (1964: 78).

All inferences from an ontogenetic to a phylogenetic process are, of course, suspect procedures. The very young *Homo sapiens* does indeed contain the innate developmental instructions which program his phasial capacity; yet the experiential side is that of learning to adapt within a code already established and in use by adults. In phylogenesis, the template for speech was itself in process of being written into the DNA code. Although, on the one hand, the young hominid was learning to cope with his environments, C (and A), on the other hand, the adult protohominids were themselves evolving their environment C, and at any given moment of geological time they were all on a par in the conditioning process.

Yet there are two features in the ontogenesis of the speech behavior in *Homo sapiens* which, I think, furnish valid comment to phylogenetic speculation, to wit: (1) the development of general principles instead of an item-by-item addition. This is consistent with what is being learned about the knowing of universals and the recognition of categories at even early evolutionary levels. (2) "Naming" could not have been a first step in the origin of speech. This notion— still held by some individuals today—seems to derive from another, and fallacious, notion that this is the initial in speech acquisition by children. If a beginner says "cup," he is uttering a "sentence" rather than a word. There is a distinction between iconicity and name or word.

The endocasts of Australopithecines and Pithecanthropines are tantalizingly suggestive; but they are uncertain at best. All that we might say with safety is that their surfaces permit the possibility that the owners of their originals possessed a speech configuration—they spoke—but the intellective order of symbol making was a low one, in measure as the parieto-temporo-occipital cortex was inadequate.

Perhaps it is not without significance that the earliest Hominidae could shape a stone tool, and even develop a shapeliness; that long ago Neanderthalers could assemble bear skulls about an "altar"; while pictographic art is a matter of but a few recent decimillennia. Yet quite possibly they all spoke, after their several fashions.

A NOTE ON HEMISPHERAL ASYMMETRY

Space-time as a fundamental of (human) behavioral organizing has been formally recognized by Gooddy (1964) and by Gooddy and Reinhold (1952, 1953, 1961, 1963) in a series of papers at once psychological and neurological. What is more particularly arresting is their attributing congenital deficiency of space orientation plus congenital dyslexia in otherwise normally intelligent children to a failure of their hemispheres to complete the functional asymmetry which, in adults, is signaled by the dominance-subordinance characteristic where speech formulation is involved (Gooddy and Reinhold, 1961).

On entirely other grounds, this writer arrived at a closely similar conjecture. (Dr. Gooddy and the writer later discovered that both had been influenced by the ideas of Dr. Walther Riese—and both of us believe that his 'Principles of Neurology" has been under-appreciated.) This author's (1964) paper, presented in 1962, may be summarized thus:

Both hemispheres receive, assumably, exactly the same perception editings via the thalamic nuclei and reticular formation. (We assume this until a differential transmission from the thalamus itself may be indicated.) They are also in intercommunication via commissures. They have no anatomical dissimilarities to which any significance may be attached. They seem not to have tangible functional inequivalence during earlier postnatal ontogenesis; the inequivalence becomes only gradually effective, and early injuries result in what some neurologists speak of as the minor hemisphere "taking over" functions from a crippled major hemisphere. This laterality appears independent of right- and left-handedness (and there really is no reason why we should have expected otherwise).

The minor hemisphere (usually the right), moreover, is known not to be idiotic in matters of phasia, despite the overshadowing role of the dominant hemisphere.

We are beginning to understand how the nervous systems of animals abstract universals from particulars; how spatial and temporal interconversions are effected; how the improved scannings by the evolutionary successions of cortical refinements build up to symbol. But the final effect is the detachment of symbol from a here-now base: In man at least it is emancipated from space-time connotations. This may be finalized by a nonidentical, asymmetric reciprocation between the hemispheres.

This is not to say that the asymmetry alone has produced the emancipation. There are other factors at work—as, for instance, indicated by hallucinogenetic activities even in limbic mechanisms. The asymmetric performance of the supralimbic system must have been a gradual evolution; it has had a capstone effect.

Clearly psychological experiments upon split brain macaques and cats, and clinical observations of humans who have undergone hemispheral dividings (Akelaitis, 1944; Basser, 1962, Goodglass and Quadfasel, 1954; Hillier, 1954; Humphrey and Zangwill, 1952; Roberts, 1955; Sperry, 1958, 1961), are to be watched with lively interest.

BIBLIOGRAPHY

Akelaitis, A. J. 1944. A study of gnosis, praxis, and language following section of the corpus callosum and anterior commissure. *J. Neurol:* **1**:94–102.

Alajouanine, T. 1956. Verbal realization in aphasia. *Brain* **79**:1–28.

Ashby, W. R. 1960. "Design for a Brain." Wiley, New York.

Basser, L. S. 1962. Hemiplegia of early onset and the faculty of speech with special reference to the effects of hemispherectomy. *Brain* **85**:427–460.

Bay, E. 1962. Aphasia and non-verbal disorders of language, *Brain* **85**:411–427.

Beer, S. 1959–60. "Cybernetics and Management." Wiley, New York.

Bentley, A. F. 1941. The factual space and time of behavior. *J. Philosophy* **38**:477–485.

Bertalanffy, L. v. 1950. The theory of open systems in physics and biology. *Science* **111**:23–29.

———. 1956. General system theory. *General Systems Yearbook* **1**:1–10.

Bishop, G. H. 1956. Natural history of the nerve impulse. *Physiol. Rev.* **36**:376–399.

Bonin, G. v. 1942. The striate area of primates. *J. Compar. Neurol.* **77**:405–429.

———. 1950. "Essay on the Cerebral Cortex." Charles C. Thomas, Springfield, Ill.

———. 1952. Notes on cortical evolution. *Arch. Neurol. Psychiat.* **67**:135–144.

Brain, Lord 1961. "Speech Disorders." Butterworth, Washington.

Brazier, M. A. B. 1964. The electrical activity of the nervous system. *Science* **146**:1423–1428.

Bruner, J. S. 1957. Neural mechanisms in perception. *Psychol. Rev.* **64**:340–358.

Coghill, G. E. 1938. Space-time as a pattern of psycho-organismal mentation. *Amer. J. Psychol.* **51**:759–763.

Conrad, K. 1954. New problems of aphasia. *Brain* **77**:491–509.

Count, E. W. 1958. The biological basis of human sociality. *Amer. Anthropologist* **60**:1949–1085.

———. 1958–59. Eine biologische Entwicklungsgeschichte der menschlichen Sozialität. *Homo* **9**:126–146; **10**:1–35, 65–92.

———. 1964. Phasia: on the phylogenesis of speech. "Proceedings of the Ninth International Congress of Linguists, Cambridge, Mass, August 27–31, 1962." Mouton & Co., The Hague.

———. 1967. The lactation complex. *Homo* **18**:38–54.

Critchley, McD. 1953. "The Parietal Lobes." Edward Arnold, London.

Denny-Brown, D. 1956. Positive and negative aspects of cerebral cortical function. *North Carolina Med. J.* **1917**:295–303.

———, and B. Q. Banker. 1954. Amorphosynthesis from left parietal lesion. *Arch. Neurol. Psychiat.* **71**:302–313.

———, and R. A. Chambers. 1958. The parietal lobe and behavior. *Res. Pub. Asso. of Nervous and Mental Diseases* **36**:35–117.

———, J. S. Meyers, and S. Horenstein. 1952. The significance of perceptual rivalry resulting from parietal lesion. *Brain* **75**:433–471.

Dethier, V. G. 1964. Microscopic brains, *Science* **143**:1138–1145.

Dewey, J. 1896. The reflex arc concept in psychology. *Psychol. Rev.* **3**:357–370.

Dubois, E. 1897. De verhouding van het gewicht der hersenen tot de grootte van het lichaam bij zoogdieren. *Verhandelingen der Koninklijke Akad. van Wetenschappen, Amsterdam* **5**:10ff.

———. 1898. Über die Abhängigkeit des Hirngewichts von der Körpergrösse beim Menschen. *Archiv. Anthropol.* **25**:123ff.

Ehrenwald, H. 1931. Störung der Zeitauffassung, der räumlichen Orientierung, des Zeichnens und des Rechnens bei einem Hirnverletzten. *Z. gesamte Neurol. Psychiat.* **132**:518–569.

Frank, L. K. *et al.* 1948. Teleological mechanisms. *An. N. Y. Acad. Sci.* **50**:187–278.

Frings, H. and M. Frings. 1964. "Animal Communication." Blaisdell, New York.

Galambos, R. 1959. Electrical correlates of conditioned learning. "The CNS and Behavior, 1st Conference." Josiah Macy, Jr. Foundation, New York.

Goldstein, K. 1947. Organismic approach to the problems of motivation. *Trans. N. Y. Acad. Sci.* April, 218–230.

——. 1947–63. "The Organism." Beacon Press, Boston.

Gooddy, W. 1964. Some comments on the significance of retrograde amnesia, with an analogy. *Brain* **87**:75–86.

Gooddy, W. and M. Reinhold. 1952–53. Some aspects of human orientation in space, I. *Brain* **75**:472–509; II. *Brain* **76**:337ff.

——. 1963. Some aspects of human orientation in space, III. In: L. Halpern, ed., "Problems of Dynamic Neurology." Jerusalem.

——. 1961. Congenital dyslexia and asymmetry of cerebral function. *Brain* **84**:231–242.

Goodglass, H. and F. A. Quadfasel. 1954. Language laterality in left-handed aphasics. *Brain* **77**:521–548.

Gregory, R. L. 1961. The brain as an engineering problem. In: W. H. Thorpe and O. L. Zangwill, eds., "Current Problems in Animal Behaviour." Cambridge University Press, Cambridge.

Hall, A. D. and R. E. Fagen. 1956. Definition of system, *General Systems Yearbook* **1**:18–28.

Harlow, H. F. and C. N. Woolsey, eds. 1958. "Biological and Biochemical Bases of Behavior." University of Wisconsin Press, Madison.

Hayek, F. A. 1952. "The Sensory Order." University of Chicago Press, Chicago.

Hebb, D. O. 1959. Intelligence, brain function and the theory of mind. *Brain* **82**:260–275.

Herrick, C. J. 1956. "The Evolution of Human Nature." Harper, New York.

Hillier, W. F. 1954. Total left cerebral hemispherectomy for malignant glioma. *Neurology* **4**:718–721.

Hockett, C. F. 1960. Logical considerations in the study of animal communication. In: W. E. Lanyon and W. N. Tavolga, eds., "Animal Sounds and Communication." AIBS, Washington, D. C.

——, and R. Ascher. 1964. The human revolution. *Current Anthropol.* **5**:135–168.

Humphrey, M. E. and O. L. Zangwill. 1952. Effects of a rightsided occipito-parietal brain injury in a left-handed man. *Brain* **75**:312–324.

Jackson, J. Hughlings. 1958. Selected Writings of J. Hughlings Jackson. Basic Books, New York.

Jasper, H. 1949. Diffuse projection systems. The integrative action of the thalamic reticular system. *EEG and Clinical Neurophysiol.* **1**:405–420.

Kennedy, C. H. 1927. The exoskeleton as a factor in limiting and directing the evolution of insects. *J. Morphol.* **44**:267–312.

Klüver, H. 1952. Brain mechanisms and behavior with special reference to the rhinencephalon. *J. Lancet* **72**:567–574.

——, and P. C. Bucy. 1939. Preliminary analysis of functions of the temporal lobes in monkeys. *Arch. Neurol. Psychiat.* **42**:979–1000.

Kubie, L. S. 1953a. The central representation of the symbolic process in psychosomatic disorders. *Psychosom. Med.* **15**:1–7.

——. 1953b. The distortion of the symbolic process in neurosis and psychosis. *J. Amer. Psychoanal. Ass.* **1**:59–86.

——. 1953c. Some implications for psychoanalysis of modern concepts of the organization of the brain. *Psychoanal. Quart.* **22**:21–68.

Ladygina-Kohts, N. N. 1923. "Issledovaniye poznavatel'nykh sposobnostey shimpanze." GIZ, Moscow.

——. 1959. "Konstruktivnaya i orudiynaya deyatel'nost' vysshikh obyezan." Izd. Akad. Nauk SSSR, Moscow.

Lashley, K. S. 1952. Functional interpretations of anatomical patterns. *Proc. Ass. Res. Nervous and Mental Diseases* **30**:529–547.

Lenneberg, Eric H., ed. 1964. "New Directions in the Study of Language." M.I.T. Press, Cambridge, Mass.

———. 1967. "Biological Foundations of Language." Wiley, New York.

———, I. A. Nichols and E. F. Rosenberger. 1964. Primitive stages of language development in mongolism. *Proc. Ass. Res. Nervous and Mental Diseases* **42**:119–137.

Lettvin, J. Y., H. R. Maturana, W. S. McCulloch and W. H. Pitts. 1959. What the frog's eye tells the frog's brain. *Proc. Inst. Radio Engineers* **47**:1940–1951.

Lorenz, K. 1935. Der Kumpan in der Umwelt des Vogels. *Z. Ornithol.* **83**:137–213, 289–413.

Luria, A. R. 1962. "Vysshiye korkovyye funktsii chelovyeka i ikh naruzheniya pri lokal'nykh porazheniyakh mozga." Izd. Moskov, Univ., Moscow.

———. 1963. "Mozg chelovyeka i psikhlicheskiye protsessy." Akad. Pedagog. Nauk, RSFSR, Moscow.

McCulloch, W. S. 1948. A recapitulation of the theory. In: L. K. Frank *et al.*, "Teleological Mechanisms" (=*Ann. N. Y. Acad. Sci.* 50). 187–278.

MacLean, P. D. 1949. Psychosomatic disease and the "visceral brain." *Psychosom. Med.* **11**:338–353.

———. 1954. The limbic system and its hippocampal formation. *J. Neurosurgery* **11**: 29–44.

———. 1955. Studies on the limbic system (visceral brain) and their bearing on psychosomatic problems. In: E. D. Wittkower and R. A. Cleghorn, eds., "Recent Developments in Psychosomatic Medicine." Lippincott, Philadelphia.

———. 1958. Contrasting functions of limbic and neocortical systems of the brain and their relevance to psychophysiological aspects of medicine. *Amer. J. Med.* **25**: 611–626.

Magoun, H. W. 1963. "The Waking Brain." 2nd ed. Charles C. Thomas, Springfield, Ill.

Marler, P. 1961. The filtering of external stimuli during instinctive behaviour. In: W. H. Thorpe and O. L. Zangwill, eds., "Current Problems in Animal Behaviour." Cambridge University Press, Cambridge.

Maslow, A. H. 1966. Isomorphic interrelationships between knower and known. In: G. Kepes, ed., "Sign, Image, Symbol." George Braziller, New York.

Moore, J. A., ed. 1965. "Ideas in Modern Biology." Natural History Press, New York.

Mountcastle, V. B., ed. 1962. "Interhemispheric Relations and Cerebral Dominance." Johns Hopkins Press, Baltimore.

Neumann, J. v. 1958. "The Computer and the Brain." Yale University Press, New Haven.

Nielsen, J. M. 1962. "Agnosia, Apraxia, Aphasia." Hafner, New York.

Ogle, K. N. 1962. The visual space sense. *Science* **135**:763–771.

Ombredane, A. 1951. "L'aphasie et l'élaboration de la pensée explicite." Presses Universitaires de France, Paris.

Papez, J. W. 1937. A proposed mechanism of emotion. *Arch. Neurol. Psychiat.* **38**: 725–743.

Penfield, W., and T. Rasmussen. 1955. "The Cerebral Cortex of Man." Macmillan, New York.

———, and L. Roberts. 1959. "Speech and Brain Mechanisms." Princeton University Press, Princeton.

Pitts, W. H., and W. S. McCulloch. 1947. How we know universals. *Bull. Math. Biophys.* **9**:127–147.

Pribram, K. H. 1958. Neocortical functions in behavior. In: H. F. Harlow and C. N. Woolsey, eds., "Biological and Biochemical Bases of Behavior." University of Wisconsin Press, Madison.

———, and L. Kruger. 1954. Functions of the olfactory brain. *Ann. N. Y. Acad. Sci.* **58**: 109–138.

Prosser, C. L. 1965. Levels of biological organization and their physiological significance. In: J. A. Moore, ed., "Ideas in Modern Biology." Natural History Press, New York.

Riese, W. 1950. "Principles of Neurology" (="Nervous and Mental Disease Monographs"). New York.

Riesen, A. H. 1947. The development of visual preception in man and chimpanzee. *Science* **106**:107–108.

Roberts, L., 1955. Handedness and cerebral dominance. *Trans. Amer. Neurol. Ass.* **80**:143–148.

Rose, J. E., and C. N. Woolsey. 1949. Organization of the mammalian thalamus and its relationship to the cerebral cortex. *EEG and Clinical Neurophysiol.* **1**:391–404.

Rosenblueth, A., N. Wiener, and J. Bigelow. 1943. Behavior, purpose, and teleology. *Philosophy of Sci.* **10**:18–24.

Schrier, A. M., and R. W. Sperry. 1959. Visuo-motor integration in split-brain cats. *Science* **129**:1275–1276.

Sebeok, T. A. 1962. Coding in the evolution of signalling behavior. *Behavioral Sci.* **7**: 430–442.

———. 1965. Animal communication. *Science* **147**:1006–1014.

———. 1967. Animal communication. "International Encyclopedia of Social Sciences."

Shannon, C. E., and W. Weaver. 1949. "The Mathematical Theory of Communication." Illinois University Press, Urbana.

Sharpless, S. and H. Jasper. 1956. Habituation of the arousal reaction. *Brain* **79**:665–680.

Sperry, R. W. 1961. Physiological plasticity and brain circuit theory. In: H. F. Harlow and C. N. Woolsey, eds., "Biological and Biochemical Bases of Behavior." University of Wisconsin Press, Madison.

———. 1961. "Cerebral Organization and Behavior." *Science* **133**:1749–1757.

Thorpe, W. H., and O. L. Zangwill, eds. 1961. "Current Problems in Animal Behaviour." Cambridge University Press, Cambridge.

Trevarthen, C. B. 1962. Double visual learning in split-brain monkeys. *Science* **136**: 258–259.

Turner, O. A. 1948. Growth and development of the cerebral cortical pattern in man. *Arch. Neurol. Psychiat.* **59**:1–12.

Vowles, D. M. 1961. Neural mechanisms in insect behaviour. In: W. H. Thorpe and O. L. Zangwell, eds., "Current Problems in Animal Behaviour." Cambridge University Press, Cambridge.

Walker, A. E. 1938. The Primate Thalamus. Chicago University Press, Chicago.

Wiener, N. 1949. Time, communication, and the nervous system. In: Frank, *et al.*, "Teleological Mechanisms" (=*Ann. N. Y. Acad. Sci* **50**). 187–278.

———. 1950/1954. "The Human Use of Human Beings." Houghton-Mifflin, Boston.

Wittkower, E. D., and R. A. Cleghorn, eds. 1955. "Recent Developments in Psychosomatic Medicine." Lippincott, Philadelphia.

Yakovlev, P. I. 1958. Remarks at the *First Conference on the Central Nervous System and Behavior.* Josiah Macy, Jr. Foundation, New York.

Yerkes, R. M., and A. W. Yerkes. 1929. "The Great Apes." Yale University Press, New Haven.

ACKNOWLEDGMENTS

Permission to quote from authors and works is gratefully acknowledged herewith, as follows:

To Professor MacDonald Critchley and Edward Arnold (Publishers), Ltd.: MacD. Critchley, "The Parietal Lobes" (1953).

To The Josiah Macy, Jr. Foundation: the remarks by P. I. Yakovlev, in the *First Conference on the Central Nervous System and Behavior* (1958).

To The M.I.T. Press: E. H. Lenneberg, "New Directions in the Study of Language" (1964).

To The Princeton University Press: W. Penfield and L. Roberts, "Speech and Brain Mechanisms" (1959).

To The University of Texas Press: C. J. Herrick, "The Evolution of Human Nature" (1956).

To Williams and Wilkins Co.: D. Denny-Brown and R. A. Chambers, "The Parietal Lobe and Behavior" (Research Publications of the Association for Nervous and Mental Diseases, XXXVI, 1958).

5 *An Essay on Phasia*

On the Phylogenesis of Man's Speech Function[*]

PREFATORY NOTE

This essay may be better understood if the wider context of its placement be first stated.

In 1951 we debated this problem: The natural history of any animal other than man assumes that the animal's life-ways are an aspect of its biology; whenever those ways have been explored systematcially, they prove to be characteristically patterned or configured. By what logical right do we ever except man from this rule?

Yet this has been done since time immemorial; it is continued into cultural anthropology. About this matter, more will be said later. Here, suffice it that the investigation led to the concept of the "biogram." After a number of years of study and oral presentation of the idea, two articles were published (Count, 1958, 1958/59). They submitted a framework of a comparative vertebrate sociology, conceived as an aspect of vertebrate morphology, and therefore involved evolutionally. In no way did it appear that man had escaped from the framework which also embraced his phylogenic relatives; it did appear that man's "culturized" life mode was expressive of his "biogrammatic" position; a *Weiterbildung* of, and not an escape from, a vertebrate-mammalian-primate biosociology.

[*]From *Homo* **XIX**, 3–4: 170–227, 1969.

Obviously, this raises a host of questions. For instance, the evolution of the architecture of a nervous system which the medical student cannot comprehend unless he humbles himself to examine the brain of a shark and that of a salamander—yet a system which, at man's level in any case, is capable of extremely idiosyncratic performances. Structure is meaningless without functional context.

Immediately, there appeared the paradox that man's place in nature (including the surroundings which he has built up for himself) is at the heart of all anthropological query—yet the evidence relevant to the problem posed (except, of course, for the fossil finds) has been gathered almost entirely by the scientists of other disciplines. The investigation of "biogram" took on the shape of looking at the findings of ethologists, experimental psychologists, neurologists, and others through the eyes of an anthropologist—not in critical examination of their work, but in the hope of seeing better what anthropologists in their turn might be learning about man.

Expectably, some critical things could be said. These other scientists were shaping their inquiries for their own ends: at best what they were discovering responded to the anthropologist's queries but partially. On the other hand, today much of the research by anthropologists would have a different guise, if they were but acquainted with these other domains.

For his part, this student fastened upon two problems of man which promised, each in its way, to test the validity and fruitfulness of the "biogram" approach. His acquaintance with man's sociocultural patternings led him to the intuitive conclusions, first, that nothing is more elemental and more fraught with phylogenic implications than "familialism"; second, that nothing is more distinctive of man, and more fraught with sociocultural significance than man's capacity for symbol making and for channeling this into speech ("phasia").

Two brief articles on the "humanization" of vertebrate-mammalian-primate familialism have appeared (Count, 1967a, b). A preliminary paper on phasia has appeared (Count, 1964/1962). A lengthier study is in press (Count, 1968a). The present study is conceived as a companion piece to the last.

We cannot close this note without expressing profound appreciation of the editors of *Homo;* most especially of Dr. Schwidetzky, for her interest and her very helpful effort, without which this essay would not now be happily in print; to Priv.-Doz. Heinrich, of the Psychiatric Clinic of Mainz University, for his kindly reading of the manuscript; and to my good friend Dr. Gerhardt von Bonin, whose comments saved me from my most egregious errors.

0. INTRODUCTION

It is evident that anthropology—however specific it may often be in dealing with data—aims at being ultimately a co-ordinating science, somewhat as a legitimate holding corporation co-ordinates constituent companies. We anthropologists will never know China as intensively as a Sinologist does, or prices, credit, and banking as well as an economist, or heredity with the fulness of the genetic biologist. But we face what those more intensive scholars only glance at intermittently and tangentially, if at all: to try to understand in some measure how Chinese civilization and economies and human heredity, and some dozens of other highly developed special bodies of knowledge do indeed interrelate in being all parts of man—flowing out of man, centered in him, products of him.

(Kroeber, 1953, p. XIV).

0.1

There is only one extant primate species who engages in conversation, and, in addition, relies heavily upon it for resultful transactions with his fellows. Hereinafter, we shall term the speech function "phasia." The phenomenon thus places as a very major problem of anthropology.[1] Paradoxically, anthropology has done almost nothing toward accounting for its evolution.

Why this has been so is an interesting question, but it lies outside the economy of this essay. On the other hand, it is well known that the speech codes of *Homo sapiens*—his languages, their acquisition during postnatal ontogenesis, their disorders and pathologies—have been explored in great breadth and depth by a number of scientific disciplines, including anthropology. But this essay is an inquiry into a phylogenesis; hence these matters too lie outside its intent. Yet they do bear importantly upon the inquiry; they must therefore be considered on occasion.

A phylogenic inquiry into phasia collides with an ultimately insurmountable barrier: Only one species of one genus of the family Hominidae has survived the Ice Ages—and no fossil specimens of some quasi-phasias have been recovered along with the osteal fragments from Late Tertiary–Early Quaternary primates. At best, therefore, our inquiry remains forever a speculation. To some scientists, it therefore will seem futile; others—perhaps more philosophically inclined—will permit its validity, provided it conforms to concepts within scientific canon. Ultimately, it is a matter of taste. This stu-

---

[1]We use "anthropology" under its American definition.

dent considers a speculation upon the phylogenesis of phasia not only scientifically valid but an obligation of anthropology.

Our essay is a denial that man's capacity for speech is an unaccountable *nova* in evolution. Probably every scientist would grant that phasia must have emerged out of antecedents, out of some primordia *(anlagen);* what we are insisting upon is that any biological phenomenon which is amenable to scientific consideration at all must contain within itself some clues to its genetic history; the problem is to find the clue to those clues.

Clearly, it is the very conspicuous discontinuity between human and alloprimate systems of phonic communication which underlies all the difficulties. Yet there are those who doubt that the pursuit is therefore hopeless.

An infant science, of very recent birth, is that of zoosemeiotics—a companionate exploration by linguistic anthropologists and field students of animal behavior (whether or not they admit to being ethologists). There is a rationale: Phasia is assumable as being a particular way of organizing behavior by a particular primate, via sonic mechanisms (derived from a very ancient amphibian ancestry), and this validly suggests references to the thesaurus of alloprimate call systems (see Altmann, 1965; 1967, especially the articles by Struhsaker, Sebeok, Altmann [No. 17]; Bastian, 1965; Hockett, 1959; 1960a; 1960b; Hockett and Altmann, 1968; Hockett and Ascher, 1964; Sebeok, 1962; 1965; 1967; 1968).

It is a real gain, furthermore, when phasia is recognized as being but a particularized case within the more general and comprehensive phenomenon of communication between animals, and when we recognize that we cannot hope for understanding of the particular unless we base it upon the more comprehensive.[2]

Meanwhile, it is especially to the ethologists that we owe the insights and the cryptographic techniques by which the codes of animal behavior are being "cracked." Indeed, even the genetics of the not-learned aspect of behavior (and all behavior is deeply rooted in this matrix) is being probed (cf. Dilger, 1960; 1962a; 1962b; 1962c; 1964).

However, science first entered upon the problem of speech from a direction utterly different from that of natural history; namely, that of the medical clinic, which is confronted with the aphasias, the agnosias, the epilepsies. What the pathologies of brain may contribute to an account of the phylogenesis of speech differs not at all in

[2]Of course, this attitude is not new. It goes back at least as far as Darwin: "The Expression of the Emotions in Man and Animals" (1872). There exists a respectable literature in the subject.

principle from what the medical sciences may contribute otherwise and in general to the history of the human body. The clinical experience and literature are rich indeed—and hardly known at all to anthropology.[3] In the present essay, we shall attempt to bend some of these findings to phylogenetic ends.

It could not be done, but for another science which is partly an outgrowth of those experiences, partly a recurving of behavioral science upon physiology: experimental insults to brains of other vertebrates, particularly of mammals, most particularly of alloprimates. Thus, deficits associated with artificial, localized lesions in monkey and ape cerebra become comparable with the lesions in man. Not only are the similarities and differences richly suggestive, but they raise the very question of what constitute similarities and differences, of the precise nature of behavioral homology, of equifinality wherein outwardly similar behavior-segments may be induced from non-identical neurologic mechanisms. It is instructive to discover in man and monkey similar behavioral deficits—but including additional and characteristic speech defects in the one primate and their absence in the other.

In man, there is an ontogenesis of phasia, and speech deficits during ontogenesis have a character distinct from that in adults. This is understandable: In the latter case the deficit supravenes upon a definitive cytoarchitectonic; in the former, upon a brain still undergoing development. This insures that an appeal from phylogenesis to ontogenesis is problematical at best, and always strewn with booby-traps. We have come to realize that a very small-brained human learns to speak whereas to a larger-brained ape it seems never to occur to make the attempt; for during the phylogenesis which we may term the humanization process some further instructions came to be written into the human DNA code. Yet this very fact, we submit, suggests a line of genetic exploration for the future; and we may still compare patiently the ontogenesis of cortical cytoarchitectonics in man and ape, and juxtapose the respective behavioral deliveries. Most of this work, too, remains for the future.

0.2

So we come back to Profesor Kroeber's appraisal of anthropology. It was spoken in the context of cultural anthropology; it holds no

---

[3]Practically any treatise on the speech disorders contains some historical account of the growth of insight into the structure and function of brain. For an excellent historical treatise on the subject, consult Ombredane, 1951.

less in yet wider context. The principle was stated by Egon von Eickstedt (1936; English translation in Count, 1950) in what we choose to regard as a manifesto. The present writer has attempted a statement in like vein: "A major task of anthropology is to account for the origin of *man:* not just the evolution of his bodily architecture and his biological processes in the narrower sense, but man as an entire entity: the *primate* who formalizes every one of his biological processes with rituals; who regulates and channels his behavior via complex social institutions: who thinks and speaks in symbols; who finds satisfaction in singing and in carving distorted figurines; and whose very tools are esthetic; the *creature* whose mentation is such that, even primitively he can worry as to whether the stars are friendly; who can become willing to die while supporting abstractions; or torture and kill another of his own kind for the same abstraction; and who can be simultaneously a son, a husband, a father; a hunter who turns over his kill to some one else; an *animal* sensitive to absurdity; an *organism* who can commit suicide; who can conceive of death yet deny its existence. We have a wealth of descriptions as to how these phenomena operate in societies past and present; but—whence did these phenomena arise and gather themselves? Where are the *anlagen* —the primordia—in the subhuman Primate level? Here is the more fundamental question. Anthropology today is indeed a shrewd discipline: it has yet a long way to go before it achieves profundity" (Count, 1964–65; 1967—but here altered slightly by the editor).

It should be apparent that a *Ganzheitsanthropologie*—an anthropology of the whole—must contain a *bioanthropology* conceived along broader lines than the traditional *physical anthropology.* Nonetheless, certainly its maw would not have the capacity to swallow all the other sciences—neurological, behavioral, physiological, biochemical, medical—which apply themselves to the human problem. All of which would suggest that an edifice of man-science, analogous to those of sideral science and of earth-science, remains to be built.[4]

0.3

The foregoing remarks are not so far removed from the specific task in hand as they may appear to be. This is an essay in holism; its

[4]There is no intention of discussing blueprints of its architecture. But at least it will hardly be denied that there is room for anthropologists who, although inexpert in neurology or in Sinology, yet understand reasonably well what those disciplines have to say—and for other scientists who can appreciate the anthropologists' dialect.

thought owes much to von Uexküll, von Bertalanffy; to Kurt Lewin, Kurt Goldstein, W. Ross Ashby, Norbert Wiener; to numerous others who also recognize that an information of the whole cannot appear autogenically out of an information of the parts, and that how to effect the integration at a next higher level is indeed a problem, not an assumptive matter. If the phylogenesis of phasia has stood impregnable to scientific attack, it is at least possible that this is due to failure to view it in holistic dimensions. We shall attempt to see one body of evidence in the light cast by another body: We search for integrations.

In the latter attempt, we shall fail. For success belongs to the future, and to many minds. We trust, nevertheless, that to outline a strategy of attack, will not be effort misplaced.

We shall proceed in this wise:

1. Phasia represents a particular coping by the human organism with information secured from its environment. This makes of it an ecological proposition—which calls for a reconsideration of "environment."

2. We may paraphrase this generalization more narrowly and precisely: The CNS (central nervous system) may be treated as a "system" in the more technical sense of general systems theory. The performance of the CNS, moreover, is reducible to the organism's ways of analyzing space-time and programming itself accordingly. Phasia is a highly elaborate version of the ways.

3. The CNS—more particularly, the brain—is the "machine" (in Ashby's sense) which expresses the methods. It will be necessary to examine certain cardinal structurings and their functions.

4. All these obtain, in varying degrees of complexity, among non-human vertebrates (we are more specifically interested in alloprimates); they must be brought up to the human level. The entire process, when it passes to the human level, develops pervasively the complexion of symbolopoesis (the symbol-making process, taken as a neuropsychological phenomenon).

At no point along the way dare we lose from mind the realization that what we are considering is organic system undergoing biological evolution. Consequently, we are driven to consider "behavior" as but the symptomatology of neurologic process.

For us, the "black box" of behavior science, as well as that of communication theory, is the central concern.[5]

[5]This topic has been stated more explicitly in Count, 1968a. The surveys of neural mechanisms in that essay, moreover, are not being duplicated in the present one.

1. MAN-SCIENCE

We are witnessing today a search for new approaches, for new and more comprehensive concepts and for methods capable of dealing with the larger wholes of organisms and personalities. The term *organism-as-a-whole* has been used, along with *holism, synholic,* and similar expressions to recognize the patterned, organized structure-function activities, internally and overtly, of living organisms. . . . We are formulating and critically examining the new concepts and methodologies, not only for obtaining data but for ordering and interpreting their inter-relationship. We are establishing new criteria of credibility with which to test the validity of these new findings, as well as to elicit new and hitherto unsuspected relationships from older findings. We are, in brief, constructing a new conceptual frame of reference for scientific investigation in the life sciences.

As I see it, we are engaged today in one of the major transitions or upheavals in the history of ideas, as we recognize that many of our older ideas and assumptions are now obsolescent and strive to develop a new frame of reference to give us clearer and more comprehensive understanding of the basic processes underlying all events.

In this transition, many of our long-cherished convictions and expectations must be revised—some to be wholly discarded as archaic and replaced by others more consonant with our new insights and a larger conceptual grasp of the dynamics of events, especially in the life sciences.

The principle of indetermination—that we cannot simultaneously measure both the position and velocity of a particle—implies more than a methodological limitation. It indicates a wider and more fundamental situation in biology, where we must recognize that the dynamic processes which we should like to study cannot be isolated by the investigator from the organic field in which they operate, without sacrificing much of what should be observed and measured.

(Frank, 1948: 190, 192, 193.)

This is our preliminary position.[6]

1.1

1. Phasia represents somehow a *Weiterbildung* of (allo)primate phonic communication.

2. Phonic communication, in any tetrapod, is a special modality of its more general capacity for communicating.

3. Communication represents an *ad hoc* organizing of behavior in confrontation with situation.

---

[6]And see 1968a.

4. The situation typically includes or involves members of one's own "kind" (usually, conspecifics, whatever their sex or age).

5. Communication therefore is an ecological phenomenon.

The rest of this essay shall invert this logical order of listing; for the inversion is more amenable to evolutionary consideration.

1.2 A Reconsideration of Ecology

We postulate, as an axiom, that the minimum completely viable universe of discourse is that of organism-within-environment; anything less is an arbitrary abstraction which is useful only temporarily, and intolerable beyond some point.

Traditional ecology is a study of how organisms cope with the energies of a positively entropic universe situated outside themselves. Such ecology leaves unconsidered an enormous fact: *How* the organism does this is a matter of processing information.

It has been the great accomplishment of cybernetics and of information theory to show that the entropic trend of energy and the character of information are related mathematically as mutual negatives (see note 1; also, 2.2).

It follows that organisms relate to their environments, somehow and simultaneously, in terms of positive and negative entropy. To Schroedinger (1956: 67–73) we owe the celebrated statement that a living organism "feeds upon negative entropy." The present essay reduces to a variation upon this theme.

We may place, obliquely to this, von Uexküll's acute analysis of the organism's environment as its *Umwelt*, its "phenomenal world." Certainly, a horse, a mouse, a fly in the same meadow possess three different phenomenal worlds. The *Umwelt* is the physical universe passed through the analyzing screen of the animal organization.

In the next section, we shall have something to say about the animal as a self-organizing system; we reserve for it, and for its successors, the demonstration that although the energies of the universe present constraints within which the organism must "choose," it is the organism itself which has the initative. We shall avoid as far as possible the attitude that the organism "responds" to a "stimulus" from the "environment"; we shall assume the position that it is a property of living system to organize an *Umwelt* by executing autogenic choices.

Now we find that the organism copes with yet another universe: its own internal organization. Physiology lies in this domain, for it is the study of how organism copes with the energies, originally derived from the external universe, but now lodged within. But again we discover that it is a matter of processing information quite as well as of energy.

Still speaking diagrammatically, an alimentary-respiratory-excretory mechanism is the animal's device for processing chemical energies; a nervous system is its device for processing physical information. The "voluntary" moiety thus appears as the mediating channel to the external *Umwelt;* the autonomic mediates the internal. The CNS (central nervous system) effects ultimate coordination of this self-organizing system.

A matrix begins to suggest itself; but there is yet another universe to consider: that composed of one's own kind: the "social environment." In the nature of things, it is mixed in with the physical universe that constitutes the raw materials of the *Umwelt;* the same "voluntary" nervous system mediates it. But there is a sharp distinction: The constituents of the "social environment" are identical in character with the animal who is under discussion (for convenience, term it "ego"); and *all possess the same code of communication.* By contrast with the physical universe, here *dialogue* takes place: Any unit may initiate a coded message, any unit may "respond," in the legitimate sense of that word.

1.3

Our matrix therefore has this form:

"Ecosystems"		A. Physical "Universe"	B. Internal "Universe"	C. Social "Universe"
	E Energetics	E A	E B	E C
	I Information	I A	I B	I C

Fig. 5–1 The "Umwelt"

Notes on the matrix:

The cells represent logical categories or frames of discourse. Thus, the activities of animal organisms which ecologists treat place essentially in EA; those of behavioral psychology, in IA, and so on.

We can think of no activity of animal organism which does not place in some cell (ambit) or other; conversely, it is not likely that there are animals for whom one of the cells would be an empty category.

However, the matrix thus far is alien to the principle of holism. It is a dissection, and dissections entail the loss of the information which transcends parts and characterizes the relationships which describe a whole. Were we to imagine the cells assembled as facets of a cube, with a webbing of internal connections, we should have a more adequate model for our expanded definition of organism-in-environment.

We emphasize that the cell contents and their interconnections are those of processes, not of products or results (cf. Frank, 1948: 193f.).

In this essay we are concerned only with the I-array. It is the array wherein nervous activity occurs. The phonic communication which eventually converts to phasia localizes in cell IC; yet it could never come into being ontogenetically as well as phylogenetically, but for the antecedent developments within IA and IB. Which is a way of saying that animals could not communicate unless they had organized an *Umwelt* which becomes a basis of transaction (see note 2). It may be observed, in passing, that "ego's" interests focus in column B.

2. SOME THEORETICAL CONSIDERATIONS

Science stands today on something of a divide. For two centuries it has been exploring systems that are either intrinsically simple or that are capable of being analyzed into simple components. The fact that such a dogma as "vary the factors one at a time" could be accepted for a century, shows that scientists were largely concerned in investigating such systems as followed this method; for this method is often fundamentally impossible in the complex systems. Not until Sir Ronald Fischer's work in the '20s . . . did it become clearly recognized that there are complex systems that just do not allow the varying of only one factor at a time—they are so dynamic and interconnected that the alteration of one factor immediately acts as a cause to evoke alterations in others, perhaps in a great many others. Until recently, science tended to evade the study of such systems, focusing its attention on those that are simple and especially reducible.

In the study of some systems, however, the complexity could not be wholly evaded. The cerebral cortex of the free-living organism, the ant-hill as a functioning society, and the human economic system were outstanding both in their practical importance and in their intractability by the older methods. . . . But science today is also taking the first steps towards studying "complexity" as a subject in its own right.

(Ashby, 1963: 5.)

The new notion that has been added is that no system is random in itself, but can become random only by losing its identity in a set, or ensemble, of systems. More than that, an ensemble is not adequately defined by the mere listing of the individual systems it contains, but requires the notion of the distribution of these systems. This notion of distribution is equivalent to the notion of probability.

(Wiener, 1948: 199.)

It should be noticed that as soon as some of a system's variables become unobservable, the "system" represented by the remainder may develop remarkable, even miraculous properties. A commonplace illustration is given by conjuring, which achieves (apparently) the miraculous, simply because not all the significant variables are observable. It is possible that some of the brain's "miraculous" properties—of showing "foresight," "intelligence," etc. —are miraculous only because we have not so far been able to observe the events in all the significant variables.

(Ashby, 1963: 114.)

La fixité du milieu intérieur est la condition de la vie libre.

Claude Bernard, *fide* J. Barcroft: "Features in the Architecture of Psychological Function."

We are convinced that any inquiry into the phylogenesis of phasia cannot prosper without the conceptual tools of systems theory, cybernetics, information theory. It would manifestly be absurd to attempt any recapitulation of these. We shall be the richer, nevertheless, when we consider brain mechanisms, if we have first steeped ourselves in their thought modes.

2.1 Living Systems and Automata as Organizers: Comparison and Contrast

Structurally organisms are mainly colloidal, and include prominently protein molecules, large, complex and anisotropic; machines are chiefly metallic and include mainly simple molecules. From the standpoint of their energetics machines usually exhibit relatively large differences of potential, which permit rapid mobilization of energy; in organisms the energy is more uniformly distributed, it is not very mobile. Thus, in electric machines conduction is mainly electronic, whereas in organisms electric changes are usually ionic.

Scale and flexibility are achieved in machines largely by temporal multiplication of effects; . . . In organisms spatial multiplication rather than temporal is the rule; the temporal achievements are poor. . . .

If an engineer were to design a robot, roughly similar in behavior to an animal organism, he would not attempt at present to make it out of proteins and other colloids. . . . The movements of the robot could readily be much faster and more powerful than those of the original organism. Learning and memory, however, would be quite rudimentary. In future years, as knowledge of colloids and proteins increases, future engineers may attempt the design of robots not only with a behavior but also a structure similar to that of a mammal. The ultimate model of a cat is of course another cat, whether it be born of still another cat or synthesized in a laboratory.

(Rosenblueth et al., 1943: 23.)

We may partially translate this into the dialect of systems theory. A real machine has "organization properties" and "object properties." In an artifactual computer, however, there is no interaction between it and a computer program. "The computer world, technicalities apart, is not concerned with real time or decay of real parts that goes on as time passes. . . . The physical "fabric" [see Beer, 1959, Ch. XVII— E.W.C.] of the computing machine is irrelevant to the programme or organization so that the physical stability of the control systems that embody the prescribed central units may be taken for granted. But, when dealing with the computing machine that is a real brain, the fabric *is* relevant." (Pask, 1966: 10f.; and see note 5.)

2.2

We pick up Schroedinger's remark that living systems feed on negative entropy.

He recognizes further two "mechanisms," both stochastic, which characterize systems: One produces order from disorder, a further one produces order from order. "The 'order from order' principle" he says "is the real clue to the understanding of life" (op cit. 78. And cf. Quastler, 1958b: 189).

Von Foerster is convinced that there is yet a third—"order from noise" (1960: 43–46). It is worth noting; however, our treatment will be content with Schroedinger's second mechanism.

We cannot help feeling, nevertheless, that Schroedinger's duality of "mechanisms" is a trick of phrase rather than two classes of some sort; that instead we should be thinking *processually,* and see one antientropic principle continuing to operate throughout organic evolution—effecting a continuous succession of further orderings.

At all events, order-from-order permits an indeterminate progression of degrees of orderly complexity. In the present section, we propose to move Schroedinger's idea—whether in his terms or ours—to the level where it is translatable as a "self-organizing system coping with space-time." For this, we need a rationale of "self-organizing system" (which, however, we shall leave to the references cited herewith); (Yovits and Cameron, 1960, particularly von Foerster, 1960;

Pask, 1965: 32–39); also, some discussion of "space-time," which follows shortly.

2.21 But first, we must fill out a prescription for a "teleological mechanism."[7] Ashby defines the living organism as a "machine"—requiring redefinition a "machine" (Ashby, 1960; particularly, Ch. 3).

An organism as machine adapts by first securing information from its surroundings, and therewith it forces its essential variables to operate within some proper limits, by treating the environment. This is also definable as a process of "learning"; and this is the way a "random mechanism" is motivated, not merely to achieve a preset goal but to search for goals (purposes) to achieve. Wiener has pronounced this acute observation to be one of the great philosophical contributions of this day and also one of high technologic promise (Wiener, 1954: 38).

2.3 Space-Time

Let us assume a living system as characterized at once by Schroedinger, von Foerster, Ashby, Pask, confronting a universe other than its own internality. (We need not distinguish, at this level, between A and C environments.) Paraphrased, the organism is a cybernetic machine (in Ashby's sense) which interacts with a space-time continuum—whatever definition we may arrive at for the latter term.

2.31 We must content ourselves with a very fragmentary definition, if only it be useful. For we are pointing toward the fact that if in man that area of neocortex, roughly identifiable as "Wernicke's area," temporo-parieto-occipital cortex, angular-supramarginal gyri, etc., be functionally disturbed, either by lesion or electrostimulation, there are interruptions or distortions of the capacity for spatial and temporal analyses, for apprehensions of parts of one's own body, and completion of "verbal gestalts" (in Conrad's sense—Conrad, 1954); and that the roughly homologous region in the macaque, experimentally insulted, shows suggestively comparable deficiences (mutatis mutandis, of course; cf. Denny-Brown and Chambers, 1958).

Coghill's (1938) attempt to define "space-time as a pattern of psycho-organismal mentation," and Herrick's (1956) attempt to paraphrase and eleborate upon it, have been touched upon in the 1968 a study; we shall not repeat. Eventually, we shall find Gooddy and

[7]See Frank et al., 1948. Although Ashby is not happy with any use of "teleological," we are doing no violence to his thought.

Reinhold coming to grips with the problem at the human level (Gooddy, 1958, 1959, 1964. Gooddy and Reinhold, 1952, 1961, 1963).

Whatever be the actualities behind the fact that the nervous system of any animal including man operates upon a "here-now," and also that the "past" is inextricably part of "now" by virtue of hysteresis[8]— it is not a Newtonian or a Euclidean space-and-time that are processed. We may find it useful to "read into" reality this kind of formulation—as per Eddington's remark that the mathematics is not in the universe until we put it there (*fide* Herrick, 1956: 30).

Bentley (1941) (who appraises the conceptions of James, Pierce, Dewey, Lewin, Brown, Koffka) asserts the autonomous right of modern psychology to construct a behavioral space-time upon the premise that "adaptations are events . . . of complex organic-environmental situations." An organism's behavior is both "durational" and "extensional."

2.32   The mathematics which we put into the universe—if we may follow after Bachem—reflects an "astigmatism" built into our brain; whence we emerge with some peculiar quantifications. "Most physical dimensionless constants are very close to unity. . . . If, however, the most universal velocity appears as 3.10^{10} cm/sec, it seems that the fundamental units of length and time are incorrectly chosen" (Bachem, 1952: 497).

The cause of the "astigmatism," Bachem insists, is neurophysiological. "Spatial cognition is epicritic . . . [there is] fine discrimination due to the local sign of our tactile and visual receptors and their cortical representations. . . . Temporal cognition is partly non-sensory or idiognostic and partly protopathic . . . [which latter term] refers to the poor discrimination by internal, general senses. Time must be considered as our most primitive category for cognition. The ever-present 'now'—the almost momentary conscious present—is the only content of the crudest consciousness, neurophysiologically represented in the mesencephalic and diencephalic border area of the brain. The continuum of our subjective time, flowing past the present 'now,' serves as a linear receptacle for all our feelings, sensations, and thoughts, and thus must have developed simultaneously with these elements of cognition" (op. cit. 498).

An "astigmatism" of our brain which Bachem does not cite is that which has produced our immensely elaborate mathematics of quantity and number; the while by comparision a mathematics of quality and

[8]May we suggest *mnema* as a term holding forth promise to analyses?

structure is as yet but very poorly developed (cf. Boulding, 1956: 11; who, however, also points out that such a mathematics is on the way. In fact, general systems theory itself is an illustration of this). This, we believe, is at least one reason why science has not yet succeeded in converting space-time into an effective universe of discourse which is simultaneously that of physicist, psychologist, neurologist. What we are trying to point out is that if we eventually hope to understand phasia as an expression of symbolopoesis, and symbolopoesis as a human way of coping with space-time—this is our intuitive hope—then we must pray for the simultaneous mathematics of number-and-quantity and of quality-and-structure. Shortly, we shall find the frog's retinal networks speaking to the frog's brain in a "vocabulary" of four "words" (Lettvin et al., 1959)—and certainly, although they tell us of "Newtonian" space and time, this is not their "idiom." Intensity, movement, shape are not built up by the retinal networks from the quantities which enter into their formalizings in physical mechanics. How networks actually do apprehend the vectors of time and space, has been beautifully hypothesized by McCulloch and Pitts.[9]

Eventually, what animals succeed in doing is to organize their space-time into ego, non-ego; the latter being differentiated into range (environment A) and alter (environment C). And meanwhile, we shall be trying to maintain a correction of the mathematical astigmatism which Bachem attributes to our brain/minds.

2.4   Redundancy in the IA—IC Environments

Hitherto, we have assumed a living machine relating to external environment, without exploiting the distinction between A and C universes which our matrix has registered.[10]

When in a universe there exist two units of a kind, possessing a code in common, the outputs of one unit convert into inputs of the other (see note 6). There is "message." There is "communication." This obviously occurs in the C-universe; whether it does in the A-universe is for us not a problem of prime concern.

In 1968a, we attempted to derive "communication" from the state-

[9]McCulloch and Pitts, 1943; Pitts and McCulloch, 1947 more especially. They do not apply general systems theory (the articles antedate its development); yet significantly, they require a symbolic logic as well as integral calculus. And cf. Brain, 1963: 392: "Time as a relationship of order, may well be represented by a coding in the nervous system based on spatial organization—one aspect of the problem of serial order discussed by Lashley." (For the latter, see Lashley, 1951; 1960.)
[10]The B-universe has received some notice implicitly in terms of "fabric."

ment that animals "query" their environment. This obtains in the A-universe quite as truly as in the C-universe; but these two universes do not "respond" in the same way.

In both universes, a vertebrate (*pace* any other animal kind) exploits heavily the redundancy component of information.[11]

No great deal of reflection is required for seeing that, at any moment the animal's *Umwelt* could overwhelm it with information. The information or message, arriving from any or all possible sources except that of particular interest, constitutes "noise." Then, by Shannon's Theorem of the Noisy Channel,[12] "if a certain amount of information is to be transmitted with perfect reliability in the presence of noise, then it is necessary to provide at least as much redundant information as the amount of equivocation introduced by the noise; furthermore, this amount will be sufficient if the coding is maximally efficient."

Yet the "equivocation" is as much a matter of the quality of the brain mechanism, as it is of anything else; for the meaning ("sema") of any message resides in the "fabric" of the animal system—not in the physical ambience.

The "semanticity" problem lies at the heart of that of symboliform messaging; information theory is as yet far from ready to handle it. In 1968a, we remarked that information "rides" energy, "sema" rides information, organismal messages are "honest." The semanticity of a code is not a defining property of messaged information: The telephone engineer is not concerned with the question of whether English is being spoken and what is being said. Quastler has remarked that "amount of information is in general related to the utility of being informed"—and that " 'amount of information' in a statement is related to its capacity of carrying *semantic* information" (1958b: 1964). This assuredly applies to Ashby's definition of a "machine" which quests for purpose. And this is as far as we can go.

2.5   Signature

A principle which has some derivative relation to redundancy is what its discoverer terms "signature."[13] Redundant information reduces un-

---

[11]For brief formalized definitions of "redundancy," consult, e.g., Weaver, 1949: 104, 110; Quastler, 1958a: 33; Pask, 1965: 32.

[12]Quoted from Quastler, 1958: 34. See also Weaver, 1949: 111 f. For the full mathematical treatment, see Shannon, in Shannon and Weaver, 1949: Part II. See also Cherry, 1957: Ch. 5, Sec. 4.

[13]Quastler, 1958: 33f.; 1964, Ch. 2. In the latter reference, he extends it down to the level of macromolecules; he also develops a formalized definition of it.

certainty. In the presence of much "noise," its requirement can be high. Can there be an economy, an efficiency, of redundancy information? "A given amount of redundant information in a message can be used for error checking the more effectively, the more evenly it is related to all parts of the message" (1958: 33f.).

Perhaps it can be illustrated very simply. You can readily expand *"Mr E W Count"*—if you already possess a certain prior coding—into a certain fuller spelling and save the printer some redundant labor. *You will unerstand this centense inspite of its erors and you can korekt it 4 me.* You possess the coded information, "This is English," and (for the first example) the registry of the present writer's name elsewhere in this essay. (In addition, you can correct the sentence the more easily, because you are not being compelled to struggle with the design-analysis of my handwriting!)

The "signature" principle, we believe, promises a great deal toward the elucidation of the successive abstractions whereby a brain reduces an otherwise overwhelming amount of information to a degree of practicable precision. If we understand Quastler, we dare say that a "signature" measures the *adequacy* of information. And we surmise that fundamentally it gets down to the very neurology of cyto-architectonics, circuits, and networks; that *mnema* serves as a signature check upon newly entered information. At the eventual level of symbols, we can again appeal to Quastler (1964: 32): "A Symbol is a signature of the information in a real event, by virtue of some code which may be entirely arbitrary; an operation with a symbol does not necessarily involve the physical intervention of a referent, as when I speak a word. A signature implies the direct presence of the entity, and a carrier of a signature, the direct action of this entity."

2.6

What, then, is the quality of the brain mechanism? "The brain is not an accurate organ. Its memory is poor, its recognition is poor, its sensory input doesn't work very well, its motor activity isn't very well organized until one becomes skilled. This is not a good computer. What it does is to respond variably over a range. There is an advantage in the circumstance that it doesn't always do the same thing to the same stimulus. If it misses once in a while it may learn something about how to operate more usefully. . . .

"The ability to make mistakes connotes the ability to make choices over a range not accurately defined, and so find new ways of doing things, and that is probably one of the virtues of the imperfections of the nervous system" (Bishop, 1960: 146. See note 7).

The brain secures redundancy (1) by way of a multiplicity of channel modes (somaesthesis, vision, audition, etc.); (2) by cross-referring edited information; (3) by checking it against editions of previous information ("mnema," hysteresis). This occurs in the telencephalon-diencephalon-mesencephalon of all vertebrates; at the mammalian-alloprimate-human levels that are added in cross-modal referrings by the archepallium, mesopallium, neopallium, "supralimbic" cortex; plus the matchings effected by two cerebral hemispheres which "reciprocate" in ways understood as yet but imperfectly.[14]

How vertebrates exploit redundancy behaviorally is easily illustrated. The man-eating shark—we postulate it to be in that homeostatic state called "hunger"—first "hears" (via lateral-line system) its potential target, and heads anadromously toward it; reaches the range of chemotropic source (olfaction)—a further positive = cybernetic reinforcement; finally sights its victim, and swims about it in an ever-tightening spiral. The herring-gull chick pecks for food at the parent's bill—but varying the color, the shade of the bill as well as of a certain patch on it, induces varying degrees of uncertainty in the pecking.

The more complex the phylogenic level of brain mechanism, the greater the capacity for involving the situational *context* in the processings of information. The balancing of redundancy with novelty becomes an exceedingly complex affair; and the parameters of context remain still the most baffling part of the communication problem. It becomes possible (even before the human level is reached) for a recipient of messages to choose to treat them at one time as novelty, another time as noise; as when I find that the sight of your lips moving disturbs my hearing what you say; yet, if I am uncertain of your sounds, your lip movements become a help (Count, 1968a). One music connoisseur closes his eyes, another watches the pianist's fingers. Tomorrow, I may have difficulty recalling the coloratura's aria heard tonight; show me the score, and it will be recalled. At all events, it is this "poor computer" which, at the human level of elaboration, becomes pervadingly symbolopoeic; how, as yet we know not. We are more likely, some day, however, to comprehend the "how" if we assume the imperfections to have been not a liability but an asset.

The brain, or CNS, as a self-organizing system, monitors itself. This, of course, is a cybernetic statement; and it calls for further clarification. "A random system of interactions may yield generalized patterns that are unpredictable, and alternate paths may be stabilized in different amounts. A random system of reacting elements, such as a brain

---

[14]The vertebrate CNS is distinctive in its combination of "interconnection" and "projection" systems of integration. Cf. Vowles, 1961: 22–25. And see section 4.35.

is useful if it is monitored—that is, if some particular solution is selected, if a monitor freezes the output at some point. In a brain a certain randomness of interactions among neurons may give the basis of plasticity, mass action, and similar phenomena. At a particular output, however, a behavioral act occurs, according to instructions contained in its genetic constitution, experience, and immediate environment" (Prosser, 1965: 368).

3. BRAIN

I would like to state parenthetically that, if all other reasons were lacking, which they are not, the continuing need for parameters other than performance with which to specify level of behavioral organization is sufficient to link the future destinies of psychology and basic biology . . . the gain sought is in classes of information.

(Halstead, 1947: 247.)

It is to the credit of human intelligence and creativeness to have conceived a doctrine as a mighty instrument for the discovery of natural phenomena and yet borrowed the first principle of this doctrine not from facts, which we worship too much, but from a scheme or design of our own, which we underestimate too much.

(Riese, 1950: 86.)

The primary development of the association, as well as the peripheral system, is centrifugal; that is to say, toward the receptor fields in the sensory elements and toward the motor field in the association elements. Consequently, the individual acts on its environment before it reacts to its environment.

(Coghill, 1930: 345.)

In the case of our brain, it is certain from the chemistry of our chromosomes that our genes cannot specifically determine all the connections of our neurons. What they do is to specify a relatively simple machine, which goes on to build a more complicated machine, which elaborates a third and so on, until the last prescribes our most complex structures, like the cerebral cortex. Von Neumann has suggested that the plan is something like this: the earlier machines are never completely superseded or separated from the final machines, but serve to tend them. When they find any part preoccupied or out of order, they shift the problem to be solved to portions of the newer structure of the brain that are free and able to solve it.

(McCulloch and Pfeiffer, 1949: 374.)

Our mode of life has been achieved through eons of evolutionary change, during which the conservative and relatively stable organization of the brain stem has been supplemented and amplified by the addition of cortical apparatus with more labile patterns of action, resulting in greater freedom of adjustment to the exigencies of life. In all behavior there is a substrate of innate patterns of great antiquity, and in practical adjustments these primitive factors are manipulated and recombined in terms of the individual's personal experience. Memory and learning are pre-emiently cortical functions but these cortical capacities have not been given us by magic, and we want to know how they have been developed and the roots from which they have grown.

(Herrick, 1948: 122.)

3.1   On Neural Nets and Universals

We remarked earlier (2) that a central nervous system does not process the information of space-time in Euclidean or Newtonian terms. The language of perception is quite otherwise (see note 8). Every sensory event is unique; it occurs here and now, it strikes upon a specific population of neuronal units. Yet the very immediate reception is in terms of categories and changes of state. We shall examine this matter.

3.11. "The translation of outside information into pulse intervals of various frequencies," says von Foerster (1963), "is universal. That is, all sensory modalities will code their information into the pulse language, which is not only understood but also spoken by all other nerve cells. Indeed, it is the only form of communication between neurons and it is the only way in which all our experiences, thoughts, feelings and ideas are represented."

In a network of neurons which transmits information one to another, every neuron can become either excited or inhibited by another: the "all-or-none" principle of neurology, which translates into the "on-off" or "1-0" of binary, digital computings.[15]

"Every pair of neurons converging to a third is an associative proc-

---

[15]At this point—a *caveat*. The brain is no mere digital computer. Analogical computations are involved quite as well. (Cf. Bishop, 1956: 380; also, Bruner, 1957.) Let us keep clear that digital-analogal computations are techniques of operative mathematics, not descriptions of natural history. The point requires emphasis, since some students have been victims of a confusion; for instance, in the speculation that analog mechanisms were phylogenically the earlier and digital mechanisms the later evolution (Sebeok, 1962: 439). The present essay seeks never to use the dialect of computation beyond the limit where it brings risk of ambiguity.

At present, we are trying for an account of that aspect of a total processing by neurological mechanism or system which is most readily describable in a digital dialect. This is because what we are discussing is real effects of electrical pulsations. The whole subject of the biochemistry that must be responsible for all brain activity —from the ionic exchanges within an axon to the pharmacology of the uncus—is being totally ignored herein, with grave injustice; less because it has not yet reached the stage of development comparable to the biophysical aspect than because of this writer's ignorance.

ess, is a pair of premises leading to a conclusion, is a set of particular cases from which a generalization is abstracted by induction. Every pair of diverging branches from a neuron is a set of particulars derived from the general."[15a]

3.12   There exists a justly celebrated report on "what the frog's eye tells the frog's brain."[16] There are in the frog's retina four fairly distinctive but commingled kinds of fibers, possessing characteristic structural and functional properties. (In consonance with the description by von Foerster and by McCulloch and Pitts), each kind delivers aggregatively and respectively, one of the following results: (1) contrasts of illumination, whatever the intensity (within proper limits)—making possible the discernment of edges; (2) curvature of an edge, irrespective of illumination contrast; (3) motion of an edge; (4) sensitivity to a rapid reduction of illumination. (There is a residual fifth, less well understood.)

The axons, at first bundled, become very much tangled within the optic nerve; they interbraid. Eventually, in the tectum, each of the four kinds terminates in a particular lamina. Each kind, moreover, has its own speed of conduction. Each lamina "maps" the retina; all four are "in registration."

The authors comment (p. 150 f): "The eye speaks to the brain in a language already highly organized and interpreted instead of transmitting some more or less accurate copy of the distribution of light on the receptors. . . . The operations thus have much more the flavor of perception than of sensation, if that distinction has any meaning now. That is to say that the language in which they are best described is the language of complex abstractions from the visual image."

[15a]Platt, 1956: 195. A lively and nontechnical exposition of the process occurs in von Foerster, 1962; 1963. For a formalized account, see McCulloch and Pitts, 1943. In the optic system there are network relays successively in retina, tectum or superior colliculus, lateral geniculate body, occipital neocortex. In such series of operational levels, clearly the information processed in any immediate predecessor may be considered an "environment" for its successor (cf. von Foerster, 1962: 34). He adds (ibid.): "[therefore] information of the 'self-state' of the system can be processed equally well. . . . In the normal person information of 'self-states' is usually coded [in such a way] that they are distinguishable from true environmental information. In some pathological cases, however, we know that this distinction collapses. In hallucinations, the patient, for instance, 'hears' that invisible chickens are talking to him, etc."
[16]Lettvin et al., 1959.—H. H. Maturana's "The functional organization of the pigeon retina" (In: "Information Processing in the Nervous System") has not been available to me.

3.13 Another landmark study appeared twelve years earlier (Pitts and McCulloch, 1947). Its thought manifestly is a direct ancestor of that just treated; but it treats of the cortical mechanisms whereby "universals" are known at the mammalian level. The proposition is this:

> Genes can predetermine only statistical order, and original chaos must reign over nets that learn, for learning builds new order according to a law of use.
>
> Numerous nets, embodied in special nervous structures, serve to classify information according to useful common characters. In vision they detect the equivalence of apparitions related by similarity and congruence, like those of a single physical thing seen from various places. In audition, they recognize timbre and chord regardless of pitch. The equivalent apparitions in all cases share a common figure and define a group of transformations that take the equivalents into one another but preserve the figure invariant. So, for example, the group of translations removes a square appearing at one place to other places; but the figure of a square it leaves invariant. These figures are the *geometric objects* of Cartan and Weyl, the *gestalten* of Wertheimer and Kohler. We seek general methods of designing nervous nets which recognize figures in such a way as to produce the same output for every input belonging to the figure. We endeavor particularly to find those which fit the histology of the actual structure.
>
> (op. cit. p. 127 f; see also pp. 130, 133, 137, 146;
McCulloch and Pitts, 1943: 129–132; McCulloch and Pfeiffer, 1949: 374).

Roughly speaking, the difference between the four-word thesaurus of "universals" which the frog's eye speaks, and the far more complex thesaurus of a mammal, is that of the frog's processing terminal being its (mesencephalic) tectum, while the mammal carries its analysis further into thalamocortical transactions (see note 9).

Pitts and McCulloch, however, deal a little more fully with acoustic than with optic processings; we switch over to this modality: The mechanism (we have sketched it in note 10) "recognizes chord and timbre independent of pitch." It provides for "exchangeability of time and space. . . . Any dimension or degree of freedom of a manifold or group can be exchanged freely with as much delay in the operation as corresponds to the number of distinct places along that dimension" (op. cit. p. 130).

"These procedures are a systematic development of the conception of reverberating neuronal chains, which themselves, in preserving the sequence of events while forgetting their time of happening, are abstracted universals of a kind. . . . By systematic use of the principle of the exchangeability of time and space, we have enlarged the realm (of properties) enormously. The adaptability of our methods to unusual forms of input is matched by the equally unusual form of their invariant output, which will rarely resemble the thing it means any closer than a man's name does his face."[17] It should be added that a neuron network performs also the converse of time-into-space exchange (McCulloch and Pfeiffer, 1949: 374).

3.2 An Evolving Computer Called Brain

3.21 In that most remarkable essay—written, noteworthily, during the gestation period of cybernetic science—Rosenblueth, Wiener, and Bigelow (1943)[18] reasoned thus:

Active behavior is either purposeless (random) or purposeful. "Purposeful" denotes an act directed toward a goal—"a final condition in which the behaving object reaches a definite correlation in time or space with respect to another object or event" (op. cit. p. 18). And "when we perform a voluntary action what we select voluntarily is a specific purpose, not a specific movement" (p. 19). "All purposeful behavior may be considered to require negative feedback" (ibid.)—it requires some return information from the goal which thus acts as a corrective to error deviation in the act being performed. Such behavior may be extrapolative (predictive) or nonextrapolative (nonpredictive). An example of the former: a cat pursuing a mouse runs toward the place where the mouse will be—not to where it is. This is a first-order prediction; throwing a stone at a moving target is a second-order prediction: two paths must be foreseen. Predictive behavior requires the discrimination of at least two coordinates, a temporal and at least one spatial axis. Prediction will be more flexible, however, if the behaving object can respond to changes in more than one spatial coordinate. A capacity for doing this will reside in the properties of the sensory receptors and of the internal organization of the subject. (RWB speculate that a rat or a dog cannot integrate input and output for a predictive action of third or fourth order.) "It is possible that one of the features of discontinuity of behavior observable when comparing humans with other high mammals may lie in that the other mammals are limited to predictive behavior of a

---

[17]Op. cit. p. 146. Incidentally, these appraisals are done on mammalian data, not merely on human. The authors' speculation was strongly criticized by Lashley (1952: 541).

[18]Cited, hereinafter, as RWB. We summarize by borrowing, as far as feasible, their own phrasings.

low order, whereas man may be capable potentially of quite high orders of prediction" (p. 21).

Very shortly we shall examine the matter of extrapolative powers in nonhuman vertebrates; but at the moment there is the matter of the discontinuity in orders of prediction between man and nonhumans. Quite presumably, the neuropsychologic evolution between Australopithecoid and *Homo* would dispose of the discontinuity. It would convert into an account of increment in degrees of prediction. We could, with considerable confidence, query the possibility that symbolopoesis, for one thing, is a function of degree of predictive capacity.

We yet would not have gotten very far unless and until the theory of "degrees" of integration had developed beyond the condition where it now lies. *Fide* Prosser (1965: 368 f): "an aspect of the wholesparts problem, qualitative differences and informational bridges between levels of complexity of organization, [has] scarcely been approached by information theory. This is at the heart of emergent evolution. . . . Extrapolation[19] (from one level to a next) requires bridges of information that may be very limited as compared with the knowledge about each of these levels per se."

And it is, we believe, very unlikely indeed that the "degrees" of RWB—which are logical, not natural functions—would represent "step-mechanisms."[20] Granted that for its emergent evolution gene mutations had to occur; it holds nevertheless that it is systems—not "traits"—which evolve. We still must imagine a continuity of generations throughout the prolonged geological time when homination was occurring, and when there was no tangible saltation in the levels of complexity of organization, in the IA and IC ambits.

3.22   In a series of most ingenious experiments, Krushinsky (1965) and his collaborators have probed the extrapolative capacity of sample birds and mammals.[21] The essential requisite was that of confronting the subject with a situation of utter novelty—so that prior conditioning could not operate and the innate capacity for a problem-solving would lack such constraint; that is the subjects were assumed to be quite naive.

A food vessel was passed across the limited field of vision, and then

[19]It should be clear that "extrapolation" is not being used by Prosser in the same way that it is used by RWB.
[20]For a relevant treatment of step-mechanisms, consult Ashby, 1960: Chs. 7, 9, 22.
[21]See his bibliography, ibid. The experiments he reports have much more of interest than what we are reporting here.

it disappeared and continued behind a wall of moderate length. Would the subject pursue a quest, to the successful point of passing the length of the wall, turning its edge, and arriving at the food behind it? There are certain rather obvious requisites for success. The subject must select relevant features from out of a large context, apprehend their relationship, determine their laws of change. Naturally, we do not expect to encounter the same pattern of motions by pigeon and dog in solving the problem—as RWB said, "when we perform a voluntary action what we select voluntarily is a specific purpose, not a specific movement." Noteworthily, crows did about as well as dogs; cats somewhat less so; hens and rabbits much less so, and approximately equally; pigeons worst.

There are a number of striking features about all this. (1) In every case, the animal had to take its directional cue from the direction traveled by the food, retain it after the food had disappeared, turn away and follow, with no further feedback, that direction, but in parallel; round the terminal edge of the wall with some "expectation." (2) The quality of performance did not correlate with the presence or the absence of cerebral hemispheres. (3) On the other hand, the gyrencephaly of rabbit, cat, dog increases in that order; and the crows possess certain brain complexities beyond those of hens or pigeons. Obviously, whatever their "mentations" they cannot be processed alike in animals with hemispheres and those without.

At all events, the "orders of prediction" certainly surpass the second order which RWB postulated for a cat pursuing a mouse. And we are prepared, we believe, to see behind this some time-space exchange as suggested by Pitts and McCulloch; but now the associations are incommensurably more complex than are the analyses performed by a Heschl's gyrus or striate area. At this juncture, the behavioral evidence is far in advance of the neurophysiology which eventually must be brought to support it.

3.23 At least, we are sure that back of it lie a phylogenesis and an ontogenesis wherein mechanisms have diversified out of an antecedent lesser diversity. We revert to Pask's (1966: 12) list of "fabric properties."—

The brain is a heterogeneous system: It comprises "minimal packages" which embody, severally, the control units which perform specific types of computation. (We never lose sight of the fact that there is no point-to-point registry of a particular computation as a particular unit of behavior.)

The essay of 1968a sketches the functional levels of the CNS as reticular formation, thalamocortical traffic, limbic system, neocortex, supralimbic lobe; it will not be repeated (see note 10).It hardly needs saying that this corresponds but very little to the phylogenesis or the ontogenesis of the system. New "packages" have never been "added on" to an antecedent, simpler system—as can be done with the construction of automata;[22] instead, it is "packages" which generate further, subsidiary "packages"; so that the computations are carried beyond their previous stages. (This lies at the heart of the remarks in note 10.) "Each time a new part is added to a system a qualitatively new information function appears. As long as one deals with a single variable, the problem is one of *efficient use of existing variations*. A two-part system introduces *relations between parts;* a three-part system, *relations between relations;* a four-part system, *relations between a part and a complex of relations*" (Quastler, 1958a: 39).

We thus arrive at *qualitative novae* of information. The permutative possibilities increase exponentially (see note 11), assuming even that the character and complexity of the constituent parts at any of these levels remain constant. In the real vertebrate brain, however, they do not remain constant. The cerebral cortex obviously is vastly more complex in any mammal than it is in the most advanced reptile; but thalamocortical traffic demands that the mammalian thalamus be correspondingly more complex. On the other hand, there is no note-worthy advance in the complexity of limbic lobe from primitive mam-mal to most advanced; indeed the structural complexity of the speci-fically olfactory portion of the telencephalon has diminished in man, the while his "associative" portion has developed the cerebral hemis-pheres. Some features of brain are most copious in Tarsius, less so in chimpanzee, least in man. These matters fit Ashby's remarks (see quotation, heading our section 2).

A crucial implication is to be drawn from all this. Frequently it is said (and even by the best of its students) that when in the course of evolution a new element of CNS mechanism supravenes, it "takes over" the function of elements already present at earlier evolutionary levels. Illustratively, in mammals the occipital lobe supposedly takes over the function of completing vision analysis which in the frog went no farther than the tectum.

The truth of such statements goes only this far: Both frog and mam-mal must finalize whatever vision analyses they make before using

[22]Unless we would make a trivial, and spurious, exception of the gradual incorpora-tion of the rhombencephalic portions of the neural tube which form the posterior part of the brain stem and are gained at the expense of the spinal cord; which process is not completed until we arrive at the reptilian level.

the information in programming an action based (in part at least) upon it. Krushinsky's birds and mammals solved the same problem and programmed behavior which bore resemblances and led to the same ultimate success. Yet as to their brain mechanisms, they all possessed indeed the common vertebrate heritage, upon which however their evolution had built diagnostic distinctions. The solution of the problem was done by nonidentical mechanisms. (The efficiency, to be sure, was unequal.)

But the "coarse grain" of the experiments did not bring out the complexities of the analyses which undoubtedly obtained differentially in, say, dog and crow respectively. (In all fairness to the experiment, such was not its intent.) The experiment demonstrated that all these animals could achieve a certain moderate level of order of prediction. There are nevertheless capacities for analyzing visual information which a mammal possesses and a bird does not. To illustrate:

Konrad Lorenz' (1952) jackdaws displayed the same hostile behavior toward a man (himself) in possession of black bathing trunks as toward a cat carrying a dead daw in its jaws. We notice two points. (1) The daw carried its object analysis no further than an identification of something which (to us) shows as limp, black, and of a certain size; (2) the object is attached to what by virtue of the attachment is a predator. (Lorenz himself was otherwise always "on friendly terms" with his daws.) There was, in other words, a recognition-interpretation of a situation-gestalt without a prior complete analysis of its constituent ingredients. If we could construct some comparable situation for a dog, we may be sure that his analysis would be very different—and probably would have a greater range of unpredictability.

But to return to brain mechanisms: The mammalian homologue of the frog's tectum is quite as efficient as the latter's; indeed, something is known of its analytic performances. Neurologically speaking, what Brodmann 17 accomplishes is to carry the analysis of visual information beyond what is done by lateral geniculate body and by superior colliculus. And those have already "prepared a better report" for the striate area than the frog's tectum could have done.

We are trying to emphasize that we must avoid a certain logical pitfall. If we say "the cerebral hemispheres now accomplish what brain-stem structures once did for an animal's performance," the subject of our sentence belongs in neurologic science and our predicate in behavioral science. In other words, jackdaws and dogs never behave alike, even when their performances have logical parallels and they achieve comparable goals.

Let us give this point its final abstraction. "Nothing," says Bishop (1956: 395), "could be more conservative than the persistence of the general plan of the chordates to the extent that Herrick could outline in the larva of Amblystoma precursors of all the main structures of the primate. The success of the vertebrate nervous system seems due not so much to the virtues of this fundamental plan, however virtuous, as to the capacity it has shown for almost infinite elaboration of its details. But in this flexibility of differentiation little has been discarded and the higher vertebrate still performs some of his 'lower' functions with machinery quite as primitive as that of his ancestors. Even the cortical neurone, except for some elaboration of its processes and connections, probably still functions in its various parts quite like the neurone of the lowly vertebrate before a cortex had been invented. The cortex still operates largely by means of connections characteristic of primitive neuropil."

4. HOMINATION[23]

Suppose that we were asked to arrange the following in two categories— *distance, mass, electric force, entropy, beauty, melody.*

I think there are strongest grounds for placing entropy alongside beauty and melody, and not with the first three. Entropy is formed only when the parts are viewed in association, and it is by viewing the parts in association that beauty and melody are discerned. All three are features of arrangement. It is a pregnant thought that one of these three associates should be able to figure as a commonplace quantity of science. The reason why this stranger can pass itself off among the aborigines of the physical world is that it is able to speak their language, viz., the language of arithmetic.

Eddington: "The Nature of the Physical World."
With thanks to W. Weaver (1949: 117.)

I feel sure that Eddington would have been willing to include the word *meaning* along with beauty and melody; and I suspect he would have been thrilled to see, in this theory that entropy not only speaks the language of arithmetic; it also speaks the language of language.

(Ibid. "Entropy"
Weaver seems to use sometimes as a paraphrase for "information.")

4.10 We have reached a point where our search for the origin of phasia must confine itself almost exclusively to the cerebral hemis-

---

[23]This anglicizes the Spanish *hominiación.* We prefer it to the usual "humanization," for it permits a technical use untrammeled by the numerous vulgate usages which have a priority in the other form.

pheres; more narrowly, to the neopallium. The limitations are forced upon us, not by information theory or by theoretical biology, but by the kind of empirical evidence that has been collected.

4.11 Practically all we know about the cortical mechanisms responsible for speech in any way comes from studies of their disruptions—pathological or electroencephalographic. But we are questing phylogenesis—biologic evolution. To move this kind of evidence over into so different a frame of discourse resembles something of a topologic transform; or, if you please, steering an automobile in reverse while watching the driver's mirror before you. It can be done, it has to be done; but it demands a skill.

The neocortex, with its six cytoarchitectonic laminae, is strikingly homogeneous all over, in its fundamentals; the local differences being rather a statistical matter.[24] Yet these effect the qualitative-analytic differences which eventuate in "mentation." And the processes within these *differentiae in similitudine* continue on their general way; if an utterance is formulated thereby, it is never but a selective, partial formulation of what is going on. The brain mechanisms never cease all other activity in order that they may concentrate upon producing a particular act. There are no "speech centers."

The statistical character of the local differences shows up, moreover, as functional foci with fading peripheral zones and indeterminate borders: "Functional fields" overlap; there are areal fade-outs and fade-ins of performances.

When a cortical area has been injured, its mechanisms (a) cannot process "normally"; (b) process "abnormally," chemically and electrographically. Moreover, their normal functionings may be those of inhibiting or of otherwise moderating (monitoring) transmissions as well as of transmitting; indeed, cortical mapping shows local zonings of such inhibitioning.

4.12 Now we may try for a rough overview of the cortex functioning under phasial deficit; we shall imagine that we can move a lesion over its surface, and watch for performance deficits, as they too fade in and out.[25] (In the following, ordinarily the left hemisphere is intended.)

---

[24]For the cytoarchitectonic distinctions, see Bailey and von Bonin, 1951. And see note 12.
[25]This device, we discover, is not really novel; its earliest invention seems to be Freud's in his "On Aphasia" (Zur Auffassung der Aphasien, 1891). See note 12. In our overview, we have elected to adapt from Luria, 1966a (1962), Part II. This stricture

I Superior Temporal Region

4.121 (1) Auditory cortex (Brodmann 41; thereupon, 42): various phonemic indiscriminations; with Brodmann 22 involved—some loss of understanding of direct object-attributes, yet with preservation of a generalizing capacity.[26] If the lesion involves temporal but not occipital cortex, the victim may be incapable of coping with voiced numbers yet remain very reliable with written numbers.

(2) Occipitoparietal and occipital regions (lower Brodmann 39, transiting to 19): Inability to recognize very simple objects by sight, yet ability to do so by touch; misidentification of a whole, because a detail has been seized upon and a whole extrapolated from it. The visual-analysis deficiency seems marked (visual agnosia) as Brodmann 19 becomes involved. "A lesion of the parieto-occipital divisions of the cortex may cause important disturbances in the synthesis of individual elements into simultaneous groups,' as Sechenov originally pointed out. These disturbances lead to considerable changes in visual perception, in spatial orientation, in the performance of certain logical-grammatical operations, and in calculation of functions evidently closely associated with disturbances of the complex forms of spatial analysis and synthesis. . . . The patients in this group eagerly began to tackle the problems presented to them, without showing those defects of attention and of the regulating role of the spoken instruction that characterize patients with a lesion of the frontal lobe. . . . Although they find difficulty in individual logical-grammatical or arithmetical operations, they nevertheless preserve the general scheme of reasoning . . . which Bruner and his associates, and Miller, Pribram and Galanter call the 'general strategy' of thinking" (Luria, 1966a: 162, 163 *passim*, or 1962: 140, 141 *passim*. The citations are to Bruner et al., 1956 and to Miller et al., 1960).

"A distinctive feature of these disturbances of spatial synthesis, primarily those accompanied by a lesion of the dominant hemisphere, is their association with special speech disorders. . . . Patients with a lesion of the . . . parietotemporal-occipital divisions of the left hemisphere exhibit signs of disturbed spatial synthesis and spatial orientation not only in relation to visual perception and activity, but also in

---

is but a practical one; for the literature is mountainous. The Brodmann-area identifications are partly ours—wherever Luria's seemed obscure. We have intercalated some comments and occasional other citations. Bibliographic note: we have consulted both the English translation, which is on the whole excellent, and the Russian original. [26]This we believe to be noteworthy, since sometimes it is supposed that the "higher" or "more complex" functions disintegrate first. We have noted earlier that "categorization" applies in some way even to very primitive, fundamental neural processings.

regard to the more complex forms of activity proceeding at the level of speech processes" (1966a: 153 or 1962: 132).

A lesion of this area is responsible for "semantic aphasia." There is, for one thing, a disability in recalling the name of an object; but it is unlike the amnestic aphasia from a temporal lesion—where the difficulty derives from an "instability of the sound image of words." This does not obtain in the parietal cases: Rather, there is failure in logical constructiveness, whether or not verbalism is involved. "Place a triangle below a circle" leads to drawing first a triangle then a circle; but there is no attempt to relate their positions. "Father's brother," "brother's father" will elicit the reaction that "father" and "brother" are clear enough—but they cannot grasp relatedness that binds them further. (1966a: 157 or 1962: 136.)

It is interesting to compare Luria's juxtaposition of behavior deficits and topography of lesions, with a discription by Miller *et al.* of normal adult behavior when subjects were test-assigned some matchings of concepts with hypotheses: "Some people tackle the problem verbally, symbolically; others want to manipulate the objects to group them perceptually this way and that; a few can alternate between the abstract and the perceptual strategies" (op. cit. p. 164 f). This suggests that there may be idiosyncratic emphases in adults' enlistment of their Brodmann 22, 39, 19, etc. Idiosyncrasies are, of course, masked out by statistical populations. Luria's total subjects numbered well-nigh a thousand (battle casualties).

Luria concludes that disturbances of intellectual processes in the superior temporal region are highly specialized, due not to some kind of defect in "symbolic function" or "abstract thinking" (these are not seen as operable concepts) but apparently to disturbance of definite kinds of spatial syntheses (1966a: 164 or 1962: 143); defects, however, not of immediate spatial perception but of "spatial ideas."

II Sensorimotor Region

This approximates Brodmann 3, 1 and 2, 5, 7, 40, which for somaesthesis analogizes approximately with 41 and 42 for audition, and 17 and 18, 19 for vision. (As with these, tactile sense factors out to more elementary psychophysiological components. Tactile agnosia subtracts from the summary editing within the parietal region a capability of identifying shapes, textures, weights.) The region includes, further, Brodmann 4, 6, 8, 44. Luria considers this entire area as having a complex unity, which secondarily breaks down into the conventional two (1966: 176 or 1962: 151)—which is quite understandable, from ontogenesis as well as from phylogenesis. In the adult, their function-ings continue to overlap.

Motor aphasia comprises a host of various difficulties in articulating and vocalizing whatever it is about a language sample which must have been assembled and readied for utterance. It is effected by a lesion of a region of precentral cortex in the "dominant" hemisphere, yet the victim retains the capacity for uttering noises. The incapacity to articulate learned patterns and the innately determined capacity to phonate, are consistent with the anatomical facts that the pharyngeal structures and the oral musculature lie on the midline axis of the body, and that even their bilateral innervation overlaps. But there are also some interesting transmodalities involved in the articulation of speech. Ordinarily, utterance incapability is accompanied by derange-ment of writing capability, and there is some loss of capacity for understanding words and phrases. A cybernetic impoverishment seems indicated; for normal youngsters, when learning to write, make more mistakes if they are not permitted to articulate the sounds of the letters. Motor aphasias, moreover, cause confusion of homoarticulate phonemes (e.g., "l" and "n") (Luria, 1966a: 189 or 1962: 162 f).

Here Broca's first, classic case of motor aphasia still is instructive —despite the fact that the particular extent of the involved lesion was not accurately determined at the time. Broca's patient manifested what we shall call, for want of a better term, a paraplegic quality about his utterances, for they were reduced to a repetitive "tan, tan." Luria sees this kind of thing as a disruption of the "internal syntactic scheme" (1966a: 210 or 1962: 180), a reduction to a "telegraphic" style—where single "words" burst out which seem substitutes for sentences.

Recently, he has made a discovery that bids fair to have importance not only to clinical neuropsychology but to our own problems. "Pa-tients whose active speech has suffered in consequence of acousticog-nostic defects or defects of the kinaesthetic base of the speech-act show noticeable difficulty in finding the necessary articulations; yet as a rule they preserve the general melodic structure of an utterance. Countrariwise, patients with 'kinetic motor aphasia' who have pre-served distinctive articulation usually lose the melodic structure of utterance, and even in later stages of recovery their speech retains remnants of telegraphic style and usually remains melodically inex-pressive" (Luria, 1962: 181. Translation ours. See also 1966a: 211).

Linguists have assigned the "melody" of speech to the domain of "paralinguistics" or of "semeiotics." This seems to fit the logic of their analytic techniques; but the biologist who would speculate on the phylogenesis of phasia cannot but incline to inverting the categorization: Perhaps we should see in speech (as the linguist defines it) a *"paramelodic"* elaboration.[27]

Injuries to the superior region of the premotor area induce difficulties of coherence and fluency. As patients themselves have managed to testify—"Sometimes a word that should come after comes before, you say it and you don't know what to do next—all the fluency is gone" (op. cit. p. 206 or p. 176). Injuries to the inferior region (which includes "Broca's area"—Brodmann 44) result in quite a different kind of disorders. Each phoneme or syllable must be engineered with effort, and with indifferent success; varietal capabilities are narrowed down; a success may convert into a helpless perseveration —all other choices of articulation are shut out. In the severest cases, articulation fails completely. The "internal syntactic scheme" has collapsed. In late stages of recovery—if these occur—"telegraphic style" begins to emerge; recovery may go no further. A patient relates the story of his casualty: "there . . . front . . . and the . . . attack . . . then . . . explosion . . . and then . . . nothing . . . then . . . operation . . . splinter . . . speech, speech . . . speech" (op. cit. p. 210 or p. 180).

Intellectual processes are disturbed by injuries to regions of the premotor area; as might be expected, they are very imperfectly understood. Confronted with a long passage—"I don't understand the first time. If I read it through once I grasp only a few words and do not understand what it means. . . . I have to read it many times to pick out ideas and put them together, and then I can understand it" (op. cit. p. 216 or p. 185).

The difficulty, despite superficial resemblance, is not the same as that from certain parietal difficulties. "Not only is the process of evolving the speech design disrupted . . . but also the process of coagulating the structures of speech which is indispensable to grasping the sense of the text. In both cases we are involved with a disruption of the *dynamics* of the speech processes and not with that disintegration of specific logicogrammatical structures which is encountered in patients with semantic aphasia" (1962: 185. Translation ours. See also 1966a: 216).

III Frontal-Lobe Areas

Knowledge about frontal-lobe activity has lagged far behind that about the rest of the neocortex; the history of neurologic science

---

[27]We have noticed, informally, in infants of but a very few months of age—after lalia had set in but echolalia still was in the future—a quite unmistakable and really "skillful" "echomelodia" of its mother's utterances. Lalia itself is always melodic.

makes this accountable. Extirpation of the lobes in dogs destroys the (motor) syntheses for goal-directed behavior, the capacity for choosing between alternatives, the capacity for evaluating the effects of their own actions. Humans with extensive frontal lesions cannot initiate a prodromal action. They can perform a simple task if the preconditions are set up: if there is a cue. And they may be incapable of ceasing the motions once the goal of task has been reached (e.g., they continue to strike a match after it has been lit.) For complex tasks, there can be no programmatic resolution. Selectivity is gone—that monitoring which enlists a balancing between suppression and activation. A proverb cannot be grasped as being metaphoric—it is taken in an immediately literal sense, and its disjected details lead off into irrelevant associations; it is difficult to bring the patient back to the point.[28] And Luria characterizes the disturbances as those of "selective logical operations" (op. cit. p. 287 or p. 245 f).

4.122   DISCUSSION.   Spatial limitations have compelled us to drastic oversimplifications. We have done no more than suggest the simultaneous presence of phasial and nonphasial behavior deficits stemming from one and the same lesion; but it must do. Nonetheless, we would emphasize that, unless and until an organism-as-system, human or other, disintegrates completely, it continues to attempt integrative copings in confrontation with situation. We choose "not a specific movement, but a specific purpose." This very general principle appears at the level of speech disabilities, repeatedly and in characteristic guises, from one individual case to the next. Illustratively, if the aphasic can still speak, yet cannot dredge up the specific word (usually a noun), he hunts through a field of associated ideas, perhaps hitting upon a synonym; he may be aware, and frustrated, if he cannot do so; pleased if he succeeds. He employs, in other words, *Umweg* strategies. "In general," say Schuell, Jenkins, Jiménez-Pabon (1964: 114), "aphasic patients make the same kinds of errors nonaphasics make under conditions of fatigue or inattention, but with far greater frequency. In other words, there seems to be evidence of a system with lowered efficiency."

Moreover, these samplings excerpted from Luria's characterizings should have suggested at once how symptoms fade in and fade out as we move a lesion over the surface of the cortex: Visual information contributes ineffectively to the analytic-synthetic process in proportion as the lesion is situated in Brodmann 18, 19; recall, or the search for the precisely identifying words stumbles or halts if temporo-parieto-

[28]1966a: 250 ff. or 1962: 214 ff. A notion of the great variety of possible symptoms cannot be conveyed in our brief essay.

occipital cortex (roughly, Brodmann 22 or supramarginal gyrus or Wernicke's area) is involved; the plan of a paragraph read, the planning of speech motorization, become unmanageable under involvement of Brodmann 6 and as we transit to 8 and 44 and then other areas of frontal lobe.

If we would speculate on the phylogenesis of phasia, it is doubtful that we can afford to ignore these qualitative features of speech. Here is the capacity for organizing thought, in terms hinted by the performances. For, whatever sort of "proto-grammar" we care to assign in our imaginations, to the evolving line of Australopithecoids, we shall have to posit some fairly high order of extrapolative capacity.

But we have no justification for assuming for the evolution of brain from ape to man anything other than that the cerebral cortex has evolved holistically, synergetically. It may or may not be significant that the frontal lobe of man bears about the same quantitative ratio to his entire cortex as in the case of the rhesus while his parietal cortex shows a slightly better ratio (see Appendix). This *steadiness of ratios* strongly suggests that whatever the primary-projection areas of the monkey's cortex analyze, is adequately synthesized into cognitions by temporal and parietal cortices, and there is a corresponding capacity for planning generated by frontal areas; that the much greater capacity of man for doing all these things lies in a ubiquitous increase of the parts while their interrelations have remained approximately constant. It is to be hoped that some day we shall be in a position to consider these things in terms of psychophysiologic performance of identified mechanisms—instead of applying measurements of crude mass to such delicate, massless properties, as our foregoing comments have forced us to do. At the other end of this spectrum, the logical categories of linguistic analysis afford no clues as to how the regional performances of the neocortex have continued to elaborate further and maintain their reciprocal monitorings—and have eventually permitted phonemes, morphemes, syntaxes.

At all events, despite the welter of syndromal features that issue from the clinic, it appears that they can be sorted approximately about two focalities: Insofar as cortical lesions entail any speech disorders the postcentral areas are in general agnosic, the precentral areas apraxic or anarthric. Alajouanine (1956. See particularly, Figs. 2, 3. And see Brain, 1961a: 50) assigns to these two groupings the loose and noncommittal labels, respectively, of Wernicke's and Broca's aphasias.

Introspection tells us that if we would form an utterance, we must assemble some semanticity into a relationship, codify it and program it into a serialized delivery. The sequence is not rigidly linear: A preceding phase does not have to be letter-perfect and complete as *sine qua non* cue for its immediate successor. As the delivery proceeds, there is a servo monitoring. We may start a sentence before we know exactly what will be the final word choices—yet these choices will lie within the constraints preimposed by an anticipative syntaxis. Nevertheless, we can, within limits, alter even the subsectional construction as we go along.[29] And furthermore, we can think out sentences without being compelled to convert them into externalized phonation at all. Or, I can bypass the vocal utterance of this sentence, and construct instead a series of graphic-art designs which have now been placed upon this sheet of paper (symbols of symbols). Or, I could interrupt the writing of this sentence and finish it vocally. And capacity for thinking out something to say bears no appreciable correlation with facility to articulate it vocally. Girl babies, on the average, develop the latter facility earlier than boys; it continues to be slightly higher in women than in men throughout life; yet there is no evidence that symbolopoeic thinking develops earlier in girl infants than in boy infants, nor farther. The congenitally deaf are no less capable of learning linguistic symbolopoea than the acoustically viable. While this neither confirms nor denies a validity to Alajouanine's dichotomy, it is consistent with it.

4.13, 4.131 Conrad studied the brain injuries of German battle casualties of World War II, and attempted a systematic interpretation in terms of gestalt-emergence and cortical topography. He concluded that "the meaning of aphasia is the failure to develop verbal gestalts to their final gestalts. Thus there is failure in the development of

(a) Verbal gestalts in the process of verbalization out of the preverbal (aphasia of Broca).

(b) Verbal kinetic gestalts in the process of motor execution as kinetic motor tunes (pure word-dumbness).

(c) Verbal gestalts in the process of perception of the auditory gestalt (pure word-deafness).

[29]Let us try to clarify this difficult statement. When I start a sentence, my choices follow a Markoff series. Each word I utter narrows my range of choices for the next. Yet the succeeding term is not contingent upon the immediately preceding one only. Much of my sentence as a holistic proposition already has some degree of plan before it starts. This seems to be an example of a *Vorgestalt*. But when I start a sentence, I do not need to have its entire vorgestalt brought to the status of a definitive gestalt before I can begin to utter it. Indeed, I may not know what word I shall choose to finish it with, until the moment I utter it. My sentencing monitors itself as I go along with it. There is always a residual of "surprise" up to the very end of the Markoff-chain process which marks my sentence.

(d) Verbal gestalts in the process of perception of the content of meaning, out of the auditory gestalts (sensory aphasia).

(e) Verbal gestalts in the process of the voluntary evocation of names (amnestic aphasia) (1954: 501).

Conrad's order appears to be that of an utterance formulated and delivered, and passing from its originator to a receiver; both of them are aphasic, but differently.

His mappings rather distinctly support the pre-and post-central dichotomy; in that (a) and (b) tend to localize in Brodmann 6, 4, 3, 1, 2 and lower-anterior 40; (d) has a temporo-parieto-ocipital distribution; (e) has a scattered representation in post- and pre-central cortex but not, on the whole, in the proper areas of primary sensory perception.[30]

4.132 DISCUSSION. We believe that this bears upon the phylogenesis of phasia in the following manner. Phasia must be the outcome of two (not unrelated) facilitations: a semantic assembling and a vocalized externalization. The first belongs rather to Luria's superior-temporal and frontal regions; the second goes with his sensorimotor (plus the "premotor") region. Cf. Alajouanine's Wernicke and Broca aphasia-types.

If we turn for a moment to chimpanzees—our cousins are proving to have surprisingly more symbolopoeic capacity than they ever seem to convert into a phonated code. Their inferior pre-central cortex, by tests, has a much higher threshold for electrostimulation than ours has. Apparently, they not only "think less acutely" than we do, but they apparently are not very interested in "saying what they think."

4.2 "Eigenraum—Fremdraum"[31]

4.21 The Vertebrate Ego We propose to attempt carrying the idea of a "self-organizing system" from the point where it was left in section 2, into a state where it will have relevance for our phylogenic considerations of neurologicàl and behavioral matters.

A vertebrate—for that matter, an insect too, and perhaps any and every animal—organizes its *Umwelt* as a part of its self-organizing. That is, its relatedness has its self as a focus, as a reference. This statement seems obvious and trivial—until it is probed.

---

[30]We might have surmised this *a priori*. "Amnestic aphasia" is more carefully analyzed by Luria (op. cit.); it should not have the same complexion pre- and post-centrally. Class (c) is not particularly represented on Conrad's mappings.
[31]"Self-space–alien space." "*Eigen-*": literally, cognately, "own."

A universe can be defined in terms of physics, without involving any summative, focal reference point to which all its vectors must bend. We shall term it, therefore, "indifferent." Now place an organism in it. The universe remains "indifferent." But now we have a focal reference point; now everything there is to say about the universe, if we remain within our new frame of discourse, is bent to this new focality. Here we have the origin of *meaning*.

Whether Ashby's ultrastable goal-questing Homeostat could be shown to have the complex property which now ensues in an animal organization, we lack the capacity for saying. What can and does happen now, in the case of the animal, is that it organizes itself and its *Umwelt* simultaneously, at least partly by a process of discrimination, respectively into a self-space and an alien space. At the most advanced levels of evolution, this produces a "body schema," which carries cognition to the level of conception. Alien space, however, is not left without further differentiation; for the animal develops a "home" and "range" ("territorialism"). We need not analyze this idea further.[32] "Home" may have actual spatial dimensions and properties (and so may "range"); but whether or no, it always has psychological dimensions and properties.

"Home" may be physically no more than a "lair," with no alternations applied to it; yet, the more we go into the matter with respect to any animal, the more likely it proves to be that the animal *does* effect some changes—it adapts the physical spot to itself, as much as the converse. And an aggression by an intruder upon its home is treated promptly as an aggression upon itself. No artifactual automaton (no Homeostat) does either of these things.

In fact, more than food an animal needs a focus of self-orientation. It is commonly termed "security"—by which usually is meant the emotional state of the animal that results from establishing a certain set of homeostatic conditions. But within the frame of the present discussion, we prefer to term it self-orientation. It implies some degree of goal-already-achieved, some successful "effort-after-meaning."

A hungry animal will not eat unless it is certain of the situation as it sees it, and judges it. A new born infant will not feed until and unless its environment contains no more than a minimum amount of novelty. If the situation contains a high quantity of novel information—high "surprise value"—there is suggestion that its higher-center pathways become "jammed." The organism cannot cope with it.

Whatever may hold, then, for animals without nervous systems, as

---

[32]It is mentioned in Count, 1958, 1958-9.

soon as we have reached the phylogenic level where they occur, we have at least the ingredients for an ego where the animal organizes its own corpus plus its immediate and its more distant surroundings, simultaneously as being one continuous proposition. How much "ego" animal psychologists might discover in a Coelenterate, we of course do not know; we assuredly have it at the insect and the vertebrate levels; and these animal morphologies construct ego configurations quite *sui generis*.

Something further takes place. An ultrastable system called organism evolves during its lifetime (ontogenesis), according to a DNA scheduling which is a property of the system solely. (This does not, of course, rule out the fact that the developmental potential requires environmental parameters if it is to be realized.) When the vertebrate exchanges its intraoval or intrauterine environment for the physical universe, among other things it summons a new set of input modalities to cope with novel parameters. Of those projected to neocortex, the fundamental modality remains that of somaesthesis; it is indispensable, as vision and audition are not. It is quite possible for a congenitally blind (and deaf) human to organize an adequate self-space/alien-space dyad from somaesthetic parameters, but not, in all probability, conversely. Vision and audition thus exercise a role that is confirmatory and a contributor to precision, during processes of analysis and feedback. There is an element of redundancy.

The normal human infant, at age 5 months, has begun to "discover" his own body. His feet and toes become visible, and attention-summoning. They belong to his *"Fremdraum"*—which is beginning to have cognition. His *"Eigenraum"* is "visceral" still. Eventually, when visual analysis and somaesthetic analysis effect a transmodal integration, the limbs will be transferred to his body schema which is forming.

Is this accompanied by any symbolopoeic effort? We do not know. At all events, it is definitely prephasial. By comparison, if the ontogenesis of body schema in alloprimates has been studied at all, we are uninformed about it. It definitely exists in the immature chimpanzee. Has it a symbolopoeic ingredient? Again we cannot say. It definitely remains nonphasial.

It is relatively simple to understand that a congenitally blind human, to whom sight has been given suddenly by an operation after a number of years, must yet fall back upon touch and manipulation to recognize an object, and must effect a visual gestalt by plodding through a selection of optic details; indeed, perhaps never effecting with facility and assurance a complete transmodal synthesis.[33] Here we can safely presume that the concepts which the congenitally blind can program into phasial code have not included visual abstractions in their building, although the capacity for symbolopoeic programming into phasial code is intact.

The situation is different in the case of the patient with parietal disorder which deranges the *Eigenraum–Fremdraum* system; as, for instance, when he refuses to acknowledge his arm as a part of himself, even when the examiner forces him to trace it visually. "I can see what you show me, but I cannot feel it; and I must trust my feelings." Transmodal verification has been lost, and somaesthesis has prior authority over vision. It hardly needs pointing out that this is no mere reversion to an early level of ontogenesis; it does, we think, point up the delicacy and tenuousness of the *Eigenraum–Fremdraum* differentiation, which must be prerequisite to the emergence of phasia in ontogenesis.

As for any phylogenic relevance, we are left to suppose that an alloprimate possesses as clear a discrimination of the dyad as man has; but without man's symbolopoeic affection, or his self-consciousness, whatever that may on analysis prove to be, or how it developed (see note 13).

No artifactual machine has yet been built wherein the sum of its performances results in its transformation into a considerably different set of relationships which are more complex than the early state whence they elaborated; but this is a vertebrate property *par excellence*. So the vertebrate during its ontogenesis never returns to a former state. This is emphatically true of those with the most evolved CNSs. So the animal probably never completes its organization of its *Umwelt*. Up to this moment, we have assumed no more than the IA ambit; but as soon as we include the IC ambit, the problem of organizing an *Umwelt* is greatly aggravated. There is no further complication at the perception-cognition *étape;* but at the human level at any rate, conception-ideation appears to require the intercommunication which is possible only where there is reciprocative exercising of a shared code at some level of cortical efficiency above that of an ape. This involves most intricately the supralimbic cortex post- and pre-centrally; the differences between these two cortices have been sketched earlier.

[33]Study of this matter has progressed since von Senden (1932), whose work remains fundamental. See also Hayek, 1952. A selected and updated bibliography is appended in von Senden, 1960.

Before completing this point let us turn for a moment to the onto-genesis of the social hymenopteran ego. Its definitive behavior shows a high degree of stereotypy, and a low degree of plasticity. (Apparently, a degree of plasticity is gained from the summative behavior of the colony; but this is only of incidental interest here.) The larval behavior is lost when in the pupal state there occurs a very extensive transform—morphologically, systemically, topologically considered. The newly hatched adult falls to tending the hive cells without any instruction; a few days later, on schedule, it ceases this and turns to foraging. And so on. Behavioral ontogenesis is catenary; at least, there appears to be very little known about transitional transforms of behavior or of hysteresis effects *(mnema)*.

By contrast, the vertebrate's ego in its adult state is the quotient of a very involved hysteresis formulation. It is anything but a catenary, of linear function. And we must understand its *Eigenraum–Fremdaum* polarity in this light. We must understand vertebrate communication as interaction among individuals who are "living" this kind of polarization. We must understand phasia as this kind of intercommunication *par-excellence*.

4.22 The Homination of Space-Time All that has been said earlier about space-time analysis by animals is applicable to man. It is reasonable speculation that its primitive qualities have persisted; but additionally and further, as though by a kind of topological transformation its functions have developed ideations. By what processes the bridging has been effected is altogether unknown today; we may gather some hints nevertheless.

To the best of our knowledge, no one else has attacked the problem side of human space-time analysis with such disciplined imagination as Gooddy and Reinhold;[34] and their interest is born of their immediate and down-to-earth clinical experience with its aberrations. Of this they have had experience of two kinds: the pathological derangements of brain functionings, and congenital disorders in otherwise sound children. (In what follows, the discussion is ours, but supported from their writings.)

4.221 SPACE They report (1952: 483–492) a most spectacular case of human disorientation which, despite the fact that its diagnosis remained uncertain up to the time of writing, gives an excellent idea of what can be entailed. We abstract:

[34]See the bibliography. Cited in our text as GR.

A 44-year-old (right-handed) nurse developed sudden falling down to the left. The left homonymous field of vision was lost; she could not frown, nor protrude her tongue on command. There was tactile inattention in the left arm and hand. When she tried to read, on reaching midline the right half of the printed line "shunted" leftward, making her dizzy and nauseated. An object placed in the left hand, although identifiable, made that hand feel heavier and larger than the right. She found it hard to cross the midline of her body—as was disclosed when she was asked to draw on paper the petals about a daisy-head. In this and in other tests she could not transfer an object across her midline unless she changed hands. Taking an object in the left hand drove the right hand irresistibly to come up and seize it too. The reading difficulty progressed to where she read with the page upside down, unawares. Objects in space appeared to her upside down; it bothered her. Asked to spell words, or to recite the alphabet, she promptly did so in reverse. She began writing from right to left with her right hand, sometimes *but not always* mirror-imagewise; upside down and mirror-wise simultaneously; but not mirror-wise with the left hand. She showed some capacity to write simultaneously with both hands—left to right. As vision deteriorated, she began also to hear sounds as though they arrived from the space on the opposite side of her body. Sometimes she was aware of the difficulty.

As reported, her symptoms of derangement in autotopognosis were relatively mild—those extremely bizarre manifestations, wherein, for instance, the victim fancies her leg as being someone lying beside her in bed, etc., were not there. Nonetheless, spatial disorientation seems never to be confined to either *Eigenraum* or *Fremdraum* alone. (The distinction is a clinical heurism, not one of neuropsychological functioning.)

4.222 "Predictive behavior requires the discrimination of at least two coordinates, a temporal and at least one spatial axis." Of course, all bodies exist in a space whose minimal description requires three axes indifferently; and existence is durative by definition. But the motions of animals are products of constraints: the directions they elect to travel are preferential, and functions of the body's symmetries.[35] Pronograde animals have difficulty moving backwards or sidewise—usually, they solve the problem by moving along the circumference of a circle (which remains referred to the body). But man

[35]Shall we say—animals treat space astigmatically?

can move radially, rotate about his vertical axis, less easily about his transverse and front-to-back axes—and these motions induce vertigo. "Orientation . . . implies the ability of the human individual to integrate all and perceive certain of the sensory impulses arising from his entire body and to relate one set of sensory information to another. . . . By this means a man is able to appreciate the form and position of his own body in relation to the outside world (and this in terms of a longitudinal axis and mirror-image symmetry). . . . Orientation involves relation to a fixed point. The afferent stimuli upon which orientation depends are not static but flow ceaselessly from the body and outside world throughout the life of an individual. The "fixed points" are therefore fixed only for a given moment in time. . . . *Orientation and movement are both inseparable. Both have their origin in sensation.* . . . [They] must involve the entire nervous systems of the organism, and a defect of a part involves disorientation of the whole. . . . An individual becomes disorientated (1) when the integration between the two halves of his body is disturbed, and especially when he is deprived of the power of contrasting one against the other; (2) when he loses the ability to perceive sensory impulses arising from one half or part of his body, and as a result is also unable to perform parallel or rotary movements with, or in relation to, that part . . . in space" (GR, 1952: 477ff, *passim*).

Sensations (GR) are a product of motion judgments. They originate as waves propogated along nerve fibers to the brain. "It is remarkable that the most recent advances in physics and philosophy appear to indicate that objects are motion complexes. We are able to recognize such complexes or patterns of motion, abstract them, and endow them with symbolic descriptions, such as words, gestures, musical notation, mathematical formulae, and so on" (GR, 1953: 343). When, furthermore, we are aware that we have moved or are moving, it is a judgment not relative to gravity but to rate of change; that is, to acceleration. Indeed, all stimuli are perceived as rates, duration, direction—as parts of universal motion (op. cit. p. 347, p. 349). "We suggest that the stream of afferent impulses arising from one-half of the body and formed into complex motion patterns of the cortex are contrasted by the mind (at conscious and unconscious levels) with the motion patterns from the other half of the body, the dynamic representation of one part, say to the hand, being contrasted against that of another, say the arm and these in turn are contrasted against the trunk and head and lower extremities. A man orientates himself in space by means of his knowledge of one half of the body in relation to the other, of the position of one portion of a limb in relation to the other parts. Location of stimuli is thus dependent upon cortical motion patterns, each one differing from the next, which represent the limbs and the body of a man. . . . A person perceives space in relation to his body—to the body as a whole and to its individual parts. . . . *Space is an idea,* a product of mind" (op. cit. 360, 362).

On such basis, GR classify spatial disorientation thus:

1. Defective two-point discrimination.
2. Visual and tactile "inattention" and disorientation.
3. Disorders of postural sensibility.
4. Disorders of voluntary movement ("apraxia").
5. Disordered appreciation of solid form ("astereognosis").
6. "Autotopagnosia."
7. Right and left disorientation (while symbol knowledge is retained).
8. Finger agnosia.

(We interject that most of these, perhaps all, may be induced in monkeys by experimental ablations of cortex. But GR's second group involves symbol systems.)

1. Difficulties in the understanding and expression of written and spoken language.
2. Difficulty with calculation.
3. Difficulty with mathematical or geometrical symbols.
4. Difficulty with drawing (op. cit. p. 352).

Clearly, GR are arguing from a symptomatology to a philosophic rationale, with references, along the way, to neural dynamics. The functionings of nerve populations as they produce these symptons are not handled—even today it remains a task for the future. We have not yet reached the goal to which Halstead summons (see heading quotation, section 3).

4.223 TIME How animals—including man—treat space has been studied much more than how they treat time. At this point we are not concerned with the ontogenetic process, wherein a system changes programmatically during a time scheduling, so that ultimately its function pattern summates as a "mature" state, which must be definable partly in terms of hysteresis. Instead, we are concerned with time as one of the integral dimensions upon which the organism must operate as it copes with universe and organizes its *Umwelt* in its effort after meaning.

Actually, this constitutes two quite distinguishable subjects: (1) The treatment of any information by the nervous system requires time

—a matter of neural networks performing computations, wherein the fabric of the machine participates as a relevant factor; (2) "the coding and decoding of information about time itself" (Brain, 1936: 390ff).

The latter subject belongs to symbolopoesis. The first of the subjects ties back into what has already been said in section 2. In a series of studies, Gooddy has derived "the brain as a clock" as a particular case of the "internal clocks" which are functions of the rhythmicity which is inherent in any and all organic systems. "All that is necessary for a clock is 'the detectable phenomena of accurate repetition'."[36] We have noted earlier that Gooddy and Reinhold paraphrase sensation as motion—indeed, that perception itself is somehow a matter of the second derivàtive (d^2y/dx^2). The rhythmicities of bodily systems, moreover, are not constants—certainly, metabolic states vary, and even may become unstable under "parametric jamming."[37]

It is easy to illustrate the clocking by a living body. To the ill person, time "drags"; also, to a bored person—but not from the same physiological rhythmicities. That biological time has nothing immediate to do with sidereal time shows amply in the ontogenetic growth rates; but also in phylogenesis, for basically the same reason: Homination has included the lengthening of life span, delayed maturations which allow the requisite time for *Weiterbildungen* in the brain mechanisms over those of apes, etc. How little we are prone to take cognizance of the time dimension may be emphasized precisely at this point: A human can undoubtedly "size up" a very complex situation "instantly"—taking no more time to do so than an ape would while reaching a much less involved "sizing-up." Some humans are "slow thinkers," others "lightning calculators." Although there have been a few experiments to test a correlation between speed at reaching decisions and capacity for processing degrees of complexity, what they seem to have demonstrated best (in our opinion) is an inadequate philosophy of time on the part of the experimenters.

Gooddy, however, observes acutely that when memory, foresight, judgment, intelligence, behavior, concentration, reasoning are deranged under cortical lesion—obviously, all very different aspects of mentation pattern—they possess the common feature of a loss of "timing" (op. cit. p. 1143). But now we have definitely passed beyond the point where we are considering the elemental chronology of physiological vectors, which underlie all those conceptual ideational

---

[36]Gooddy, 1958: 1140. See also 1959. Gooddy and the present writer have made the mutual discovery that they are indebted to the philosophic insights of Riese (see Riese, 1950).
[37]Our term.

performances, and have reached these performances themselves. "Thus when memory fails we find a defect of recall and arrangement of time past. A failure of concentration is an inability to maintain a "fine-scale" sensorimotor activity ranged immediately about the present. Foresight, judgment, and reasoning imply a failure of forward memory or "prediction." When these powers are lacking, it is easy to show that the patient can no longer estimate odds of probability concerning future events on the information available from the past" (ibid).

We have already met some of the "building-blocks" of this capability for treating the time axis: Pitts and McCulloch's manifold which exchanges space for time and vice versa; the extrapolative capacities in space-time of Krushinsky's birds and mammals. At the level of Gooddy's patients, we seem to be dealing but with neocortical matters. But this is not accurate. Prediction does indeed organize a here-and-now in terms of a generalized past (it does not matter, when I summon, for instance, the words "All people think" that they were acquired at different time points in my ontogenesis—and that each has undergone numerous revisions since first acquired) for meeting a future situation-as-envisaged. But it can be shown that retrograde amnesias, pre-epileptic "dreamy states," and *déjà vu* reach down into the clockings at least of the limbic mechanisms (see note 14).

4.224   We shall linger further but briefly with clinical phenomena.

A patient has obvious time disturbances if he grossly misjudges time duration in any of a number of possible ways; if his speech is slowed down, if he "perseverates." It is not obvious (from the clinical reports I have read) that the examiner has paid close attention to the precise time order of the seriation as the patient constructs the details of a drawing he is instructed to make; or the order of the seriation with which he comments upon a Rorschach blot. Such features obviously indicate the gating in a sequential patterning. Linguists, on the other hand, are very familiar with the organizing of a gating, since all utterances are a configured gating of a very complex kind; the meaning of an early 'morpheme is not completely grasped until later relationships appear—there is a time lag; the syntax of the code that is a character of any and every language system. Moreover, every gating is quite vulnerable to disarrangements, which certainly root in some timing disturbances of brain mechanisms.[38] Indeed, but for this phenomenon, which is extremely common among all "normal" indi-

---

[38]Cf. Freud, "The Psychopathology of Everyday Life."

viduals, there would be very little if any of those alterations in languages which form the substance of historical linguistics: the anticipations that effect umlaut; the inversions (*arbol, albero,* admiral); infixes (IE ablaut, etc.); and so on.

It were not amiss to expand Ehrenwald's *primitiver Zeitsinn* to approximate Gooddy's concept of "internal clocks"— the rhythms and periodicities of the body viewed as mechanisms; which include among others the nervous system. That an EEG wave should represent some envelope[39] of summary firings of cortical neurons, means that it demonstrates the abstractings which are being done in that *étape* of the information processings which nerve fields are ceaselessly performing. Still, we need carry this aspect no further; it has served to indicate that space analysis without time as a dimension is not feasible in a life system—where the fabric is an integral feature of the processings.

Ehrenwald summarizes his scheme in Table 5-1 (op. cit. p. 566. Translation ours).

(*"primitiver Zeitsinn"*)	(*"gnostische Zeitauffassung"*)
Disturbance of the primitive time sense (altered cortico-subcortical balance.) Cf. experimental sleep and hypnosis inductions; the Bowman and Grünbaum cases. Time-sense disturbance under mescaline intoxication (Behringer, Mayer-Grosz); disturbance of "immanent experience of duration" in melancholics, etc. (E. Strauβ).	Disturbance of the gnostic time conception. (a) Primary-ordinate[a] disturbance type (bilateral threshold constellation). (Cf. principal case in his article). (b) Agnostically induced type (diffuse brain injury. Induction from diencephalic-mesencephalic lesion in Gamper's sense). Cf. cases of genuine Korsakow syndrome.

[a]Capability of conceiving chronological sequence and order of events.

It will be seen that Ehrenwald's dichotomy dissects Gooddy's "personal time-sense." And indeed at the human level, where his Category II assuredly exists, one can never be certain but that both categories are always involved in personal time-sense disturbances whatever the etiology; and that failure to identify either is likely to be the fault of the test battery. At all events we remind ouselves again that the *Weiterbildung* of the neocortex emerges from the stepped-up

[39]We must accept responsibility for inserting this term.

effectiveness of thalamocortical relationship; and that the neocortex, however functionally normal, must always process as best it can the kind of information it receives from the thalamus. There seems no alternative explanation for those behaviors (Category I) where the patient responds intelligently yet with bewilderment to the examiner's tests; whereas a disturbance of Category II possesses a quality of dementia.

4.225   TIME AND MEMORY.   The time problem obviously is a formidable one. Clearly, it far transcends the trivial statement that a neural transaction, like every natural transit from one state to its successor, takes time. It is equally clear that, whether along a nervous track or an artifactual computer circuit there could be no determination of the present by the immediately preceding state but for persistence of some kind of "momentum." However, it is beyond the scope of this essay—and beyond the capacity of its author—to treat significantly the neurology of memory[40] as an order of time. Yet several notes seem desirable. (1) My brain is as insensate to its own time processing as to its spatial processings; a kind of neuropsychologic Heisenberg principle seems to take effect: I cannot perform a mentation and simultaneously be a spectator of the performance. I can run a kilometer and pace myself from my wristwatch; but I cannot think out this sentence while watching the minute hand of a clock to see how long it takes me—let alone try to speed it up or slow it down. (2) The bilateralities of my corpora quadrigemina and neocortical sensory registration insure that I shall analyze my space in terms of right and left halves—however I may bring them together. But time has no right and left halves for me to analyze. It seems true nonetheless that my two ears do not perceive identically in time the pitch-and-timbre of a tone which is being recepted as sonic wave frequencies: I can tell the direction whence the sound is coming. (3) At the level of "gnostic time conception," there are the startling experiences of Dr. Penfield's operative patients who, under faradic stimulation of "interpretive" cortex of the temporal lobe (spots of Brodmann 22, 21 and perhaps significantly, close to the transition to 38), had uncontrollable and vivid "flashbacks" which coexisted simultaneously and consciously so along with their experience of here-and-now—including fidelity to the tempo to the original experience, now dredged up to consciousness in the "flashback" (Cf. Penfield, op. misc.)

[40]This writer considers that Lord Brain has written a treatment that has classic stature, titled "Neurological and psychological time": see pp. 390–395 in Brain, 1963.

The point to mentioning these matters here (however lightly and fragmentarily) is that whenever anthropologists speculate at all about the phylogenesis of phasia, they treat it as some kind of response to a present stimulus only. But this is not the way that nonhumans as well as humans have experience.

Pribram and associates ablated discriminatively the "rhinecephalic" archi- and mesocortical structures of the temporal lobe of macaques, but preserved the neocortical portions. The subjects maintained normal capacity for visual choosing and preserved their performance of tasks learned prior to ablation. But capacity for transferring prior experience to a new problem had disappeared: "problems that are responded to as *equivalent* by the normal monkey are treated as *novel* by these monkeys with temporal lesions. . . . The results of the experiments suggest that these medial forebrain structures deal not only with the organism's stability with respect to his internal milieu, but also to his performance, over time, with regard to his external environment." In a similar vein, the lizard who suns himself and thus readies his internal steady state, which facilitates necessary motion, "is tracking his internal environment over time, instead of the location of events external to him. . . ." [Here lies] "the difference between mechanisms that provide stability (invariance, constancy) in space vs. those that provide organisms with stability in time. . . ." "Habituation of operation appears as a *critical, initial* step in the memory process. . . . Only by remembering, in some form or other, can organisms maintain their stability in time" (Pribram, 1962: 108, 109, *passim,* rearranged).

We are suggesting that to account for the phylogenesis of phasia, we should begin here, and think of the neocortical operations—which seem to be tacitly assumed by those who attack the problem from a behavioral or linguistic premise—as instrumental to something much broader and organic than but their phasial symptomatics.

In fact, even after we have probed the archi- and mesocortices, we have not touched bottom. "In spite of the striking presence of spatial coding in the central nervous system . . . this type of coding is not the only one. Even in some rather primitive parts of the mammalian brain stem, e.g., the reticular formation, some sensory information seems to be subjected in part to temporal coding" (Kuypers, 1962: 30f).

4.23 We shall not repeat here what has already been said (1968a) concerning the build-up of body image and of space image, with their implications for symbolopoea and, hence, for phasia. Some features from that material and that appearing in this essay, may now be brought together and restated on the basis of our *Umwelt* matrix; and always with reference to the relevant CNS mechanisms:

1. The I–non-I polarization has its residence particularly in that deeper region of temporal lobation where the more archaic pallium (limbic structures) and the more evolved pallium (neopallium) conjoin. Both the discrimination between and the "fusion" of *Eigenraum* and *Fremdraum* are activated here (*fide* Kubie, 1953a). Or—there is a bridgement between IB on one hand, and IA, IC on the other. "But for this, we should be like disembodied spirits." (MacLean, see note 14.)

2. Symbolopoesis cannot be merely a neocortical function; it is profoundly a functioning of this mechanismal totality (cf. Kubie). We must expect that dream-language and phasia are organically related.

3. Insofar as space-time analysis is a neocortical function, the clinical evidence about man and the experimental ablations upon monkey bear too close an array of resemblances for us to reject the conclusion that the analyses are basically homologous, that cortical topography is somehow functionally as well as cytoarchitectionically comparable (cf. Denny-Brown and Chambers).

4. Catarrhine monkeys, apes, and man possess approximately the same ratios of pre- to post-central supralimbic neocortex, which suggests that they should maintain approximately the same balances in processing whatever information they receive from the cortex that traffics with the thalamus. In these matters, man indeed has a quantitative advantage, by virtue of larger neuronal populations etc., from the further complexity of cell-assemblies that this makes possible. (Cf. Hebb, 1949, 1959.)

Of course, this leaves a host of questions unanswered—but also raises some new ones. Rather obviously, for instance, apes do "think" —as far as any observation of behavior can testify.[41]

5. The many and contrastive behavioral differences arising respectively from frontal and post-central traumata are very familiar to the clinic (and some suggestion has been given, *ante*). With respect to body-image—not only is postcentral (more particularly, parietal) cortex active in its build-up, but, understandably, in its maintenance. And

[41]Were we humans incapable of expressing thought verbally or artistically, we would have very fragmentary evidence, merely from watching each other behave, as to our mind contents. In fact, this remains true, despite our phasial equipment. There was a time when the mentations of animals were overestimated, because of a facile anthropomorphizing. The reaction—wholesome at the time—against this probably has led us to underestimate them. We are becoming more informed as to the factors involved, and hence more capable of a reevaluation.

hence, under lesion not only is there unawareness of spatial phenomena (in monkey as well as in man) but unawareness of unawareness (in man: anosognosia).[42] It is the post-central (sensory-projective) cortex that is concerned with the build-up of body image (Critchley, 1953: 225, 232).

4.3 Functional Asymmetry of the Cerebral Hemispheres

4.31. General Remarks 4.311 As originally planned, this essay was to have considered the topic of nonidentity between the right and left neocortices in their contributions to phasia, which has led to appellations of "dominant" or "major" for one (more commonly, the left) and "subordinate" or "minor" for the other. We decided against it, because hemispheral "laterality" is presently undergoing energetic research, interpretation is in flux (Mountcastle, 1962; Ettlinger, 1965), and the topic at the same time is too important for half-measures. By the same token, however, a "minimum residual" must be set down, shaped as a "suspended hypothesis."

4.312. Were we to commence with rock-bottom fundamentals (and the more serious our intent the more necessary this would be), we should find that cerebral bilateral asymmetry is secondary upon its bilateral symmetry; which in turn is a particularity of the axial relations of our physical form as a whole; that to possess a bodily geometry which departs from sphericity in such a way that we possess an anteroposterior and a dorsoventral axis necessarily imposes a transverse axis which, as it crosses the anterposterior axis, generates a mirror-image replication on each side. The geometry of the body determines how the organism will interpret universe as *Umwelt*. Bilaterality in a vertebrate does not necessarily subserve everywhere some common functional principle. Possession of two kidneys may, so to say, be but an accident of the (mirror-imaged) double body architecture—an imposition of solid geometry. The CNS is initially a hollow tube, on the mid-dorsal line of the elongate, cylindroid body; its mirror-imaged bilaterality is an internal differentiation. (Cf. annelids, arthropods.) The specializations which accrue along the mid-dorsal axis during phylogenesis—tectum, cerebellum, telencephalic pallium—are geminal, by virtue of this geometric predisposition. Thus the limbic lobe is geminally constituted—yet one-sided destructions seem to result in no functional impairment.

[42]Denny-Brown and associates emphasize this point. See his idea of "morphosynthesis" and its disturbances.

A metallic artifact can be machined to a bilaterally symmetric exactitude within a very narrow range of error tolerance. An organism is constituted of statistical aggregates: its mirror duplication has a larger degree of randomness, a lower degree of constraint; therefore some degree of bilateral inequality is a rule. In measure, then, as a pair of mirror-imaged units become more complex internally, as well as correspondingly complex across their interchange, there is the opportunity—the inevitability, in fact—that they should evolve some functional inequivalence. The cerebral hemispheres play back to each other information that has already undergone equivalent abstractions. This is quite a different matter from a playback between neocortex and intrinsic thalamic nuclei.

4.313   It is not difficult to appreciate the rationale of decussating channels, whereby information from a universe situate on one side of the body's midline is transmitted to the other side; and of an impar mechanism straddling the midline plane of the body, which integrates (cf. centrencephalic system). It is less easy to rationalize the processing of the information gathered from one side by a machinery situate almost entirely on the other (it is contralateral). Whatever be the complete explanation, it all appears to add up to a correction of the informational "astigmatism" that must result from the fact that, unless a sensitive body is a sphere, information cannot be received without some distortion.

In the most primitive vertebrate brains (to say nothing of invertebrates), the mechanisms which embody focalized sensory modalities are pairs, mirror-imagined, at their peripheral, receptive ends, and at their processing ends are situate on the contralateral sides of the midline. The pairing principle persists into the ultimate level of neopallial evolution. Commissural interrelations—which "correct" an otherwise unrelieved contralaterality—have continued to obtain between the pairings of archepallium and mesopallium; the great bulk of neopallial interconnection is represented by the corpus callosum.

Perhaps the basic reason for the mirror-imaged doubling by the cerebral hemispheres is the geometric constraint first imposed upon a primitive neural tube: Once bilaterally founded, there was no other way for it to continue an evolution. As far as we are informed, we see no validity in reasoning that the arrangement represents an achievement of maximum theoretical efficiency; we can see validity in reasoning that once the constraints were set and entered upon, the pairing of what eventually constituted the hemispheres followed from the fact of their paired anlagen; and the CNS has "done what it could with the equipment it already possessed." And we recall that such a system is not aiming, teleologically, at an ideal, or maximum possible, efficiency, but at "managing to commit as many errors as it can get away with."

4.32 The belief—the widespread conviction, indeed—that the organizing and delivering of speech is a role of but one hemisphere, the other maintaining or developing a silence, goes back, as we know, to Broca's clinical studies a century ago. This heurism has been immensely fruitful, although no neurologist would hold to it any more—which conforms with the general truth that the greater bulk of permanent scientific achievement has lain in ascertaining what is not so.

The evidence leading to the induction that speech resides in but one hemisphere comes from the fact that phasia is disordered, it even ceases altogether, from traumata to the one but not (or, at any rate, less so) to the other. To be sure, a trauma which merely destroys a portion of brain mechanism, as with a battle casualty, has not the same effect as a disease lesion which not only destroys a portion but may poison the remaining, sound tissues. Clearly, in any system of relays, the next relay can process only the information it receives. If the message is faulty, it is handicapped. At very best, it can compute-report the faultiness to other elements in the hookup; and the whole system may search for a paraphrasic correction—with more or less success. But in either foregoing case, the student infers what a normal role must be from matching the totality of a deficient performance against the totality of a "normal" performance. This certainly leads to insights—indeed, it is often the only way whereby a clue turns up; yet it has the weaknesses of its own strength. Now, any neurologist will point out that the disruption of a complex function from a local defect does not mean that the function indicated by default actually resided in that spot. It would be quite another thing nevertheless were we in a position where we could watch the machinery performing normally, and could witness what was actually happening here or there. The method of discovery by default, therefore, is a negative one; it is applied *faute de mieux*.[43]

[43]It should not need saying that this in no wise is intended in depreciation of the ingenious and thoughtful applications of the method—but for the fine insights it has wrested from incomparably the most complex phenomenon known in the entire universe, the human brain, this essay (and all others on phasia by the present writer) would have no content. The strength and the limitations of the method are splendidly exemplified in Geschwind, 1965—which to our knowledge is the most recent and a noble landmark along the same pursuit in which the present study is trying to participate.

4.33 Throughout our treatments in this essay of neural mechanism and behavioral delivery, we have been dogged by the same difficulty which affects the professionals of these matters. Suddenly we discover that our idioms lapse from a neurophysiology and shift into a psychology. The ultimate source of the ensnarement—it is actually unavoidable—is our Occidental tradition of the mind/body problem. Thus, "the doctrine of cerebral dominance is based on pathological (and not on uncontested physiological) observations; namely on *disordered* speech. . . . Nothing seems indeed to be more difficult than to resist the temptation of thinking and speaking in terms of a localization of *functions,* although the facts available admit only of localization of *symptoms.* 'Aphasia,' 'alexia,' 'agraphia,' etc. are symptomatic and psychological, not functional and neurophysiological. The most reasonable appraisal, at the level of pathologic behavior, of the supposed dominance in (usually the left) hemisphere is that it is the more vulnerable to trauma in the matter" (Riese, 1950: 61, 65).

In the monograph just cited—a beautiful and, we believe, undeservedly neglected work—Riese attributes the original "vulnerability" doctrine to Hughlings Jackson (see particularly Ch. XII), which has it that the highest nerve centers are at once the latest phylogenic arrivals, therefore the least stabilized as yet. (May we paraphrase?—evolutionally, the least "seasoned.") It is a debatable speculation; we abstain. Riese, however, develops "vulnerability" more usefully.[44] Toxic agents, for instance, have selective effects upon the cells of nervous structures; this is sufficient to localize some dysfunctionings. Other agents may be weaknesses of the circulatory structures. At all events, the problem is not that of the individual's "dominant" hemisphere being functionally structured in another way, but of whether the speech mechanisms, however constituted, are deranged from lesions of that hemisphere more readily than from lesions of the other.

All of which amounts to saying that, because disturbances to one (usually, left) hemisphere interrupt phasia, this by no means indicates that the other (usually, right) is failing to contribute, in an equal degree, if not in identical manner; and that quite surmisably it is the method of discovery-by-default which may require a reappraisal by those best qualified to make it.

Some "not so" features will be listed:

1. There are no known cytoarchitectonic or neurophysiologic differences which distinguish the respective hemispheres. Size discrepan-

---

[44]He follows Holmes (1947): "Introduction to Clinical Neurology."

cies are slight, and so are features which accompany such discrepancy as there is; and no functional implications are derivable from them.[45]

2. Handedness and cerebral dominance for speech no longer appear as being correlated. (Cf. Goodglass and Quadfasel, 1954; Roberts, 1956; Zangwill, 1960. And see note 15.)

3. Since phasial defaulting due to damage to the "dominant" hemisphere in early life may be recouped by the "subordinate'" the latter can hardly be a phasial idiot.[46]

4.34 The principal commissure whereby neocortical information is exchanged interhemispherally is the corpus callosum—exclusively a part of the neocortical evolution. In the most primitive mammals the bulk of the post-central neocortex consists of the primary-projection areas for somaesthesis, audition, vision, plus their adjacent fields wherein the primary information is processed further, to complete whatever imagery the animal is capable of. If we treat these primary projection areas as points, then the respective secondary processing areas would surround them as concentric radiations, and eventually must have frontiers which meet each other; thereupon permitting some "pooling"[47] of their processed information, such as it is. The product thus has the character of a transmodal integration. But in the most primitive mammals, this "association" cortex is slight and not well differentiated. The primary-projection areas obtain their information from the "extrinsic" nuclei of the thalamus.

These neocortical fields exchange information interhemispherally via a primitive corpus callosum—essentially, therefore, it is a servomechanismal channel. In the higher mammals, the "pooling" areas increase in size and matching capacity. Correspondingly, the thalamus develops its "intrinsic" nuclei. These "pooling" areas continue their interhemispheral exchange.

Those mammals whose brains have evolved the farthest—the higher primates particularly—show a further elaboration in the midst of the "pooling" areas of neocortex. This is Yakovlev's "supralimbic" cortex, which traffics essentially *intra se* only. It handles information that has undergone extreme abstraction and is very remote from the other end of the processual axis, where the information from the universe

[45]Cf. von Bonin, 1962. Geschwind (1965: 275) speculates, though without much assurance, that the discrepancies might have significance. It would favor a theory he has in mind as to man's monopoly of speech.
[46]The matter is discussed in Penfield and Roberts, 1959. See also Basser, 1962.
[47]Our term.

is being converted into space-time analyses. There is corticocortical traffic between the post-central and frontal supralimbic cortices per hemisphere; how much interhemispheral exchange there is, still is uncertain.

These differential callosal traffickings appear to explain, in part at least, some aspects of the results obtained from split-brain experiments and lobectomies. The distinction between sensation and perception has been leached of its meaning at that end of the neuropsychological continuum which begins in the sensory-receptor organs themselves; by like token, perception-cognitions have no delimiting boundary; and, in measure as supralimbic functionings become powerful, conceptualization ("gnosis"?) emerges. We can see why Goldstein appraised the primary analytic fields as more peripheral, those of higher orders of abstraction as more central. Furthermore, conceptualizing requires the feedbacks of memory.

With this, we have reached a frontier of knowledge. That general area of the supralimbic cortex, identified variously with or as Wernicke's area, angular and supramarginal gyri, Brodmann 39 and 22, appears, as we have noted, to traffic but little if at all, across the corpus callosum. Stereognosis, autotopognosis are "lodged" contralaterally in the hemispheres, but their spheres of recognition end, severally, at the body's midline. It is as if, so to say, nature had anticipated the split-brain experimenters by supplying a built-in case of it; if nevertheless we normally effect a total, integrated space-time continuum, perhaps Penfield would attribute it to the centrencephalic system.

And perhaps, further, here is a clue to that very familiar, yet strange phenomenon—the so-called behavioral "dominance" of one hemisphere. A trauma in the region of the angular and supramarginal gyri, or an electrostimulation there, interrupts the effective completion of a gestalt—an object is recognized, but its name cannot be recalled and attached to it. This occurs (usually) in the left hemisphere but not in the right (adults); that is, that area where space-time becomes generalized into a universal concept ("table" possesses a very definite configuration, despite its indeterminate latitude for size, shape, color, texture etc., and also a considerable background of unrelated contexts, but devoid of any temporality; so that I can even exploit it as a metaphor) must remain underanged, if I am to focalize this into a sonic, a phoneticized, seriated program—a "verbalization." And if my "dominant" hemisphere fails me suddenly, I cannot summon the other to deliver it (no matter if the "subordinate" should contain all the requisite information *in archivo*).

After all this has been said, the fact remains that there exist two quasi-equivalent computers, structurally a pair of mirror-images, which receive identical information from thalamus and limbic systems; and they can intercommunicate, play back to each other (according to a system of constraints which is a property of their organization); and so they can match their computings, whether at the *étape* of primary projection or that of recondite abstraction. (We have noted, in section 2, that a living system called a CNS obtains a degree of certainty out of random error by multiple computation.)

Surmisably, we should have *less,* not more phasial power if our two hemispheres behaved as a two-barreled shotgun, instead of the way they do. To argue from analogy (since now we cannot transcend the speculative realm), our cognition of space-depth is due to the fact that our occipital lobes must process slightly contradictory reports from our retinas. By analogy, the gestalt of symbol represents matchings at a very high order of abstraction of information. The moorings to a literal space-time are loosened—prerequisite to conversion back, in grammarized utterance, to the concretenes of another kind of here-and-now. In the midst of the whole course, where the moorings of space-time are the loosest, the two hemispheres seem to be "out of phase"with each other. Perhaps it has been a requisite for symbol.

4.35 We resume a topic mentioned, then abandoned, in section 2.6.

The relations between brain stem and the cerebral hemispheres—particularly, thalamocortical traffic—are essentially projection systems. Corticocortical traffic exploits the interconnection principle. (These are, of course, simplistic characterizations.)

Over the phylogenetic course, the vertebrate CNS has effected a series of levels of transmodal information integrations by exploiting these two principles or systems. Confining our attention to the selachian, the protomammalian, and the advanced mammalian levels, we may witness a succession of devices wherewith this series of animal organizations, while retaining the phylogenically older ones, yet proceed to add on a further device for carrying the abstracting to a new integrative level. In so doing, an earlier system becomes one part in a later and more embracive whole. The new whole is defined by a new body of information constraints (cf. Quastler, Prosser); the parts alter their own constraints in conformity with the new couplings established.

We may attempt to summarize the evolution of the capacity in the vertebrates' CNS to query an *Umwelt* in this fashion.

1. The selachian gathers information by successively adding in the modalities of "audition," "olfaction," "vision." Some interconnective association-processsing occurs in the dorsum of the encephalon; there are servomechanisms; assuredly there is also "feedback through the environment as an analog of brain functioning," as suggested by Bishop. Such "image" as all this must effect, can hardly have back of it any fine-grained detail; as the animal approaches its prey, the image must increase in intensity—as symptomatized by the animal's mounting excitement—but hardly in novelty.

2. At the reptilian level, an additional processing commences, which achieves full development at the mammalian level, by virtue of an archi- and a mesocortex; that is, by virtue of a "limbic system" (in MacLean's sense). This development, structurally, remains essentially the same in the mammalian order, including man. It is capable of quite a variety of organizings, which register as the repertoire of emotional states which seem common to mouse, cat, monkey, man (see note 14). If we allow to the selachians a certain degree of cross-modal perceptive association, at the mammalian level this is retained; but we now have also some cross-modal cognitive associations. The texture of the cognitions must depend upon the deliveries of the archi- and the mesopallium, but further, upon the efficiency represented by the degree of neopallial development and its relations with the more primitive pallia.

Now it becomes important to distinguish between *sharpened perceptive-cognitive* analyses and *enhanced capacity for conceptualizations*. When a brain casualty is tested for his capability in discriminating by touch between the embossed outlines of simple geometric figures, it is a matter of literal and concrete spatial cognition. If he (or a sound individual or a monkey) is tested to see whether he can first effect a perception-cognition of a certain figure by vision, and then recognize the same by touch, he is being queried as to his capacity for *extrapolating* from a spatial analysis (cognition) which has been fed by one sensory modality to a spatial analysis (cognition) which is being fed by another, by enlistment of memory engrams. It is this sort of thing, we believe, that Geschwind discusses as cross-modal transfer.

But the symbolopoesis which effects a conjunction of word with thing-cognited is of quite another level of abstraction and integration; and here we encounter another instance of what Prosser (1965: 366 f) indicates as our lack of knowledge about bridges of information for passing from one level of organization to one of next-higher order. We have now passed beyond *cross-modal perception-cognition* trans-

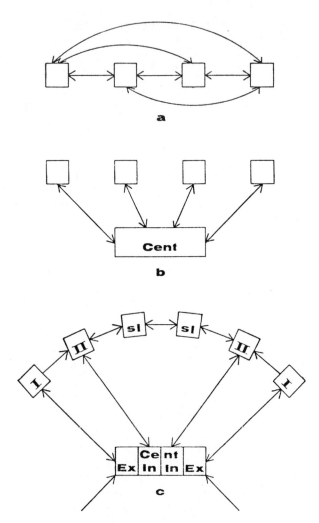

Fig. 5–2 "Interconnection" and "projection."
The rectangles symbolize either Pask's "packages" or neuronal aggregates functioning as some kind of unit; e.g., thalamic nuclei or neocortical nets or regions. Double-
headed arrows: two-way channelings; single-headed: one-way channelings. a:
Interconnections. Every additional unit increases the dyadic relationships in a
geometric ratio. The units are equivalent by hypothesis. b: projections. Every additional unit (in the upper array) increases the dyadic relationships in arithmetic ratio,
with "Center," which increases its capacity by the same arithmetic ratio. c: The two
principles combined, as in the mammalian brain. Only sensory-perceptory inputs
indicated. Legend: *Cent* may be equated with thalamus. *Ex:* extrinsic nuclei. *In:*
intrinsic nuclei. I: primary sensory-perceptory projection regions of the neocortex.
II: regions of further, derivative analyses. SI: supralimbic cortex. All three diagrams
neglect Quastler's principles of relational increments (1958a: 39. And see our 3.23).
(Vowles, 1961: 22 ff. Figures a, b adapted from his Figure 3.)

fer to a *cross-model conception* transfer. This is quite a different matter.

And, as we have come increasingly to know, since von Senden's day (if not earlier), this capacity does not have to wait upon a full battery of cross-modal perception transfers before it can operate with full power of its own.

4.36 GR have reported (1961) a most suggestive case of a ten-year-old boy who, normal otherwise, showed subnormal capability for reading and writing. Purely psychological blocking was readily eliminated from the diagnostic possibilities; they concluded that the difficulty represented a genetic fault of ontogenesis. He read slowly, using his fingers to follow letter by letter; had little trouble with long words but difficulty with three- or four-lettered ones, often reversing some of the letters. Clinically, he showed confusion in seriation when asked to recite a set-series (e.g., months of the year). In space analyses other than those of spellings, he also showed right-left nonorientation. He had, that is, weak ability for translating symbols deriving from one sensory modality into those from another; especially, for converting spoken symbols into written ones.

And GR theorize that the difficulty stems from a failure on the part of the two hemispheres during postnatal maturation to achieve criterion in the ratio of functional asymmetry between the hemispheres.[48] "The cerebral defect may be related to a too close similarity of function, that is a lack of asymmetrical function of the two hemispheres" (op. cit. p. 241).

Admittedly, the boy (and the authors stress that his condition is probably far more frequent than it is realized) was quite capable of speech at criterion level. *Prima facie,* then, the dysfunction appears to be one of stereodysgnosia, rather than one of phasia.

In the light of all that has been said hitherto, however, this objection cannot be final. On grounds of systems theory, we recognize that the transformations of a system such as occur when a living system matures, are not linear, catenary, but somehow topological. That is, during the course of ontogenesis of the speech function, we do not have to wait for the completion of a set of building blocks *seriatim.* It is empirically established, for instance, that a child is speaking long before one hemisphere becomes completely "dominant"—whatever meaning we may care to give this term. Space analysis of some degree may well be, both ontogenically and phylo-

---

[48]Phraseology ours. (We are setting aside their assumption that handedness and phasial laterality are related: Their principal point can stand without this propping.)

genically, prerequisite for the evolution of speech, albeit the matured "idea of space" may be years in the offing. Indeed, we recognize that the speech function participates in the playback whereby cognition continues into conception.

And we cannot emphasize too many times that we shall never unlock the riddle of the phylogenesis of phasia by searching for some one key factor. "We've got to return to the concept of *gestalt,* of a constellation of events, in time and space."[49] But for the supralimbic neocortical expansion, the further expansion of temporo-parieto- occipital differentiation within it, plus the asymmetric playback between the two cerebral neocortices we can say with assurance that there never would have come about the conceptualizations, the semanticity, the grammarized encodings of phasia. If there had never occurred the lowering of thresholds, the phonic facilitations, perhaps even the shiftings in the inhibitory role of cortical mechanisms, the utterance of speech would never have occurred. Again there comes to mind Ashby's profound and incisive remark, "There are complex systems that just do not allow the varying of only one factor at a time—they are so dynamic and interconnected that alteration of one factor immediately acts as a cause to evoke alterations in others, perhaps in a great many others" (1963: 5). We need add only that among the factors mentioned above, no one of them can be selected as having a chronological priority and therefore as the cause which evoked the others. And even if that were possible, once the set of factors was in process of changing, each member became a cause to all the others, and all the others converged to change each and every member of their configurations. We must pursue *constellations of events.*

5. AN APPENDIX

Some comment on comparative volumetrics of the brain is unavoidable, if for no reason other than that endocranial capacity of fossils is about the only datum which fills the gap between anthropoid and *Homo.* Taken out of all context, the gap seems spectacular; and this subjective impression has induced some students to appraise the cerebral expansion of man as anomalous, even "explosive" (the adjective has been applied); whence the further deduction that some great "selective pressure" had developed; which has led to further speculations as to what it might have been.

[49]Fremont-Smith, in "The Central Nervous System and Behavior," 2nd Conference, p. 99. Quoted out of context, but without misapplication.

This note is directed toward a correction of this chain, of which every link is without substance.

The human brain contains about 10^{10} or 2^{33} cells, and its total weight may be set here at 1400 g. Let us arbitrarily assume the weight of chimpanzee brain, 400 g, as the quantity antecedent to homination —since it is the ape-to-man gap that has led to the above-stated appraisal. Let us assume further, that cell sizes and their aggregative density remain constant throughout the phylogenesis. This assumption is quite false; but when we drop it, later on, it will only strengthen our line of argument.

Then a 400 g brain would have contained 2^{31+} cells. This means that, from some period in the Tertiary to the advent of *Homo sapiens* (or of Rhodesian or Neanderthal man) in the Pleistocene, less than two further mitotic divisions added to a basis of 31 would have been adequate to bridge the volumetric gap between 400 g and 1400 g, and a temporal gap of more than a million years. If, in addition, we were to start with the chimpanzee's seven-month gestation, and raise it to the human nine months, we would have allowed the requisite ontogenetic time without altering any physiologic tempos.

A number of years ago, we attempted what was to have been a first study of the brain-weight/body-weight ratios of mammals, with particular reference to the primates, in order to reach some judgment as to man's place among them. The study (Count, 1947; see Scholl, 1947) was tellingly criticized by Scholl—deservedly so (indeed, Scholl was more graciously restrained than he need have been), for it had attempted a statistical treatment that was to have made its point intelligible to the nonstatistically-minded student of human evolution; it failed to meet statistical criteria and it was also too recondite for the readers it sought to reach. Nevertheless, we believe its core idea to be sound (although here we must not indulge in a defense). If so, then among primates man places as having about the size of brain to be expected of a primate having his bodily size, while extant giant apes appear rather as "microcephals" of the Primate Order. (Incidentally, the formula developed would assign to Australopithecines, assuming an average brain weight of 600 g, a body weight of about 20 kg. Buettner-Janusch [1966: 146] assigns to them a weight of 25 kg.)

Let us recognize that the ratios of brain weight to body weight among mammals have often been studied under erroneous assumptions (e.g., by Dubois). But the volumetric or ponderal relations are there nevertheless. And if we recognize that an individual organism is a system, and its brain a particular "package" within that system (Pask), then we cannot avoid the conclusion that its spatial totality reflects one aspect of its substance for processing the information it will quest for at any time within its *Umwelt*. The brain as a machine is a summation of many variables. In the "sequence" Tarsius—Cercopithecus–Anthropoid–*Homo* some of the variables may diminish, others increase.

Brain size—volumetric, ponderal—is, so to say, an *envelope* of variables. Provided the variables are of a certain configuration (e.g., let them be the consequence of the DNA programming that is distinctive for *Homo)*, the total quantity of material involved may have a wide range of tolerability. For example, in *Homo,* a brain of 2000cc and one of 1000 cc may function on a par; it is, on the other hand, imaginable that 1000 cc in *Sinanthropus* was below this parity, because such features as we shall mention shortly lay in *Sinanthropus* outside the range characteristic of *Homo sapiens.* But it still holds true that there are physical limitations to what neurons can do, which are functions of spatial limitations. An insect brain is tiny; in spite of its much smaller neurons, it cannot approach the cellular populations contained in a vertebrate brain. The neuron cannot develop a great arborization of dendrites. The vertebrates are unique in their device for introducing a circulatory system into the very interior of their nervous structures, thus providing eventually for an indeterminate expansion of neuron populations and therefore of available choices.

Between the brains of ape and man, there exist many differences of cytoarchitectonics which, although their specific meaning for the behavioral deliveries of these two primates is unknown, cannot but be meaningful somehow.Some examples follow.[50]

The average size of the cortical cells (eulaminate, agranular, koniocortical) increases from Tarsius to *Homo* but not by constant ratios, the greatest discrepancy lying between chimpanzee and man. Cell density is likewise lowest for man. The upshot is that the number of cells in the human cortex totals about 6.9×10^9, upon a brain weight of 1450 g; while in the chimpanzee there are 5.5×10^9 cells upon a brain weight of 350 g. Rather obviously, the discrepancy lies not so much in an increase of cortical cell population in man but in the enlargement of the cells and their wider spacing—which would allow for greater dendritic plexification, and presumably more latitude of computations. Within these grosser differences, details show lesser

---

[50]It is well known, of course, that the study of regional cytoarchitectonics of the mammalian cortex reaches back to the nineteenth century. Undoubtedly, the finest body of studies on the primate cerebral cortex are those by Baily, von Bonin, and their associates. See the bibliography under their names. Our essay, at this moment, is relying upon an excellent study of neuronal quantity by Shariff (1952).

discrepancies; they appear, however, to add up. The primate neo-cortex has developed the very effective supragranular layers beyond those of other mammalian orders. There is but a slight absolute increase in the thickness of the isocortex from Tarsius to man, while the body weight has increased enormously; so that in fact, the *ratio* here strongly favors Tarsius over *Homo*. Within this thickness, the granular layer remains approximately constant (it diminishes slightly in man); absolute supragranular and infragranular thickness together increase but slightly from Tarsius to *Homo;* they appear to maintain a steadiness of ratio between them.

If to these overall differences are added the greater regional differentiations in the cytoarchitectonics of the neocortex, from Tarsius to *Homo*—the laminae differ statistically, in relative sizes of their cells, etc.—we arrive at a set of structural configurations which, although undoubtedly not exhaustive (and *pace* biochemical differences) may be summed as major differences in respective brain weights. It is a problem of holism. And these differences are in their turn but a partial product of the total differences in bodily dimensions and in Gooddy's "clocks." We daresay that only a primate of man's system of "clocks" could have developed a brain capable of phasia.

Throughout this essay, references to ontogenesis have been held to a minimum, because it is a speculation in phylogenesis. But the further the probing into an evolution, the less possible this becomes, for the obvious reason that, say, the differences between a chimpanzee and a man are occurrences, not states. The occurrences are the processes of ontogenesis; an adult is but the terminal expression of them.

Very happily, while this essay was in its earlier stages, there appeared Lenneberg's superb study on the "biological foundations of language" (1967), which very effectively substantiates these assertions. Certain features apply immediately to what we have just been discussing (see op. cit. pp. 170–175; pp. 67–71).

The human postnatal ontogenesis has a time span of 18 years; that of a chimpanzee, 11 years. Converting from sidereal time to biological time (cf. Gooddy's "clocks"), Lenneberg shows that at birth the chimpanzee's brain already has approximately 60% of its definitive weight, while man's has less than 25%. The approximate weights are, respectively, 250 g and 350 g. A chimpanzee's birthweight is about ½ that of man; the respective adult weights may be taken as about 47 kg and 64 kg.

By mid-childhood—respectively, 4 and 7 years—man has caught up with the chimpanzee in terms of percentage of definitive brain weight.

The two animals follow an identical schedule of percentage increment to body weight, when this is referred to biological time span.

At birth, the mitotic dividing of brain cells has practically ceased. The growths therefore reflect increase of size in the neurons themselves and their population densities; at growth terminal, we have the quantitative differences given in Shariff's data.

In man, onset of language Lenneberg sets at before age 3 years; in the chimpanzee, of course, it never occurs. In a human nanocephal, language onset occurs after age 6 years. At time of onset, the normal child has a brain weight, approximately, slightly less than 1100 g; the nanocephal, approximately 350 g. But histologically, the cortical cell sizes and the population density are within normal human range. The number of cells therefore is very much smaller. Yet eventually, all of them acquire the rudiments of language, including speaking and understanding, and the majority master the verbal skills at least as well as a normal 5-year-old child (Lenneberg 1964: 84).

EPILOGUE

In this essay, we have sought to show that the phylogenesis of man's most distinctive property need not be altogether a permanent riddle.

That it is a highly speculative essay, is obvious. We have sought, not so much for clues to the solution, but for clues to the clues.

In the long run, it will not matter if the speculations themselves prove untenable. All that may be expected is that the argument will have indicated with a minimum of error the direction which the query itself must take. We shall ask for nothing more.

SUMMARY

The process whereby a certain primate line underwent "humanization" is a cardinal problem of anthropology. Process and problem must be viewed as holisms.

Within these, the phylogenic emergence of "phasia"—the speech function—is of cardinal importance. Anthropology has made no noteworthy contribution to its elucidation.

Despite the obvious impossibility of ever finding fossil specimens of speech as accompaniments of palaeoanthropological recoveries, intellectually valid speculations are feasible, from the findings of zoo-semeiotics, child development, clinical, and primate-experimental neuropsychology. For, phasia must be assumed as a *Weiterbildung* in evolution upon whatever brain mechanisms and their functionings operated at a subhuman primate level. This essay, however, omits discussions of zoosemeiotics and the genetic psychology of children.

Phasia is assumed to be an *ad hoc* coping with situation as the organism analyzes the situation. This at once places it as an exercise of *information ecology* (in contradistinction to the *energy ecology*, which is the conventional meaning of ecology). A matrix of ecologies is submitted as a base upon which to apply information theory and systems theory to a treatment of the living brain as a unit of discourse within a "self-organizing system."

The vertebrate brain obtains an adequate degree of certainty out of randomness by multiple computations which it then matches. Its inputs are multimodal, wherefrom its possessor determines novelty and redundancy from messages. The vertebrate brain-as-machine combines projection arrangements with intercommunication arrangements in its couplings of neural networks and circuits. These principles are traceable throughout the phylogenic course, from selachians to mammals. The course expands from transmodal perception associations through cognitive integrations to the eventual "transmodal conceptualizations" which are the essence of symbolopoea.

A neurological sequence is suggested. Neural networks compute "universals" at least at the amphibian level; they appear to possess this as an intrinsic property at any level. The limbic system of mammals performs at a more abstract level. The neocortex carries abstractions to a conceptive level; it plays back to the limbic cortex (and there are other playbacks).

The whole process is viewed in the essay as one of space-time analysis at successive abstractive levels, which have been phylogenically determined. There has occurred a gradual resolution of a body-schema orientation, which becomes the referent for an *Eigenraum–Fremdraum* definition. The process occurs long before the human level is reached; phasia becomes a kind of logical conclusion or a final *Weiterbildung* of the process. The capacity for analyzing space-time operates within an *Umwelt* that does not necessarily involve members of one's own kind; phasia represents negotiations with an *Umwelt* composed of one's own kind, and who reciprocate by using the same code.

Brain traumata, epilepsies, etc. appear to give substance to this view. The view seems to elucidate also the ontogenic scheduling of phasia. Some notes on the comparative cytoarchitecture of neocortex in apes and man suggest that the respective volumetrics of the brain summarize—they are an "envelope of systems"—differences lodged in the respective DNA codes. This emphasizes *relational* differences rather than featural differences.

The essay seeks, not for clues to the emergence of phasia, but for clues to such clues.

NOTES

1. Boltzmann in 1894 characterized entropy as related to "missing information"— "inasmuch as it is related to the number of alternatives which remain possible to a physical system after all the macroscopically observable information concerning it has been recorded." (Weaver, 1949: 95 n) Mathematically stated,

$$\text{entropy} = k \log D$$

where k is Boltzmann's constant (for its derivation, see any textbook of physics) and D is a measure of disorder. Statistically, disorder is a state of randomness, that of "high probabality." Then D^{-1} becomes a measure of order; therefore

$$- (k \log D)$$

expresses information, or "negative entropy."

See further, Schroedinger, 1956: 67–73; Cherry, 1957: 212–216; Quastler, 1958a: 21; Wiener, 1954, *passim;* 1949, Ch. III; Weaver, 1949: 95 ff. And see Note 3.

2. Symbolopoea certainly is a far vaster topic than this essay can handle. The least we can say about it is that a cardinal distinction of phasia from alloprimate phonic communication is its relatively very heavy symbolopoeic burden. How our matrix is applicable, therefore, to the symbol-fraught, culturized human life mode, aside from phasial considerations, deserves a note.

Primitive world views, in the Frankforts' happy aphorism (Frankfort and Frankfort, 1946) treat the universe as a Thou rather than as an It. (The latter characterizes the scientific attitude.) We may say that such an attitude operates upon phenomena of the A-environment as if they belonged in C. The histories of religions, of philosophies, of science tell of shifts from one ambit to the other. The child mind behaves analogously. The cultural anthropologists could raise an interesting discussion about the placement of the numerous varieties of cannibalism or slavery. The "lactation complex" (Count, 1967a) could be treated in like manner; here, the mother-offspring mutualism definitely shifts its ambit location over the years. Psychiatrists could contribute much comment on the persisting confusions in the human psyche as it attempts to relate itself to the several environments.

Perhaps it needs stating that the behaviors of an animal within IA and IC respectively are distinctly different, yet without the animal's being "aware" that they are distinctive. Dogs and crows do not engage in dialogue with trees or rocks (although dogs bay at the moon). But humans do—in primitive rituals, and also at highly sophisticated levels of poetry. In the case of man we may presume that in early childhood there exists an as yet undeveloped capacity of distinguishing between denizens of environments A and C; but when at maturity this has developed, there exists a positive capacity for confusing or reamalgamating already differentiated categories.

There is a further distinction between A and C which is fundamental to culture. The complexity of the physical universe, as far as we know it, is constant; science merely continues to discover that it is more complex than hitherto realized. The complexity of the human social universe continues to become genuinely more complex. At the descriptive level, which is where the culture historian operates, this is obvious. It can be rationalized further, however, under the analyses of cybernetics and systems theory. For the evolution of brain mechanisms has entailed increments of constraints, of degrees of freedom of choices, readjustments in positive and negative feedback, the opening up of previously closed systems of behavior sequence; shifts from simple-probabilistic to highly complex-probabilistic systems (Beer's terminology).

The logical principles involved, however, do not constitute a *nova*. The social universe of any mammal is genuinely more complex than that of a lizard. If the social universe of *Homo erectus* was indeed more simple than that of a Bushman (quite presumably it was), then this would be a rough measure of the difference in the evolutionary degree of their respective brain developments. This degree of difference, on the other hand, does not obtain between Bushman and European—both specimens of *Homo sapiens*. By like token, Bushman speech is essentially as full-statured as Indoeuropean; whatever their differences of complexity, these are not at all of the same order as between the supposable "archaephasia" of *Homo erectus* and the definitive phasia of *Homo sapiens*.

Environments A and C are, obviously, spatially and temporally intermingled; they are negotiated via the same sensory reception and motor programming. Despite this fact, even at the level of nervous system they are far from identical.

For organism and its A environment do not reciprocate as an identical pair. To the organism, the exercise is a coded one, primally in its DNA schedule; the physical universe remains "indifferent." And it is a "constant." All negentropy or anti-entropy occurs within the organism. In this sense, the relationship is a "monologue." *Per contra* the organism and its C-environment constitute a dyad. There is a "dialogue" between paired identities. There is a "mutualism."

Let this mutualism be spelled out further. Its character can change in time, for both members of the dyad are systems whose variables or functions change—a property of living system. Here are some illustrative cases:

(1) Lactation complex. (Mother: infant.) The early and principal objective is the transfer of an energy source from one conspecific organism-or-system to another. The energy source is complex-homogeneous. The information which "rides" the energy is complex-heterogeneous, programmatic, contextual. The members of the dyad reciprocate, but inequivalently (cf. Count, 1967a).

(2) Coitus. Energy transfer is negligible. The essential objective is mechanical transfer of (1/2 of a dyadic) code. But the transfer has no intrinsic effect upon the transaction (a unique case). The transactors are reciprocating equivalents, but nonidentical. But the *context* of the transactors are reciprocating inequivalents.

(4) Language instruction. The case resembles, though but partially, the preceding. The transactors may also be reciprocating equivalents (two adults).

3. It were unfitting to extend the scope of this essay to an account of the origin of living system itself; yet, since phasia itself is placed in a somehow culminative position along an anti-entropic continuum, its logic may be pursued, if desired, into the following: Blum, 1961; Quastler, 1964a; Yockey *et al.*, 1958; Prosser, 1965. The "order from order" principle carries through nucleic acids, proteins, living cells, cell associations, cells yet more elaborately structured for processing information in a metazoan. Nervous system occurs at this last level.

The argument is stated explicitly by O. D. Wells: ". . . except for rapidity of transmission the functions of a nervous system are already inherent even in uni-cellulars, where metabolic gradients, phase differences, differential permeability, etc., serve as fore-runners of a nervous system, with no marked break. The presence in all animals of a chemical transmission system in terms of the output of the ducted and ductless glands, chemical activators in the blood such as secretin, and the product of large molecules by other large molecules such as antibodies by gamma-globulin, or proteins by DNA-RNA, illustrate that there are many other channels of transmission of information besides a nervous system. A further argument suggests that an autonomic system and its control of the inside environment was antecedent to a central nervous system, and leads to the conclusion that the reference frame of a common outside environment comes into existence only through the development of distance receptors, a central nervous system, and a language, which make the environment and must map the 'inside' environment as a projection 'outside' " (Wells, 1963: 257).

How neurons process information can be dealt with no more than cursorily in this essay. (Some features are sketched in Count, 1968a. Consult: Bishop, 1956; Bodian, 1962; Brazier 1952, 1964; Bruner, 1957.) How nervous networks edit information, the functioning of reverberating circuits, comprise a special and large body of literature; consult, however, von Foerster, 1960a, 1963; Pitts and McCulloch, 1947.

Wells' statement (discovered only considerably after the formulation of our matrix) ties up the following relevent essentials:

(1) The nervous system is but one specialized instrument for relating to a universe. It follows that it is subordinated to a particular set of constraints, which confine its degrees of freedom of choices.

(2) Implicitly, its information processings must be expressable as an interplay of digital and analogical computations.

(3) There is an adumbration of the course whereby environments B and A become differentiated. A certain phylogenic priority goes to environment B; and we have a hint as to the ontogenic course whereby *Eigenraum* and *Fremdraum* become differentiated.

For our appreciation of the "grass roots" of phasia, it cannot be overemphasized that man never succeeds in completing this differentiation; indeed, we would make bold to say that, despite his superlative neocortical expansion, his diencephalic and limbic mechanisms anchor him down quite as securely as is the case with the alloprimates. The visceral bedding of symbolopoesis may be appreciated from Kubie, 1953a, b, 1955b, 1958; MacLean, 1949, 1954, 1955, 1958.

4. Some potential ambiguities require clarification. We are speculating upon the evolutionary emergence of a certain observable, extremely complex behavior peculiar to man. One course which we might attempt is that of researching the "call systems" of alloprimates, with the hope that they might be broken down and reassembled into some kinds of thesaurus; thereupon, we would attempt to construct a model wherewith we might extrapolate or interpolate to the human structure. This procedure has been followed notably by Hockett and Ascher, by Hockett, and by Altmann separately and cooperatively.

We have chosen, instead, to probe the biological mechanisms whose exercise results in the behavior. Consonantly, we have adopted the postion that it is not traits, but systems, which evolve.

Strictly speaking, of course, a "system" cannot "evolve" unless its details alter somehow. We need details. The palaeanthropologist can do no more than unearth fragmentary "traits"—never "systems." Systems are inferred. This essay, moreover, is not addressed to systems theorists (however welcome would be their reading of it) but to anthropologists and kindred minds.

In 1968a, we gave some indication as to why we are neglecting "natural selection" in this research. To recapitulate: Students of human palaeanthropology frequently invoke it ritually to account for a presumed trait change: "Selective pressure" (they may say) favored the reduction of canines with the invention of weapon-tools, and/or the discovery of fire. And so on.

We shall state our criticism baldly. This is *explicatio ignoti per ignotum*; it risks the trap of circular reasoning; it confuses spatiotemporal association of occurrence (small canines, artifacts) with correlation; correlation with some cause-effect, forgetting that correlation is an admission of ignorance. Ritual explanation—to use the dialect of information theory—is "noise."

A matter of principle is at issue here; wherefore, a further remark. The "tooth-tools-fire" ensemble is being used here merely to illustrate an established way of thinking, with which a synholic approach is at variance. Because we are considering systems, we are very much concerned with the constraints which are the properties of a whole and not those of the parts taken discretely (Quastler, 1958c: 400; Prosser, 1965: 366 f.). But we must first establish our "universe of discourse." In cybernetic dialect, this is "the totality of possible assertions about the variables and their relations to one another." (Pask, 1965: 29). And a system is an "identified universe of discourse" (op. cit. pp. 33, 29). We believe that the approaches of this essay do not violate this prescription.

On the other hand, "tooth," "tool," "fire" may be considered unitary variables within three respective systems; but the information content for the connections between them does not exist, other than as it is invented by the student. What is the "identified universe of discourse"?

Per contra, we can attempt for the time being to follow the evolution of systems without involving ourselves with questions of their adaptability to environments—of what compelled them to change as they did. Theoretically, we cannot maintain this position permanently, for the cybernnetics of living organisms relates them to the ambience of their inputs and outputs. We treat them as self-organizing systems—by permission of Schroedinger's order-from-order mechanism—but we remember that this abstracts (see Pask, 1965; von Foerster, 1960).

And unavoidably we use "system" in two utterly different technical senses—that of anatomy and physiology ("central nervous system") and that (or those) of systems theory, cybernetics ("self-organizing system"); even simultaneously—when we contemplate the CNS cybernetically. We hope it does not lead to ambiguity of presentation.

5. Pask (1966: 12–14) has spelled out the properties of biological fabric from the cybernetic standpoint:

"1. As a result of maturation and development, biological fabric becomes partitioned into discrete packages . . . (such as an individual, a tissue, a region of the brain). The minimal package of *fabric* is that which embodies the minimal component in the cybernetic model, namely the control system that embodies one control unit. All viable packages . . . are integral multiples of 'minimal packages'. . . ."

"2. Within a given package of fabric, there is an activity restriction. . . . This limits the rate at which physical operators may be applied to a certain maximum value and imposes a limited data processing capability of the sort that is known in the specific sensory motor systems of man."

"3. Certain types of biological fabric also manifest the property that the rate of operator application has a definite minimum value. This sort of fabric embodies those control systems that are 'active' control systems . . . it is also manifest in the curiosity drive of many animals and the minimum rate at which man must receive data from an input that occupies his attention."

"4. Biological fabric is abraded by haphazard perturbations, and the structures embodied in it will decay unless they are repaired. . . ."

"5. Biological fabric is malleable or adaptable in the sense of Ashby and the stable configurations are goal directed control systems."

"6. [Proceeding beyond No. 4] . . . operator applications are required in order to maintain a stable configuration of fabric. . . . More stable physical configurations are less readily modified by relevant transformations as well as being, by definition, less readily modified by haphazard events; that is, more stable configurations have greater inertia." (Pask lists further a No. 7 and a No. 8; they would need inclusion were our study electing to proceed with operational applications.)

There are further noteworthy distinctions.

(1) Artifactual computers actually have no "memories." (This really is at variance neither with RWB's nor Pask's assumption about "memory"—nor are their respective uses of the term in conflict.) What these computers do is process ciphers. Mackay is tellingly severe about this; the "remembering" by computers is "poetical talk," "ani-

mistic superstition." The confusion is one of logic; eventually traceable to false issues behind the mind-brain controversy. "The undeniable dualism of human nature is one of 'aspect' rather than 'stuff.' Mental and physical categories are logically complementary, and careless mixing of them can lead to nonsense. . . . Some claims made for computers are nonsensical in this respect. Neither brains nor computers (*qua* physical systems) think, feel, perceive, decide, etc. These are the activities of people, not of brains. This does not mean that the artificial production of conscious beings is necessarily impossible, but only that it is not guaranteed merely by the imitation of conscious bodily behavior; even our ability to specify the requisite behavior remains to be shown" (Mackay, 1965: 331 f).

By corollary, perhaps, the capability of "recalling" has never yet been built into the "memory" of an artifactual computer. Moreover, even if we knew in complete detail how the brain is organized, and could incorporate into a model even what information is furnished by the proteins, the model would at best but *simulate* human intelligence. "If we did have design principles for an intelligent artifact, these principles might be radically different from those incorporated in the human mechanism" (Maron, 1965: 122, 125 f).

(2) In characterizing any living system, its history must be included (cf. Mayr, in Schaffner, 1955: 17); there is no comparable relevancy in an account of how an artifactual computer was constructed. That is to say, hysteresis is a determining dimension of the character of a living system.

This has been studied and repeatedly asserted by Rashevsky (see particularly, Vol. II, Chs. VII, VIII). "The circumstance that a system possesses several configurations of equilibria shows already that its actual configuration is not determined uniquely by the specification of the external constants. If under given external conditions the system is one of the several possible configurations of equilibrium, and if a small disturbance displaces the system from this configuration, then the system will again return to it after the disturbance is removed. But a sufficiently strong disturbance may bring the system into a different configuration of equilibrium in which it remains even after the disturbance is removed. It will now require a disturbance in the opposite direction to bring the system back into its original configuration. . . . Such very complex physicochemical systems as are exemplified by living organisms are likely to possess many equilibria configurations and to exhibit hysteresis. The above-discussed dependence of the final state of a system on the rate of variation of the external parameters suggests an interesting possibility for the interpretation of the failure to produce an organism artificially. The evolution of the organic world took millions of years. Starting with some particular configuration of organic molecules, the slow changes in the environment resulted finally in the formation of a simplest living cell. It may be quite possible for us to obtain in the laboratory the same original configuration of organic molecules and subject them to exactly the same variations of the environment. Yet the end-result may be quite different unless those changes are as slow as to require millions of years. The slowness of the geological changes may be the thing responsible for the origin of life on our planet" (op. cit. pp. 69, 72 f. Cf. Goldman, in Yovits and Cameron, 1960: 121).

(3) An artifactual machine which could replicate itself, *once it exists,* theoretically is not beyond constructing. But it has not become possible to conceive of one which would "create" itself. (Blum, 1961: 475).

6. Usually the C-universe of any animal is comprised of conspecific individuals. This need not be rigidly true. In general, if the codes of two individuals have some viability between them, they behave to each other accordingly.

My dog once cornered a badger. The two faced each other and dialogued in snarls and stances. The dialects of their codes were not identical, yet they were unmistakably carnivore. My dog could not have so dialogued with a horse or a deer. He and I dialogued—but first we had to learn something of each other's codes.

The principle, in fact, extends to conspecifics. Human adult and infant possess, genetically, the ingredients of a common code. But a mother and infant establish dialogue on a basis where this code-in-common stands at two different developmental stages of configuration. This same principle is exemplified by the general capacity of the brain to make mistakes and, connotatively, to "make choices over a range not accurately defined." (See Bishop, in the main text, 2. 6).

7. "The optimum amount of redundant information will be not that which makes all errors vanish, but that which minimizes the sum of the cost of errors plus the cost of redundant information, plus the cost—in information units—of error checking. . . . [An organism] will commit as many errors as it can get away with, and use the minimum of redundant information needed to hold errors to this level." Quastler, 1958 a: 190. See also McCulloch, 1960.

The neuron assemblage which is the brain seeks safety in numbers; its errors conform to stochastic process. Neurons die continually throughout life, and there are no postnatal mitoses to restore the population. The brain, however, does multiple parallel computations and compares results. Whence the reliability, purchased at the cost of redundance. But for this, the middle-aged human would be much less "intelligent" than the very young adult.

8. Discussion of this point belongs in neuropsychology, where it has received ample attention. It is basic to gestalt psychology. In an extraordinarily charismatic essay, Hayek (1952) argued boldly that perception already is a classifying process. This has been amply confirmed empirically.

It were quite inappropriate, in this essay, to define sensation, perception, cognition, and attempt to effect transitions from one to the next. These topics are certainly germane; but they belong in a much lengthier treatment. We content ourselves with mentioning von Senden, 1960; Goldstein, 1963; Hebb, 1961. From reception of a "stimulus" to its final disposal by operation of brain mechanism, there is a continuity of principle: an editing and abstracting by identifiable neuronal populations. Nonetheless, at every new relay, the information is in a different state. It is known empirically how the states differ, for instance, in the successive Brodmann areas 17, 18, 19 of the neocortex.

Our objective is different from that of any neurologist and/or psychologist. We are in search of an evolutionary natural-history outline for the peculiarly high capacity of man for elaborating symbols and expressing them as such.

9. This is stated advisedly. Hughlings Jackson's appraisal of the cerebral cortex as embodying the highest level of integration or mentation, which has supravened upon a hierarchy of lower ones, seems no longer helpful toward understanding brain performance. Rather, the emphasis must shift to the traffic between thalamus and cortex. "We wonder," remarks Lord Brain, "if there is any meaning in asking whether the cortex or the diencephalon of an artist or a poet, or indeed of any human being, is the 'higher,' and whether one should not conceive of the relationship between these two parts of the brain, not as a hierarchy, but as an integrative unity such as that represented by the yin and yang symbols of Taoism, intertwined in their self-embracing circle" (Brain, 1958: 452).

To neurologists, the shift in appraisal no longer is a novelty. It was, for instance, Penfield's clinical experiences which led him to translate thalamocortical traffic as the "centrencephalic system." (See the bibliography. Penfield and Roberts [p. 207 f] quite definitely attribute speech performance to this coupling.) "The most logical subdivision of the cortex," says von Bonin, "is that based on thalamocortical relations since the afferent impulses determine the functional importance of a given part of the cortex" (1950: 51).

There are indeed speech disorders emanating from lesions of the thalamus; often they are hard to diagnose differently from certain cortical syndromes. This is understandable, in view of the thalamocortical interplay. Indeed, as far as it has been followed, there appear to be no cortical destructions which do not entail retrograde degenerations into the thalamus (supralimbic cortex excepted?); the functional, syndromal implication is obvious. In brief, if we confine our etiology of speech disorders to considerations of cortex, we are not covering the phenomenon. It is the limitations of empirical data which constrain us to do so—not the fact of biology.

Since we are directing address not to the neurologists but to our fellow anthropologists—layman speaking to laymen—we shall take the liberty and the risk of diagramming.—

Suppose that we possess, in a room of fitting size, a very complex computer. We program it, and we obtain from it the reports of which it is capable. But we become dissatisfied: Surely, if somewhere within the circuitry of our black box we could intercalate some elements which might effect yet finer analyses before the final output is due, might we not obtain a far more sophisticated report? But now we find that such intercalations comprise a relatively enormous bulk; therefore we build a large annex, and carry cables from our original machine through an opening and thereby couple our systems. Nevertheless, it is our original computer which ultimately delivers the output we require..

Like all analogies, this cannot be pushed beyond the limits of its intent. Our thalamus does not process olfactory information, which retains its primitive position in the brain mechanism. On the other hand, the autonomic information which the thalamus receives from the hypothalamus is not passed on to the cortex. The cortex processes only such information as telencephalon and diencephalon "choose" to relay to it; yet, the diencephalon is concerned with programming a comprehensive course of total-organismal action.

We have mentioned that in 1968a, there is a sketch of brain mechanism as it pertains to the totality of the speech function; it is presented as reticular system, thalamocortical traffic, limbic system, neocortex, supralimbic lobe. Such presentation, however, masks a very long phylogenetic history. And the full force of meaning in the account of how the brain disposes of information which it is capable of treating as input, cannot be felt unless this history is included. There is hysteresis. Another diagram perhaps will be tolerated.—

The vertebrate brain—primitive or advanced—manifests a series of five regions; only the first three need concern us here: telencephalon, diencephalon, mesencephalon. The telencephalon receives the olfactory channel and processes its input. The optic channel enters the diencephalon, traverses it, and its input undergoes its first processing in the mesencephalon. The acoustic channel, although it first reaches the brain a little farther back than regions being considered, delivers its input to the mesencephalon also, close to the optic processer.[51]

How mesencephalon and diencephalon process optic and acoustic inputs is a very complex story; it reaches down even to the most primitive of the fishes. The diencephalon places *between* telencephalon and mesencephalon. Eventually (incipiently in Amphibia, clearly in Reptilia, very pronouncedly in Mammalia), that region of the diencephalon which processes optic and acoustic inputs (thalamus) effects a further processing relationship with the processing mechanism of the telencephalon; and it is from the latter that the cerebral hemispheres develop. (The olfactory inputs are not being considered for the moment.) In all known mammalian brains, then, optic and acoustic information is processed by the diencephalon before it can proceed into the cerebral hemispheres; the olfactory information is processed within the basic telecephalon and then transmitted directly to the cerebral hemispheres.

In this sketch, the feedback relations have been ignored; and much remains to be learned about them. Nonetheless, this elemental separation between olfactory processing on the one hand and optic-acoustic on the other, has fundamental significance for the buildup of "mentation"—a matter to which psychiatrists can testify, as well

[51]Each of these channelings has a different phylogenetic history; they took shape millions of years apart, under different ecologic conditions. Their integrations within the mammalian hemispheres were achieved later still.

as neurologists. (See, for instance, MacLean, 1949, 1954, 1958. There are interesting olfactory symptoms preceding epiliptic ictus in the "rhinencephalon.")

We can think of no more fundamental fact about the morphology of the thalamo-cortical relationship than the following: (1) The thalamus contains, among its "packages" (Pask), neuron relays from mesencephalic stations which have partially abstracted visual, auditory, and somaesthetic information. The thalamic nuclei are, respectively, the lateral geniculate body, the medial geniculate body, ventrolateral and arcuate nuclei. They relay their processings respectively to the cortical striate area (occipital, Brodmann 17), Heschl's gyrus (temporal, Brodmann 41), postcentral gyrus (Brodmann 3). The thalamic nuclei, because they receive these outside channels are termed "extrinsic." These corresponding cortical areas are "primary-projective"; their abstractings radiate to the succeeding zones—the information progressing through a localizing, an analyzing, a further distributing. (2) These successive processings in nonprimary zones of the cortex interrelate with other definite thalamic nuclei, which have no relay traffic from another region of the brain stem; hence they are termed *intrinsic*. (3) Eventually, these abstractive successions converge upon a further cortical area in their midst, where the brain effects final syntheses before programming a consequent action. This is Yakovlev's "limbic lobe" area, which does not traffic with the thalamus at all, but only corticocortically. See Fig. 2c. (And see the figures in Count, 1964/1962.)

This completes the account of the neocortex as an intercalated annex of the thalamus-as-computer.

One might expect that injuries of the "extrinsic" cortex would produce more serious behavior deficits than those to "intrinsic" cortex; since the latter can process only what it receives from the extrinsic. And indeed, this is corroborated from experimental ablations on the cortex of rhesus (see Pribram 1958).

10. From the medial geniculate nucleus in the thalamus, specific afferent axons bearing chordal impulses sweep up through the cortical laminae of Heschl's gyrus; they bend diagonally, passing through lamina IV (Gennari, Vicq d'Azur). Indigenous neurons, small, dense, occur as bundles, vertically. Nonspecific afferent axons also ascend from the thalamus, vertically through all the cortical laminae. They synapse with a matting of horizontally strung fibers which on the average are layered at a right angle to the above-mentioned indigenous fibers. Thus, lamina IV constitutes a manifold. The aforesaid nonspecific afferents supply the alpha-rhythm sweep, up and down through the cortex—this rhythm presumably performing "a temporal scanning of the cortex, which thereby gains, at the cost of time, the equivalent of another spatial dimension in its neural manifold" (Pitts and McCulloch, 1947: 133).

The manifold is thus a "translator" of the impulses ascending from the medial geniculate body. Thereupon, the translations are relayed down into lamina V, where they are "added." The resultant is transferred by associative efferents to neighboring associative cortex, where the mechanism repeats the performance; the cytoarchitecture, however, has its own idiosyncratic details; but they are of a secondary nature.

The point-to-point principle, however, which begins with the gamut of receptors in the organ of Corti, carries through (as in the analogous case of the optic registry in the occipital cortex). the afferents from the medial geniculate body are positioned in Heschl's gyrus so that the lower tones excite the outer-forward end, the high tones the inner-rearward.

The authors admit that their interpretation is considerably hypothetical; at all events, it demonstrates the character of the phenomenon and problem.

11. There occurs a striking conversation in the transactions of the IX American Conference on Cybernetics (see Bowmann, 1953). We abstract some of it.—

Suppose a black box having m input and n output channels. The possible combinations of these amount to:

$$2^{m \cdot 2^n}$$

Assume a million fibers in the optic nerve: $m = 10^6$. Assume $\frac{1}{10}$ that number of output channels: $n = 10^5$. [52] Then

$$2^{m \cdot 2^n} = 2_{10^6 \cdot 2^{10^5}}$$

—by comparison, Eddington estimated that the total number of protons and electrons in the cosmos approximates 2^{256}.

We may note that such figures would apply to the chimpanzee's black box as well as to man's. The text of our essay indicates that unpredictability resides yet further in the permutations that occur inside the black box, between input and output, and involving also hysteretic contributions. Behavioral plasticity and orders of complexity move in universes of such orders of magnitude.

12. It is common knowledge that in the most primitive mammals the topography of the neocortex has the regional localization of primary optic, acoustic, sensori-motor projections; that between these there develop, by a kind of intercalation, an "association" cortex. In phylogenetic course, the intercalations expand—effecting even more precise further editings of the primary information as received—and the three primary projection regions are forced even farther apart. The sensorimotor is indented by the rolandic or central fissure: Another "association" cortex develops anterior to the sensorimotor cortex. The three primary projection areas receive inputs from the thalamus; they process it and transmit it to the secondary areas for further processing. The eventual imagery (visual, auditory, somaesthetic) is not fully developed until this has happened. The three primary projection regions therefore constitute a tripolar topography; between them lies a "basin" into which the information "drains." Here the intermingling effects a cross-referencing, and syntheses can be built up which no longer are bound by the constraints of space-time. Memory traces ("engrams"?) function as monitors.

This should aid us to understand why it is that, in proportion as a lesion lies more closely to a source of primary projection analysis, the corresponding information modality is more affected, and vice versa. If the lesion is closer to the source of auditory radiation, for instance, there may be difficulty in comprehending spoken words: They may resemble the undifferentiable speech of an unknown language. And so on. The affectations are a matter of degree. If we could move the lesion about, one defect within a total comprehension presumably would disappear while another begins to appear.

The frontal associative cortex manifests what we shall call, for want of a better term, a plan-role, using this word in a sense consonant with that of Miller, Pribram and Galanter. Consistently with what has just been said, the closer the lesion locates toward the premotor area, the more difficult it becomes for the patient to synthesize a program of action; as Luria has indicated.

13. Geschwind (1965; see particularly pp. 275, 611, 641) has argued the proposition that the key to man's speech capability lies in his unique facilty for effecting cross-modal associations, which involve the inferior parietal lobule. Here the traffic is but intra-neocortical—there are no limbic connections. (This we have noted already, as a characteristic of Yakovlev's "supralimbic" lobe.) It is this capacity in man which renders possible the development of speech, in that it is agentive in attaching "names" to objects (Geschwind, 1965). *Per contra*, "in sub-human forms the only readily established sensory-sensory associations are those between a non-limbic . . . stimulus and a limbic stimulus" (op. cit. p. 275). He speculates further that in man the left hemisphere is readier to perform intra-neocortical cross-modal associations than the right is.

Clinical data suggest further that "language" is not "comprehended" by Wer-nicke's area but rather that this region serves to arouse associations elsewhere,

[52] I have taken the liberty of revising the original figures, which assumed $1,000,000 = 10^7$.

probably by way of the inferior parietal region. It illustrates also that speech is not created in Wernicke's area; instead the latter serves to transform what has come from the remainder of the brain into language (op. cit. p. 633. Geschwind's "Wernicke's area" apparently is a smaller spot than that designated conventionally.)

Prima facie, this seems consonant with what we have emphasized on previous occasions (Count, 1964 [1962], 1968a, and this essay); namely, that it is no accident that the conceptualizing which converts into a grammarized utterance is completed in that area of the parietal lobe which also completes stereognosis and autotopognosis. Geschwind's speculation appears to be pinpointing what we have been treating as space-time analysis.

Closer inspection raises some questions, however, which we proffer not in refutation, but because we rather suppose that they would have to be met before his hypothesis could become acceptable.

(1) Cross-modal transfer of training intra-neocortically appears to occur in monkeys (Burton and Ettlinger, 1960; Ettlinger, 1960)—albeit under the provisions and criteria of the experiments, less readily than in man. But neither does such transfer occur in man without considerable effort. If in phylogenic speculation over phasial emergence, one were to give to Geschwind's proposition the weight which it seems to urge, then one would be led to conclude that our present phasial facility has developed from the presence in incipient man of a computative capacity which even at the *Homo sapiens level* is exercised only with effort.

(2) How cross-modal association and phasial capacity develop apace in very early childhood, how they relate reciprocally, is a research problem still for the future. However, it cannot now be said that until and unless the child has first effected intra-neocortical integrations from cross-modal transfers, he cannot move on to an organizing of speech. The speculative conclusions about the cause-effect coupling of these two processings have been drawn from observations on matured brains; and the neocortical area in question achieves maturity only after more than a decade. Meanwhile most of the objects seen and named by the child afford no opportunity for cross-modal verifications. Moreover, the pinning of a name to an object is about the last, not the first, episode in the series of events whereby a child completes his space-time analysis. What is apprehended first is a situation, not the objects which contribute severally to it. The Indoeuropean-speaking child is trained to emphasize nouns in his learning; were he a Navajo, he would be trained to "name" actions. "Sitting," "walking" do indeed afford opportunity for associating information from more than one modality; but it cannot be argued that thalamocortical and limbic neocortical traffic is inadequate to account for it. That is, there is nothing we can see about phasia which is inexplainable without the particular intra-neocortical role that Geschwind emphasizes. For analyzing space-time and promoting it to phasia, it may have proven an asset, but not a determinant.

We are not arguing that intra-neocortical traffic does not contribute to the build-up of phasia whether ontogenetically or phylogenetically; as far as our layman's judgment allows, intra-neocortical or supralimbic traffic may offer the cross-modal association as an agent of an added redundance, a further verifying or matching process; but its *relative* importance must remain as yet an open question.

14. We cannot afford to leave the role of the limbic lobe in the build-up of space-time analysis in so vague a condition.

The essential conservatism about the evolution of this structure has nearly a century of investigations behind its realization. (See, more particularly, Klüver, 1952; MacLean, 1949, 1954, 1955, 1958, 1959; Papez, 1937.) Externally, the behaviors of nonhumans due to local stimulations of limbic structures resemble those elicited in man; of course, the subjective aspect is accessible to the student in man only. The limbic system is heavily responsible for psychosomatic disorders—which means also that capacity for having such disorders at all is a reflection of a high-order evolutionary achievement by the mammals.

MacLean (158: 614, 623) appraises the successive phylogenetic expansions of archicortex, mesocortex, neocortex, which culminate with the mammals as being like a series of ever finer-grained television screens. By this token we seem justified in saying that they represent a progressing effectiveness in assigning novelty and redundance to multimodal information, after that information has undergone some degree of editing.

MacLean has striven nobly to bring out the character of what this editing produces. There is a primitiveness about the discriminative perceptions and their recombining in a next-order synthesis, when "redness" can bring together blood, fainting, fighting, flowers (MacLean 1949: 348); or, to a child a leaf "tastes" green (op. cit. p. 344). (Snake: penis; room: vulva-uterus.) This, it strikes us, is cross-modal, not at some perception-level, but at some cognitive one. And MacLean sees in this capacity the further capacity for "tying up symbolically a number of unrelated phenomena, and at the same time (a lack of) analyzing ability of the word-brain to make a nice discrimination of their differences. . . . Perhaps it were more proper to say [that the limbic-visceral-brain] was an animalistic and illiterate brain." (Ibid.)

It seems to us that with the advent of these ever finer-meshed pallial scanners it is not just space that is further analyzed, but, in a certain way, time also. That is, the effects of past experiencings become more available in the programming of the next performance. A hysteresis effect upon brain mechanism translates as memory in behavior. The hippocampus in the limbic system is but one synaptic remove from the neocortical portion of the temporal lobe. The amygdala appears to be agentive in retaining the memory of an immediately previous experience; so that in the face of a persisting situation, the mammal resolves it partly on the basis of a "delayed loss of the immediate past."[53] Generalizing from specific experiences includes, shall we say, a "retro-recognition." Pribram's sound baboon, when offered a lighted match, would burn his mouth and face investigating it; he would not repeat it with the next lighted match (offered him immediately); a baboon with the amygdala extirpated repeated the disastrous performance indefinitely.

Phasia is a form of report upon an *Umwelt* whose organization is extremely high. Its phylogenesis could hardly have been possible if there had not already been available to it this dimension of time. Needless to say, once *Homo* had evolved the phasial capability, a pathological condition of the amygdala would have no destructive effect upon the capability; it would, however, greatly disturb the way in which phasia would be put to use, now that there exists a superadded neopallium.

Because introspective reporting is available from *Homo*, we have most instructive reports about the subjective side when epilepsy strikes the amygdala or the uncus; those published by Hughlings Jackson[54] are classic, particularly the case of "Z" (op. cit pp. 399–405, 458–463)—himself a physician. In the latter, evidently the neocortex could continue to perform a diagnosis, write it up with considerable competence—yet with no *post-facto* recollection. But the epilepsy effected a temporal disorientation—a "dreamy state," *déjà vu*, pre-ictal forebodings (and certain other symptoms). It is noteworthy that the neocortex presumably retained considerable capability for space-time analysis; it continued to program with some competence a grammatical and semantically relevant phasial sequence—yet a *feeling for self within spatio-temporal ambit*[55] was seriously disturbed. As nearly as this permits any inference, it is this kind of quality which perhaps the mammals acquired when they evolved their limbic lobation. There is here—if we may generalize—a resolu-

---

[53]Our term. This falls in with Pribram's speculation: See his remarks in "Second Conference. The Central Nervous System and Behavior" (Josiah Macy, Jr. Fdn., 1959): 194 ff.

[54]Originally reported: Brain (1888) **XI:** 179 ff; Brain (1898) **XXI:** 580 ff. See Jackson, 1958 (1931): **I:** 385–405, 406–411, 458–463.

[55]We ask the reader's indulgence for our phrasing—which stands *faute de mieux*.

tion of space-time into an *Eigenraum–Fremdraum* that is heavily charged with whatever symptomatizes as "emotion." And—whatever this may be worth—we find it impossible to imagine the more precise space-time analyses which the neocortex makes feasible, and which eventually induce phasia, as ever becoming phylogenetically possible without the antecedent existence of the limbic analyses. As yet, there exists no proof for this; we can imagine it as a potential area of research.

And—dare we suggest that music appreciation may rely heavily upon the activity of the limbic lobe?

15. Blau (1946) has amassed impressive evidence from early man's shaping of his tools, that he already had developed a motor preference in his right hand over his left. Blau's further argument that directional preference in writing was correlated with this, however, is far from convincing.

The early Semitic scripts go in either direction. Circular inscriptions for example, in early Greek, run clockwise or counterclockwise. Some archaic Greek was written *boustrophedon*. Chinese was written columnarly, from top to bottom, the columns arranged from right to left.

What, apparently, does not occur, is writing that begins at the bottom and works up. Such a direction would, of course, cover up all that precedes—much as writing from right to left with the right hand, and conversely, will do. There may be substance in this; but we deem it too simplistic. There is a more plausible possibility.

Alloprimates paint "fans" of lines which converge from a distance upon a focus approximating the midline of the body; they almost always are drawn centripetally (see Morris, 1962: 95 f). It is also the directional order whereby a chimpanzee pulls wads of nesting materials toward itself. Clearly, it represents mechanical constraints of spatial treatment; but this does not rule out the possibility that, additionally, there may be psychological constraints of body-schema orientation.

When the human hand holds a writing instrument—stylus, pen or other—the forearm is pronated, the palm therefore faces toward the body's midline plane, whether the writing be vertical or horizontal. It is a mechanical constraint of spatial treatment.

Meanwhile, as we have noted, handedness does not correlate with hemispheral dominance for speech; we have noted also what transpires in supralimbic cortex while conceptualization is being mobilized for an utterance can hardly be presumed to correlate with the motorizations of appendicular musculatures—their interhemispheral arrangements certainly are different.

BIBLIOGRAPHY

Alajouanine, T. 1956. Verbal realization in aphasia. *Brain* **79**:1–28.

Altmann, J. 1966. "Organic Foundations of Animal Behavior." Holt, Rinehart and Winston, New York.

Altmann, St. A. 1965. Sociobiology of rhesus monkeys. II. Stochastics of social communication. *J. Theoret. Biol.* **8**:490–522.

———. 1967. "Social Communication among Primates." University of Chicago Press, Chicago.

Ashby, W. Ross. 1960. "Design for a Brain." 2nd ed. Wiley, New York.

———. 1963. "An Introduction to Cybernetics." Wiley, New York.

Bachem, A. 1952. Brain astigmatism: a discussion of space and time. *Amer Scientist* **40**:497–499.

Bailey, P., and G. v. Bonin. 1951. "The Isocortex of Man." University of Illinois Press, Urbana.

———, G. v. Bonin, and W. S. McCulloch. 1950. "The Isocortex of the Chimpanzee." University of Illinois Press, Urbana.

Basser, L. S. 1962. Hemiplegia of early onset and the faculty of speech with special reference to the effects of hemispherectomy. *Brain* **85**:427–460.

Bastian, J. 1965. Primate signaling systems and human languages. pp. 585–606. In: DeVore, ed.

Beach, A. A., D. O. Herb, C. T. Morgan, and H. W. Nissen. eds. 1960. "The Neuropsychology of Lashley. Selected Papers" McGraw-Hill, New York.

Beer, St. 1959. "Cybernetics and Management." Science Eds., New York.

Bentley, A. F. 1941. The factual space and time of behavior. *J. Philosophy* **38**:477–485.

Bishop, G. H. 1956. Natural history of the nerve impulse. *Physiol. Rev.* **46**:376–399.

——. 1960. Feedback through the environment as an analog of brain functioning. In: Yovits and Cameron, 1960: 122–146.

Blau, A. 1946. "The Master Hand." Research Monographs, Amer. Orthopsychiat. Assn., No. 5, New York.

Bliss, E. L. ed. 1962. "Roots of Behavior." Hoeber, New York.

Blum, H. F. 1961. On the origin and evolution of living machines. *Amer. Scientist* **49**:474–501.

Bodian, D. 1962. The generalized vertebrate neuron. *Science* **137**:323–326.

Bonin, G. von. 1945. "The Cortex of Galago." University of Illinois Press, Urbana.

——. 1950. "Essay on the Cerebral Cortex." Charles C. Thomas, Springfield, Illinois.

——. 1951. The isocortex of Tarsius. *J. Compar. Neurol.* **95**:387–428.

——. 1962. Anatomical asymmetries of the cerebral hemispheres. In: Mountcastle, ed.

——, and P. Bailey. 1947. "The Neocortex of *Macaca mulatta*." University of Illinoise Press, Urbana.

——, H. W. Garol, and W. McCulloch. 1942. The functional organization of the occipital lobe. *Biol. Symposia*, No. 7.

Boulding, K. 1956. General systems theory—the skeleton of science. *General Systems Yearbook* **1**:11–17.

Bowman, J. R. 1953. Reduction of the number of possible Boolean functions. *Trans IX Amer. Conf. Cybernetics*. New York.

Brain, R. 1958. The physiological basis of consciousness. *Brain* **81**:426–455.

——. 1961a. "Speech Disorders." Butterworth, Washington.

——. 1961b. The neurology of language. *Brain* **84**:145–166.

——. 1963. Some reflections on brain and mind. *Brain* **86**:381–402.

Brazier, Mary A. B. 1952. Expanding concepts in neurophysiology. *Arch. Neurol. Psych.* **67**:545–549.

——. 1964. The electrical activity of the nervous system. *Science* **146**:1423–1428.

Bruner, J. S. 1957. Neural mechanisms in perception. *Psychol. Rev.* **64**:340–358.

——, and A. Goodnow. 1956. "A Study of Thinking." Wiley, New York.

Buettner-Janusch, J. 1966. "Origins of Man." Wiley, New York.

Burton, D., and G. Ettlinger. 1960. Cross-modal transfer of training in monkeys. *Nature* **186**:1071–1072.

Cherry, C. 1957. "On Human Communication." M.I.T. Press, Cambridge.

Coghill, G. E. 1930. Correlated anatomical and physiological studies of the growth of the nervous system of Amphibia: IX. The mechanism of association of *Amblystoma punctatum*. *J. Compar. Neurol.* **51**:311–375.

——. 1938. Space-time as a pattern of psycho-organismal mentation. *Amer. J. Psychol.* **51**:759–763.

Conrad, K. 1954. New problems of aphasia. *Brain* **77**:491–509.

Count, E. W. 1947. Brain and body weight in man: their antecedents in growth and evolution. *Ann. N. Y. Acad. Sci.* **46**:993–1122.

——. 1950. "This Is Race." New York.

——. 1958. The biological basis of human sociality. *Amer. Anthropologist* **60**:1049–1085.

———. 1958–9. Eine biologische Entwicklungsgeschichte der menschlichen *Sozialität*. *Homo* **9**:126–146; **10**:1–35, 65–92.

———. 1964, 1962. Phasia: on the phylogenesis of speech. *Proc. IX Internat. Congr. Linguists, Cambridge, Mass.,* 1962: 440–446. Leyden.

———. 1967. Toward a comparative vertebrate sociology: groundwork for a bio-social anthropology. **VII** *Congrès international des sciences anthropologiques et ethnologiques,* 1964. **IV:** 140–148. Moscow.

———. 1967a. The lactation complex. *Homo* **18**:38–54.

———. 1967b. A note on incest and the origins of human familialism. *Homo* **18**: 78–84.

———. 1968a. Animal communication in man-science: an essay in perspective. In: Sebeok, 1968.

Critchley, McD. 1953. "The Parietal Lobes." Edward Arnold, London.

Dancoff, S. M., and H. Quastler. 1953. The information content and error rate of living things. In: Quastler, 1953: 263–273.

Denny-Brown, D., and B. Q. Banker. 1954. Amorphosynthesis from left parietal lesion. *Arch. Neurol. Psychiat.* **71**:302–313.

———, and R. A. Chambers. 1958. The parietal lobe and behavior. *Res. Publ. Assn. Nerv. Ment. Diseases* **36**:35–117.

DeVore, I. ed. 1965. "Primate Behavior: Field Studies of Monkeys and Apes." Holt, Rinehart and Winston, New York.

Dilger, W. C. 1960. The comparative ethology of the African parrot genus *Agapornis*. *Z. Tierpsychol.* **17**:649–685.

———. 1962a. The behavior of lovebirds. *Sci. Amer.* Jan. 1962.

———. 1962b. Behavior and genetics. In: Bliss, 1962.

———. 1964. The interaction between genetic and experimental influences in the development of species-typical behavior. *Amer. Zoologist* **4**:155–160.

Eckerstrom, R. E. ed. 1963. International Design Conference, Aspen 1962. Zeeland, Michigan.

Ehrenwald, H. 1931. Störung der Zeitauffassung, der räumlichen Orientierung, des Zeichnens und des Rechnens bei einem Hirnverletzten. *Z. gesamt. Neurol. Psychiatr.* **132**:518–569.

Eickstedt, E. von. 1936. Ganzheitsanthropologie. *Z. Rassenk* **3**:1–9. See Count 1950.

Ettlinger, E. G. ed. 1965. "Functions of the Corpus Callosum." Boston.

Ettlinger, G. 1960. Cross-modal transfer of training in monkeys. *Behavior* **16**:56–65.

Foerster, H. von. 1960. On self-organizing systems and their environments. In: Yovits and Cameron, eds., 1960.

———. 1962. Circuitry of clues to Platonic ideation. In: Muses, ed., 1962.

———. 1963. Logical structure of environment and internal representation. In: Eckerstrom, ed., 1963.

Frank, L. K. 1948. *Foreword* to Frank et al.: 189–196.

———, G. E. Hutchinson, W. K. Livingston, W. S. McCulloch, and N. Wiener. 1948. Teleological Mechanisms. *Ann. N. Y. Acad. Sci.* **50**:187–278.

Frankfort, H., and H. A. Frankfort. 1946. *Introduction* to Frankfort et al.

———, H. A. Frankfort, A. Wilson, Th. Jacobsen, and W. A. Irwin. 1946. "The Intellectual Adventure of Ancient Man. University of Chicago Press, Chicago.

Geschwind, N. 1965. Disconnexion syndromes in animals and man. *Brain* **88**:237–294; 585–644.

Goldstein, K. 1939, 1963. "The Organism." American Book Co., New York.

Gooddy, W. 1952, 1958. Time and the nervous system: the brain as a clock. *The Lancet,* 31 May, 1139–1144; 26 December, 1155–1156.

———. 1964. Some comments on the significance of retrograde amnesia, with an analogy. *Brain* **87**:75–86.

———, and M. Reinhold. 1952, 1953. Some aspects of human orientation in space. (1) Sensation and movement. *Brain* **75**:472–509; (2) The dynamic nature of nervous activity. **76**:337–426.

————, and M. Reinhold. 1961. Congenital dyslexia and asymmetry of cerebral function. *Brain* **84**:231–242.

————, and M. Reinhold. 1963. Some aspects of human orientation in space. (3) The sense of direction and the arrow-form. In: "Problems of Dynamic Neurology." Jerusalem.

Goodglass, H., and F. A. Quadfasel. 1954. Language laterality in left-handed aphasics. *Brain* **77**:521548.

Halstead, W. C. 1947. "Brain and Intelligence." University of Chicago Press, Chicago.

Harlow, H. F., and C. N. Woolsey. eds. 1958. "Biological and Biochemical Bases of Behavior." University of Wisconsin Press, Madison.

Hayek, F. A. 1952. "The Sensory Order." University of Chicago Press, Chicago.

Hebb, D. O. 1949. "The Organization of Behavior." Wiley, New York.

————. 1959. Intelligence, brain function and the theory of mind. *Brain* **82**:260–275.

Herrick, C. J. 1948. "The Brain of the Tiger Salamander, *Amblystoma tigrinum*," University of Chicago Press, Chicago.

————. 1956. "The Evolution of Human Nature." University of Texas Press, Austin.

Hiller, W. F. 1954. Total left cerebral hemispherectomy for malignant glioma. *Neurology* **4**:718–721.

Hockett, Ch. F. 1959. "Animal languages" and human language. In: Spuhler, ed., 1949.

————. 1960a. Logical considerations in the study of animal communication. In: Lanyon and Tavolga, 1960.

————. 1960b. The origin of speech. *Sci. Amer.* **203**:88–96.

————, and St. A. Altmann. 1968. A note on design features. In: Sebeok, ed., 1968.

————, and R. Ascher. 1964. The human revolution. *Current Anthropol.* **5**:135–168.

Jackson, J. H. 1958, 1931. "Selected Writings." (James Taylor, ed.) Basic Books, New York. (Reprinted; original publishers: Hodder & Stoughton, London.) 2 vols.

Jeffress, L. A. ed. 1951. "Cerebral Mechanisms in Behavior." Wiley, New York.

Kennedy, C. H. 1927. The exoskeleton as a factor in limiting and directing the evolution of insects. *J. Morphol. Physiol.* **44**:267–312.

Klüver, H. 1952. Brain mechanisms and behavior with special reference to the rhinecephalon. *The Lancet* **72**:567–574.

————, and P. C. Bucy. 1939. Preliminary analysis of the temporal lobes in monkeys. *Arch. Neurol. Psychiat.* **42**:979–1000.

Kroeber, A. 1953. *Introduction* to: "Anthropology Today." University of Chicago Press, Chicago.

Krushinsky, L. V. 1965. Solution of elementary logical problems by animals on the basis of extrapolation. pp. 280–308. In: Wiener and Schade, eds.

Kubie, L. S. 1953a. Some implications for psychoanalysis of modern concepts of the organization of the brain. *Psychoanal. Quart.* **22**:21–68.

————. 1953b. The distortion of the symbolic process in neurosis and psychosis. *J. Amer. Psychoanal. Ass.* **1**:59–86.

————. 1955a. The problem of specificity in the psychosomatic process. In: Wittkower and Cleghorn, eds.

————. 1955b. The central representation of the symbolic process in relation to psychosomatic disorders. In: Wittkower and Cleghorn, eds.

————. 1958. "Neurotic Distortion of the Creative Process." University of Kansas Press, Lawrence.

Kuypers, H. G. J. M. 1962. Comments. In: Mountcastle, ed.

Lanyan, W. E., and W. N. Tavolga. 1960. "Animal Sounds and Communication." *Amer. Ins. Biol. Scis., Publ.* No. 7. Washington.

Lashley, K. S. 1951. The problem of serial order in behavior. In: Jeffress, 1951; also, in Beach *et al.*, eds., 1960.

————. 1952. Functional interpretations of anatomic patterns. *Proc. Ass. Res. Nerv. Ment. Diseases* **30**:529–547.

Lende, R. A. 1963. Cerebral cortex: a sensorimotor amalgam in the Marsupialia. *Science* **141**:730–732.

Lenneberg, E. H. ed. 1964. "New Directions in the Study of Language." M.I.T. Press, Cambridge, Mass.

———. 1967. "Biological Foundations of Language." Wiley, New York.

Lettvin, J. Y., H. R. Maturana, W. S. McCulloch, and W. H. Pitts. 1959. What the frog's eye tells the frog's brain. *Proc. IRE* November, 1940–1951.

Lorenz, K. 1952. "King Solomon's Ring." Methuen, London.

Luria, A. R. 1962. "Vysshie korkovyye funktsii chelovyeka." Izd. Moskov, Univ., Moscow.

———. 1963. "Mozg chelovyeka i psikhicheskie protsesy." Akad, Pedagog, Nauk, RSFSR, Moscow.

———. 1966a. "Higher Cortical Functions in Man." Basic Books, New York (Translation of Luria, 1962).

———. 1966b. "Human Brain and Psychological Processes." Basic Books, New York (Translation of Luria, 1963).

———, and F. Ja. Yudovich. 1959. "Speech and the Development of Mental Processes in the Child." Humanities, New York.

McCulloch, W. S. 1957. The stability of biological systems. In: "Homeostatic Mechanisms." Brookhaven Symposia in Biology No. 10.

———. 1960. The reliability of biological systems. pp. 264–281. In: Yovits and Cameron.

———, and J. Pfeiffer. 1949. Of digital computers called brains. *Sci. Monthly* **69**: 368–376.

———, and W. Pitts. 1943. A logical calculus of the ideas immanent in nervous activity. *Bull. Math. Biophy.* **5**:115–123.

Mackay, D. M. 1965. A mind's-eye view of the brain. pp. 321–322. In: Wiener and Schade, eds.

MacLean, D. 1949. Psychosomatic disease and the "visceral brain." *Psychosom. Med.* **11**:338–353.

———. 1954. The limbic system and its hippocampal formation. *Neurosurgery* **11**: 29–44.

———. 1955. Studies on limbic system ("visceral brain") and their bearing on psychosomatic problems. In: Wittkower and Cleghorn, eds.

———. 1958. Contrasting functions of limbic and neocortical systems of the brain and their relevance to psychophysiological aspects of medicine. *Amer. J. Med.* **25**: 611–626.

———. 1959. The limbic system with respect to two basic life principles. "The Central Nervous System and Behavior, 2nd Conf." Josiah Macy, Jr. Fdn., New York.

Maron. 1965. Cybernetics, information processing, thinking. In: Wiener and Schade, eds.

Miller, G. A., E. Pribram, and K. H. Galanter. 1960. "Plans and the Structure of Behavior." Holt, Rinehart and Winston, New York.

Moore, J. A. ed. 1965. Ideas in Modern Biology." Doubleday, Garden City, New York.

Morris, D. 1962. "The Biology of Art." Knopf, New York.

Mountcastle, V. B. ed. 1962. "Interhemispheric Relations in Cerebral Dominance." Johns Hopkins Press, Baltimore.

Muses, C. A. ed. 1962. Aspects of the theory of artificial intelligence. *Proc. 1st Internat. Symp. Biosimulation,* Locarno, 1960.

Ombredane, A. 1951. "L'aphasie et l'élaboration de la pensée explicite." Presses Universitaires de France, Paris.

Papez, W. 1937. A proposed mechanism of emotion. *Arch. Neurol. Psychiat.* **38**: 725–743.

Pask, G. A. 1965. The cybernetics of evolutionary processes and of self-organizing systems. Ass. Internat. de cybernétique. Namur, Belgium.

————. 1966. A cybernetic model for some types of learning and mentation. (Mimeographed typescript.) To be published in the Proceedings of the Bionics Symposium, Dayton, Ohio, 1966.

Penfield, W. 1952. Memory mechanisms. *A M A Arch. Neurol. Psychiat.* **67:**178–198.

————, and H. Jasper. 1954. "Epilepsy and the Functional Anatomy of the Human Brain." Little, Brown, Boston.

————, and T. Rasmussen. 1950. "The Cerebral Cortex of Man." Macmillan, New York.

————, and L. Roberts. 1959. "Speech and Brain Mechanisms." Princeton University Press, Princeton.

Pitts, W., and W. S. McCulloch. 1947. How we know universals. *Bull. Math. Biophy.* **9:**127–147.

Platt, J. R. 1956. Amplification aspects of biological response and mental activity. *Amer. Scientist* **44:**180–197.

Pribram, K. H. 1958a. Comparative neurology and the evolution of behavior. In: Roe and Simpson, eds.

————. 1958b. Neocortical function in behavior. pp. 151–172. In: Harlow and Woolsey eds.

————. 1962. See "Discussion," in Mountcastle, ed.

Prosser, C. L. 1965. Levels of biological organization and their physiological significance. p. 357–390. In: Moore, ed.

Quastler, H. ed. 1953. "Information Theory in Biology." University of Illinois Press, Urbana.

————. 1958a. A primer of information theory. pp. 3–49. In: Yockey et al., eds.

————. 1958b. The domain of information theory in biology. pp. 187–196. In: Yockey et al., eds.

————. 1958c. The status of information theory in biology. pp. 399–402. In: Yockey et al., eds.

————. 1964. "The Emergence of Biological Organization." Yale University Press, New Haven.

Rashevsky, N. 1960. "Mathematical Biophysics: Physico-mathematical Foundations of Biology." Dover Publications, Inc., New York.

Riese, W. 1950. "Principles of Neurology. Nervous and Mental Disease Monographs." Williams & Wilkins, Baltimore.

Roberts, L. 1956. Handedness and cerebral dominance. *Trans. Amer. Neurol. Soc.* **76:**43–50.

Roe, A., and G. G. Simpson. eds. 1958. "Behavior and Evolution." Yale University Press, New Haven.

Rosenblueth, A., N. Wiener, and J. Bigelow. 1943. Behavior, purpose, and teleology. *Philos. Sci.* **10:**18–24.

Schaffner, B. ed. 1955. "Group Processes. Transactions of the First Conference." Josiah Macy, Jr. Fdn., New York.

Schiller, C. H. ed. 1957. "Instinctive Behavior." International Universities, New York.

Scholl, D. 1947. (Review of Count, 1947.) *Nature* **159:**269.

Schroedinger, E. 1956 (1944). "What Is Life? and other Scientifiic Essays. Doubleday, Garden City, N. Y.

Schuell, H., J. J. Jenkins, and E. Jiménez-Pabón. 1964. "Aphasia in Adults." Hoeber, New York.

Sebeok, T. A. 1962. Coding in the evolution of signaling behavior. *Behavioral Sci.* **7:**430–442.

————. 1965. Animal communications. *Science* **147:**1006–1014.

————. 1967. Art.: "Animal communication." In: Internat. Encycl. Social Scis.

————. ed. 1968. "Approaches to Animal Communication." The Hague. In press.

Senden, M. von. 1960. "Space and Sight." Free Press, New York. (The English translation by Peter Heath, of Raum- und Gestaltauffassung bei Operierten Blindgeborenen, 1932).

Shannon, C. E., and W. Weaver. 1959. "The Mathematical Theory of Communication."

University of Illinois Press, Urbana. Also, *Bell System Tech. J.* 1948, **27**:379–423, 623–656.

Shariff, G. A. 1953. Cell counts in the primate cerebral cortex. *J. Compar. Neurol.* **98**:181 ff.

Spuhler, J. N. ed. 1959. "The Evolution of Man's Capacity for Culture." Wayne, Detroit.

Thorpe, W. W., and O. L. Zangwill. eds. 1961. "Current Problems in Animal Behavior." Cambridge University Press, Cambridge.

Uexküll, J. von. 1921. "Umwelt und Innenwelt der Tiere." Berlin.

———. 1928. "Theoretische Biologie." Springer, Berlin.

———. 1934. "Streifzüge durch die Umwelten von Tieren und Menschen." Springer, Berlin.

Vowles, O. M. 1961. Neural mechanisms in insect behavior, pp. 5–25. In: Thorpe and Zangwill, eds.

Weaver, W. 1949. Some recent contributions to the mathematical theory of communication. In: Shannon and Weaver, 1949.

Wells, O. D. 1963. Irrelevance of a "nervous system." In: Wiener and Schade, eds.

Wiener, N. 1948a. "Cybernetics." 1st ed.

———. 1948b. Time, communication, and the nervous system. In: Frank, *et al.*

———. 1954. "The Human Use of Human Beings." 2nd ed. Doubleday, Garden City, New York.

———, and J. P. Schade. eds. 1963. "Nerve, Brain, and Memory Models. Progress in Brain Research." vol. 2. Elsevier, Amsterdam.

Wittkower, E. D., and R. A. Cleghorn. eds. 1955. "Recent Developments in Psychosomatic Medicine." Lippincott, Philadelphia.

Yakovlev, P. I. 1958. "First Conference on the Central Nervous System and Behavior." Josiah Macy, Jr. Foundation, New York (Remarks, pp. 401–407).

Yockey, H. P., R. L. Platzman, and H. Quastler. eds. 1958. "Symposium on Information Theory in Biology." Pergamon, New York.

Yovits, M. C., and S. Cameron. eds. 1960. "Self-Organizing Systems." Pergamon Press, Oxford.

Zangwill, O. L. 1960. "Cerebral Dominance and its Relation to Psychological Function." Edinburgh.

ACKNOWLEDGMENTS

Permission to quote from authors and works is gratefully acknowledged herewith, as follows:

To The University of Chicago Press: A. L. Kroeber, *Introduction to:* "Anthropology Today" (1953).

To Dr. Harley D. Frank, executor for the estate of L. K. Frank, and The New York Academy of Sciences: L. K. Frank, in Teleological Mechanisms (*Annals,* vol. L, art. 4, 1948).

To John Wiley & Sons, Inc.: W. R. Ashby: "Introduction to Cybernetics" (1963).

To The University of Chicago Press: W. C. Halstead: "Brain and Intelligence" (1947).

To The University of Illinois Press: C. E. Shannon and W. Weaver: "The Mathematical Theory of Communication" (1948).

To Basic Books, Inc.: A. R. Luria: "Higher Cortical Functions in Man" (1966).

To Dover Publications, Inc.: N. Rashevsky: "Mathematical Biophysics" (1960).

To The Johns Hopkins Press: the remarks by K. H. Pribram, in V. B. Mountcastle, editor: "Interhemispheric Relations and Cerebral Dominance" (1962).

To Professor C. Ladd Prosser, and The National Academy of Science and Doubleday & Company, Inc. (The Natural History Press.): C. L. Prosser, in J. A. Moore, editor: "Ideas in Modern Biology" (1965).

To Dr. George H. Bishop, and Pergamon Press, Inc.: G. H. Bishop, in: M. C. Yovits and S. Cameron, editors: "Self-Organizing Systems." (1960).

6 Myth As World View[1]

A Biosocial Synthesis*

About a million years ago (it is the dimension of the time, not its precise point, that is relevant) some members of the primate order reached a level of brain organization, of corresponding psychic complexity, where the *representation of reality* not only could occur, but apparently was by nature of the case inevitable.

The meaning of "representation" actually will occupy all of this

*From: "Culture in History." Essays presented to Paul Radin. Stanley Diamond, ed. Columbia University Press, New York, 1960.

[1]"World view" is an attempt to translate the German *Weltanschauung*. Although I had been using this term before "discovering" Dilthey, I think I mean the same thing essentially as he does. It is described thus by H. A. Hodges ("Wilhelm Dilthey: an Interpretation," p. 160): "Outlook. *Weltanschauung*. There is no adequate English equivalent, and I have often used the German word. In Dilthey it means a complex of ideas and sentiments comprising (a) beliefs and convictions about the nature of life and the world, (b) emotional habits and tendencies based on these, and (c) a system of purposes, preferences, and principles governing action and giving life unity and meaning. The Weltanschauung of a person or a society includes that person's or society's answer to the fundamental questions of destiny which Dilthey calls the *riddle of life*."

Although I certainly have no intention of divorcing the *Weltanschauung* of the individual from that of the society which provides him the matrix for his own, and concur that at any time a culture is embodied in its carriers, I must confine the efforts of the present essay to *Weltanschauung* in society or societies.

essay. It is a process of symbolization, of symbolopoea. Symbol has been declared the very "roots" of myth,[2] and it has also been denied to myth altogether.[3]

The contradiction lies less in the authors' conceptions of myth than in their definitions of symbol. We shall adopt Professor Bevan's use of the word, who in turn begins with Professor Whitehead:[4] " 'The human mind' [says Whitehead] 'is functioning symbolically when some components of its experience elicit consciousness, beliefs, emotions, and usages, respecting other components of its experience'. . . . A symbol certainly, I think, means something presented to the sense or the imagination—usually to the sense—which stands for something else. Symbolism in that way runs through the whole of life."

For the purpose of this study, the statement gives us adequate definition of symbol; for we are concerned with the symbolic process as a creative social force, rather than with a philosophy of symbolism or a metaphysic; granted nonetheless that it is hardly possible to treat the one without reference to the other.

A science of mythology must pose the following questions:

1. In the evolution of man, when and under what circumstances did the capacity to symbolize come into being?

2. What symbolopoetic ingredients produced whatever we define as "myth"? Or, what are the sources of "myth"?

3. What shall we settle upon as properly includible under "myth"?

4. What place has mythopoea had in the building of cultural configuration?

5. As a cultural configuration is transformed (through elaboration, transmutation, dissolution), what happens to its myths?

The array of questions is enough to show why as yet there exists no science of mythology, but only discrete studies of myth materials

---

The anthropologist who in his definition of myth comes closest to Dilthey's conception of *Weltanschauung* is, I think, B. Malinowski. See his "Myth in Primitive Psychology." This places me in substantial agreement with Malinowski—as far as he goes; I do not accept as narrow a definition of symbol as he seems to hold—as will appear in the main text; and I am at pains to demonstrate that to assume myth and ritual as separate entities before adducing their similarities and relationships is an inverted procedure. Malinowski, moreover, confines his exposition to the situation of primitive man, although he does indicate that the same processes are at work in high civilizations. In this I agree; but in a proper treatment of *Weltanschauung* we cannot afford to neglect the high civilizations, and they shall not be neglected in this essay.

[2]Susanne Langer. 1942. "Philosophy in a New Key." (Harvard University Press, Cambridge).

[3]Bronislaw Malinowski. 1926. "Myth in Primitive Psychology." p. 19. (W. W. Norton, New York).

[4]Edwyn Bevan. 1957. "Symbolism and Belief." p. 11. (The Beacon Press, Boston).

by literary essayists, historians, psychologists, folklorists (taken in the broadest sense). Equally well the questions suggest the difficulty of bringing about an organized and comprehensive discipline of mythology—ranging as it must, at one end of its spectrum, over the operations of a peculiarly powerful mammalian brain, and at the other reaching the artist's appreciation and insight. But no less does the very scope and magnitude of such a proposed discipline urge its importance for a holistic appraisal of man. The present study (within the strictures of the circumstances that have elicited it) must remain but suggestive; it cannot even cover all of the aspects.

II

The capacity to symbolize is known certainly only at the human level of cerebral development. Possibly, however, it exists rudimentarily at the lesser levels of ape and even of other mammals. It is wholesome to keep this in mind; for it saves us from assuming too glibly that the capacity is some kind of unaccountable and mystical *tertium quid* which man completely refuses to share with his humbler fellow-creatures. Nevertheless, it is certain that in no society but man's is symbolopoea all-pervasive, all-important, a *sine qua non* for his very being.

A little farther along, we shall examine (though all too briefly) the organic seat of some of the activities that play into the symbolopoetic edifice. Suffice it here that the endocranial casts of the earliest and lowliest Hominidae permit us the respectable guess that the capacity to symbolize, to mythologize, to speak genuine language belonged already to those early levels of humanization and that they had had simultaneous and common origin and development. If so, then mythopoea is coeval with humanity and indeed an aspect of human morphology.

The problem of mythopea has yet another naturalistic side. How an organism relates with its environment is the subject of ecology. But an organism is no passive *tabula rasa* whereon environment writes as it pleases. The organism—as biopsychologists in particular know full well—meets it in a very real way and to a very significant extent on the organism's own terms. That is to say, we may consider the universe as a vast system of energies; it is the peculiar constitution of the organism itself that converts energies into "stimuli." There is nothing intrinsic about a light wave that makes of it the source of visual experience; it does not compel eyes into existence; the intrinsicality of vision resides in the organism. Nay more: Organisms (and this is truer the more elaborate their neurological constitution) can "elect" to "ignore" or "give attention to" certain energies and phenomena which they are quite capable of perceiving. The energies called "light" are externally given; their mode of treatment by the organism is an autogenous matter.

Thus out of the natural surroundings an animal organizes a world within which it acts. This is what lies behind von Uexküll's distinctions of *Umwelt* and *Merkwelt*. It follows that richness of *Merkwelt* is a function of neuropsychic elaborateness. It follows further that only a symbolopoetic neuropsyche can trace regularity in the courses of the stars because it is concerned about them somehow; only to such a psyche can it matter whether the universe is friendly or not. At this level of evolution, *psychoecology* becomes a very real and a tremendous province within the total life activities of a certain organism's *Umwelt* and *Merkwelt*.

The Neuropsychic Basis of Symbolization

The endocranial casts of fossil Hominidae, fragmentary evidence though they be, are precious and tantalizing hints of a psychic life that vanished beyond recovery a million years ago. And it has been but a very few years since the brains of extant men were still refusing to give up to the minds of other extant men their secret for producing the life of the mind which the psychologists were seeking to probe. Symbolopoea declined to discuss with visitors its neurophysiological housekeeping.

All is no longer utter darkness, though full daylight is not yet at hand. Psychoanalysis brought insight into the interplay of the conscious and the unconscious, the rational and the irrational, the symbolisms of dreaming—forcing even a reexamination of those terms. From a diametrically opposite approach has come comparative neurology, and especially neurosurgery. The two expeditions do not yet walk arm-in-arm; but at least they are within hailing distance.

We shall assume the findings of psychoanalysis and other "depth" psychologies, since they are so readily accessible.[5] A treatise on brain

---

[5]For "basic readings," as they pertain to symbolization and mythopoea, consult: S. Freud, "The Interpretation of Dreams" (available, among other sources, in A. A. Brill, ed., "The Basic Writings of Sigmund Freud," The Modern Library, New York E. Fromm, "The Forgotten Language" (available now in paperback, The Grove Press, New York); C. Jung, "Psyche and Symbol"; P. Mullahy, "Oedipus: Myth and Complex" (Hermitage Press, New York).

architecture is far beyond our scope, nor is it even desirable. On the other hand, the "hailing distance" is pertinent to the naturalistic approach with which this study has begun.[6]

The Brain as Psychic Purveyor The central nervous system of all vertebrates receives information from both the external and the internal environments—from the physical surroundings and from the bodily systems. It processes both kinds conjunctively; it organizes and distributes a response; some of this is assigned to remain within the organism (such as accelerated heartbeat, visceral tonus) and some of it to perform upon the external environment (such as running). The messages which thus activate the internal environment are mediated by the "autonomic" nervous system. The messages which begin and end where the animal effects contact with the external environment are mediated by the "voluntary" nervous system. These two systems are brought into effective conjunction (to speak simplistically) in the diencephalon—one of the major and basic portions of the brain.

All this is neuropsychic process. Under proper conditions a portion of it—but never more than a small portion—can be "conscious." Another, and far vaster portion, never can rise to the level of "consciousness." Between the two lie matters that are more or less amenable to being summoned into consciousness. All levels are involved simultaneously in the symbolic processes, as will be brought out further below. Mythopoea will remain largely a mystery until it has been accounted for on this multivalent basis.

The cerebral hemispheres are an adjunct to the brain which are possessed only by mammals. All vertebrates, on the other hand,

[6]There is no literature in this field that is not purely technical; hence the synopsis in the main text which otherwise would be overly extensive for an essay of the present scope. The following are essential titles:

L. S. Kubie. 1949. Instincts and homeostasis. *Psychosom. Med.* **X:**15–30; 1953a. The distortion of the symbolic process in neurosis and psychosis. *Psychoanal. Ass.* **I:**59–86; 1953b. Some implications for psychoanalysis of modern concepts of the organization of the brain. *Psychoanal. Quart.* **XXII:**21–68; 1953c. The central representation of the symbolic process in psychosomatic disorders. *Psychosom. Med.* **XV:**1–7; 1954. The fundamental nature of the distinction between normality and neurosis. *Psychoanal. Quart.* **XXIII:**167–204; 1956. Influence of symbolic processes on the role of instincts in human behavior. *Psychosom. Med.* **XVIII:**189–208.

P. D. MacLean. 1949. Psychosomatic disease and the "visceral brain." *Psychosom. Med.* **XI**(6):338–53.

H. W. Magoun. 1952. An ascending reticular activating system in the brain stem. *A. M. A. Arch. Neurol. Psychiat.* **67**(2):145–55.

W. Penfield. 1952. Memory mechanisms. *A. M. A. Arch. Neurol. Psychiat.* **67**(2):178–98.

F. Schiller. 1952. Consciousness reconsidered. *A. M. A. Arch. Neurol. Psychiat.* **67**(2):199–227.

possess those basic portions of brain which carry out the functions just outlined. This can mean only that, deep below the surface, below the obvious of the symbolopoetic processes, and therefore of the mythopoetic phenomena, there feed into these mechanisms neuro-logic energies that are more ancient even than the mammals, let alone the primates and the line of man. Whatever, then, be the function of the cerebral hemispheres, it must be in the nature of something added to an ancient base. It is necessary that we examine a little this more ancient base, which in the lower vertebrates is the total brain, but which at the mammalian level we may term, roughly, the "brain stem," or "archaic" brain. We shall pay special attention to its two anteriormost portions: the *telencephalon* and the *diencephalon*.

In all vertebrates, the telencephalon receives the olfactory stimuli; besides this, its "roof" contains tracts by which these and the stimuli received by other portions of the archaic brain become associated by interstimulation. In other words, stimuli become related, so that the animal may organize a response.

The olfactory region of the telencephalon is the rhinencephalon. But this region is not so simple as that would suggest. For the sense of smell is to be viewed as one element in a more complex mechan-ism; one which comprises taste and other oral sensations, and visceral sensations including sexual. The life mode of an animal is a reflex of its psychoneural structuring; in the lowest vertebrates this olfactory-oral-visceral complex means that the animals move through a world of smell-taste-visceral sensations.

From fish to man this primitive mechanism is never lost. In the course of evolution others arise, they interpose connections with it, they come to overshadow it—but they never erase it. MacLean there-fore has named it the "visceral brain." In psychosomatic health and disease it is fundamentally involved in the production of the elemental emotional tonus of a mental state. Both psychologist and mythologist will immediately appreciate MacLean's observations:[7]

In primitive forms the visceral brain provides the highest correlation center for ordering the affective behavior of the animal in such basic drives as obtaining and assimilating food, fleeing from or orally disposing of an enemy, reproducing, and so forth . . . it will serve to point up the problems discussed . . . if it is first indicated how the primitive brain perhaps ties in with behaviour that has been so often described as primitive, or infantile, in patients with psychosomatic illness. Psychiatrists have resorted to these adjectives probably because so much of the information obtained from these

[7]MacLean. 1949, p. 344.

patients has to do with material which in a Freudian sense is assigned to the oral and oral-anal level, or, as one might say all inclusively, the visceral level. In practically all the psychosomatic diseases such as hypertension, peptic ulcer, asthma, ulcerative colitis, that have been subject to fairly extensive psychiatric investigation, great emphasis has been placed on the "oral" needs, the "oral" dependencies, the "oral" drives, etc. of the patient. These oral factors have been related to rage, hostility, fear, insecurity, resentment, grief, and a variety of other emotional states. In certain circumstances, for example, eating food may be the symbolic representation of psychologic phenomena as diverse as 1) the hostile desire to eradicate an inimical person, 2) the need for love, 3) fear of some deprivation or punishment, 4) the grief of separation, etc. It will be useful to refer subsequently to the *excessive* oral manifestations of hostility and anger as "visceral aggression"; of insecurity and fear, as "visceral fear"; of a feeling of dependence, as "visceral need", etc. It is to be noted that many of the seemingly paradoxical and ridiculous implications of the term "oral" result from a situation, most clearly manifest in children or primitive peoples, where there is a failure or inability to discriminate between the internal and external perceptions that make up the affective qualities of experience. Visceral feelings are blended or fused with what the individual sees, hears, or otherwise senses, in such a way that the outside world is often experienced and dealt with as though it were incorporated. Thus the child looking at a leaf may say, "It tastes green." Or the primitive may attribute a feeling of anguish to a squirming animal in his stomach. . . .

The diencephalon, which lies immediately behind the telencephalon, is very complex. In one way or another it eventually receives the stimuli that enter the body via all portions of the nervous system other than the olfactive. Buried deeply within it is a major portion of the reticular system. In recent years this has come to be considered the very essential region where the animal's entire response is at last brought together and organized, and it is somehow very much involved in the production of the state of consciousness.[8] Penfield terms this great coordinating mechanism seated in the depth of the diencephalon, the "centrencephalic system." To and from the diencephalon run pathways connecting it with all other parts of the brain. It is reciprocally connected with the cerebral hemispheres, and its hypothalamic region contains the terminals of the autonomic system.[9]

[8]This statement, unfortunately, must remain purposely vague. Neither "consciousness" nor "integration of response" can be localized as simplistically as the remarks might imply. The point is that there now exists real evidence that these regions are essential to the particular functions mentioned. In the mammal with its superaddition of cerebral hemispheres to the "archaic" brain, integration must also be viewed as a harmonious reciprocation between the centrencephalic system of the diencephalon and the cortical areas with which it is connected.
[9]See Magoun, 1952; Penfield, 1952.

The cerebral hemispheres have evolved out of the association area in the roof of the telencephalon. From fishes to reptiles there is a series of these developments (archicortex, paleocortex, mesocortex); from reptiles to mammals this development is climaxed by the relatively enormous neocortex. Some, but far from all, of the information that enters the archaic brain is transmitted to these hemispheres. Here it is subjected to a final and elaborate scanning; it is filed in the archives of memory, chiefly in the temporal lobes. Recent and remote experiences are synthesized; reasoning is applied. The product is passed back to the diencephalon for final organization into a total response. Intermediate between the neocortex and the diencephalon lie the portions of cortex that have evolved from fish to reptile. The microstructure of all these several regions reflects the fact that both phylogenetically and ontogenetically they present successive levels of development; their contributions to the total psychic recipe, as far as these have been identified, seem consistent with this fact. In his behavior as well as in his physical structure, man never gets away from his vertebrate family history.

In the temporal region of their cerebral hemispheres, the primates are particularly well developed; the brain swells into a pair of large temporal lobes. Here are the archives of memory. Furthermore the rest of the neocortex on the one hand and the visceral brain on the other are intimately tied up with them—in fact, the terminations of the visceral brain are incorporated into the base of the lobes.

For decades, experimental neurologists have exposed the cerebral cortex of various animals; and, by applying electrodes to different regions, they have mapped out something of what each contributes to the sum total of behavior. In more recent years, neurosurgery—particularly in the hands of Dr. Wilder Penfield—has been uncovering the psychic meaning of the temporal lobe in man. That the temporal lobe must contribute heavily to symbolistic activity, he has demonstrated dramatically.[10] He remarks, eventually:

> One of my former patients once wrote to me asking whether at the time of operation I had been stimulating her subconscious mind when I produced in her a recollection of the past. I was amused for a moment. Then I was startled for these records become something like that. Perhaps her suggestion was not far from the truth. The great body of current experience seems to be forgotten but it is not lost, for the little strips of record that the electrode activates reproduce experiences that are clear and accurate in every detail. There is much evidence from other sources that we make sub-

[10]See especially his Studies of the cerebral cortex of man. In: "Brain Mechanisms and Consciousness; A Symposium." Charles C. Thomas, Springfield, Ill., 1954. See pp. 294f.

conscious use of them. Yes, the continuous strip of current exeperience is converted into a subsconscious record and one might well say that it forms the neuronal basis of what has been called the subconscious mind.[11]

It should be clear by now that any symbol is a composite, in which archaic and highly evolved ingredients have merged: the symbolizations of everyday life, the fantasies of the waking state, the dreams of sleep, the tales and rituals of primitives and of sophisticates are blendings of the "rational" and the "irrational."

[The] "ancient brain"—much of which lies in the depth of the temporal lobe, with its dreamy states of psychomotor epilepsy and its body-memories —has extensive relationships with both neopallium and hypothalamus. . . . [It is] a crossroads or association for both *internal* and *external* perceptions arising from the eye, the ear, the body wall, the apertures, the genitals, the viscera. These reach the temporal lobe via the diencephalon. Smell reaches it directly. Here, then, within the temporal lobe and its connections, is the crossroads where the "I" and the "non-I" poles of symbol meet. It is impossible to overestimate the importance of this fact that the temporal lobe complex constitutes the mechanism for integrating the past and the present, the phylogenetically and ontogentically old and new, and at the same time the external and internal environments of the central nervous system. It is through the temporal lobe and its connections that the "gut" component of memory enters our psychological processes and the symbol acquires its dual pole of reference. Thus in the temporal lobe and its deeper primitive connections is the mechanism for the coordination and integration of all of the data which link us to the world of experience, both extero- and interoceptive. It is by means of this temporal lobe complex operating through a bipolar symbolic system that we are able both to project and introject. It makes of the temporal lobe and its intricate bilateral and autonomic connections, which MacLean has called the "visceral brain," the central nervous organ which can mediate the translation into somatic disturbances of those tensions which are generated on the level of psychological experience. It might even be called the psychosomatic organ.[12]

The meaning of symbol from the standpoint of a neuropsychology may now be summarized in Kubie's words:[13]

(a) There is the symbolic function by means of which in thought and in speech we represent abstractions from experience. Here the term "symbolic function" is coextensive with all higher psychological functions, and especially with concept formation.

(b) There is the symbolic function with which we are all familiar in figures of speech, metaphors, slang, poetry, obscenities, puns, jokes, and

[11]*Ibid.,* p. 303.
[12]Kubie, 1953b, p. 31.
[13]Kubie, 1953a, pp. 67ff. Kubie also reproduces this passage in 1953b, pp. 39ff.

so forth. Here the concept behind the symbol is translated into some other mode of expression; but the relation between the original concept and the symbol remains relatively transparent, except when it is obfuscated in varying degrees for "artistic" purposes, as in the obscure realms of modern art and modern verse. This use of the symbolizing capacity of the human psychic apparatus characterizes that type of function which Freud called *preconscious* or the *descriptive subsconscious*. It reaches its most systematic development of course in the intuitive processes of the creative artist and scientist.

(c) Finally, there is the more limited psychoanalytic use of the term "symbolic function" where the symbol is a manifest representation of an unconscious latent idea. Here the link between the symbol and what it represents has become inaccessible to conscious self-inspection.

For *symbol,* in the psychoanalytic sense, we might reserve some special term; but since all three are aspects of the symbolizing capacity which is the unique hallmark of Man, and since the three merge and overlap one with another, not to have one generic name for them would obscure the essential continuity of all "symbolic functions" from one end of the spectrum to the other . . . it is important to recognize the continuity of these three kinds of symbolic function: since it is because of the continuity that every symbol is a multivalent tool. That is to say that simultaneously on conscious, preconscious, and/or unconscious levels every direct or indirect representation of any conceptual process will in all circumstances, if in varying proportions, be literal, allegorical, and also "symbolic" in the dreamlike or psychoanalytic sense. Consequently, in actual daily use symbols are simultaneously charged with meaning in all three ways and on all three levels. This makes of every symbol a chord with a potentiality of at least nine simultaneous overtones.

This continuity will be clear if we consider the various ways in which the symbol snake can be used. First it can represent a real snake, or the species Snake as a whole. Here it does not matter whether the spoken word or the written word or drawing or model of a snake is used as the symbol. Secondly, the symbol snake can be the snake of the Garden of Eden, or the traditional snake-in-the-grass of melodrama. Such an allegorical reference to external evil and to conscious conflicts over instinctual problems will be clear to everyone. Finally, however, there is the use of the same symbol as the manifest representative of some unconscious latent idea, of which "penis" would be a typical clinical example, plus all the urges and conflict-laden struggles which center around this latent idea. There can be no hard and fast lines between these three major types of symbolic usage; and whenever we use the symbol snake at all, there will be a simultaneous excitation of all three levels of meaning in varying proportions. In other words, every moment of thought and feeling involves simultaneously the activation of a literal, an allegorical, and a dreamlike meaning of the symbolic representative of all of the percepts which are relevant to that amount of psychic activity.

A science of mythology is not yet equipped to deal with the myth systems of the world to the very penetrating degree that this quotation suggests; regretfully, we are forced to leave the problem thus suspended. We can at least gather up the signposts of a biological approach to mythopoea thus:

1. Symbols are multivalent in any given instance.

2. The symbolic process is a very complex neuropsychic evolute; it is both symptom and reflex of an edifice that has been compounded both phylogenetically and ontogenetically of primitive materials that represent a succession of elaborations.

3. We may reasonably suppose that emergence of the symbolizing function is what has brought culture out of no-culture.

4. By corollary, technology and social regulation are presumably coeval with it, and their development is bound up with it.

5. We may not simply equate symbol with metaphor, with *pars pro toto,* or with any other substitutive procedure; although these complicated procedures can and do occur in symbolopoea. We must first see the symbol as a reifying integral, first as a means for contacting reality, and not as a device designed to shut out reality. It is extroversion quite as much as it is introversion, if not more so. Like the proverbial furskin of stone age man, it is intended first of all to make possible a coping with a demanding environment, one which could not otherwise be coped with; secondarily, it can of course be converted into an escape mechanism. It depends not upon the garment but upon the wearer.

6. The focus must be upon the neuropsychic root of the symbolic process, and away from any classification based upon kinds of symbols or upon the sociocultural purposes they may serve.

7. Consequently it is the oneness of folktale, ritual, myth-tale, as products of a common symbol-making matrix, that must be grasped first; whereupon these several formal categories are seen as secondary, and even artificial.

8. Mythopoea is an activity of psychoecology.

9. World view begins in psychoecology.

Toward a Definition of Myth

Prolegomena—Myth and Science: Event to Process A major contribution to our present-day perspective on man has come from cultural anthropology:the concept of culture itself.[14]

[14]Paradoxically, even among anthropologists there is no universal agreement on its definition. The question is reviewed magnificently by A. L. Kroeber and C. Kluckhohn. 1952. Culture: a critical review of concepts and definitions. *Papers of the Peabody Museum in American Archeology and Ethnology,* **XLVII:**1.

Cultural evolution may be read in terms of its success in finding regularities or dependabilities in the world it deals with. These regularities or dependabilities are the ground fabric of both personality development and cultural configurations. Recognition of this fact, whether conscious or not, has generated in the last quarter-century or so the discipline of Personality-and-Culture—the flourishing hybrid of psychology and cultural anthropology. A little thought will show that personality and culture actually are inseparable; world views of a person and of his culture reciprocate. Nonetheless, the hybrid discipline has not yet come to exploit the resources of the data of mythology; and such exploitation would be a department of mythology as a science.

However, the mythology of the person must in this essay be set aside. We shall deal only with that abstraction, culture. And we return to the question of dependabilities as they are envisioned by a culture.

To most, if not all, primitive cultures the universe is somehow numenal; it has been so likewise to many cultures that were not primitive. Now, in a given culture, not only do its carriers display a certain basic personality structure,[15] but there is likely to be some kind of personality ideal that gives direction to as well as being a product of the value system and the goal structuring of that culture. The numina, when they become personified or personalized, are likely to express both of these patterns of personality. Some such numinous personalities are no better nor worse than the individuals that make up the society; others are projections of what is most to be admired and desired in personality; yet others may be the ideal-in-reverse. More-than-human powers may attach to any of these categories; other-than-human though not necessarily superhuman powers may characterize still others. It will be obvious that personality pattern and numenal powers form a two dimensional plotting; a warp-and-woof for the numenal scheme of a given culture and society. It has been argued that it is man's anxieties and frustrations that motivate the "discovery" of a dependable numenal universe: the womb of the gods is the brain-and-psyche of man. There is also widespread recognition that anxiety/frustration alone is too slender a basis for erecting an explanation for a numenal projection upon the universe; however, we can afford to pass up this discussion. At any rate, we are at a juncture where theology, psychology, anthropology triangulate; and it is enough for us that, by conceiving spots of the universe as dependable, the mythopoets went on to invest it finally with the regu-

[15]For the meaning of this technical term, see A. Kardiner. 1945. The Psychological Frontiers of Society." Columbia University Press, New York.

larities that made science possible. It is likewise true, and also pertinent here, that a numenal universe was both conceptual reflex and matrix of the "sacred" society in which the myth-makers lived and which they also abetted. Science, on the other hand, is the product of "secular" society. But science never could have come into existence but for the antecedent recognition that regularity existed. Science invested this legacy when it began to examine the nature of regularity. Regularity is the common denominator that is abstracted from events.

What "happens" is event, never process. An event is unique, yet it has repetitive vectors. This is the basis of learning, of habit, of generalization; in its most elementary dimensions, it is apprehendable even by protozoans. A situation likewise has its vectors; for situations are the product of events. Situations impress one at first as a static matter, while events are dynamic. We have traveled far, however, in the last two centuries—we are today becoming incapable of conceiving static, changeless situation; only situations that change more or less rapidly. To primitives and to ancients, permanence of situation was fully assumable; it changed so slowly that to him who was in the midst of it came the illusion that it was static. Yet even though he conceived it thus, he found room within it to act repetitively himself, and to assume that others would do likewise. So even a world believed to be static can be a stage for repetitive event. It is not itself a regularity; but it harbors regularity.

In this matter ancient Mesopotamia and Egypt are an instructive study in similarity and contrast. The metaphysic of the Mesopotamian cosmos (if we may apply "metaphysic" to the ages "Before Philosophy") featured repetitive event: The world wore out every year and had to be reestablished in crisis. It was the duty of man to cooperate with the gods in this annual task, else the world would revert to a primeval unorganized state. With the Egyptians it was different. The metaphysic of their cosmos was eternal stability, established once and for all in the beginning of things. Within this closed system the gods and the life cycles of men traveled undisturbed. It seems that the Egyptian cosmos was a situation; the Mesopotamian was a series of repetitive events.

In either case there were regularities, yet they both were the regularities of event, however those ancients visualized them. Neither Egyptian nor Mesopotamian seems ever to have visualized actual process that utilizes events as illustrations of its working. This was finally done by the Greeks.

To see process behind a succession of events is to abstract, for as we have noticed, it is events, not processes, that "happen." Mythopoea behaves, in fact, in the opposite way, as can best be seen in ritual.

For ritual is a contrived event. Though every event is really unique and irrecoverable, together they can have similarity over a series that is a tolerable substitute for identity. Ritual event would have no meaning and no efficacy if its elements were never performed more than once. So ritual seeks to turn event itself into a regularity; that is, it seeks to capture and encase some cosmic regularity within its "event-ness."

The Greeks discovered process by swinging a high-powered lens upon the regularities of events to discover the details of their tissues. When events become illustrations of processes, it no longer matters if the events are specific acts of particular gods. Why the god performed the deed, whether he may be expected to do so again, or persuaded or dissuaded, becomes an irrelevant matter. Our focus becomes the concatenation that describes the course of what transpired, but only if the concatenation may be generalized and every specific event that illustrates it may be safely forgotten. And if we may count on the process we need not pause to inquire whether or not the universe is numinous; yes or no, the matter is irrelevant. And within a frame of reference where the numinous has no weight, there is nothing to be worshipped. This is what the authors of "The Intellectual Adventure of Ancient Man"[16] are referring to when they contrast the ancient view of the universe as a *Thou* and the modern attitude toward the universe as an *It*. The universe-as-It we may term a "secularization"; conversely, the universe-as-Thou belongs to a "sacred" mythology. Paradoxically, there can still be such a thing as a "secular" mythology. Meanwhile, to continue speaking the language of mythology, when the Greeks turned away from questions of the world as divine will to problems of the world as process, they became Prometheans who committed the Great Irreverence.

The term carries no invidious intent; it is used neutrally. It is true that Promethean mankind has paid dearly for the questions which the Greeks began to ask of the universe; yet I doubt if any steady-minded person would have the world again as though those questions had never been asked. So the steady-minded must join the Greeks in their Great Irreverent act.

For it were idle to regret having eaten of the Tree of Knowledge and having been driven forth upon stony ground. The Great Irreverence has brought what has been described as "the emancipation of thought from myth."[17]

True—yet not true enough. For again we are confronted with para-

---

[16]H. and H. A. Frankfort, J. A. Wilson, Th. Jacobsen, W. A. Irwin. 1946. University of Chicago Press, Chicago.
[17]Ibid.

dox. On the one hand the emancipation went even further than they indicate; on the other, had the emancipation proceeded to the limits of its logic, it is likely that it would have done away with the artist.

The further emancipation just mentioned is simply that our spectrum of reality has been lengthened at both its ends. Dr. Warren Weaver[18] points this out when he says that there are three "degrees" of problems that science has faced, or must face: (1) problems of *simplicity,* such as a pre-twentieth-century science was able to formulate successfully in terms of two simultaneous variables; (2) problems of *disorganized complexity,* in which the number of variables is enormous and undeterminable; whereupon the calculus of variations —statistics—takes over successfully; and (3) problems of *organized complexity,* in which occurs "a sizable number of factors which are interrelated into an organic whole." For the latter, says Weaver, adequate tools are still to be made.

We may note that prescientific man never conceived problems of the first two degrees. Such problems are purposeful abstractions, scientific formulations. Rarely, or perhaps never, in nature are there any actual two-variable situations. True, primitives often treat a situation *as if* it held but two variables: If the sun shines, the earth will bring forth. But they always have the common sense to allow for what in statistical parlance we might call "residuals." To the primitive the residuals are incalculable and unpredictable, and it is precisely in this area where he is likely to set up his ritual operations. As for problems of the scope and nature handled by statistics today—they are simply inconceivable outside a scientific matrix.

The world-as-problem with which nonscientific men cope belongs within Weaver's third "degree": that of "organized complexity." This range of reality lies between the other two; and to the scientist it would appear in such terms as these:

What makes an evening primrose open when it does? Why does salt water fail to satisfy thirst? Why can one particular genetic strain of microorganism synthesize within its minute body certain organic compounds that another strain of the same organism cannot manufacture? Why is one chemical substance a poison when another, whose molecules have just the same atoms but assembled into a mirror-image pattern, is completely harmless? Why does the amount of manganese in the diet affect the maternal instinct of an animal? What is the description of aging in biochemical terms? What meaning is to be assigned to the question: Is a virus a living organism? What is a gene, and how does the original genetic

[18]Science and complexity. *Amer. Scientist* **36**(4):536 ff.

constitution of a living organism express itself in the developed characteristics of the adult? Do complex protein molecules "know how" to redupli-
cate their pattern, and is this an essential clue to the problem of reproduction of living creatures? All these are certainly complex problems, but
they are not problems of disorganized complexity, to which statistical
methods hold the key. They are problems which involve dealing simultaneously with a *sizable number of factors which are interrelated into an
organic whole*. They are all, in the language here proposed, problems of
organized complexity.

On what does the price of wheat depend? This too is a problem of
organized complexity. A very substantial number of relevant variables is
involved here, and they are all interrelated in a complicated, but nevertheless
not in a helter-skelter fashion.

How can currency be wisely and effectively established? To what extent
is it safe to depend on the free interplay of such economic forces as supply
and demand? To what extent must systems of economic control be employed to prevent the wide swings from prosperity to depression . . . ?

How can one explain the behavior pattern of an organized group of
persons such as a labor union, or a group of manufacturers, or a racial
minority . . . ?

These problems—and a wide range of similar problems in the biological,
medical, psychological, economic, and political sciences—are just too complicated to yield to the old nineteenth-century techniques which were so
dramatically successful on two-, three-, or four-variable problems of simplicity. These new problems, moreover, cannot be handled with the statistical
techniques so effective in describing average behavior in problems of disorganized complexity.[19]

In all this catalogue there speaks the idiom of science. Yet the
dimension of reality is precisely that within which life has always been
lived. And this is the dimension which the nonscientific world view
has always met. Given but the requisite background of knowledge,
they are the kind of question any ancient Mesopotamian would have
asked.

It has ever been and seems destined ever to be the dimension
where the artist has created. The artist remains a mythopoet outside
the sphere of the Great Irreverence. For no matter what his beliefs,
disbeliefs, doubts, or the subjects he treats, his world still remains
numinous—in that, at the core of him he is an interpreter of man
to man.

Orientation In English, the word "mythology" has two different
meanings. Mythology is the discipline whose subject matter is myth;

[19]*Ibid.*, p. 539.

mythology is the corpus of myths held by an individual or a society. The meaning of both rests upon a definition of myth.[20]

For over two thousand years myths have been identified, interpreted, debated; and on only one point have scholars agreed: myths are a form of literature (in the broad sense of the word) about gods or demigods. The problem becomes that of explaining the gods and their deeds. At the same time, many students have noticed the substantive connections between myths and rituals.[21] But they had already committed themselves to the assumption that myth and ritual are nevertheless separate entities. Therefore, which is older than the other? One must have promoted the origin of the other; but which did which?

Discussions of this assumed problem relied for their data almost entirely on the documents of the Mediterranean and Levantine worlds. Then anthropology began to report cultures in which one or the other category was almost wholly absent; instances appeared where rituals received mythic reinforcement; others, where myths generated rituals.

Out of this welter of seeming contradictions came the realization at last that there can be no monolithic explanation for the origins of myth and ritual. The trouble had lain not simply in the nature and quality of the data on which the arguments had rested, but in the premises that backed the reasoning—even in the logic itself.

Since we should have no discipline of mythology today but for its pioneers, it would be ungracious to let them be judged by hindsight. Nevertheless, the venture has been dogged by semeiotic or phenomenological fallacy that cannot be overlooked. It will help clarify this fallacy, if we borrow by analogy from medicine and psychiatry.[22]

Scientific medicine never classifies diseases as headache, stomach ache, cough, rash, fever diseases. Nor would modern psychiatry classify as different illnesses the phobias and the compulsives, the manic and the depressive states, or distinguish as fundamental the compulsives that drive a man to hurt himself from those that drive him to hurt others. Equally misguided would it be to dichotomize

[20]A brief but excellent treatment of the history of mythology is that of Richard Chase, "The Quest for Myth." See also Ernst Cassirer, "The Myth of the State," Part I.

[21]See Clyde Kluckhohn. 1942. Myths and rituals: a general theory. *Harvard Theol. Rev.* **XXXV**(1):45–79 for an excellent review of this question. See also "Myth," by Ruth Benedict, in "Encyclopedia of the Social Sciences (New York, 1933).

[22]Kubie has criticized psychiatry precisely for the same fallacy, and this has suggested the analogy. *See particularly* 1953a, pp. 59ff., and the references cited there; "The fundamental nature of the distinction between normality and neurosis." This is a model of analytic and expressive clarity.

mental disorders deriving from biological dysfunctions and those deriving from injurious social experiences. "In between the causal chains and the consequences we recognize specific pathological processes within the body, which are set in motion by the causative chain, and which ultimately mediate the end results. It is this peculiar constellation of pathological processes with its own idiosyncrasies which is the 'disease entity.' "[23]

Since this essay is developing the point that the essence of mythology is the mythopoeic process, which is symbolic activity, which is psychoneurologic, perhaps we have a case of parallelism as much as a case of analogy to that of psychiatry—although nothing can be farther from our intention than any suggestion that mythopoea is a pathological phenomenon.

The point is that myth and ritual are not two basic and separate categories, somehow related secondarily. No more may we place one of the categories as ancestral to the other, or as antedating the other. That in one culture myth is extensively present while ritual is not, that in another the situation is the reverse is an interesting fact about the culture—but for establishing a principle about the evolution of myth and ritual it carries no weight. Nor is it a fundamental distinction that one tale is told for its entertainment value while another is taken seriously, or that one has no further consequences while the other leads to concerted social action. These notions lead to difficulties that will be taken up later.

With these strictures in mind, we pass to the problem of a practical scheme for analyzing the structure of myth, after the manner of the grammarians; that is, we shall seek a grammar and a semantic of mythology.

A "Grammar" of Mythology[24]   We shall include as the corpus of mythology all rituals, all narratives commonly accepted as myths,

---

[23]Kubie, 1953a, p. 62f.

[24]This attempt at a "grammar" is a purely empirical matter. It represents a system of categories which I first developed to aid my students in mythology to a workable architecture beneath a mass of inchoate data. It is hoped that the system will help rather than hinder a science of mythology, but to such a science it pretends to do no more than supply a "prolegomenon." Dr. Claude Lévi-Strauss has been developing what seems a most promising method of analyzing the structure of myth-tales. He starts by breaking down a tale into the elemental movements of its motifs. These he sorts and rearranges in a kind of matrix, and from this pattern he apparently is able to force the emergence of the theme treatment. Thus he claims that he comes upon the essential meaning of the tale. (*See* The structural study of myth, in "Myth: a Symposium," Thomas A. Sebeok, ed. ["Bibliographical and Special Series of the American Folklore Society, V."], Philadelphia, 1955.) In doing this, Dr. Lévi-Strauss

plus folk tales and any other literary pieces in which world view is treated as such (even if unconsciously); and by the same token, all other documents that likewise express myth material. Thus we include Sumerian cylinder-seals, vase paintings of the deeds of Heracles, statues of deities, emblazonments such as the Persian Sol Invictus, the Chinese Yang/Yin, the Buddhist Wheel. We must do this because no discourse on mythology can ignore them, or even fail to recognize them on occasion as of fundamental importance.

Within this corpus, mythopoea expresses itself by way of three idioms: *myth-tale* (the word "tale" may be used alone if the meaning is unambiguous), *rite* and/or *ritual*, and *monument*.

MYTH-TALE, RITUAL, MONUMENT. It might be called a sociological accident that myth and folk tale have traditionally been considered two separate categories of primitive or unsophisticated literature. The two genres were first set up as distinctively different; only after a long time was their essential and more basic oneness discovered. The reason for this was that the sophisticated classes of Europe knew the lore of the Greeks insofar as it was treated by Homer, Hesiod, and Plato, but they despised the lore of the European peasantry. Such, in general, was the situation until the nineteenth century, when the upsurge of nationalism brought an interest in folklore. Suddenly Europe saw in its peasantry the chthonic virility from which sprang the strength of its nations—a curious twist to primitivism and a perennial theme of certain mythologies. The lore of the common folk went into anthologies—tales, songs, music—and issued forth again in symphonies and tone poems, patriotic verse, romances, and insurrections.

Were we writing the history of Christianized Europe in terms of its mythology, here would belong a chapter on myth and folk tale and the stratification of social classes. It would develop in this way: When the pagan folk of Europe became Christianized, their ancient paganisms were shattered. Christianity is rather peculiar among the socio-cultural systems of the world in that it stresses belief in certain

---

has progressed beyond anything I have undertaken systematically. But his analysis is confined to myth-tales, and the tale seems to be coextensive with his definition of myth itself. We seem to be traveling different roads; and neither of us vitiates the work of the other.

The present "grammar" attempts to remain amenable to the humanistic approach while making way for a scientific approach. It is an article of the writer's faith that the very stature of cultural anthropology as a science requires it never to cease being a "humanity." With the possible exception of psychology, this makes it the only science of which this can be said. Of no part of cultural anthropology can this be truer than that which enters the land where dwells the psyche of man.

dogmas. Translated into the language of mythology, it identifies adherence to religion with intellectual assent to articles of *Weltan-schauung*.[25] The invading mythology therefore attempted to annihilate the indigenous mythology. The invader was kept intact by institutional backing, a thing which the indigenous mythology possessed but feebly. The invader had originated under urban cultural conditions; it succeeded best in the cities in extirpating the indigenous mythology, and best therefore where it could attack the indigenous views by counterposing positives. But the indigenous mythology of pagan Europe harked back even to Paleolithic times; it therefore possessed a chthonic side for which there was little if any counterpart in the cities. This material survived among the peasantry because the invading system had no positive counterpoise; only negatives—intellectual tabus, mere denials of validity, prohibitions to believe.

It was this truncated mythology that European scholars rediscovered in the nineteenth century. It did not appear to be a mythology at all. It had no cosmology of its own, no recognizable deities attached to the rituals (later research found they were still there), many tales with no particular point except entertainment. At the same time, scholars discovered the Indo-Europeans, linguistically as well as mythologically. The Eddas and the Vedic hymns, the fragments of Celtic and Slavic tale and monument were seen as relics of a common pagan past, of beliefs once held but, at least as far as Europe was concerned, long since repudiated. The repudiated or forgotten is myth; current extra- or anti-canonical beliefs held by the peasant class are folklore.

This rapid sketch is severe and simplistic, to be sure. Lest the truth it seeks to convey thereby be vitiated, we must add immediately that the Christian and the pagan mythologies had also blended, but again this process succeeded in the rural areas far better than in urban, as the folk festivals of Europe still testify so amply.[26]

Myth, folk tale, legend, saga, Märchen, and the like are convenient labels for genres of the "low tradition" of Occidental culture. We might say that the Occident possesses a "front yard" mythology within its "high" tradition, while its "low" tradition contains its "back yard" mythology.

[25]Ruth Benedict has expressed this point with beautiful succinctness. See her article, "Myth," in the *Encyclopedia of Social Sciences*.
[26]An example of what can come of such mutual acculturations has been done into a charming book by Dr. Sula Benét: "Song, Dance, and Customs of Peasant Poland" (Roy Publishers, New York, n. d. [ca. 1952]). Here is the community's seasonal round, replete as its life is with ritual dramatization at every juncture, and also the ritual in the biography of the individual as he too passes through the drama of his own life.

Most of the world, however, has not undergone a metamorphosis of its world views parallel to that of the Occident. This began to appear when the anthropologists returned from the field with the literatures of many primitive cultures. The deductive scheme that had been made to fit the literatures of European culture failed to work among these exotics. Folk or fairy tales do not represent a more primitive level of cultural evolution than myths; the entertainment value of the former as against the seriousness of the latter is not a fundamental distinction; wishful thinking is present in all.[27]

What, then, is a myth-tale? It is any narrative that expresses world view, no matter what the external, the literary form may be, or the motivation behind its telling. And we shall include hymn and poem insofar as they are informative. If once they were given credence by the ancestors, and are now told more lightly, then the problem becomes one of inquiring into the status and condition of a people's beliefs that makes this so, which is a subject more fruitful than the task of determining the most appropriate genre lable. It is the tones of the chord, not its overtones, that must be heard first.

Certainly, were we to push this definition to its rigidly logical conclusion, all literature would be myth. Presumably no one can tell a story without disclosing something of his own world view or that of his culture. This difficulty cannot be helped. But then, no category in the field of mythology is determinate. For a grammar of myth, it is not a serious problem. As a practical matter, we may agree to include all tales wherein world view can be explicitly demonstrated, plus other literary forms that have obvious mythologic direction.

There is yet another stricture that must be disposed of. Commonly, myth-tales are thought of as narratives involving gods or demigods and the supernatural world. This too runs into anomalies. Primitive men do not draw a line between a natural and a supernatural world— even when they recognize that their own hoeing of a field is matter-of-fact while the god contributes another ingredient to the crop. "Natural" and "supernatural" are terms from our own thought-idiom. They help us to grasp the factors in a total situation where primitives are involved; but they help us not at all if we wish to get inside the mind of primitive man. They are not free from our cultural egocentricity. Further, if we define myths as tales about gods and the like, we must conclude, logically, that myth dies when belief in gods and

[27]Fortunately it is no longer necessary to spend effort validating these assertions. They would be accepted by most anthropologists today, and, I believe, by most folklorists. The matter is adequately and effectively summarized by Stith Thompson, in Myths and folk tales, in "Myth: a Symposium," pp. 104–10.

a supernatural world dies. Why this is an unsatisfactory conclusion will be clear after we have treated the subject of themes; for the moment, suffice it that if a myth is a narrative about gods, then its touchstone is motif—that is, a concrete feature told about them. And this kind of thing necessarily dies if the god dies: The myth-tale dissolves. Yet what the narrative has been trying to say is thematic, often a profound observation about the tragedy of man; the motif proves to have been but the vehicle that carried the theme. Such a theme lives on to be handled by the most sophisticated of men, even if carried by other kinds of motif. So the gods disappear; yet the myth remains. This is what is likely to happen in a secularized society. Sophisticates are inveterately mythopoetic, but they come to use their own sets of idioms.[28] The reason why mythology is commonly coupled with religion is that most societies are sacred, they rest within a numinous universe. But there is such a thing as secular mythology.

For a grammar of mythology it is immaterial whether ritual preceded myth-tale or vice versa; whether one can occur without the other; whether they are coeval in origin; whether there is no general rule but all possibilities obtain.[29] The essence of the matter is that the one cannot be dealt with adequately without the other. If the basis for defining myth is psychological, then ritual and myth-tale are but two cardinal modes of expressing myth. Where both are present in a culture, both express the same world view, even if a ritual occurs with no tale attached to it, or the tales occur with no ritual. Both treat the same numinous universe; both see cause and effect in terms of event, not of process; for both a natural-supernatural dichotomy does not exist; the assumptions about the nature of man and of his position in the universe are identical. The only essential difference seems to be that the tale satisfies some intellectual demand, while ritual satisfies some action demand.

So when we encounter a culture which has much ritual but practically no myth-tale, or a rich thesaurus of myth-tale but little ritual, we do not ask: "Why does one culture possess so much mythology while the other lacks it?" or: "How did people elaborate so much ritual without ever developing a supporting mythology? Instead, we ask: "What is there about this culture that leads it to develop this idiom of mythopoea and not the other?" Whichever is present, we

[28]Not *categories* of idioms: these abide: tale, ritual, monument.
[29]For divergent views of this set of problems, *see* Lord Raglan, Myth and ritual; and Stanley Edgar Hyman, The ritual view of myth and the mythic, both in "Myth: A Symposium."

have some kind of index as to how the culture approaches its numinous universe. This is a cultural problem, and it is hardly different, essentially, from the question as to why the English have produced such magnificent literature, but (since Purcell) no great music to range beside Bach and Beethoven—yet Händel found in England the more congenial environment for his creativity. At all events there is nothing about ritual or myth-tale as such that compels the other into existence. Where the one does evoke the other, we have a problem of culture event, not one of mythopoeic principle.

We may treat *ritual* as the more generic term, *rite* as an element of ritual. Rites may compound into rituals; the simplest ritual contains but one rite. The one rite, however, can be repeated an indefinite number of times: the repetitiveness itself may then be a feature of the ritual.

Actually, a ritual obtains its efficacy from the fact that it is a repetition. Much of the force of a Roman Catholic Mass, of a Christmas ceremony, of Ramadan, of Yom Kippur, of an Australian corroborree lies in its time binding: It is because it has been done indefinitely back in the past, and also because it is destined still to be done in the future, that it is efficacious. And the rite of baptism or of circumcision which can occur but once in the lifetime of the individual is efficacious precisely because it has been and will be practiced regularly on all others of the group.

In what follows we had best include, anticipatorily, a mention of monument. When tale and ritual occur conjunctively, they reinforce each other, as with the Ojibwa or Menomini Midewiwin, the Christian Mass, the Jewish Passover. Monument—the symbolic paraphernalia of the ritual—reinforces both. The Midewiwin ritual is not commemorative of the myth, even though the ritual may have originated in the dream or vision of a shaman. The etiology, to be sure, is not idle: It does serve to bind the ritual into a cosmic scheme. The Christian Mass has certain external resemblances to the Midewiwin: There is an efficacy that emanates from a deity above, and which is transmitted down through the mediation of initiate individuals. The process started in one initial event, where the divine made junction with the human. To transmit the efficacy the event is symbolistically recalled or dramatized. The efficacy itself lodges in the monument, the migis shell, the Host. But behind these externalities there is a fundamental difference of world view. The Greek mysteries often postulated that, although man and god were different, somehow they still had proceeded from a common substance: The mystery brings man back to partake of the divine; a mystic union occurs. There seems to be no evidence of such an idea in the Midewiwin. The Passover is frankly commemorative. There is not an efficacy that is being mystically transmitted from a sacred event. The event certainly does serve to rationalize the ritual; but the ritual gains its points from its being a continuing act of obedience to a God whose nature is to demand obedience. In the Christian Mass, on the other hand, the words, "Do this in rememberance of me," do not stress the command nature of their speaker; there is, rather, more of a prescriptive plea. A continuing efficacy will flow forth if you will but do this, but to respond must be your choice.

In all cases, however, if a myth-tale attaches to the ritual in such a way as to give it rationale, it is believed that the event is the historic initiator while the ritual is a continuator of a regularity.

Both myth-telling and ritual use the "props" of monument, that is, paraphernalia, either as tools of emphasis or because the monument itself contains an efficacy that is indispensable to the performance. The pectoral or altar crucifix captures the same event which is told in a tale and is being reenacted every time a Mass is said, and which also appears, in a special way, but once a year, on Good Friday.

The basic technique of myth-telling is recitation. But it may employ gestures; it may also display some article around which the tale is woven. Such things enhance the dramatic emphasis. They are monuments, as well as a part of language. The basic technique of ritual is gesture. But ritual also makes use of recitation; when it does, it is converting recitation into a form of gesture. Tale and rite, then, may both use the same paraphernalia; the difference lies in the way they do it. To borrow an analogy from physics—myth-tale holds symbol energy as a potential, while ritual is symbol energy kinetically expressed. Tale is mythology verbalized; ritual is mythology acted.

We need not pause to discuss such matters as magic versus religion, or the apotropaic, supplicative, coercive, sympathetic, or other class of rituals. Such features belong to the study of primitive religions. They are indeed pertinent to discussions of the various cultural settings which elicit one or another ritual motivation, but they are not fundamental categories; to use them as though they were, and to erect a classification of rituals upon them, is to commit the semeiotic fallacy.

But there is reason for scaling rites and ritual in terms of the levels of psychological evolution which they reflect. For the purposes of this essay, it is necessary only to apply the term "psychoecology" to Radin's succinct way of stating the matter.[30]

[30]1957. "Primitive Religion" Dover Publications, New York, pp. 7ff.

Expressed in strictly psychological terms the original postulation of the supernatural was thus simply one aspect of the learning process, one stage of man's attempt to adjust the perceiving ego to things outside himself, that is, to the external world. This attempt did not begin with man. It is clearly rooted in his animal nature and has, from the very beginning, been expressed in three generalized formulae. According to the first one, the ego and the objective world interact coercively; according to the second, man coerces the objective world, and, according to the third, the objective world coerces man. With the coming of man there appeared for the first time a differential evaluation of the ego and the external world. That evaluation which ascribed the coercive power to man alone or to the coercive inter-action of the ego and the object found its characteristic expression in magic and compulsive rites and observances; that which ascribed this coercive power to the object found its characteristic expression in the religious activity.

We can arrange this hypothetic evolution, from magic to religion, in four stages:

1. The completely coercive and unmediated. Here the relation between the ego and the objective world is almost in the nature of a tropism.

2. The incompletely coercive and unmediated. Here a measure of volition is imputed to the object.

3. The reciprocally coercive. Here volition is imputed to both the ego and the object.

4. The non-coercive. Here the ego is regarded as being in conscious subjection to the object.

In other words, we are dealing here with a progressive disentanglement of the ego from an infantile subjectivism; the freeing of man, as Freud has correctly observed, from the compulsive power of thought. But this freeing of man from his compulsive irrational anchorage did not take place in that intellectual vacuum with which psychologists so frequently operate, but in a material world where man was engaged in a strenuous struggle for existence.[31]

THE TECHNICAL ELEMENTS OF RITUAL.   Gesture, we have noted, is a basic technique of ritual. Gesture may be movement; it also may be

---

[31]As long as we do not take "coercive" and "stages" in too rigid senses, this seems to me a most valid statement of the case. Dr. Radin himself is very free from such rigidity of thinking; hence the following strictures are *caveats* directed anywhere but at him. (1) The "stages" must be considered as but scale-markings along a continum. (2) "Coercion" is but our own interpretive figure of speech; it does not necessarily portray the intent of the primitive who began exercising it. The raw act of seizing any living thing, whether plant or animal for the purpose of eating it is not a coercion on the human level any more than on that of any carnivorous or frugivorous animal. The making of the first knife out of a piece of flint was not a coercion of the material. Before we can have magic rite, just as before we can have a material technology, we have just technique. In other words, even back of Radin's stage one, there is a still more primitive and undifferentiated one. He seems to be suggesting it in his remark about "almost . . . a tropism."

pose. Dance is its most intricately developed form; it exploits both kinds of gesture. All or any part of the body may be enlisted; facial expression, of course, is included.

Dance emphasizes and elaborates upon the time dimension— tempo and rhythm. It is phylogenetically an ancient talent, for we can hardly withhold from the rhythmic troopings of chimpanzees the label of dance. But among these artless cousins of ours there is no clear evidence of symbolization. And to be sure the dancing of *Homo ludens* can be spontaneous and nonrepresentational—perhaps just because he has had dancing ancestors among the alloprimates. Equally obvious is it that he can freight his dancing very thoroughly with symbolic content.

Symbolized gesture is a form of iconography. It can be diaphoric,[32] or it can be metaphoric. But its dependence upon the time dimension associates it with music and recitative, and sets it off from sculpture and painting, which may turn even movement into pose (and use pose itself thereby to express and hold that about movement which otherwise would be but momentary and lost). On the other hand, symbolized gesture dissociates itself from music and associates itself with sculpture and painting in that it treats pose and movement visually and not acoustically (when feet are stamped we have rudimentary music). When gesture and its evolute, dance, exploit their resources to the limit, they develop subtle balances between motion and pose: Time is presented both as flow and as duration.

Song and instrumentation are congenial to both ritual and tale; that is, song and instrumentation are morphemes of ritual; but to tale they are not so intrinsic as they may become to ritual. When song and instrumentation are used with or in a tale, they raise its dramatic impact. Epics are chanted and accompanied. The tale may be broken off with interjected refrains. But when these things happen, we are witnessing a far more complex phenomenon than a mere and bare narration: recitation has gone over into a form of ritual (*sive* drama). A hymn of praise to a deity, a national anthem like "The Star-Spangled Banner," when performed, are really complex pieces of mythology whose analysis would take us far beyond the scope of the present study.

MONUMENT.[33] A monument is a concrete, that is, seizable, object or device which may serve to focus or orient the personality of the

[32]See Philip Wheelwright, The Semantic approach to myth, p. 97, in "Myth: A Symposium."
[33]This is the least fortunate of the three terms for idioms, but it must do *faute de mieux.*

believer. It may be portable; it may be large and immovable; it may be actually used in a ritual, or it may simply stand to recall tale or ritual. Most monuments are visual and even material; many are acoustical; probably no bodily sense is exempt from being enlisted in making monument. The following are all monuments:

The Christian cross and/or crucifix, whether erected in stone on a hillside, atop a church edifice, as the centerpiece of an altar, as a pectoral worn by priest or lay person, in the guise of gesture ("making the sign of the cross")

The stone effigy of the Civil War veteran in city square or on village common

The Lincoln Memorial in Washington

Lenin's body in its mausoleum

The Queen of England

Ritual masks

Priestly garb and altar paraphernalia

The caduceus of the medical profession

The American national emblem

The national anthem

Any psalm or hymn performed ritually

Scriptural and other formulations in rituals

Ritual dance steps and postures

Ritual incense

Roast lamb at a Passover feast

What makes these objects samples of myth-idiom is the attitude developed toward them. They are charged with mythologic meaning. While most of the samples just given are sacred, others are secular—demonstrating that there is such a thing as secular mythology. And finally, as we have already noticed, an entire, complex ritual or cele-bration—such as Christmas—may itself become a monument. How inseparable ritual and monument may be, we realize when the priest stands before an altar: Together they become a complex monument. They are a node where the human microcosm effects a junction with the macrocosm that is the "universal Other."

The great traditional religions, such as Judaism and the liturgical bodies of Christendom, have developed architectural ediflces so richly symbolic that they have become epitomic monuments of their re-spective world views. They express cultural climaxes. At the other end of the line stand the altars on high places, and the Plains Indians' buffalo skull painted half black, half red. The Midewiwin lodge of the Ojibwa and Menomini is a reflex of an aspect of their cosmic scheme.

Both officiating priest and the scheme of the lodge are attempts, each in its way, at *mimesis* or *methexis*.

MOTIF, THEME, MORPHÉ. Let us regard tale, ritual, monument as the warp of myth through which travels a weft: motif, theme, morphé. Furthermore, the warp is idiom, while the weft is semantic content.

For motif we shall adopt Stith Thompson's definition: It is "the smallest element in a tale having a power to persist in tradition."[34] The definition is quite adequate in its own right, but there is a further, cogent reason for accepting it: Antti Aarne and Stith Thompson together have advanced the analysis of motif so significantly that we cannot do better than work within their edifice.[35] To this we may add Thompson's description of a type: It is a complete tale that is "made up of a number of motifs in a relatively fixed order and combination . . . . Most animal tales and jokes and anecdotes are types of one motif. The ordinary Märchen (tales like Cinderella or Snow White) are types consisting of many of them."[36]

What a motif is, and what it does, may be brought out if we turn to that of the earth diver.[37] We find this character hovering or floating over a primal world ocean or flood in company with another supernatural being. The latter bids him dive to the bottom for earth; after several mistrials he fetches it up; his companion scatters it over the face of the waters, and it becomes the dry land. This seems to be the most widely diffused single motif in the entire repertoire of the world's mythology. It occurs across Eurasia and North America, from Finland to New York and Quebec; it is found again in India and southeastern Asia. A reasonable case can be made for its being a genuine example of diffusion from a single source—Irano-Chaldea. It this be true, then all of its variations record, however scantily in any particular instance, the fact that there have been very many psychocultural differences among its recipients and its transmitters. Yet no matter what these differences may be, the act of earth-diving persists throughout.

---

[34]"The Folk-Tale," p. 415.
[35]See esp. Antti Aarne, Verzeichnis der Märchentypen, FF Communications No. 3 (translation by Stith Thompson, The types of the folk-tale, FF Communications No. 74); Stith Thompson, "Tales of the North American Indians" (Cambridge, Mass., 1929); "The Folk Tale" (see Appendix); Motif-index of folk-literature, FF Communications Nos. 106–9, 116, 117 (published also in Indiana University Studies, Nos. 96–97, 100–1, 105–6, 108–10, 111–12).
[36]See E. W. Count. 1952. The earth-diver and the rival twins. In: "Indian Tribes of North America: Proceedings of the 29th International Congress of Americanists, III." Sol Tax, ed. University of Chicago Press, Chicago.
[37]Ibid.

Clearly an earth diver must have a sea into which to dive; *per contra*, a sea (as a feature of a tale) is in no need of an earth diver. In fact the primal ocean occurs in Chaldean mythology quite without an earth diver; in this untrammeled form it transmitted itself to Western Semitic mythology. Both as a matter of literary analysis and as a historical development, the earth diver is, so to speak, a dependent variable, while the primal ocean is an independent variable.[38] Together, they form a compound motif.

A theme is a mythopoeic attitude toward life, or an interpretation of it. Thus, gods fear men, or are anxious lest men become too godlike in power. This is the reason why YHWH-'IHM drove Adam and Eve from Eden, and why he confounded the language of men when they built the ziggurat of Bablyon; it has a meaningful similarity to Aeschylus' interpretation of Zeus' persecution of Prometheus. Men, on their part, will defy the gods to wrest power from heaven, though the attempt kill them. Here we have two themes, often brought together as obverse and reverse: the jealousy of gods, and Prometheanism. Some themes may be designated from the forms they take in Greek mythology: Orphean, Promethean, Oedipan, Dionysian; also, *phthonos, nemesis, moira, hybris*. For others the labels vary: power quest, primitivism, Yang/Yin, the dualism of good and evil, rebirth out of death.

We might say that themes represent the philosophic broodings of the mythopoet. And so it is to be expected that the same or an equivalent theme will occur in two or more unrelated cultures, carried by utterly dissimilar motifs. When this happens, we may term the respective cases in the cultures thematic allelomorphs. This makes it possible, for instance, to compare Job and Prometheus, a most revealing contrast in the Hebrew and Greek tempers as to *Weltanschauung*.

In fact, it is the kind of themes that engage the thought of a culture, and the way in which they are treated that give enduring substance to the study of myth. This applies both to the *Weltanschauung* of any particular culture and to cross-cultural comparisons. Themes endure, though gods die and motifs change their shape. Prometheus is as eternal as mankind. But for the durative character of theme, Ernest Jones could not have written "Hamlet and Oedipus," Jean

---

[38]The primal-flood motif is probably continuous with both the biblical *tohubohu* of Genesis I and the deluge of Genesis VI, but collaterally so, in that the source of both the biblical and Eurasiatic-American branchings presumably is Mesopotamian-Iranian.

Anouilh "Antigone," Thorton Wilder "The Bridge of San Luis Rey," Herman Melville "Moby Dick," Thomas Mann "Doctor Faustus."[39]

A morphé is a figure about whom or which thematic material may cluster until this figure takes on an enduring character. The mother-goddess is a morphé, whether in the guise of Inanna, Astarte, Venus, or Isis. Utnapishtim and Noah are allelomorphs of one morphé, so are Enkidu and Samson. In the first two cases the different guises of the morphé are generically related; in the case of Samson and Enkidu their only relationship is via the common theme of primitivism: They represent a male chthonic strength. The serpent at the base of the Tree of Life is a morphé that has been known from Sumerian times down to the caduceus of medicine.

Sometimes one and the same feature of a myth may be treated both as a morphé and as a motif. The mother-goddess who mourns for her dying son, the thaumaturgic twins or boon companions, the hero are cases in point. It depends upon the focus. The sorrowing mother-goddess with her dying son is thematic when the two characters together embody a certain philosophic idea. But a tale about them can diffuse as a motif; the idea they embody may suffer attrition; eventually another theme may be inserted into the motif instead. This was the fate of the earth-diver morphé as the motif associated with it diffused over the globe. Further examples of morphaé are:

The Trickster

Satan (highly composite and paradoxical)

The Phoenix

The Chinese Dragon

The Minotaur

Eden

[39]Stanley E. Hyman, in The ritual view of myth and the mythic, in Myth: A Symposium" (p. 93f.) says: "What such modern writers as Melville or Kafka create is not myth but an individual fantasy expressing symbolic action, equivalent to and related to the myth's expression of a public rite. No one, not even Melville (let alone Moritz Jagendorf) can invent myths or write folk literature." If we define myth as a form of folk literature, then there is nothing more to be said. It is not at all clear what is meant here by Melville's not being able to "invent" myth. And if to "individual fantasy expressing symbolic action" is to be denied the label of mythopoea, then there are no myths at all. How else did Gilgamesh or the story of Adam come into existence? Shall we deny myth status to the initiatory tale of the Midewiwin, if we discover that it originated as a shaman's vision? Or to the vision that started the Ghost Dance? If we start with the premise that mythopoea is a process now dead in sophisticated culture, then the case is closed before its hearing. But thereupon we are faced with the task of explaining the phenomena generated in modern man from the same psychological wellsprings, and of finding new technical terms to fit; and all the while we are postponing a reckoning with the dictum that "plus ça change plus c'est la même chose."

World Mountain
Tree of Life
Cosmic egg

A morphé clearly can embody several themes at once; theme and morphé reinforce and elaborate each other. It is interesting that morphaé are more likely to be sustained by ritual than by tale; tales may be totally absent, or at least superfluous. Erda, the Katcinas, Mawu, YHWH need no specific tales to keep them alive. On the other hand, a morphé may so enlist the imagination of a folk that it gathers a cult and also an endless number of informal folk tales. This is most notably true of the Virgin Mary; although without her Son it seems that she would be meaningless, the cult actually attaches to her and not to her Son.

Let us return to the collection of tales that features the earth-diver motif. It has the advantage of being widely diffused and no more than moderately complicated; at the same time it alters not only in motif details but also in theme and morphé.

The earth-diver tales are everywhere cosmogonic. We should suppose, therefore, that they have been taken seriously wherever they are told. There is no way to verify the point, but there is nothing about the shape of any version that would lead us to suspect otherwise. But the tales demonstrate with equal probability that their audiences were often entertained. From a few spots where they have been collected we have versions that are elaborate, rich in details of world view, and built into lengthier cycles with much other thematic material and with other "types" (in Thompson's sense). Over most of the area the forms that have been recovered are much simpler and seem to be no more than "That's How" stories.

Apparently they first took shape in the early centuries of our era when missionaries from the Iranian plateau-country spread dualistic cosmogonic ideas into Central Asia, where they impacted upon primitive indigenous paganisms. A little later Nestorians and Buddhists were active in the same country. In general the upshot has been Christianized versions among the Cyrillic Slavs and a Buddhistic overlay among the Mongols and Tatars, while a deeper stratum is Zervanitic or Manichaean. In all cases, the actors are the local deities.

The Cyrillic Slavs have long been under the influence of the Eastern Orthodox churchly doctrines, so that theoretically they should know also the Genesis tales which are official and canonical. Here, then, the earth-diver cosmogony co-exists with the official teaching; yet its status is on a level comparable to that which it occupies among most American Indian tales.

Among the Cyrillic Slavs, the actors are God and Satan (the diver); among the Cheremiss, Yuma and Keremet; among the Tatars, there are various names for God and Devil, and so on. In America the actors are always members of local cycles: Manabozho, Wisaketcak, Old Man, Eagle, and Crow, water birds and water mammals, etc. It is very noteworthy that even in versions like those of the Slavs, it is not the tale that sustains the theology, but the theology that sustains the tale. God and Satan do not depend upon the earth-diver story for their acceptance among the Slavs—although this does not preclude the possibility that the repetition of the tale reinforces belief in deities who are thereby made graphic in terms that the people can comprehend. But after this has been said it remains true that God and Satan, like other folk-tale characters that have taken graphic shape, attract about them stories both old and new. This is likewise characteristic of Trickster, Brer Rabbit, John Henry, Samson, St. Nicholas, the Christ Child and the Virgin Mary.

The tale, including its dualistic feature, is very widespread in America. But in the Old World, this dualism is thematic: the antagonism between the primal principles of good and evil which, paradoxically, brings the world into existence. The tale traveled to America, but no Persian missionaries came with it: The meaning of the rivalry has been almost or entirely leached out. The tale comes to reside, undistinguished, in the general corpus of American Indian folk literature. But the motif has thus been set free to be freighted with new thematic material, and this has happened in at least three independent cases. The Arapaho, the Mandan, and the Confederate Iroquois, each in their own way, have reset the tale in public rituals, and have embellished it with esoteric or official symbolic details. Such consideration was never accorded in the Old World where the folk were under the dominance of one or another of the larger, sophisticated religious systems.

The foregoing sketch serves to indicate how motif, theme, morphé relate, and yet preserve degrees of freedom. They change accordingly, as they diffuse across cultures; they change also as they travel across the centuries within any single culture.

The Progression and Elaboration of Myth

A grammar of mythology can concern itself only with the externalities by which tale is elaborated to epic, ritual to ceremony and theater (drama particularly), and with the complete myth cult. The far profounder study belongs to the humanists, the *Philologen* especially.

Progression and Elaboration of Tale The chief actor or agent in a motif or a type we shall term the "principal," a more neutral word than "hero." Once a principal captures people's fancy, he is likely to become the center of numerous episodes; these compose a cycle. The variety of these principals knows no bounds: Samson, Sinbad, Marko Kraljevic, Odysseus, Väinamöinen, Coyote, Wisaketcak, John Henry, Joe Magarac, Brer Rabbit, Abraham Lincoln, Li'l Abner. They may be geminal: Lodge-Boy and Thrown-Away, Gilgamesh and Enkidu, Roland and Oliver, the Katzenjammer Kids.[40] In a cycle the character of the principal holds the episodes together. The least formal cycle is no more than a desultory collection; a more organized cycle passes the principal through a progression so that the cycle becomes a sort of biography. When this happens we have a true epic; we may trace the emergence of one or more themes which are diffused through the whole corpus and which cannot be grasped from a reading of but one sampling of the literature.

The biographical cycle commonly treats of the principal's origin, waxing, maturity, waning, and disappearance. This happens to Samson, John Henry, Gilgamesh, Barbarossa, Roland, and Oliver. It is very much a matter of the thematic treatment. Samson, John Henry, Roland, and Oliver are destroyed by their tragedy; Gilgamesh passes in the fullness of his period; Barbarossa and Quetzalcoatl have retired until times are again congenial; Joe Magarac has merged into the steel whose spirit he really is—like John Brown (and the comparison has substance), "his soul goes marching on."

There is yet another kind of compounding in which there is a succession of principals: The earlier wanes as the later one waxes. This happens among the Yurok Indians, with their Wohpekumao–K'pulayao –Kewomer sequence. Likewise with Ouranos–Kronos–Zeus; Elijah– Elisha; John the Baptist–Jesus.[41] The principle applies also to the succession of world epochs in Levantine mythologies (and a number of others, in scattered locations over the world). It is most interestingly developed by the P narrative in the Hebrew Hexateuch. These successions form dynastic cycles or epics.

Progression and Elaboration of Ritual Ritual may elaborate into ceremony. Ceremony attaches one or more rituals to an occasion, irrespective of whether that occasion takes place but once or repetitively. If it takes place but once, it nevertheless is liable to be repeated in sym-

[40]It hardly needs pointing out that some of these can be morphaé; others perhaps have not achieved that stature.
[41]See John 3:30.

bolized form. Thus, Jesus performed the ceremony of washing his disciples' feet on the eve of his betrayal. The custom itself was common etiquette, and it already contained sentimental overtone; had this not been so, the deed could not have developed the impact which raised it to a higher level of symbolism. The deed was done once, but it developed a commemorative ritual. Eventually European kings and nobles washed the feet of a selected number of indigents on Maundy Thursday as part of a ceremony. The celebration of victory by the Allies in Paris, 1945, was an opportunistic ceremony which enlisted long established rituals, such as the Roman Catholic High Mass. The inauguration of the President of the United States and the coronation of Britain's monarch are programmatic ceremonies involving rituals both successively and simultaneously.

Ritual is always dramatic, no matter how primitive[42]—hence the potential that evolved into the Greek theater and the *No* drama. In Greece the idea of theater was free to evolve out of ritual because Greek religion was not, or had not, a church. The Christian church has had for one of its ancestors the mystery religions of Hellenistic times, and in these ritual drama was enormously important. It is therefore a most natural thing that Christian church services should be dramatic rituals. A Roman Catholic High Mass, the Easter ceremony of the Eastern Orthodox Church are spectacular testimony to this fact. Quite as dramatic ceremonies were the Zagmuk of ancient Babylonia and the Day of Atonement ceremonial in the Jerusalem Temple. The ceremony is a way of converting an event (whether or not the event ever actually happened is immaterial, as long as the ceremonial participants believe it happened) into a symbol by commemorating it.

Rituals are the operational basis on which cults are elaborated. Unfortunately, "cult" is an ambiguity, and anthropologists have not been guiltless in promoting it. "Cult of ancestors" and the "peyote cult" of American Indians cannot be lumped together casually. Whatever justification there may be for so doing must lie in the fact that both kinds stress a concrete rallying point about which a complex of beliefs, attitudes, and acts is organized, so that the complex becomes a *gubernaculum vitae*.

Counterposed to this similarity is the difference in psychological focus. Those who practice the cult of a goddess or of ancestors or of

---

[42]Dr. Lucile H. Charles has analyzed most ably the dramatic nature of ritual, in a series of papers published in the *Journal of American Folklore:* Growing up through drama, July–September 1946:274–82; Regeneration through drama at death, April–June 1948:151–74; Drama in first-naming ceremonies, January–March 1951:11–35; Drama in shaman exorcism, April–June 1953:95–122.

the dead focus their service upon these as the objects of their service. The peyote button, on the other hand, is consumed to attain a group contact with a world already believed in. Consequently, some bands practice peyote-eating to consolidate the "Indian way" against white inroads, while others use it in a centralized common experience within their semi-Christian religion. The peyote serves to make these movements mutually exclusive; they have no common focus of worship. In other words, there is no peyote cult, but only numerous peyote sects, all stemming from the widespread frustration that has come from contact with a dominating alien culture.

But if the peyote cult be allowed as such, then the label extends to the Ojibwa Midewiwin also: It is the cult of the migis shell. In both shell and button there lodges a supernal potency bestowed upon mankind by deity; by its use mankind is restored to some harmonious relationship with a universal. Shell and button are vehicles, not objectives. Cult of a goddess, on the other hand, addresses service to the goddess herself. The goddess is a personified thematic morphé. Were we to seek an equation in Christian mythology with the cult of the migis shell, we should have to coin a "cult of the Host." This nonetheless remains more nearly thematic than either migis or peyote, for the Host is symbolic of a Presence that actually is being worshipped. This is not true of migis or peyote. Were the Indian article to acquire a *persona* of some sort, it would have advanced a step nearer to the orthodox meaning of cult.

But even when one narrows the term "cult" to cover only those myths which focus upon a personified thematic morphé, one discovers that it still includes two usages. The "cult of the Virgin Mary" embraces the entire range of its actual incidence, historically as well as spatially considered. As this represents a movement that pervaded Occidental culture as a whole during some of its medieval centuries, the locution frames a real universe of discourse. But within the generic use there is also a more specific one, illustratively, Our Lady of Guadalupe, in Mexico. Here the cult has grown to be the spiritualized eidolon of a nation.[43]

Occidental culture has developed yet other elaborations of ritual and tale. Briefly, the ballet is thematic material developed through the ritual of dance; it has a common ancestor with the classical Greek theater. Oratorio is musical elaboration of the epic and dramatic potential of the myth-tale; to account for it historically would re-

[43]For an account of this phenomenon, at once philosophical and understanding, consult F. S. C. Northrop. 1946. "The Meeting of East and West." Macmillan, New York, Chap. II.

quire simultaneous discussions of the evolution of the Occidental music forms, the mystery plays, and the dramatic performances staged in the medieval churches during high festivals.

Those are surely in error who would try to give some other name than mythopoea to these developments of Europe's more recent centuries. The phenomena are far more than merely aesthetic elaborations of hoary traditional material. The student of culture history senses immediately that these art forms are the couch for themes over which Europe has brooded long, and behind which she has marshaled her loyalties. And when our eyes penetrate to their core, these themes turn out to be ancients in the dress of contemporaries. The elaborations of the warp and the weft of myth just described are the designs by which we Occidentals have continued to create world view.

Theme Work[44]

The wanderer through the mythologies of the world's cultures ever comes upon pieces of landscape at once utterly new to him, yet somehow familiar. Features of topography and their mutual bearings are recognizable; the view nonetheless is quite itself and no other. Despite the diversities of motif, the earth is there as a universal mother; in death we reenter her womb. To grow up is to pass through a succession of rebirths. The female principle has the power to absorb and thus to deprive one of his virility; it is therefore to be both feared and overcome. The dead beloved cannot be brought back Death is irrevocable, because in the beginning of things a critical event decided the issue forever. And so on.

Sometimes the tales which incarnate such broodings are presumably, or even definitely, variants from a common stem: The same

---

[44]The work of C. G. Jung and his followers—notably, C. Kerényi—in the field of mythology has been so vitally significant that virtual absence of its mention so far needs explaining, the more so, since this writer has profited greatly from these authors.

In "Essays on a Science of Mythology" (Bollingen Series XXII, New York, 1949), Jung and Kerényi treat as "archetypes" the "Primordial Child" and "Kore." Maud Bodkin, in "Archetypal Patterns in Poetry" (Oxford, 1934; paperback edition, Vintage Books, 1958), applies "archetype" to discussions of "rebirth," "Paradise-Hades," the image of woman, and others. These labels include features which, in the present essay, in some cases would be identified as morphaé, in others as themes. The phenomena are real enough, whatever the method of analysis. But the writer is not at all ready to accept as valid Jung's concept of "archetype." Moreover, this essay does not attempt to explore points of divergence and similarity among different approaches, let alone attempt reconciliations between them.

motif is there as vehicle, with certain details whose repeated and independent invention is extremely improbable. In other cases, quite as certainly the tales have no connection whatsoever. On the one hand, they deal with the same life tragedy; on the other, they resolve it differently. And this is just what we should expect—knowing as we do man's neuropsychic architecture, its antecedents in primate biosociology,[45] its panecumenical adaptivity, and the uniqueness of event as being the end product of multiple, universal processes.

Themes are the heart of mythology; they demand to be elaborated further. We shall examine two that overlap extensively. Moreover, the fact that they do not coincide will bring out more sharply the intriciate nature of thematic material.

Power Quest   Even if it be assumed (and the assumption is reasonable enough) that power quest is rooted in the dominance drive of primates and therefore ultimately in that of the vertebrates in general, the quest is obviously much more highly elaborated than the more elemental stuff from which it has sprung.

A human dominance drive can take any shape that its cultural environment permits or encourages. There should be marked differences in its patterns of expression according to the way in which a society would be placed on a spectrum of cooperation–competition–individualism.[46] The drive may, of course, become obsessive as every clinical psychologist knows, as history has documented it in certain exceptional individuals, and as dramatist and novelist have treated it, from "Macbeth" and "Moby Dick" to "All the King's Men," "What Makes Sammy Run," and "Death of a Salesman."

We are dealing with something amorphous and deep-seated, capable of organization as various as personality itself. There is a very great deal of it in mythology, but it would be idle to try to determine at what point it passes from a nonmythologic to a mythologic dimension of life. It is enough for our purposes that its treatment mythopoetically be recognizable.

In Orphism and other mystery cults, and also in Christianity (for a closely related reason), the quest took the shape of a search for a mystical union with the god, in which the initiate sought to empathize with the experience of the god, and expected that the god would like-

---

[45]See E. W. Count. 1958. The biological basis of human sociality. *Amer. Anthropologist* **LX**:1049–85; also "Eine Biologische Entwicklungsgeschichte der menschlichen Sozialität" (Mainz); *Homo* **IX**(1958):129–146; **X**(1959):1–35; **X**(1959):65–92.

[46]Margaret Mead, ed. 1937. "Cooperation and Competition among Primitive Peoples." McGraw-Hill, New York.

wise empathize with him. For the seeker there was ritual prescribed by and participated in by the initiated group, and the actions of the individual were stimulated and channeled by his companions. Aside from group-directed mysticism in Christianity and also in Judaism (we cannot say as to the Orphics), there has long been recognized a private, individual kind where the individual did not follow a prescribed ritual, yet never escaped operating within the frame of his cultural pattern.

Among the North American Indians the quest was for a tutelary spirit.[47] Among the Plains Indians it was done by individuals; among those of the Northwest Pacific coast the quest followed a group-prescribed ritual.[48] Among the Pueblos the quest seems to be a kind of individual responsibility toward one's society, so that what power he gains, he "pools." Among the Ojibwa and Menomini there were the professions of Wabeno, Jesakkid, and Midè—the first two being individualistic and primitive shamanisms and the last a society of initiates. (Some Wabeno and Jesakkid were initiates in the Midè lodge.) It is to be noted that among the Plains Indians a spirit came and, so to speak, adopted the postulant, but the postulant neither became possessed by it, nor did he ever enter empathetically into the experience of his tutelary. (For that matter it seems that no American Indian ever sought to empathize with the life of his tutelary.) On the Northwest Pacific coast the spirit took complete possession of the postulant, so exclusively that he was no longer responsible for the behavior of his body. Among the Ojibwa and Menomini he received into himself a nonpersonalized shell which was efficacious because it was the gift of the deities. The mysteries of Thrace, Hellas, and the Levant featured a theophagy.[49] This never happened among the historic Hebrews.

Power quest is treated by myth-tale as well as being acted in ritual. The relationships between them are not simple. The character of the myth-tale seems correlated somehow with presence or absence of group-prescribed ritual. North America is a great striking instance

[47]See Ruth F. Benedict. 1922. The vision in Plains culture. *Amer. Anthropologist* **24**(1):1–23; "The Concept of the Guardian Spirit in North America." Memoire No. 29, American Anthropological Association; Robert H. Lowie. "Primitive Religion." Boni & Liveright, 1924; Liveright, 1948. Ch. I.

[48]It will be noted that within mystery cults and Christianity, there has been room for both quest-with-group and individualistic quest; the Plains and Northwest Indian culture areas together were a matter of either-or.

[49]Ghost Dance and peyote cults demand mention; they are peculiar and variegated hybridizations of nativism and nonliturgic Christianity. They represent the desperation of primitive cultures that are dying under the impact of Westernism, and they are messianic. Similar messianisms have occurred in South Africa and Melanesia.

of culture territory where a theme can be heavily developed in ritual yet be negligible in tale. In the Midewiwin the function of the tale is etiological confirmation of the ritual. Possibly it started as shamanistic fantasy or vision; it may be suspect of some stimulus diffusion from Christianity. Now, if a Plains Indian, a Seneca, or a Paiute has a vision which he relates, and on its inspiration founds a power-questing cult, then we have a *de facto* etiological narrative; but this clearly is not of a kind with the tale of Daedalus and Icarus, the quest for the Holy Grail, the search for the Great White Whale, or the search for immortality by Gilgamesh.[50]

Prometheanism   The power-quest theme has in many instances become involved with Prometheanism. Prometheanism is a defiance of the power of the gods—man pitting himself against a power that can destroy him, yet which he cannot harm. The theme may be enacted under high emotional, even manic drive; it may be enacted in the coolness of a "calculated risk." In either case, it is irreverent—even if in the individual it blend with, or dwell alongside of a very considerable degree of respect or reverence.

The theme receives its name from the figure developed by Aeschylus. But Promethean figures may depart far from the Aeschylean type, Job, for instance. At first glance it may seem far-fetched that Job should be placed nearby. But the claim is not that Job *is* a Promethean figure—only that he contains an ingredient of it: He comes as close to the Promethean theme as fourth-century B.C. Judaism ever gets. In the world of that day and that place, one did not challenge the absolute monarch's judgment and motives. Promethean will—this is often overlooked—is always contextual; its stature and intensity must be recognized not as absolute but as being relative to the *Geist* of the culture. The book of Job is daring for fourth-century Judea, though not for fourth-century Athens. The innocent and God-abiding protests the injustice of divine unreasonableness: indictment unrevealed, yet punishment administered; the power to mend one's ways and so be reinstated in grace is withheld, for the power comes from knowledge, and the knowledge is being refused.

---

[50]The theme, curiously enough, can be acted out epically instead of ritually, as instanced by Ponce de Leon, or by an entire people, in search for a Promised Land. This was exemplified by the United States during the nineteenth century. Not only were there writers who interpreted the westward movement as an epic with plenty of mythologic overtones, but the mythology itself became a *mystique* that was sometimes explicit and not at all subtle and that abetted the movement. See Henry Nash Smith. 1950. "Virgin Land." Harvard University Press, Cambridge. Also paperback edition: Vintage Books, 1957.

In "Prometheus Bound" and in Job, Greek and Hebrew arraign God.

Very unhappily the rest of Aeschylus' trilogy has been lost; so that how he resolved the issue can only be surmised. At any rate, Aeschylus was himself enough of his own Prometheus to have conceived this arraignment of Zeus. For it is Zeus, fully as much as Prometheus, if not more, who is under indictment, and from the standpoint of the subsequent progress of religious thought, it is incomparably the more portentous indictment. The Book of Job does supply an outcome of the inquiry (although with ironic parallel it may have been supplied at a later time when the original ending was lost), but it comes as a reassertion that divine wisdom and ways are forever above and beyond the questioning of mortal man.

And this is as close to an arraignment of deity as the Semite dared come. It was not in him to be irreverent like the Greek, because his idea of deity and of how the universe related to deity was totally different. Hence, unlike the Greek he could not proceed to the Aschylean kind of questioning that in fifth-century Athens was already beginning to rupture a numenal universe and to engender science. For when man can question divine behavior at all, that behavior has fallen behind the march of man's sense of right. And it stands in the record that covers a half-millennium or so—from J's story of Adam to the writer of Job—that in the Semite too there lay that insubordination which even at an early date he projected into the words of YHWH: "See, the man has become like one of us, in knowing good from evil; and now, suppose he were to reach out his hand and take the fruit of the tree of life also, and eating it, live forever!51 And later: "Then YHWH came down to look at the city and tower which human beings had built. YHWH said, 'They are just one people, and they all have the same language. If this is what they can do as a beginning, then nothing that they resolve to do will be impossible for them. Come, let us go down, and there make such a babble of their language that they will not understand one another's speech.' "52

The Hebrew says: "Thou canst not know, dearly though thou wouldst." The Greek says: "I *will* know—come what may." The two attitudes travel down the ages in uneasy companionship within the Occidental world view. After all has been said, one must still live in a cosmos of *Jovis regna* or in one where the thoughts and ways of YHWH must be accepted as being as high above those of man as the heavens are higher than the earth. Or else, be destroyed, like Captain Ahab, the human who tried to play Titan.

51Genesis 3.22.
52Genesis 11.5–7.

The Occidental Promethean definitely pits himself against his universe. The mountain climber may be devout or he may be an unbeliever; in either case he arrays his human resources against overwhelming and inexorable odds, he speaks of it as "tempting fate." And when he triumphs, he writes "Anapurna." The mountain climber risks his body. There are other Prometheans who risk their immortal souls by playing cards with the Devil, if this is the way to win knowledge. The Fausts of both Goethe and Thomas Mann are versions of Prometheus after the Renaissance (as are mountain climbers, in their own way). Dr. Frankenstein plunges into the unholiness of charnel houses that he may wrest from them the power of giving life, and he looses upon earth an uncleanness as great as anything that ever came out of Pandora's box. The Promethean Captain Ahab, as we have noted, defies the lightning of heaven and the leviathan of the primal deep, and he carries mankind with him down to destruction.[53] It is quite likely that this imagery would have been far more graphic and terrible to an ancient Levantine than to Melville's nineteenth-century readers, who saw in his myth no more than a story.

Myth in Time Depth

No world view has remained unchanged indefinitely and yet continued to satisfy the thinker, reassure the man of action, and hold a society together in a common ethos. Unless we have the life of a myth traveling through time, we may be certain that we shall never understand it more than partially. The Sun Dance complex, the Midewiwin, the Trickster cycles, even the Orphic rites are elaborate institutions possessing histories that will never be known. Sometimes we are vouchsafed a few gleanings of such histories—archeological recoveries, fragments of rituals, tales, customs still rehearsed by simple folk; and they are precious indeed.

[53] In her "Ancient Myths in Modern Poets" (New York, 1910), Helen A. Clarke cites fifteen examples of Occidental authors in the seventeenth to nineteenth centuries who develop the Promethean theme. The fact is an interesting symptom in post-Renaissance Occidentalism. But she limits her cases to explicit treatments of Prometheus. Thus, that towering example of Prometheanism just cited she does not mention at all.

It would be unthinkable that an age should produce Promethean figures in its literature, yet none among its actual and living dwellers. One cannot study the life of Beethoven—particularly as it has been written about so sensitively by J. W. N. Sullivan (1927. "Beethoven: His Spiritual Development." Knopf, New York. Paperback edition: 1949a. The New American Library, New York), without feeling that here is Prometheanism at its greatest and its profoundest.

In an exemplary way Waldemar Liungman[54] has traced the diffusions with their protean changes of myth-tale motifs and ritual motifs from their Sumero-Babylonian sources to their present-day occurrences on both sides of the Mediterranean littoral. Leached of the grandeur they owned in the ancient mosaic of Mesopotamian world view, now rough-hewn to the dimensions of peasant festivities that have dodged capture by the mythoreligious system which now frames their lifeways—they bespeak processes of mutation that we can infer to some extent, though we cannot otherwise document. Here is the bulk of Europe's "backyard mythology," a mythology that often runs counter to canonical sanction.

But now let us turn to the "frontyard mythology" again—that Levantine, Mediterranean, and Northwest European blending which became the world view that has made and has been made by the civilization of the Occident.[55]

Sumerian and Babylonian cosmogony starts with an inchoate, watery abyss, vaguely personified, which engenders a succession of paired, sexed divinities; it is these who become the architects of a cosmic order and create all things including man. But to do so, they must gain ascendancy over the primal choas which spawned them.

When, sometime in the sixth century B.C., the later pre-Exilic tradition of the Priestly Code (P) had taken shape in Judah, there still was a primal, watery abyss, but it had only one deity hovering over it, and his stately series of creations climaxed in a creation of man as a bisexual pair. Deity here did not have to achieve a mastery of some thing antecedent to and huger than himself.

The Mesopotamian cosmogony proceeds as a series of great periods, each succeeding one shrinking its dimensions from cosmic to human. It is based on the dynastic successions of the land (the "king lists," etc.), and it is hardly more than a dateless chronology. Likewise, the P-tradition of Judah states a series of periods whose dimensions shrink as the contemporary is approached: from Adam to Noah to Abraham to Moses. The scheme undoubtedly has been adapted from the Mesopotamian; but the writer of P has a thesis. Each shrinkage shows a pruning: YHWH eliminates collateral lines of descendants, and saves a remnant from the earlier period with which to build the next;

[54]Traditionswanderungen Euphrat-Rhein, FF Communications, Nos. 118–19 (Helsinki, 1937–38).

[55]A caveat none the less. The above statement is diagrammatic. Actually, as we know, the "high" and the "low" traditions of Europe are not thus easily sundered. See, for instance, Richard B. Onians. 1954. "The Origins of European Thought." University Press, Cambridge.

he starts a fresh covenant with the first man of the new dynasty. These are the deeds of YHWH, in the P-tradition, the only kind of stories told about him. He "speaks," he passes his breath over the earth, but that is all. And it dawns on us that here is creation and planned control of the affairs of the world by a single deity, so that the entire account actually is the *epic of YHWH:* His *gesta* are the events of history. Here is no mere chronology; here is history and philosophy of history—the discovery of the Judean mythopoets. It is not without significance that this epic interpretation of events of the centuries came at about the time when Judah disappeared under the neo-Babylonian flood: YHWH's pruning was continuing. The very fall of Jerusalem and the exile to Babylon became an operation in this cosmic process.

Judah and Israel never contributed anything to the science of astronomy. Their tradition accepted the astronomic findings of the Babylonians, but it rejected the Babylonian astrology that had been born of those observations, and substituted a different status of God and man in the cosmic scheme. Before the middle of the first millennium B.C. had arrived, Judah had asserted that its deity alone was creator of the universe and the arbiter of all men, and also that that deity was still operating to bring about a completed divine order. It was a number of centuries more before the Greeks arrived at anything comparable and they arrived along a different route. For Zeus and his companions had not created the universe; they had only seized it as loot in warfare. It and they remained under the rule of the *moirae.* It took time for Zeus to gain control of Fate, and also to be recognized as a universal creator. But Zeus never matched the full stature of YHWH who did all this and more, for he also wrested out of his people a concentrated and exclusive dedication to himself. This Zeus never approached even remotely.

"Thy sons, O Zion, against thy sons, O Greece." During the half-millennium after Alexander the Great, one great body of world view, which we shall for convenience call Levantine, confronted another, the Occidental, then in the form of the Hellenic. Whenever great, matured cultures, each with a formulated world view of its own, face each other and are forced to devise some *modus vivendi* between them, it is an Age of Cosmopolitanism. The first age of this sort is the one just mentioned. In an Age of Cosmopolitanism the world view ceases to be identified with locale, to be coextensive with political boundaries, to posses ethnocentric deities. Instead values and principles transcend national boundaries because government and ethnos cease to be relevant—the principles are universalized. The meaning of the individual is reevaluated. The world view carries a dynamism, so that its adherents dedicate their lives to winning followers to it. In the first Age of Cosmopolitanism, Iranian and Syrian and Buddhistic missionaries penetrated inner Asia at the risk of life and limb; Jewish Pharisees "encompassed heaven and earth to make one proselyte." An unknown seer wrote the Book of Jonah. The Bundahish was an ethical cosmology.

There has been since that time only one more, a second, Age of Cosmopolitanism. It has come upon the world in but the last four centuries or so. The symptoms are here again: Matured cultures with profound world views face each other, and are forced to a *modus vivendi* between them. The individual is reevaluated; world views bid for his allegiance; missionaries seek him out. The very assumptions on which evaluations are made are rescrutinized. An Age of Cosmopolitanism is not an age of faith, but an age of search for a faith.

The Intellectual Achievement of Mythopoeic Man[56]

As the capacity to symbolize emerged in a certain primate line, its members became committed—quite unwittingly—to an "intellectual adventure." Primitive men built themselves worlds which have become the foundations for all the worlds that have followed.

Out of their tales, rituals, monuments, their motifs, themes, morphaé, they condensed concepts which have never left us, which show no indications of ever leaving, and without which we should have no art, music, philosophy, science, or religion. A sample listing of these concepts will testify to their achievement:

"I" and the "Other"
Value (as such)
Space
Time
Nature as power, and as numinous; the "Holy"
Cosmos
Permanence and transcience; continuity, tradition
Regularity in the phenomenal world
Person
Ethic
Antithesis: the antagonism and balance of opposites
Event (as such)
Relatedness, and cause-and-effect

[56]With appreciative apologies to H. Frankfort, H. A. Frankfort, J. A. Wilson, Th. Jacobsen, W. A. Irwin, "The Intellectual Adventure of Ancient Man."

Relativity
Quest
Catharsis
Conscience (guilt)
Generation, germination, birth
The irrevocability of death
Knowledge as value
Credo as value
History
Tragedy

The story of how a primate has been humanized is that of un-utterably naive young men beginning to see visions, and scarcely less naive old men dreaming dreams. As long as young men shall see visions, and old men shall dream dreams, so long will mythopoea abide with us. And when and if ever they cease, we shall no longer have either poets or engineers. For to see and to dream is mythopoea; and it is the mark of being human.

Index

Aarne, Antti, 325
Adaptation, 159 f
Adaptive radiation, 126
Aeschylus, 326, 336, 337
Age-peer group, juvenile, 26, 84–86
Agnatha, 26, 27–28
Alajouanine, 188, 191, 248, 249
Alligator, 127 f
Alloprimates, 81, 82, 217, 220, 252, 291
Ambisexualism, 17
Ametabolous insects, 10
Anadromous migration, 28
Analogues, analogy, 155, 162
Anlagen (primordia), 216
Anolis, 22, 42–44
Anthropomorphizing, 21
Aphasia, 189–192. *See also* Schuell et al.; Broca's, Wernicke's areas
Appetitive behavior, 7, 43, 71
"Archetype," 333
Armstrong, R., and the "affecting presence," xi
Arthropods, 9, 10. *See also* Insects
Ashby, R., 159 f, 161, 183, 219, 223, 224, 226, 251
Australopithecines, 151, 155, 180, 237
Autocoenosis. *See* "Self-environment"
Autotopagnosia, 192

Bachem, 227
Barcroft, 224
Barlow, 172
Bartlett, 159
Behavior primate, viii. *See also* Alloprimates
Benét, Sula, 317
Bentley, 227
Bernard, C., 224
Bertalanffy, 119, 163, 219
Bevan, 299
Bigelow. *See* Wiener
Biogram, ix, xi, 1–117, 213; insect, 8–15; vertebrate, 15–108; Cyclostomes 27 f; Chondrichthyes, 28 f; Osteichthyes, 29 f; Teleostei, 30–36; Amphibia, 36–40; Reptilia, 40–46; Aves, 46–58; Mammalia, 75–89; Alloprimates, 89–97; Man, 98–105. *See also* Lactation complex; Incest
Birkmeyer, 194
Bishop, 166 f, 230, 241
Black box, 161, 164, 219
Blau, 281
Blauvelt, 134 f
Blum, 284
Bodkin, M., 333